JOINED BY A RIVER

QUAD
CITIES

Stephen M. Miller
Publisher
LEE ENTERPRISES, INCORPORATED

Frederick I. Anderson
Editor

Roald Tweet
Editorial Adviser

E. Lawrence McDonald
Art Director

Editor's Note

This book is the result of thousands of hours of work by truly dedicated and talented Quad-Citians. Like the Quad-Cities itself, *QUAD-CITIES: JOINED BY A RIVER* is a group effort. The story is the work of nine of the finest writers this community has to offer. Each writes with a different "voice." That variety of writing styles is one of the strengths of this book, just as the variety among the individual cities of the Quad-Cities is a strength of the overall community.

Because the Quad-Cities is a collection of communities, each with its own history, as much as it is a metropolitan community, this book takes a form somewhat different from other community histories. It opens with a chapter that sets the stage for all that is to follow, moving from formation of the region's geology through the close of the Black Hawk War in 1832. Next come chapters on the founding and early development of each of the communities. The book closes with two chapters that cover the period since World War I and chart the growth of neighboring cities that grew together to become one community, the Quad-Cities.

Most of the illustrations in this book are of exceptionally high quality, considering the age of many of them. However, some — especially some of the old photographs — are of less than good quality by modern standards. The contributors made exhaustive efforts to obtain the best photographs, posters, drawings, prints and lithographs to illustrate the book. In some cases, we chose to sacrifice quality for the sake of authenticity.

ISBN 0-910847-002

Acknowledgements

It is said that one of the most honorable things a person can do is to give something back to his community. That is what we hoped to do when we began this history of the Quad-Cities. What we have achieved would not have been possible without assistance from many sources in the community. Many helped more than one of us, and we are all grateful for their assistance in helping to research the history and secure the illustrations in these pages. Institutions and individuals within them which were of special help include: Augustana College, with assistance from Marjorie Miller, director of Special Collections at the Denkmann Library; Char Hawks, with her knowledge of local Indians; and Richard Anderson, chair of the Geology Department.

Bettendorf Museum and Miriam Ingram, coordinator.

Blackhawk Genealogical Society and its members.

Davenport Chamber of Commerce.

Davenport Public Library and its Special Collections Room.

Deere & Company and Leslie Stegh, archivist.

East Moline Herald Printing Company.

Hampton Historical Society.

Historical Office, Headquarters, United States Army Armament Materiel Readiness Command, Rock Island Arsenal.

City of Moline, its department heads and the City Clerk's office.

Moline Public Hospital.

Moline Public Library.

Putnam Museum and Carol Hunt, archivist.

Quad-City Development Group.

Quad-City Metropolitan Airport.

Quad-City Times and Liz Van Lauwe, librarian.

Rock Island County Historical Society, its volunteer staff and Lucille Sampson, archivist.

Rock Island Public Library.

Silvis Public Library and Emily Wilson, librarian.

University of Illinois Library.

Upper Rock Island County Chamber of Commerce.

WOC Broadcasting Company.

Many individuals contributed to the success of this book through their special knowledge, the loan of personal photographs or their reminiscences. Those individuals include: Charles Ainsworth, Dr. Louis Arp Jr., Judith Belan, Helen Burgess, Beverly McNeal Coder, Earl "Pappy" Hall, Bess Klove, James F. Lardner, Gary Lovested, John Neubauer, Martha Jamison Peterson, Annabelle Pinner, the late Russell Rice, Frank Ross, Isabelle Smith, Lucille Tenpound, Art Voelliger and the Robert Wright family. Another group of individuals performed indispensable tasks that contributed to the production of the book: Tom O'Brien and members of his *Quad-City Times* backshop staff; typesetters Chris Martin and Sue Goetsch of the *Times* and Cindy Bruhn of Typefaces, Inc.; photographers Bill McConnell, Basil Williams and Larry Hetisimer; proofreaders LaRue Crusan, Sherry and Larry Edwards; and illustrator Richard Oberg. Finally, we must thank previous Quad-City historians and others who have written about our community and region. Their work pointed the way for our efforts.

FORMED B

BY ROALD TWEET

Here trails, vales, ridges, roads, streams, rivers and interstates
Flow together, run beside each other, are layered stratum on stratum
To be read at the shouldering bluff where Rock meets Mississippi
And cities count and recount themselves.
—HARRY STELLING, "GROUND LEVEL"

Many travelers crossing the heartland of America first view the
Mississippi River from high up on one of three interstate bridges that arch
or hang between Illinois and Iowa straight west from Chicago and the tip of
Lake Michigan. The view from the bridges extends for several miles, a wide
band of water bordered by the low bluffs and wooded hills. Here the river
reflects its Ojibway name, *missi sipi* — great water. Especially in early
morning with the river fog hanging just above the water and the valley still
shadowed, travelers will be awed as the first explorers were by the beauty of
the river. Nineteenth century European visitors invariably compared the
Upper Mississippi to Germany's Rhine Valley — and the Mississippi often
won.

A traveler crossing later in the day will discover a river not only picturesque, but at work. Railroad tracks cross on two bridges. On the water below, towboats pushing up to 17 barges of grain, coal, fertilizer and other bulk commodities move steadily up and down the marked channel, while houseboats, cruisers and sailboats play back and forth on the broad surface. An observant traveler will notice, in fact, that this "great water" is very much a managed affair, controlled by locks and dams built by the Corps of Engineers in the 1930s to permit the river to work harder. Before this aquatic staircase, the Mississippi in dry seasons was little more than a trickle.

The five highway and two railroad bridges, together with the channel below, illustrate the history of America's inland transportation. Settlers, immigrants and supplies moved in and produce and raw materials moved out of the rich Midwest, first by waterway, then by rail, and now, as with the traveler, primarily by highway. The first railroad bridge crossed the Mississippi here in 1856. In 1872, one-half mile downstream, the first wagon bridge on the Mississippi between St. Paul and St. Louis connected Davenport and Rock Island.

Water, rail and road each in turn has fed and shaped the communities the traveler would see stitched together by the bridges: a string of river towns hugging the banks on both sides. Chimneys, warehouses and storage tanks line the water's edge, interrupted now and then by levee or park. These give way to businesses stretched out along the narrow bottomland, separated from the industry by front streets, water streets or river drives. Behind the business districts, the towns march uphill to the mansions: rows of hundred-year-old homes facing the river, built by the steamboats and railroads, by logging and lumbering and by an empire of farm tractors, plows and combines. Back of the mansions the neighborhoods spread out decade by decade to the suburbs — those young upstarts that pretend no dependence on river or rail. Dotting the prairie farmland beyond lie scattered small communities, each there for a reason, but now merged into a loosely defined metropolitan area of more than 380,000 people.

Should the traveler consult a map, he would discover, before the map ran out of space for names, that these river towns had names like Davenport, Rock Island, Moline, East Moline, Bettendorf. On a very large map he might also find Milan, Silvis, Le Claire, Port Byron, Hampton; but it would take a very recent map to tell the traveler that this urban sprawl was really one bi-state community called the Quad-Cities. Most travelers have to arrive at the Quad-Cities Airport to find that out.

The Quad-Cities is a good coffee-stop distance from either Chicago or Des Moines. A traveler who left Interstate 80 for a stop at one of the small cafes inhabited by locals, and who, noticing the name on a newspaper or poster, asked "What is the Quad-Cities?" might find himself stopping longer than intended. He would learn that these were once the Tri-Cities, and later the Quint-Cities (although never, never the "Sex-Cities," someone would be sure to add), and that there is an Illinois Quad-Cities different from THE Quad-Cities. The telephone directory counts 24 communities as members of the Quad-Cities.

A traveler willing to listen would soon move on from this quibble over numbers to learn what Quad-Citians think makes them and their community different from the rest of the world. The traveler would learn that the Mississippi runs east to west in this small stretch, so that Davenport, Iowa, is directly north of Rock Island and Moline, Illinois. He would find out that bald eagles winter on area islands to fish the ice-free water below Dam 15, and that the Rock Island Arsenal is the largest in the United States. He would of course find out about the first railroad bridge on the Mississippi, which crossed from Arsenal Island to Davenport, and that the steamboat *Effie Afton* crashed into the bridge to keep rail competition away from the steamboat monopoly. He would hear how a young lawyer named Abraham Lincoln came to Rock Island to represent the railroad in the court case that followed. He would listen as the locals fought the 1965 Flood over again.

By the third cup of coffee the traveler would begin to hear names he might already be familiar with: John Deere, Weyerhaeuser Lumber, International Harvester, Caterpillar, Allis Chalmers, Alcoa, Palmer College of Chiropractic. He might learn that WOC in Davenport was the first commerical radio station west of the Mississippi and that Ronald Reagan once worked there as an announcer. The traveler might well hear that the westernmost battles of both the Revolutionary War and the War of 1812 were fought here. He would certainly find out that Black Hawk, the Sauk warrior, lived on the bluffs above the Rock River where Black Hawk State Park is now. Black Hawk's defeat in 1832 ended Indian domination of northern Illinois and opened the Quad-Cities region to settlement, to new fledgling towns such as Davenport and Rock Island.

RONALD REAGAN BEGAN HIS BROADCASTING CAREER AT WOC-RADIO IN DAVENPORT.

That traveler who stays for several days to conduct business or visit relatives would continue his education. He would learn about the golden age of steamboating which swelled the first cities, and the Rock Island Rapids which made Le Claire, at their head, an important river port. He would discover the history of the lumber barons whose acres-large log rafts choked the Upper Mississippi for 40 years as they supplied wood for the homes and barns of the Midwest. He would find the cultures still vital of those ethnic groups whose immigration shaped the Quad-Cities: Germans, Swedes, Mexican-Americans, Greeks and blacks — and so many Belgians they have their own consulate in Moline.

Above all, the traveler will sense the presence of the Mississippi River. He might cross it, fish it, ride it or eat overlooking it, but even away from it he would find that streets and ravines all lead down to the water. He would find it hard to spend several days in the Quad-Cities without taking time to stand on a levee or at a park railing, or at the Visitor Center at Lock 15, just watching the four-to-six-knot current move on one of the world's great rivers.

From time to time a traveler finds work in the Quad-Cities, or comes to college and never leaves. Only then does the new resident move beyond the collection of odd Quad-Cities trivia and begin to sense how the many separate cities, towns and hamlets connected by the Mississippi form a single Quad-Cities. The resident many live in Bettendorf, buy groceries in Davenport, see movies in Milan, dine in Moline and party in Rock Island. Together, the many communities offer a variety seldom available in more isolated prairie towns. The resident may imagine an analogy to a large university made up of small colleges, each with its own identity and purpose, but with one school spirit.

After some years of training, our traveler-turned-Quad-Citian himself might be sitting in a small Davenport coffee shop when a traveler enters, having stopped off on his way to Chicago, for a cup of coffee. "What's the Quad-Cities?" asks the traveler. "Well," says the Quad-Citian, moving to the next stool, "ever hear of Buffalo Bill from Le Claire, Iowa?"

And the process begins all over.

THE QUAD-CITIES CHAMBERS OF COMMERCE PROVIDE ONE HANDY DEFINITION OF "QUAD-CITIES": THAT REGION BOUNDED BY INTER-STATES 80 AND 280.

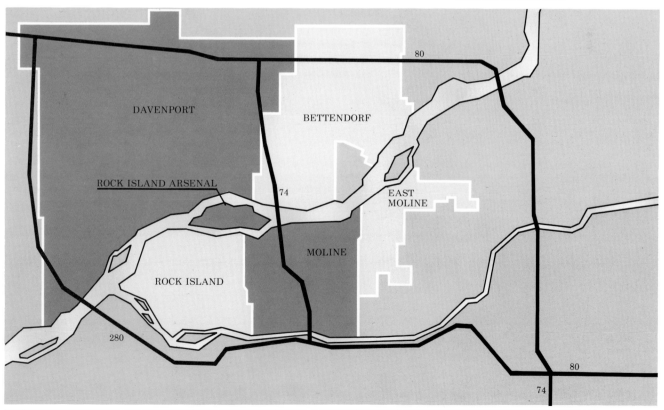

From Water Came Land and Life

From its source in Lake Itasca, the Mississippi River finds its way south, forming parts of the borders between Minnesota-Wisconsin and Iowa-Illinois. Then, at Le Claire, Iowa, and Port Byron, Illinois — the advance guards of the Quad-Cities — the river turns west in a gentle curve. Both the river and its valley narrow as the water flows west through the Quad-Cities. At Muscatine, Iowa, it turns again south on its way to the Gulf of Mexico, and both river and valley broaden out.

For 14 miles from Le Claire to Rock Island and Davenport, the Mississippi flows across a series of rock fingers stretching out from each bank. Although these Rock Island Rapids are now safely submerged under a nine-foot pool of water created by two locks and dams, they were once one of the major obstacles to river transportation on the Upper Mississippi, and for this reason were responsible for the arrival of those settlements at their head and foot which eventually merged into the Quad-Cities. Steamboats needed places to stop before encountering the rapids, places to pick up special rapids pilots who knew how to take a boat through those 14 miles, warehouses to store goods awaiting passage across the rapids in smaller boats or around the rapids by wagon.

These rapids that shaped the history of the Quad-Cities were no accident. A long time, even as geological ages go, went into them. This geological story of the rapids begins some 300 million years ago during the Devonian Period of the Paleozoic Era. A shallow sea inhabited by invertebrates and fishes covered much of inland America. The organic life in this sea extracted calcium carbonate from the water to make bone and shell. Over millions of years these collected on the floor of the sea, eventually piling up in a sedimentary bed as much as 160 feet deep. Pressure from succeeding layers of sediment turned the decomposed shells into Devonian limestone, the bedrock that underlies the whole Quad-Cities region, and which, close to the present surface, formed the Rock Island Rapids, Arsenal and Vandruff's islands, and the quarries at Le Claire and Milan that provided the stone for many area buildings.

The bedrock of Devonian limestone itself rests on other similar layers of sediment formed even earlier in the same way. The Quad-Cities rests on more than 3,000 feet of sedimentary rock above the granite basement, each formation from a sea that inundated the region. Different sediment became different rock; clay became shale, sand became sandstone and shells became limestone over millions of years of pressure.

THE LIMESTONE BEDROCK WHICH UNDERLIES THE ENTIRE REGION RISES NEAR THE SURFACE IN THE QUAD-CITIES, FORMING THE ROCK ISLAND RAPIDS AND, WHERE IT ACTUALLY DOES EMERGE, FORMING VANDRUFF'S AND ARSENAL ISLANDS.

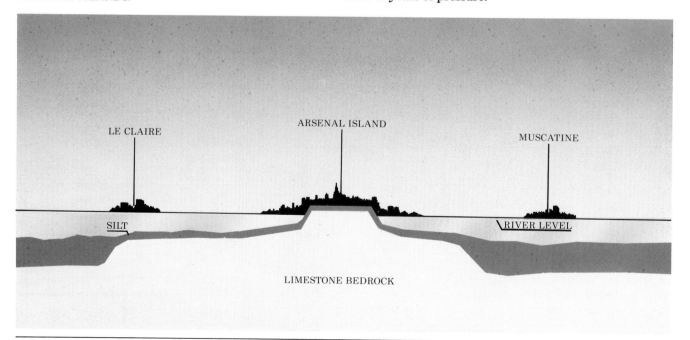

LE CLAIRE   ARSENAL ISLAND   MUSCATINE

SILT   RIVER LEVEL

LIMESTONE BEDROCK

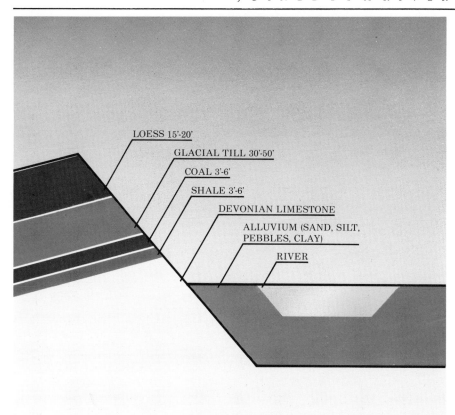

LOESS 15'-20'

GLACIAL TILL 30'-50'

COAL 3'-6'

SHALE 3'-6'

DEVONIAN LIMESTONE

ALLUVIUM (SAND, SILT, PEBBLES, CLAY)

RIVER

A CROSS-SECTION OF THE MISSISSIPPI VALLEY IN THE QUAD-CITIES REGION SHOWS THE LAYERS FROM LIMESTONE ON UP WHICH FORM THE LANDSCAPE, ALL THE RESULT OF SEDIMEN-TATION, GLACIER, WIND AND WATER.

Toward the end of the Paleozoic Era another event important in the Quad-Cities story took place. The seas receded in the later Devonian Period and gave way to shallow swamps and marshes. In the Pennsylvanian Period that followed, some 285 million years ago, forests of giant ferns and prehistoric trees sprang up in the wet land. As they died, they formed a thick layer of decaying vegetation, mixed with sand and clay deposits. Time and pressure eventually formed this layer, too. The clay became shale and within this, the vegetable matter became coal, a three-to-six-foot thick vein covering much of the Quad-Cities, and mined commercially in the outlying areas through the first half of the 20th century. Toward the end of the Pennsylvanian Period, the seas left this region permanently.

Now followed millions of years of surface erosion as the age of reptiles came and went, giving way to mammals. During this period the surface of Illinois was reduced to a nearly level plain, bringing the coal veins close enough to the surface to make strip mining possible in much of the state.

The clothing that the land in the Quad-Cities region wears on top of this rock and coal — the visible valley landscape — was put on fairly recently. A period of ice ages known as the Pleistocene Epoch covered much of North America with glaciers beginning about a million years ago. Each of the four major glaciers that reached Illinois from the north further scoured the rock above the Pennsylvanian coal formations, but each glacier, as it retreated, left debris of clay, sand, gravel and silt. This glacial till rests from 30 to 50 feet deep in the Quad-Cities area. Above this till, since the last of the glaciers, wind-blown soil — loess — sifted down until it lay 15 to 30 feet thick, providing the rich soil for Iowa and Illinois farms.

Runoff from the retreating glaciers, and later from rain, formed large rivers and tributaries, which eroded deeper and deeper channels down toward the bedrock, and even below. The Upper Mississippi Valley, with its bluffs and hills, formed this way. The glaciers also provided the main tool in shaping the Rock Island Rapids, one of the youngest geological features of the whole valley.

FOUR ICE AGES HAVE TAMPERED WITH THE COURSE OF THE MISSISSIPI RIVER. SOME TWO MILLION YEARS AGO THE NEBRASKAN ICE AGE PUSHED THE MISSISSIPPI INTO ITS PRESENT CHANNEL AS FAR SOUTH AS CLINTON, IOWA. A MILLION YEARS AGO THE KANSAN ICE AGE MOVED THE RIVER EAST TOWARD CENTRAL ILLINOIS, SO THE ANCIENT MISSISSIPPI MET THE ILLINOIS RIVER NEAR PRESENT-DAY HENNEPIN. THIS OLD CHANNEL CAN EASILY BE SEEN FROM THE AIR TODAY. THEN SOME 70,000 YEARS AGO THE ILLINOIS ICE AGE PUSHED THE MISSISSIPPI WEST AGAIN INTO CENTRAL IOWA. HERE LAKE CALVIN DRAINED SOUTH ACROSS THE DES MOINES RAPIDS AT KEOKUK. NOT UNTIL THE WISCONSIN ICE AGE 20,000 YEARS AGO DID A GLACIER DAM UP THE RIVER IN CENTRAL ILLINOIS AND SEND THE CHANNEL ACROSS THE ROCK ISLAND RAPIDS. THE QUAD-CITIES RESTS, THEN, ON THE YOUNGEST STRETCH OF THE MISSISSIPPI RIVER. THE PROCESS OF WEARING OUT A CHANNEL HAS HARDLY BEGUN. PERHAPS IN ANOTHER MILLION YEARS OR SO— UNLESS ANOTHER ICE AGE COMES TO TAKE THE RIVER AWAY ONCE MORE—THE QUAD-CITIES MAY HAVE TALL BLUFFS LIKE THOSE FROM CLINTON NORTH, OR A WIDE BROAD VALLEY LIKE THAT FROM MUSCATINE SOUTH.

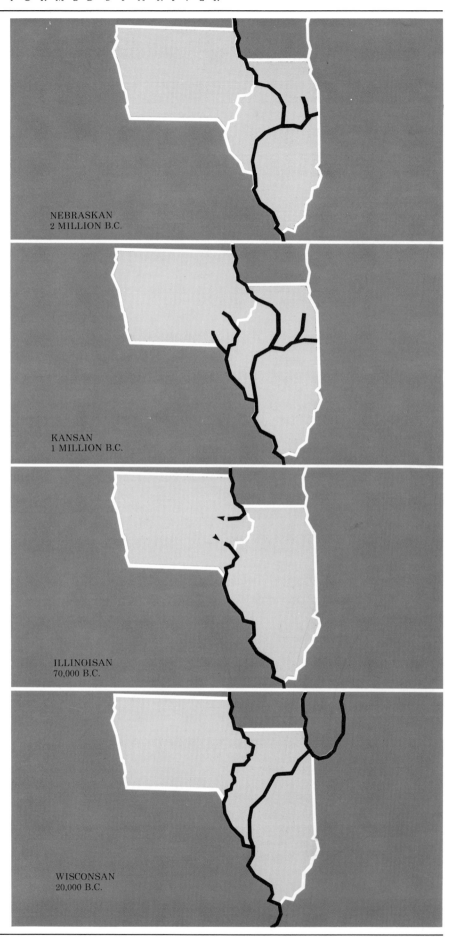

NEBRASKAN
2 MILLION B.C.

KANSAN
1 MILLION B.C.

ILLINOISAN
70,000 B.C.

WISCONSAN
20,000 B.C.

Glaciers, in fact, are responsible for the Quad-Cities being here at all. Before the first of the ice sheets arrived, the Mississippi channel ran through central Iowa where it met the present channel just south of Muscatine. The Nebraska Glacier then pushed the channel in northern Iowa east into its present channel as far south as Clinton. From Clinton north, the edge of the ice sheet forced the river over hard rock away from its natural valleys. Over a long period the river cut a channel down through the rock, creating the deep valley with formations such as the palisades near Savanna, Illinois, characteristic of the valley there. From Clinton south, the river went around the Quad-Cities.

Then the Kansan Glacier arrived several hundred thousand years ago and pushed the river east from Clinton until it met the Illinois River at Hennepin. From Hennepin, the Mississippi flowed with the Illinois to St. Louis. This old channel, part of which is now the Meredosia Bottoms, can easily be seen from the air.

The retreating Kansan Glacier left a large flat plain in central Iowa in which valleys formed for the Cedar, Iowa and Skunk rivers. These three met at Keokuk and flowed south to meet the Mississippi at St. Louis.

During the third glacial age, the Illinois Glacier moved the Mississippi back west. The glacier blocked the Cedar and Iowa Rivers to form Lake Calvin, which covered much of central Iowa.

Not until about 20,000 years ago did the Iowa and Tazewell Glaciers meet near Clinton during the Wisconsin Ice Age and force the Mississippi into its present channel across the Rock Island Rapids. Here the river was forced to cut through debris left by the glacier and through hard limestone outcroppings, a job it has only begun. As geology goes, the river through the Quad-Cities is young. By contrast, the river has been shaping its broad valley between the bluffs from Muscatine south for at least 120,000 years.

It remained for the last glacial sheet, the Mankato, arriving about 12,000 years ago, to add the final touch to the Quad-Cities landscape. Near St. Paul the Mankato ice sheet deposited huge amounts of silt, sand and gravel, which eventually filled in the riverbed and valley as far south as St. Louis. Erosion of this gravel bed lowered the river to nearly its previous level, and left a terraced flood plain between the bluffs, on which most river towns, including the Quad-Cities, were later built. These alluvial deposits also left the river itself full of constantly shifting sandbars and hundreds of sand islands covered with willow and cottonwood, which characterize the Upper Mississippi. Alluvial deposits on the flood plains reach as much as 20 feet deep, except in places such as the Rock Island Rapids, where the river channel has scoured down to bedrock.

As the last of the glaciers retreated, its melting ice forming river valleys and ravines, plant and wildlife returned. Along the bottomland or flood plain along the river, the dominant trees were those that did not mind getting their feet wet: willow, elm, sycamore, maple and river birch. Among the trees lived fur-bearing animals — deer, beaver, muskrat — and flocks of migratory birds.

Further up along the hills and bluff edges grew oak, hickory and walnut forests, home to deer, bear, turkey, elk, bison, squirrel, raccoon and rabbit. On the level land that stretched out from the bluffs on both sides of the river valley grew the bluestem or tallgrass prairie where scattered herds of bison and antelope grazed, along with gophers and prairie dogs. Although this native prairie is nearly all gone except for a few preserved swatches, the oak and hickory bluffs and the lush bottomland still look in untouched places near the Quad-Cities much as they must have looked 10,000 years ago when the first humans arrived to live on this land.

THE HOPEWELL CIVILIZATION USED SHELLS AS CONTAINERS, MADE POTTERY WITH INTRICATE DESIGNS AND CARVED CEREMONIAL PIPES IN THE SHAPES OF ANIMALS.

The Native Americans Arrive

Against the dramatic backdrop of retreating glaciers and prehistoric animals, the first humans arrived on the North American continent as early as 20,000 years ago. According to the most widely accepted theory, these ancestors of the American Indian discovered by Columbus were Mongoloid peoples from southeast and west central Asia who emigrated across a "land bridge" some 1,000 miles wide connecting Asia and North America from 26,000 to 8,000 B.C. when sea levels were low.

These hunters and gatherers spread rapidly throughout North and South America, reaching the Straits of Magellan at the tip of South America by 8,000 B.C. In North America these Paleo-Indians moved eastward, following the path of the retreating glaciers. By 10,000 B.C. a people known as the Big Game Hunters were living on the plains and had reached into the Mississippi Valley. They hunted mastodons and mammoths until these became extinct around 6,000 B.C. Then they slowly settled down in small communities, gathering nuts and berries and hunting smaller game.

The full flowering of prehistoric Indian culture in the Quad-Cities region occurred between 500 B.C. and 1,000 A.D. This was the eastern Woodland Tradition, marked by small settlements of semi-permanent villages of mat or bark-covered lodges, each holding several families or generations, and by early experiments with growing corn, squash, sunflowers and perhaps beans in small plots. In the Mississippi Valley, Woodland people lived in the oak and hickory forests bordering the rich river valleys. Here they learned the art of ceramics, decorating their pots by pressing cord or basted fiber into the wet clay. They also carried on extensive trade with other Indian cultures throughout North America and perhaps even Central America. Burial mounds in Illinois and Iowa have disclosed such artifacts as grizzly bear teeth, pendants and tools of obsidian and volcanic glass from the Rocky Mountains; copper artifacts from the Great Lakes region; and marine shells from the Gulf of Mexico and the Atlantic Ocean. The Mississippi and its tributaries must have served as a vast trade and settlement route for these Woodland Indians.

The most distinctive feature of Woodland culture, however, was the use of burial mounds by which these peoples left their record throughout the Ohio, Mississippi, Illinois and Missouri valleys. Some mounds, such as those in Ohio and along the crest of the bluffs north of Marquette, Iowa, form elaborate effigies of serpents, birds and animals, while the others, including those in the immediate Quad-Cities area, are conical burial mounds, generally modest in size. Black Hawk may not have noticed, and he certainly would not have been aware of their significance, but several prehistoric mounds were located within the bounds of the Sauk village on the Rock River.

The Burial Mound Period reached its peak with the Hopewell culture, which began in Ohio around 200 B.C. and spread from there to Illinois, Iowa, southern Minnesota and Wisconsin. The mounds of the Hopewell culture covered log tombs, often with multiple burials in addition to rich collections of artifacts.

So impressive were these thousands of mounds to 19th century historians that they invented a race of pre-Indians, the Mound Builders, to explain them. The Mound Builders were supposedly a race of advanced, civilized peoples such as those in the mythical Atlantis must have been, who were overrun by hordes of invading savage and barbaric red men, and obliterated. This theory helped salve the consciences of whites as they, in turn, overran the Indian.

But there were no Mound Builders, except for the Woodland Indians, whose descendants became the tribes of historic times. By 900 A.D. the period of mound building was over. Settlements increased in size and permanence, garden tools appeared, and horticulture increased. Burials took place in flat cemeteries. In southern Illinois, centering around Cahokia, a Mississippian culture of temple mound builders emerged and pushed north and east, ancestors, among others, of the Iroquois. Woodland culture gave way in eastern Iowa and western Illinois to the Oneota culture after 1,000 A.D. Oneota culture centered in the Mississippi Valley and spread westward into the plains and eastward to the prairies. This culture developed pottery tempered by crushed shells, intricately decorated. By 1600 the Oneota people had come in contact with European traders and were using iron knives.

From the Oneota culture came Siouan-speaking tribes in western Iowa: the Oto, Ioway and Missouri Indians. Contact with whites, and therefore with white historians, marked the end of prehistoric Indian cultures. Not only did they now become "historic" Indians; contact with whites quickly altered their locations and their lifestyles.

The Sauk and Mesquakie Indians Migrate into the Area

The Indians who came to play the major role in the history of the Quad-Cities are two tribes which most residents always name together: the Sauk and Fox. Black Hawk and Keokuk, both familiar names in local legend, were Sauk Indians. The Sauk and Fox, however, were latecomers to this area. When first contacted by French traders and explorers, the Sauk and Fox were Algonquian-speaking relatives of the Kickapoo Indians living near Montreal, Canada, where Black Hawk's grandfather was born. Though these two tribes shared a commonly intelligible language and intermarried freely, they maintained separate identities and villages, and even separate camps on joint hunts. The Sauk were the "people of the yellow earth," while the Mesquakie (the Foxes' true name) were the "people of the red earth." The name "Fox," in fact, was one of the first disservices performed by whites. The Mesquakie were hard-working hunters and farmers who lived in settled villages, but they were also quick to pick quarrels with other Indians. From their cruelty and cunning, their neighbors referred to them as Outagami. The French quickly translated this into Renard, which in English became Fox. Because of this, the Mesquakie have had to live down through history with a slur for a name. Today, however, on their own 5,000 acres at Tama, Iowa, they are once again Mesquakie.

French explorers who reached the vast region west of the Great Lakes by the early 17th century found two major language groups. In an area bounded by the Ohio, Mississippi and Wisconsin rivers, and by Lake Michigan, lived Algonquian-speaking Illiniwek Indians (quickly changed by the French to Illinois). The Illini were a loose confederation of tribes such as the Cahokia, Kaskaskia, Michegama, Moingwena, Peoria and Tamaroa. West of the Mississippi lived Siouan-speaking Ioway, Oto and Missouri Indians, with whom the Illini were constantly at war. Above the Wisconsin River lived the Siouan-speaking Winnebago Indians. Other Siouan tribes such as the Dakota lived in Minnesota.

In less than 100 years, these Indians had nearly all been replaced by the Sauk and Mesquakie in the Quad-Cities area. The story of how these two tribes got to the Rock River Valley is a small version of the larger story of white-Indian contact. For nearly every eastern Indian tribe, this is the story of a gradual push to the west and south. The fur trade, which provided much of the livelihood for the Indian once he learned to depend on white money and goods, moved in this direction as animals gave out. Encroachment by settlers not only took eastern lands by treaty or force, the cultivation of land destroyed the game resources on which the Indian lived. Competition for furs and land among French, British and Americans aided this westward movement by encouraging inter-tribal warfare. For the Sauk and Mesquakie, however, it was pressure from Indians still

SAUK AND MESQUAKIE WARRIORS, AN ENGRAVING BY 19TH CENTURY ARTIST, C. BODMER.

further east, themselves pressed by white colonization, that pushed them to the Great Lakes by the mid-17th century. The Iroquois Indians drove these and other Algonquian Indians west. The Mesquakie came to Green Bay, and the Sauk originally to Michigan, and then to Green Bay. By 1660 the French reported that the shores of Lake Superior were lined with tribes defeated by the Iroquois.

As the Sauk and Mesquakie were pushed west, they, in turn, pushed tribes already there. The Siouan Indians to the west resisted strongly and became traditional enemies of these newcomers, but the Illini to the south, besieged at the same time by the Iroquois from around the southern tip of Lake Michigan and the Siouan Indians to the west, gave way more readily. By 1700, the Mesquakie controlled a large region along the Fox River west and south of Lake Michigan. The Sauk Indians moved more westerly, coming by 1730 or so to the Rock River Valley, having already abandoned their large village on the Wisconsin River near present-day Sauk City. Their arrival at the mouth of the Rock River to construct what would become the principle Sauk village took place as early as 1730 (according to Black Hawk's own account), but at least by 1764. When Auguste Chouteau, the fur trader from St. Louis, visited it that year he found a large and settled village. The Sauk called this village Saukenuk.

THIS TAMA INDIAN WICKIUP IS MUCH LATER AND MUCH SMALLER THAN THE LODGES AT SAUKENUK, BUT THE SHAPE AND THE POLE AND BARK CONSTRUCTION REMAINED MUCH THE SAME.

The Mesquakie arrived in the Quad-Cities area by a more tragic route. Having gained control of a number of rivers used by French fur traders, the Mesquakie began stopping boats and demanding tolls for the use of their rivers. The practice grew so troublesome that the French, early in the 18th century, determined on a policy of extermination. In 1710 the French convinced the Mesquakie to settle near their fort at Detroit, but when the Mesquakie arrived they soon found themselves at war with the Ottawa allied with the French. They escaped, but continual harassment by the French eventually led the Mesquakie to seek asylum with the Iroquois. On June 1, 1730, the tribe began a trek from central Illinois around the tip of Lake Michigan to Iroquois country, but soon discovered their way blocked by tribes of Kickapoo, Mascouten and Potawatomi. The Mesquakie retreated to a rude fort near Starved Rock, which was soon surrounded. On September 8, 1730, desperate for food and supplies, the Mesquakie slipped out of their fort, only to be detected. Some 1,000 to 1,200 men, women and children were massacred, nearly annihilating the Mesquakie nation.

Some remaining Mesquakie returned to Milwaukee and the Green Bay region, but to avoid complete extermination many of the tribe chose to live under the protection of the Sauks at Saukenuk. They settled in smaller villages on both sides of the river, including the present sites of Rock Island and Davenport. The Mesquakie were not only poor in spirit, they lacked the wealth, horses and supplies that allowed the Sauks to move to winter hunting grounds in Iowa and Missouri each year. Instead, many of them went north, in season, to work the lead mines to supply the increasing white need for metal.

Although both Sauk and Mesquakie traveled widely in both large and small groups during much of the year, their location near the mouth of the Rock River remained their principal home until white encroachment, culminating in the Black Hawk War in 1832, displaced them all. The exact location of Saukenuk has been the subject of some investigation. If maps by 18th and 19th century explorers and visitors are correct, Saukenuk was located in several different places in the lower Rock River Valley, rather than being a permanent village on the bluffs along the north shore of the Rock River. It was on these bluffs by 1820 when the first local white-Indian friction occurred, but when Lieutenant Zebulon Pike visited it twice in 1805 and 1806 during his Army explorations on the Upper Mississippi, he found it south of the Rock, near present-day Milan. Other contemporary accounts and maps place it variously from the mouth of the Rock River to several miles upstream. It is likely that Saukenuk was only semi-permanent, and that it moved now and then for sanitation and because lodges wore out and needed replacing.

Permanent or peripatetic, Saukenuk was an impressive village by the 1820s. It was laid out in the shape of a right angle, with the point facing the Rock River. Here sat the chief's lodge. From this point avenues stretched out along the lines of the angle, with lodges lining both sides of the avenues. The largest of these avenues — the main street — was used for public gatherings, dances, ball games and military drills. Sauk lodges were multiple-family dwellings ranging from 20 by 30 feet to 40 by 150 feet. The lodge was an arched log frame covered with bark or mats. Contemporary accounts place the number of dwellings at from 60 to 100. Saukenuk, with its lodges, orderly streets, fences and even alleys, impressed the many travelers who stopped there.

Surrounding the village lay the horse pastures, gardens and corn fields — as much as 800 acres under cultivation. In addition to corn, the Sauk grew melons, beans and squash. Each winter Saukenuk was abandoned as the Indians moved west to their winter hunting grounds along the Cedar and Des Moines rivers. They returned in spring in time to plant crops. Having done this, the able-bodied men again left to hunt and fish for the summer, leaving the women, children and old men to weed and tend the crops. The warriors returned again from the summer hunt to harvest the crops, store them and prepare for the winter trek.

Although this idyllic seasonal life was interrupted regularly by tribal and individual quarrels with their neighbors, especially the Sioux, the industrious Sauk produced enough surplus in good years to supply horses, lead, fur, meat and as much as 1,000 bushels of grain to the area's forts and trading posts.

European Explorers Bring Change

On June 17, 1673, two birch bark canoes with seven white men led by the explorer Louis Joliet and Father Jacques Marquette floated out of the Wisconsin River, past the Wyalusing Bluffs on the left and the site of the future town of Prairie du Chien on the right, out into the current of the Upper Mississippi River. Although the Spanish explorer DeSoto had discovered the lower Mississippi much earlier, this was the first time white men had seen the upper river. "We were filled," wrote Marquette, "with a joy which I cannot express."

As the lead canoe carrying the two explorers entered the main channel, it was rammed by a large catfish and nearly upset, but not even this omen could dim the wonder of this new land. Marquette and Joliet continued down the river, but they did not find evidence of human habitation until June 25, when they came upon a village of the Illinois Indians at a spot the explorers marked as the mouth of the Des Moines River. By these and later Indians, the explorers were treated as guests.

The expedition continued south, hoping to find that the river would be the long-sought-for Northwest Passage; but 700 miles from the Gulf, they turned around, convinced that the Mississippi continued south. Guided by the Illini Indians, they returned to Green Bay via the Illinois River and Lake Michigan.

Marquette and Joliet claimed no territory for themselves or for France, but they were quickly followed by those who did, and who turned the Mississippi Valley into a battleground that saw French, Spanish, British, Americans and all of the region's Indian tribes fighting each other on varying sides for the next 150 years.

In 1678 Rene' Robert Cavelier, sieur de La Salle, received French permission to explore the Upper Mississippi region and to establish forts. He left Green Bay in 1679, explored the Illinois River and built Fort Crevecouer. From this fort La Salle sent Father Hennepin and two aides to explore the Upper Mississippi. On this trip Hennepin reached the Falls of St. Anthony, which he discovered and named. La Salle himself continued to explore the Illinois country. A year later he explored the Mississippi south from the Illinois River, reaching the Gulf of Mexico on April 9, 1682. Here he claimed the entire Mississippi and Arkansas River system for France, naming it Louisiana in honor of the French king.

French soldiers, traders and missionaries followed La Salle into the new territory, and by 1713 the French Empire in the New World extended from Quebec to the Gulf of Mexico. To keep fur trade routes open, the French built forts from Lake Pepin to the mouth of the Ohio River. Furs went overland north, too, or up the Wisconsin River to Green Bay on Lake Michigan on their way to Canada, making Prairie du Chien an important fur trade center.

French dominance of this vast inland empire did not last long. Attempts to curtail British colonial expansion west of the Allegheny Mountains, and competition for furs, led to open conflict with the British in 1754, and to the French and Indian War in 1756. Indians, even those like the Sauk and Mesquakie who were not especially friendly to the French, aided France in the war. The French and Indian War expanded into the Seven Years' War in Europe, and at its close in 1762, France had lost nearly all its power in North America. France ceded the territory of Louisiana west of the Mississippi to Spain in 1762. The Treaty of 1763 ending the war gave Britain control of the French lands east of the Mississippi. The Quebec Act of 1764 made this region part of the crown colony of Quebec. Much to the annoyance of American colonists, the act also protected Indian lands from settlement or purchase by individuals. Under the terms of this treaty, Illinois country, including the Illinois Quad-Cities area, was formally ceded to Great Britain in October 1764.

For a brief time, then, the Quad-Cities were divided between Spain and England. Hudson's Bay Company traders moved quickly into this new land with far greater organization than the loose association of voyageurs upon which the French fur trade depended.

Even as Britain was replacing France, however, she was losing her own foothold on her colonies. Discontent turned into rebellion in 1776, and this time the conflicts that had earlier avoided the Mississippi Valley came, if but briefly. As with other Indian tribes in Illinois and Wisconsin, the Sauk and Mesquakie were pulled two ways, used by both sides. They had established cordial and trustworthy trade relations with the British, but they were impressed by the Americans, too. During the war, their loyalties divided, some Sauk and Mesquakie, along with Spanish forces, aiding the Americans. Others, including those in the Quad-Cities region, allied with the British.

The Revolutionary War in Illinois centered around General George Rogers Clark and his militiamen who aided the Continental Army's more serious battles in the east by harassing isolated British fortifications in Indiana and southern Illinois. Part of Clark's purpose was to demonstrate to the wavering loyalties of the Indians both American benevolence and power. As a friendly gesture, he purchased horses from the Sauk at Rock Island, but when a force of British aided by Peoria Indians moved down the Illinois River in 1780 and unsuccessfully attacked the Spanish fort at St. Louis, Clark sent Colonel John Montgomery with a force of 250 men up the Illinois after the retreating Indians. After destroying several Indian villages on the Illinois River, Montgomery continued on to the Rock River, where he burned the villages of both Sauk and Mesquakie.

At the end of the American Revolution, the Treaty of Paris in 1783 brought the new United States all the British lands east of the Mississippi and south of the St. Lawrence River and the Great Lakes. Loyal to their Indian allies, the British insisted that this new territory be "subject to Indian occupancy," and the Americans reluctantly agreed. Peace, however, left the Indians confused. Traders of the Hudson's Bay Company continued to maintain posts in the territory, and continued to incite the Indians against the Americans. Many Indian tribes, including the Sauk and Mesquakie, had made annual pilgrimages to Fort Malden at Amherstburg, Canada, across from Detroit, where they were given presents and supplies. The Sauk and Mesquakie continued these trips after 1783, receiving continued assurances of friendship from the British, and setting the groundwork for future difficulties.

The problem of dividing up this new land lay with the Continental Congress. The original colonial charters gave each colony all the land in its borders "westward to the sea." This made present-day Illinois originally part of the colony of Virginia. In 1778 the Virginia House of Delegates created Illinois County of the entire region west of the Ohio River. Virginia ceded this land to the federal government in 1784, and other states with western lands did the same. In 1787, Congress decreed that the land bounded by the Wabash, the Ohio and the Mississippi rivers, and by the Canadian border, should be known as the Northwest Territory, and that it should be divided, as population grew, into not less than three nor more than five states. In 1800 Congress made the western section of this land Indiana Territory. The western half of Indiana Territory became Michigan Territory in 1805. Illinois became a separate territory in 1809, quickly on its way to statehood.

Meanwhile, Spain had not solidified its position in the vast region west of the Mississippi, and realizing what a tenuous hold it had, secretly retroceded Louisiana to France under Napoleon in 1800 in the Treaty of San Ildefonso. Actual transfer did not take place until 1803.

France owned Louisiana for less than three weeks. President Jefferson had gone to France in the spring of 1803, intending to buy French land near the mouth of the Mississippi in order to prevent the Spanish from interfering with American shipping at New Orleans. Napoleon, himself aware of how unprotected Louisiana was, countered with an offer to sell all of Louisiana Territory for $15 million. Jefferson quickly agreed, and on April 30, 1803, the Americans and French signed the Louisiana Purchase Treaty. From this point on, the story of the Quad-Cities region becomes an American story.

Americans Occupy the Region

French and English occupation of the Mississippi Valley and the Great Lakes had not prepared the Indians for the Americans. Neither the French nor the British forts and trading posts had been intended as the outposts of extensive settlement. Neither government intended to encroach on Indian lands, or even, except for the French missionaries, to alter the Indians' culture. Aside from the inevitable changes brought by knives, guns, cloth, beads and whiskey, Indian lifestyles changed remarkably little until the Americans arrived. These new owners wanted not only the land's wealth but the land itself.

The Indians were even less prepared for the Americans than they might have been because they simply did not understand the European concept of ownership. Indians did not own land individually or as a tribe. The Maker designated places for each tribe, and those tribes had the use of that land, but it was not owned. The idea that land could be bought or sold, or that a tribe's natural land could be transferred to someone else, was hard for the Indians to comprehend.

Trouble over land came for the Sauk and Mesquakie soon after the Louisiana Purchase. In 1804, four Sauk Indians from the Des Moines Rapids area had gone to St. Louis to plead for the release of a tribal member being held for murder. William Henry Harrison, governor of the Indiana Territory and the District of Louisiana (the north half of the Louisiana Purchase), and superintendent of Indian affairs, took the opportunity to make a treaty. On November 3, 1804, the four Sauk and another anonymous Indian relinquished all Sauk and Mesquakie lands east of the Mississippi River between the Illinois and Wisconsin rivers, as well as some land west of the Mississippi — about 15 million acres. In return they received an immediate $2,234.50 and an annual annuity of $1,000. The Treaty of 1804 further promised that the United States "will never interrupt the said tribes in the possession of lands which they rightfully claim, but will on the contrary, protect them in the quiet enjoyment of the same, against their own citizens and against all other white persons, who may intrude on them." The treaty specifically stated that the Sauk and Mesquakie could live on the land as long as the United States government owned the land. Black Hawk later implied that the Indians were drunk when they signed the treaty, but even sober, it was patently clear that since none of the five was a principal chief of the Sauk, and no Mesquakie was represented at all, the transaction was not legal. Yet it was to this Treaty of 1804 that the United States came back again and again for the next 30 years to justify the actions which followed.

The Army presence arrived on the Upper Mississippi the next year when Lieutenant Zebulon Pike was sent to begin the process of making the Upper Mississippi safe for trade and for settlement. His orders called for him to map the source of the Mississippi, to note the size and location of the Indian nations living in the valley and to record the number and kind of furs they traded. He was to note timber resources, and to select sites for three military posts between St. Louis and the mouth of the Minnesota River. If possible, he was to purchase these sites from the Indians. One of the villages Pike visited twice on this trip, and mapped for his report, was Saukenuk.

The War of 1812 Slows Settlement

Settlement would no doubt have followed Pike more closely had it not been for continued troubles with Great Britain. In spite of the transfer of the Northwest Territory to the United States, the English retained trading posts and forts in the area, and they continued to encourage Indian resistance toward the Americans. To Hudson's Bay Company posts were added the posts of a new Northwest Company formed in 1787 by British

and Scottish merchants in Quebec and Montreal to trade with Indians west of the Great Lakes.

When the New York Legislature chartered John Jacob Astor's American Fur Company in 1808, and when the Missouri Valley Fur Company opened headquarters at St. Louis in 1809, commercial rivalry on the frontier, together with smoldering English-American problems on the East coast, led to the War of 1812.

The War of 1812 divided Indian loyalties even more than the Revolutionary War had. For the Sauk and Mesquakie tribes, the split marked the beginning of the end. When hostilities began, most of the Mesquakie and a good number of Sauk, some sympathetic to the Americans and some anxious to avoid taking sides at all, crossed the Mississippi and settled down deep in Missouri Territory, or further west. Among this band of 1,500 Missouri Sauk, known as the "Peace Party," there emerged a leader sympathetic to the Americans: Keokuk.

The Sauk who remained at Saukenuk found a leader in Black Hawk. Makataimeshekiakiak, "Black Sparrow Hawk," has come down in popular legend as Chief Black Hawk, but he was neither an elected nor hereditary chief. Among the Sauks, chiefs took care of civil matters, while leaders among the warriors generally decided matters of war. As such a warrior, Black Hawk had distinguished himself. The 200 warriors who remained at Saukenuk in 1812 followed him as their war leader.

THIS OIL-ON-WOOD PORTRAIT OF BLACK HAWK WAS DONE IN 1833 BY CHARLES BURD KING, A NOTED PAINTER COMMISSIONED BY THE WAR DEPARTMENT TO DO MANY INDIAN PORTRAITS. ONE OF THE STANDARD PORTRAITS OF BLACK HAWK, DONE BY KING FOR THE WAR DEPARTMENT IN 1837, WAS DESTROYED IN AN 1865 FIRE. THIS PAINTING WAS DONE JUST AFTER THE BLACK HAWK WAR DURING BLACK HAWK'S TOUR OF WASHINGTON AND OTHER EASTERN CITIES AS A PRISONER. KING, TOGETHER WITH GEORGE CATLIN AND OTHER PAINTERS, CAME TO DO BLACK HAWK'S PORTRAIT WHILE HE WAS KEPT AT FORT MONROE, VIRGINIA. THE ORIGINAL OF THIS PAINTING IS IN THE WARNER COLLECTION OF THE GULF STATES PAPER CORPORATION IN TUSKALOOSA, ALABAMBA. IT IS THE ONLY EXTANT KING PORTRAIT OF BLACK HAWK.

According to Black Hawk's autobiography, he and his followers joined the British in the war by default. An American official promised the Sauk a large number of credits, payable at Fort Madison, but when the Sauk arrived there in late summer, they were given nothing. With no supplies for their winter hunt or for protection from the Osage Indians, they faced starvation and extermination, until a British trader arrived at Saukenuk with two boat loads of supplies.

In return, Black Hawk and his band traveled to Green Bay where they were met by the British Indian agent, Robert Dickson. Dickson threatened the Sauk with annihilation from their Indian enemies unless they joined the British, but he also praised Black Hawk, referring to him as General Black Hawk. Black Hawk, now 45 years old — old for an Indian then — and without even the power of a chief, was flattered. Before they left, Black Hawk and his followers had enlisted on the British side. Thereafter, the group of Sauk who remained at Saukenuk came to be known as the British Band, a term the Americans never let Black Hawk forget.

Black Hawk returned to the Rock River Valley and lived without incident until 1814, when he participated in two small skirmishes of the war. The first of these, the Battle of Campbell's Island, took place on July 21. By now the British had been so successful in the war that they had occupied most northern posts, including Green Bay and Prairie du Chien. In May of 1814, William Clark (of Lewis and Clark), governor of Missouri Territory and a partner in Auguste Chouteau's Missouri Fur Company, took five keelboats of troops from St. Louis to retake Prairie du Chien. Once successful, he moved his troops into a stockade which he named Fort Shelby. (It was reinforcements and supplies for this fort that Lieutenant John Campbell was taking upstream in three keelboats when Black Hawk invited him ashore at Saukenuk.) Campbell and his 33 regular soldiers and 65 rangers shared their whiskey with the Indians before retiring to their boats for the night. In the night, news came to Black Hawk of the British defeat at Fort Shelby. The British also sent six kegs of powder for the Sauks.

As Campbell poled his boats slowly against the current the next day, the Sauk followed in the thick willows along the Illinois shore. On the 21st, Campbell's boats, separated by the wind and the treacherous currents of the Rock Island Rapids, became easy prey for the Indians. Campbell's boat went aground on a low island full of underbrush. An attack force of as many as 400 Indians opened fire point blank on Campbell's boat. Black Hawk himself set Campbell's sail afire with a flaming arrow.

The two remaining barges far ahead eventually noticed the battle and returned, but the current and constant Indian fire made things difficult. One of the boats, commanded by Lieutenant Stephen Rector, managed to reach Campbell's boat and rescue Campbell and his men. Leaving behind the dead and dying, Rector's boat left in retreat for St. Louis, with Campbell himself seriously wounded. The third boat had grounded below the island on its return, and waited until it was safe to push off. Then it, too, headed for St. Louis.

In the battle, the Indians lost one warrior and one woman. The Americans lost 10 regulars, four rangers, one woman and a child, all of whom were mutilated and scalped. Campbell's boat remained partially submerged at the island, which was given Campbell's name, a reminder for many years of what British officers later called "the most brilliant victory of the war won by Indians unassisted by whites."

General Benjamin Howard, military commander headquartered at St. Louis, was upset by Campbell's defeat, but even more upset by the participation of the Saukenuk Indians. In reprisal, he determined to burn Saukenuk. In late August he sent a fleet of eight keelboats and 430 men toward the Rock River. Commanding this small army was Major Zachary Taylor, a 29-year-old regular who had already distinguished himself on the frontier. Among his captains was Samuel Whiteside, an Indian fighter from southern Illinois. Both these men would return again to participate in the Black Hawk War.

Taylor's fleet was accompanied by a party of Sioux, longtime Sauk enemies. In addition to rifles, arms included a three-pounder and two swivel guns. Taylor's plan was to pass by Saukenuk as if going to Prairie du Chien, and then drop down on the village at night.

Sauk Indians, however, spotted the flotilla when it was still below the mouth of the Rock River and sent a runner to notify the British at Prairie du Chien. The British responded with a plan of their own. They sent the Sauk back with two barges of supplies, including a three-pounder and two swivel guns, and ammunition for Black Hawk. The British commander also sent 30 soldiers to aid the Sauk. Their plan was to throw up a rude fort at the tip of the island of Rock Island, and surprise Taylor's boats as they passed this difficult stretch of Rock Island Rapids. The channel was narrow here, the current strong, and the water only two feet deep over gravel. Arriving at the island before Taylor, the British and Sauk carried out their plan. Leaving three British soldiers to aid with the large guns, the remaining British troops returned to Prairie du Chien, promising reinforcements.

On September 5, the American fleet was sighted coming up the Iowa shore opposite the mouth of the Rock River. Here, however, heavy winds forced Taylor to drop anchor at the head of Credit Island near present-day Davenport, and alter his plan of attack. He now decided to raise a white flag, arrange a conference with the Sauk, and attack the village while the conference was going on.

When the Indians avoided the white flag, some of Taylor's forces opened fire on several Sauk hidden on a small island covered with underbrush. Several Indian canoes in the area were also fired on and sunk. Then the three-pounder opened up from the Illinois shore, confusing Taylor's troops. Captain Whiteside's boat was hit by 15 shots in 45 minutes, and he retreated, followed by the other seven boats, which did not stop until they reached the Des Moines Rapids.

Taylor's defeat ended American attempts to remove British influence from the Upper Mississippi, and the war ended with British and Indians in control. The Sauk did not realize at the time that this was to be their last important victory. In less than 20 years they would be gone.

The War of 1812 concluded with a British-American conference at Ghent, Belgium, in August 1814. At first, the British tried to protect their Indian allies by proposing a buffer "Indian Territory" between the United States and Canada. When the Americans refused, the British suggested that the United States let bygones be bygones and return to conditions as they were in 1812 when the war began. This the Americans found acceptable, since the Treaty of 1804 had already given them the Sauk portion of Illinois. When the British commander at Prairie du Chien explained the peace treaty to the Indians, and they learned they had fought for nothing, they were angry. Black Hawk's request for at least one big gun to defend Saukenuk was also turned down.

The Treaty of Ghent was ratified by the United States on February 17, 1815. In March, President Madison appointed three commissioners to deal with the Indians in the west. "Deal with" meant moving them out of territory now open to white settlement.

Fort Armstrong Rises to Aid Fur Trade

After the War of 1812, the United States moved quickly to strengthen its hold on the Upper Mississippi Valley. At the instigation of John Jacob Astor and his American Fur Company, Congress banned all British traders from the United States territory in 1816. By then, the government had already projected a series of forts at Green Bay and along the Mississippi north of St. Louis to complement Fort Dearborn and Fort Mackinac, which had been reactivated. Between 1816 and 1819, Fort Edwards arose at the Des Moines Rapids, Fort Armstrong at Rock Island, Fort Crawford at Prairie du Chien, and Fort Snelling at the Falls of St. Anthony. In addition, Congress made the prairie region between the Illinois and Mississippi rivers a military tract from which land grants were made to veterans. White surveying lines now appeared for the first time on Sauk land.

In Western movies, forts protect settlers and ranchers from hostile Indians. Although these forts could have served that purpose, they were really there to keep the fur trade routes open, both against British traders and against the disruption caused by inter-tribal wars. Aside from Black Hawk's band, most Indians were friendly toward Americans.

On May 10, 1816, troops of the Eighth United States Infantry under command of Brevet Brigadier General Thomas A. Smith from Fort Independence at St. Louis arrived at the island of Rock Island to build a fort named after General John Armstrong, former secretary of war. This tip of the island at the foot of the Rock Island Rapids had been recommended by Lieutenant Pike during his explorations in 1805 because its high limestone cliffs raised it out of flood range and protected it from attack, because of its strategic location at the rapids, and because of the available water power.

General Smith discovered another advantage: the island provided its own wood and stone with which to build the fort. When his troops arrived at Rock Island, General Smith invited the Sauk and Mesquakie in the area to a treaty council. After refusing for several days, Black Hawk and the other Indians did conclude a peace treaty. The fort was being built on Sauk lands, and even according to the 1804 treaty, construction of a fort here was illegal. As construction progressed, Indians came to watch, to exchange gifts, to dance for the troops and, the whites feared, to attack. Black Hawk himself must have looked with mixed feelings on the construction at Rock Island.

THIS STEEL ENGRAVING OF FORT ARMSTRONG IS FROM MEYER'S UNIVERSUM, A SPRAWLING 10-VOLUME SET ORIGINALLY PUBLISHED IN MONTHLY PARTS BETWEEN 1833 AND 1860, AND SUBSEQUENTLY IN MANY EDITIONS IN MANY LANGUAGES. EACH MONTHLY ISSUE CONTAINED "VIEWS OF THE MOST REMARK-ABLE PLACES AND OBJECTS OF ALL COUNTRIES, ENGRAVED IN STEEL BY DISTINGUISHED ARTISTS, WITH DESCRIPTIVE AND HISTORICAL TEXT, BY EMINENT WRITERS IN EUROPE AND AMERICA."

According to popular myth, the island was sacred to the Sauk, inhabited by a great white swan that lived in a cave just under the construction site. Although Black Hawk's autobiography does not support this legend, it does suggest that the Sauk loved this island for the food it provided and for its beauty, and the building of the fort must have saddened them. The island, wrote Black Hawk, "was the best island on the Mississippi, and had long been the resort of our young people during the summer. It was our garden, which supplied us with strawberries, blackberries, plums, apples and nuts of various kinds."

Whites, too, were not indifferent to the beauty of the island and surrounding area, but they arrived at different conclusions. The Honorable Caleb Atwater of Ohio toured the Upper Mississippi shortly after the fort was completed, and concluded that the idea "that such a beautiful country was intended by its Author to be forever the occupancy of serpents, wild fowls, wild beasts and savages who derive little benefit from it, no reasonable man can for one minute believe."

Fort Armstrong was completed without trouble from the Sauk or from the Mesquakie living near the fort on both banks of the Mississippi. The completed fort was a square, about 270 feet on each side, built at the very tip of the island, so that the two open faces of the square were protected by 25-foot cliffs. At the point of these open faces stood the commanding officer's quarters, a 28-foot, two-story wood structure, with a 15-foot, one-story wing at each end, and front and rear piazzas. The officers' quarters stood along one open face, the hospital along the other. Near the point opposite the commanding officer's quarters stood a powder magazine of hewn stone.

The two landside faces of the fort were protected by stone walls eight feet high, supporting a breastwork of timbers five feet high. The three corners connected by the walls had two-story wood block houses each armed with six-pounders, the second floor diagonal for better protection. Along the inside of the stone walls were three hewn timber barracks, for three companies of men, and a storehouse. For the men serving at the fort, duty was lonely, but quite secure.

George Davenport Comes to Fort Armstrong

Accompanying the soldiers to Rock Island in 1816 were a civilian couple who were to play an important part in the history of the Quad-Cities. George Davenport had been born in Lincolnshire, England, in 1783, and had come to America in 1804. He joined the United States Army in 1812 as a sergeant, and participated in the War of 1812 and in Indian campaigns in the West. When his term of enlistment ended in 1815, Davenport entered the contract commissary service. At this time, United States troops were supplied by contract with private operators. Davenport and his wife came to Fort Armstrong to provide such service.

Davenport built a double log cabin to serve as home and store along the north shore of the island several hundred yards from the fort. Here the following year George L. Davenport was born, the first white child in the valley. Across the river, living with relatives in the Mesquakie village, was a French half-breed, Antoine Le Claire. Le Claire became the Indian interpreter for the fort, and like Davenport, went on to shape the Quad-Cities with both land and name.

Davenport branched out into the fur trade, and his trading posts were soon scattered across Iowa, Illinois and Wisconsin. He and Thomas Forsyth, who was appointed Indian Agent at Fort Armstrong in 1817 by William Clark, established excellent relations with the Indians. Forsyth, whose job consisted of paying out Indian annuities, keeping the fur traders honest and

GEORGE DAVENPORT'S DOUBLE LOG CABIN BUILT ON THE NORTH SHORE OF ROCK ISLAND IN 1816 SERVED AS HOME, STORE AND TRADING POST.

making peace between warring tribes and individuals, worked especially hard to make both Indian and white play fair.

George Davenport's business interests continued to grow. In 1825 he was appointed postmaster for the fort and the surrounding valley; that year he also established the first ferry service across the Mississippi from the north shore of the island to Iowa. Because of the current, the Iowa side needed two landings, one upstream for departures, and one downstream for arrivals. In 1826 Davenport merged his fur business with the American Fur Company and took a partner, Russell Farnham. Under the firm name of Davenport & Farnham, they built a house on the Illinois mainland.

Steamboats End the Fort's Isolation

For seven years Fort Armstrong remained an isolated outpost in the wilderness. Then, on May 10, 1823, a small steamboat approached the island. Soldiers cheered and saluted the arrival with cannon fire. The boat — little more than a steam engine on a barge — was the *Virginia*, the first steamboat that had ventured to cross the Des Moines Rapids. She was on her way to Fort Snelling with supplies, a trial run. Although the *Virginia* did go aground on the Rock Island Rapids as she left Fort Armstrong, needing a sudden rise of water to get afloat, she continued to the Falls of St. Anthony and returned. Later that summer she made a second run.

The small, frail *Virginia* was the product of American ingenuity pitted against the vagaries of America's inland waterways. Before 1811, when the first steamboat *New Orleans* came down the Ohio River to the Mississippi, travel on these rivers was clumsy and slow. Rafts and flatboats brought furs and other goods down river, after which they were broken up and sold for lumber. Keelboats could make the return trip, but only by being poled or hauled by ropes from shore at a rate of six to 10 miles per day. Supplying outposts such as Fort Armstrong or Fort Snelling was a laborious task.

The steamboat changed all that. The first powered boats could only operate in the relatively deep water below the Ohio River. Above that, especially above St. Louis, the Mississippi was shallow, full of shifting sandbars. The two stretches of rapids at Keokuk and Rock Island caused many rivermen to believe that steamboats would never be used north of St. Louis until those rapids were "improved." But river tinkerers quickly flattened out the hull of the steamboat and developed high-pressure engines which they placed on, not in, the hull. Extending out over this flat hull they built a lightweight gingerbread superstructure which gave the Mississippi steamboat the appearance of floating just above the water surface while carrying tons of cargo.

Soon steamboats were arriving at St. Louis, then at Keokuk by 1820, and, with the *Virginia's* voyage in 1823, all the way to Fort Snelling and St. Anthony's Falls — the head of navigation. Rapidly after 1823, the steamboat brought civilization to the Upper Mississippi Valley and complications for the Indians. By 1842, about 450 steamboats were operating on the Upper Mississippi, many of them already taking fashionable tourists from the east to visit the Falls of St. Anthony. Immigrants were also arriving, and when the railroad reached Rock Island in 1854, the young city became one of the three major steamboat departure centers for immigrants heading out to the farmland of Iowa, Minnesota, Wisconsin and the Dakotas.

The heyday of steamboating on the Mississippi came with the creation of Minnesota Territory in 1849. There followed a stampede of immigrants and settlers that dwarfed the California Gold Rush that same year. By 1854 as many as 175 steamboats a month were arriving and departing Rock Island. The Davenport levee was almost as busy. During the 1857 season, 1,587 steamboats arrived in Davenport, 960 of them having Davenport as terminus. At the head of the rapids, Le Claire, too, enjoyed rapid growth.

A LITHOGRAPH OF FORT ARMSTRONG FROM GLEASON'S PICTORIAL FOR FEBRUARY 26, 1853. BELOW THE FORT CAN BE SEEN THE CLIFF AND THE CAVE ENTRANCES, NOW SUBMERGED BECAUSE OF THE LOCK AND DAM SYSTEM.

Here, under a famous river landmark, the Green Tree, rapids pilots waited to be hired by passing captains to steer boats through the treacherous rapids. Le Claire also was home of the Van Sant Boatyard, one of the largest on the Mississippi and the first to develop special raftboats to tow the large log rafts coming down to sawmills from the white pine forests of Minnesota and Wisconsin.

Although the packet and passenger boats which plied the Upper Mississippi were not as spectacular as the large gingerbread palaces on the Lower Mississippi made famous by Mark Twain, they shared the same functional beauty as their larger sisters. Seldom designed with plans, the steamboats took shape on the ways as they took shape in the imagination of the builder. Yet everything was a product of river necessities. The paddle wheel was needed in water too shallow for propellers; the boats had to be high, as much as four stories, to give the pilot a long view of the twisting channel; the smokestacks raised far above the top decks to lift smoke and cinders away from passengers and from wooden decks; the filagree and gingerbread kept the boats light. The steamboat brought prosperity and people into the Mississippi Valley and spread names like Rock Island, Davenport and Le Claire across the country.

The Black Hawk War Ends Indians' Era

The last chapter for the Sauk Indians who had not left the area to settle in Iowa and Missouri was a skirmish of several months' duration known as the Black Hawk War. Rather than an isolated event, it was the culmination of pressure on the Sauk from several sources. The greatest of these was the rapidly increasing encroachment on Sauk land during the 1820s by white settlement and by the United States Government.

By the time Fort Armstrong was completed, the United States had already moved to toughen its Indian policy. In June 1815, Governor Clark had invited all the tribes along the Mississippi Valley to a conference at Portage des Sioux north of St. Louis. Black Hawk and the Indians at Saukenuk refused to appear, but the Sauk and Mesquakie who did show up reconfirmed the Treaty of 1804 ceding Illinois lands to the United States, and they promised not to interfere on the side of Black Hawk and his British Band (now numbering only about one-sixth of the Sauk nation, about 300 to 400 warriors).

USED IN SOLEMN RITUALS,
DIFFERENT SAUK CALUMET PIPES
WERE SMOKED FOR WAR, PEACE
OR SIMPLER USES.

War with Saukenuk was averted in May the following year when Black Hawk appeared at St. Louis three days after soldiers had arrived to build Fort Armstrong and, under duress, signed the treaty. On August 24, 1816, Clark concluded a treaty with the Ottawas, Chippewas and Potawatomi along the Illinois River, who claimed some of the same land claimed by the Sauk. In this treaty the tribes ceded all their Illinois land south of a line due west from the southern tip of Lake Michigan. In return, they received permission to live on former Sauk land north of the line, and an annuity of $1,000 for 12 years. This Indian Boundry Line was surveyed, slightly askew, by Sullivan and Duncan in 1819, and again, a bit further south, by Flack and Bean in 1821. The line bisected the future site of Rock Island and reached the Mississippi just above the mouth of the Rock River.

A similar treaty in 1824, signed by the Sauk and Mesquakie, confirmed all previous ones. Although several white settlers by this time had encroached on Indian land, they were few in number, and Black Hawk let them stay. The first serious encroachment did not come until 1828. The United States had come to regret the 1804 Treaty, which permitted the Sauk to remain on their land "so long as it was owned by the United States." Southern Illinois was already heavily settled, Illinois had become a state in 1818, and new settlers were eager to move into the rich northern prairies. The United States solved the dilemna caused by the 1804 Treaty by holding a Land Office Sale in 1828 and selling off several sections of Sauk lands. Both George Davenport and Russell Farnham bought land at this sale. Davenport ended up with 80 percent of the land sold, including the site of Saukenuk. From this point onward, Davenport grew cooler in his relation to the Indians. He volunteered his services to Governor Reynolds in the Black Hawk War; Reynolds appointed him quartermaster general with the rank of colonel.

The next year, contrary to the 1816 treaty with the Ottawas, Chippewas and Potawatomi, the Treaty of July 29, 1829, gave Antoine and Francis Le Claire two sections — 1,280 acres — of land north of, and bordering, the Indian Boundry Line. These encroachments gained a boost from the election of President Andrew Jackson in 1830. As a westerner, Jackson was committed to a policy of removal, which showed itself in such ways as the Indian Removal Act of 1831, dedicated to moving the Indians so far west that they would never cause trouble again.

By 1831 a large number of squatters were entering Indian lands reserved by treaty for the Indians. In 1827, the Illinois Legislature created Jo Daviess County with a seat at Galena. On February 9, 1831, another act of the legislature created Rock Island County out of the southwest section of Jo Daviess County. The Black Hawk War kept the county from being officially organized until July 5, 1833, but for Black Hawk, the end was predictable. Thomas Forsyth tried to talk the Sauk into leaving peacefully, but he was annoyed at the encroachments, too. His removal as Indian agent in 1831 for being too sympathetic to the Indians left an important gap in subsequent negotiations.

Meanwhile, rather than weakening, Black Hawk's resistance grew. He knew that alone he could not resist the invasion of soldier and settler, but he believed that his resistance would inspire other Sauk and Mesquakie, as well as neighboring Iowa and Illinois Indians, to resist. White Cloud, the Winnebago Prophet living up the Rock River near present-day Prophetstown, had promised the aid of Winnebago, Ottawa, Chippewa and Potawatomi. Just as important, the British continued to feed Black Hawk's resistance with vague promises of aid from Fort Malden via Milwaukee. Most Indian tribes had stopped their annual trips to Fort Malden by the 1820s, but Black Hawk and his band continued. This fierce loyalty to the British further annoyed United States officials.

Tension increased in the spring of 1831 when Black Hawk returned to Saukenuk from the winter hunt to find squatters living in his own lodge and others as well. Fences had been pulled down, pasture plowed up, goods destroyed. Black Hawk was patient but not accepting. There were reprisals and small fights. On April 30 and again on May 19, these new Rock Island settlers petitioned Governor Reynolds for protection. Meanwhile, 51 local white settlers formed themselves into the Rock River Rangers to aid in their own protection. On May 26, Governor Reynolds called out the state militia to remove the Indians. In order to aid this group of non-professionals, General Edmund P. Gaines, commander of the Army of the West at Jefferson Barracks south of St. Louis, headed toward Saukenuk with six companies of United States infantry. The Indians fled as he approached the Rock River in an armed steamboat, and on June 26, this combined force of regular troops, militia and rangers occupied a deserted Saukenuk and burned it down.

The next day Black Hawk crossed the Mississippi with a white flag and surrendered. On June 30, the Saukenuk Indians signed "articles of agreement and capitulation" admitting that they had broken the Treaty of 1804, and promising to move permanently west of the Mississippi. The remainder of the Sauk and Mesquakie nations, 1,500 warriors in all, had remained friendly to the United States during this skirmish. Keokuk, in fact, had come to Fort Armstrong during the conflict to reconfirm that friendship.

By the summer of 1831, the Black Hawk problem seemed to be over, but in July an event took place at Fort Crawford that turned into the fuse that lit a real war the next year. On the night of July 30, 1831, a band of Menominee Indians were camped on an island under the guns of Fort Crawford. They had come on business with Indian Agent Joseph M. Street, and business finished, they had gotten drunk. Early in the morning of July 31, they were surprised by a group of 80 to 100 Sauk and Mesquakie seeking revenge for killings earlier in the summer during an ongoing inter-tribal conflict. Twenty-five of the helpless Menomimee were killed and many others wounded.

Authorities at Rock Island wanted the offending Indians turned over to the United States, but they were refused. This small war party had been led by Quashquame, who, unlike Black Hawk, was an important Sauk chief among the British Band.

Feelings on both sides smoldered during the fall and winter of 1831-32. Black Hawk spent the winter at the traditional Sauk hunting grounds in the west, trying to convince the Missouri Sauk to join him in resisting the whites, but he was unsuccessful.

Events came to a head early in 1832. Rumors during January had Black Hawk returning or already returned. Confirmation of this came on April 5, 1832, when the Winnebago Prophet White Cloud — half Sauk, half Winnebago — came to Fort Armstrong to tell Felix St. Vrain (who had replaced Thomas Forsyth as Indian agent) that Black Hawk and his people were coming to live with him at his village on the Rock River. Vrain notified John Bliss, commander of the 60-man garrison at the fort. Bliss notified his superiors and proceeded to patch up the badly deteriorated fort.

Without being aware of this news, General Henry Atkinson, commander of Jefferson Barracks, had started out for Saukenuk on April 8 with six companies (220 men) of the Sixth Infantry. He had been ordered by the War Department to demand that the Sauk hand over the Indians responsible for the Menominee attack, or any eight to 10 Indians.

On April 10 as he reached the Des Moines Rapids, General Atkinson first learned that Black Hawk had indeed crossed the Mississippi at Yellow Banks — now Oquawka — on April 6. Here he had been met by White Cloud, and was heading for Rock Island. Atkinson's troops, coming by boat, arrived at Fort Armstrong ahead of Black Hawk, but they made no attempt

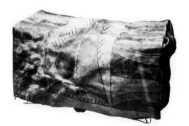

THE SAUK AND MESQUAKIE USED LEATHER POUCHES, SUCH AS THIS, TO CARRY MANY KINDS OF ITEMS.

THE ONLY KNOWN MEETING BETWEEN TWO CIVIL WAR LEADERS, ABRAHAM LINCOLN AND JEFFERSON DAVIS, OCCURRED DURING THE BLACK HAWK WAR WHEN BOTH SERVED UNDER ZACHARY TAYLOR. DAVIS, WHO WAS TAYLOR'S SON-IN-LAW, WAS A LIEUTENANT IN THE REGULAR ARMY. LINCOLN, A 24-YEAR-OLD SHOPKEEPER FROM NEW SALEM, ILLINOIS, SERVED BRIEFLY AS A CAPTAIN OF MILITIA AND LATER, AFTER HIS INITIAL ENLISTMENT EXPIRED, AS A PRIVATE.

to occupy Saukenuk or stand in Black Hawk's way. Keokuk was at the fort again, and he told Atkinson that all the Menominee murderers were with Black Hawk. Atkinson now had extra reason to go after the British Band. After again requesting Governor Reynolds to call out the state militia, General Atkinson left for Fort Crawford to get additional help. He returned with two companies of the First Infantry led by Lieutenant Colonel Zachary Taylor. Atkinson also sent messengers to the lead mining region around Galena to warn them of possible trouble.

Governor Reynolds issued his call for volunteers on April 16, requesting them to meet at Beardstown on April 22. Meanwhile, hearing reports of Black Hawk's movements up the Rock River Valley, Reynolds sent ahead two battalions of state militia under Major Isaiah Stillman of Fulton County and Major David Bailey of Tazewell County toward the Rock River on April 20. At the same time, the official United States position toward Black Hawk was hardening. Governor Clark declared on April 20 that the British Band would never "be brought to a sense of propriety until they were severely punished."

The 1,694 volunteers who gathered at Beardstown by April 22 were ready for such punishment. A majority of them were from southern Illinois, not threatened immediately by Black Hawk, and they were there to hunt Indians. Their appointed leader was General Samuel Whiteside, an earlier participant in the battle of Credit Island and by now a practiced Indian fighter.

Governor Reynolds, who accompanied these volunteers for morale purposes, decided to wait at Beardstown for supplies from St. Louis. When the supplies had not arrived by April 27, the volunteer army set out for Yellow Banks. The supplies arrived there on May 6, and 10 days' provisions were given to each man. Just as the troops were ready to march for Dixon's Ferry, a false rumor came that Black Hawk had descended the Rock River, and so Reynolds and Whiteside turned their troops toward the mouth of the river, where they arrived on May 7. They camped on a farm owned by John Blazer at the junction of present-day Ridgewood and Andalusia Roads in Milan.

Here, on May 8, the Illinois volunteers were sworn into the United States service. Among the volunteers from Sangamon County was a young New Salem store clerk, Abraham Lincoln, who was elected captain of his company. Lincoln ended up seeing no action in the war, and later described it as "a good many bloody struggles with mosquitoes," but his presence here along with Zachary Taylor and a young captain of the First Infantry, Jefferson Davis — the only time he and the future Confederate president were ever together — has added to the local Lincoln legends.

General Atkinson divided the volunteers into two groups, placing the mounted volunteers under General Whiteside and the foot volunteers, who were in charge of supplies, under Colonel Taylor. On May 9, this army of more than 2,000 set out up the Rock River.

They reached the Prophet's village the following day, and fired it when they found it empty. Black Hawk and White Cloud had moved further up the valley. The Sauk women and children had left under Winnebago escort for Lake Koshkonong in Wisconsin.

The battalions under Majors Stillman and Bailey had been at Dixon's Ferry for two days when Whiteside's troops arrived and were eager to move on after Black Hawk. Governor Reynolds still retained command of the Illinois militia, and on Sunday morning, May 13, he permitted them to go. The force of 200 moved up the Rock River, crossed at Old Man's Creek and set up camp. They were preparing supper when three Sauk Indians entered camp bearing a white flag. This may have been a ruse, as Stillman suspected, or a genuine truce offer, as Black Hawk later suggested. The latter seems more reasonable, and some historians suggest that the war could have ended here. Black Hawk had just learned that he would get no help from the Winnebagos or Potawatomi and that the promised British help at Milwaukee would not arrive. He was low on provisions. In his autobiography, Black Hawk wrote that he and his people were prepared to return across the Mississippi if White Beaver (General Atkinson) came after them.

Major Stillman took no chances. He detained the three Sauk emmisaries. When Black Hawk sent five more Indians to investigate, they encountered a scout party of 20 rangers, who pursued and killed two of the Indians. Black Hawk now decided to fight, sending Stillman into retreat toward Dixon's Ferry. A small detachment of Bailey's battalion covering the retreat were all killed in a successful attempt to prevent Stillman's forces from being wiped out. After this battle, the place became known as Stillman's Run, and the battle, the Battle of Stillman's Run.

On the same day as Stillman's retreat, Governor Reynolds issued a call for 2,000 additional mounted volunteers to replace the first volunteers whose enlistments were nearly up. The new volunteers were to meet June 10 at Hennepin on the Illinois River.

General Atkinson arrived at Dixon's Ferry with supplies on May 17, and two days later the entire army of volunteers and regulars moved out of Dixon's Ferry toward the upper Rock River. At about this time, isolated violence broke out throughout the Illinois country north of the Illinois River. Black Hawk had decided on the tactic of breaking into small groups when pursued, sending decoys to hide the location of the tribe at Lake Koshkonong, and to make the whites think he was heading toward the Mississippi. Other Indians in the region, if they did not join Black Hawk, used the occasion to vent long pent-up feelings, taking their hostility out on settlers and soldiers.

On May 23, for example, Felix St. Vrain, Indian agent at Fort Armstrong, was leading a party of cattle buyers from Dixon's Ferry to Galena when he was attacked by Sauk under Little Bear. St. Vrain was not only well liked by the Sauk, he had been "adopted" by Little Bear, and assumed he was safe. Instead, the entire party was massacred. The Sauk cut off St. Vrain's head, hands and feet, before cutting his heart out and eating it.

These scattered atrocities perplexed General Atkinson, but he decided to keep pursuing the main band up toward the headwaters of the Rock. Before continuing, however, it was time to muster out the first volunteers. This took place on May 27 at Ottawa. Three hundred of these troops, including Lincoln, volunteered for another 20 days to serve as an interim regiment until the new volunteers arrived.

While Black Hawk continued his hit and run tactics, 2,000 new volunteers gathered near Hennepin. Because of dropping river levels, General Atkinson met at Fort Wilborn, 12 miles downstream from Ottawa, and mustered them into service between June 15 and June 20. On June 15, Atkinson divided this Army of the Frontier into three brigades, generally according to the region of Illinois from which they had come. The First Brigade consisted of 962 men recruited from the southern tier of counties. The First Brigade elected Dr. Alexander Posey of Shawneetown as commander. The Second Brigade consisted of 959 men from the eastern counties, who elected as commander Milton K. Alexander, an old friend of Governor Reynolds and postmaster of Paris, Illinois. The Third Brigade, 1,275 men from the western counties, elected Sheriff James Doughty Henry of Springfield as commander. Both Henry and Alexander had participated in the 1831 campaign.

The three brigades moved out between June 20 and 23. Atkinson now had at his command some 3,200 mounted militia and 500 regulars. Aiding these from the Galena region were several Indian detachments assembled by Colonel Billy Hamilton and several hundred mounted rangers from

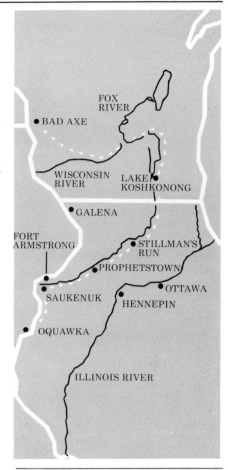

THE BLACK HAWK WAR OF 1832 WAS ACTUALLY A SLOW RETREAT BY BLACK HAWK AND HIS BRITISH BAND, PURSUED BY FEDERAL TROOPS, THE ILLINOIS MILITIA AND A LARGE VOLUNTEER ARMY. THE RETREAT TOOK BOTH PARTIES UP THE ROCK RIVER TO LAKE KOSHKONONG IN WISCONSIN, THEN WESTWARD TO THE MISSISSIPPI RIVER AT BAD AXE, WHERE, ON AUGUST 2, 1832, THE FINAL BATTLE OF THE WAR TOOK PLACE. OF THE 1,000 SAUK WHO HAD CROSSED THE MISSISSIPPI IN THE SPRING OF 1832, FEWER THAN 150 LIVED TO JOIN KEOKUK AND HIS BAND IN IOWA AFTER THE WAR.

ZACHARY TAYLOR, THE CAREER SOLDIER WHO BECAME THE 12TH PRESIDENT OF THE UNITED STATES, FOUGHT IN TWO WARS IN THE QUAD-CITY AREA. DURING THE WAR OF 1812, 29-YEAR-OLD BREVET MAJOR TAYLOR COMMANDED AN ILL-FATED EXPEDITION TO RECAPTURE THE STRATEGIC MOUTH OF THE ROCK RIVER. AFTER THAT WAR, TAYLOR LEFT THE ARMY AND TURNED TO FARMING. HE MIGHT HAVE REMAINED A CIVILIAN IF HIS COUSIN, PRESIDENT JAMES MADISON, HAD NOT PERSUADED HIM TO REJOIN. NEARLY 20 YEARS AFTER HIS BATTLE NEAR CREDIT ISLAND, TAYLOR RETURNED TO THE QUAD-CITY AREA AS A COLONEL TO COMMAND TROOPS IN THE BLACK HAWK WAR. "OLD ROUGH AND READY" WENT ON TO FIGHT IN THE MEXICAN WAR. HE LED HIS COMMAND OF VOLUNTEERS AND REGULARS TO A SERIES OF BRILLIANT VICTORIES. HIS WAR RECORD HELPED PROPEL HIM INTO THE WHITE HOUSE IN 1848 AS THE SECOND, AND LAST, WHIG PRESIDENT. HIS 18-MONTH PRESIDENCY WAS NOT PARTICULARLY SIGNIFICANT, LARGELY BECAUSE CONGRESSIONAL BICKERING OVER SLAVERY PREVENTED PASSAGE OF MANY IMPORTANT BILLS. TAYLOR DIED JULY 9, 1850, AFTER AN ACUTE ATTACK OF GASTROENTERITIS, APPARENTLY CAUSED BY EATING RAW FRUITS AND VEGETABLES, WASHED DOWN BY TOO MUCH COLD MILK AND WATER.

southern Wisconsin and the lead region assembled by Colonel Henry Dodge of the Michigan Territory militia.

Black Hawk's continued small counterattacks resulted in many skirmishes, several of which were large enough to be called battles. These included confrontations at the Apple and Pecatonica rivers and at Kellogg's Grove. Atkinson sent detachments to assist in these battles, but the main Army of the Frontier followed several routes toward Lake Koshkonong. They reached the site of Stillman's Run on July 29, and Turtles Village (now Beloit, Wisconsin) by July 3. By July 4, they had reached the lake, one of the Rock River's reservoirs. At this point, Governor Reynolds left to return home.

On July 6 the forces moved around Lake Koshkonong but were stopped in an attempt to cross a swampy area of the Bark River and mired for several days. By July 10, provisions were so low that Atkinson was forced to break up his forces to avoid starvation. He took the opportunity of discharging a large number of the volunteers (including Lincoln) who were more hindrance than help. He sent Posey's forces west to Fort Hamilton; Henry's and Alexander's brigades were sent with Dodge's rangers to Fort Winnebago for supplies and 12 days' rations. Atkinson and his regulars returned to the south side of the lake and built a small fort, awaiting supplies.

When the supply forces reached Fort Winnebago on July 12, they found a Winnebago-French half breed, Pierre Poquette, who offered to lead them to Black Hawk, now at the Rock Rapids 40 miles east. Either Dodge or Henry developed a plan to return to Fort Koshkonong by swinging north of the Rock Rapids on their way, driving Black Hawk south and west. They convinced their reluctant officers to go along with the plan, but General Alexander refused to participate in this unauthorized movement and returned with his forces to notify General Atkinson, taking 36 wagons of food and supplies.

On July 15, Henry, with 600 hand-picked troops, and Dodge with 150 headed for Black Hawk guided by Poquette and a dozen Winnebagoes. Black Hawk and his people were not at the Rock Rapids when Henry's forces arrived, but the trail grew warm further south when Henry discovered bark stripped from young trees to serve as food for Black Hawk's now starving band. Henry and Dodge pursued the Indians westward. Black Hawk was now clearly heading for the Mississippi and the safety of the Iowa shore.

The straggling Indians were finally sighted in the Four Lakes region of Wisconsin, at the site of present-day Madison. Four Sauk were killed and scalped in a chase that led across the site of the present state capitol and the University of Wisconsin, while the main band escaped northwest to the bluffs along the Wisconsin River. Here, on the afternoon of the 21st, a skirmish known as the Battle of Wisconsin Heights took place. Six Indians were killed, but the main force of Indians crossed safely over the Wisconsin River, and Henry decided to wait for Atkinson's forces before continuing the pursuit.

All three brigades united again on July 27 at Helena, a deserted town on the Wisconsin River. Using logs from the abandoned houses, the whole army crossed the river and moved toward the retreating Black Hawk, following a trail of stripped bark and the carcasses of horses dead from exhaustion. General Atkinson, angry at Henry for taking action without orders, assigned Henry's brigade to guard the baggage at the rear of the marching column.

On August 1 Black Hawk reached the Mississippi near the mouth of the Bad Axe River, opposite the northern boundary of Iowa. As they were preparing to cross, they met the steamboat *Warrior* which, unknown to them, was returning to Fort Crawford with several regulars on board from a trip to Wabasha's Village (now Winona, Minnesota) to inform the Sioux chief that their enemies the Sauk were preparing to cross the Mississippi.

WAR AND PESTILENCE !

CAPTURE OF TWO YOUNG LADIES BY THE SAVAGES

THE PRECEDING YEAR (1832) WILL BE LONG REMEM-
BERED IN AMERICA, AS A YEAR OF MUCH HUMAN
DISTRESS,

While many of our most populous cities have been visited by that dreadful disease, the CHOLERA, and to
which Thousands have fallen victims, the merciless
SAVAGES have been as fatally engaged in the work
of death, on the frontiers ; where great numbers (including women and children) have fallen victims to the
bloody Tomahawk !

AN ADVERTISEMENT USED TO PROMOTE AN 1833 ACCOUNT OF THE CAPTURE OF TWO SISTERS, FRANCIS AND ALMIRA HALL (AGES 16 AND 18) BY SAUK INDIANS DURING THE BLACK HAWK WAR. THE SISTERS WERE TAKEN FROM THEIR HOME NEAR INDIAN CREEK, ILLINOIS, IN MAY OF 1832, IN A FORAY IN WHICH 16 WHITES WERE MASSACRED. THE SISTERS WERE SOON RETURNED UNHARMED BUT THEIR CAPTURE WAS WIDELY USED ALONG THE FRONTIER TO CREATE ANTI-INDIAN SENTIMENT AND TO AID THE CALL FOR VOLUNTEERS FOR THE MILITIA.

Black Hawk recognized Captain Throckmorton of the *Warrior* and waved a piece of cotton to surrender, but he refused the captain's request to send one boat party aboard. After 15 minutes, the *Warrior* opened up with a six-pounder loaded with cannister and with musket fire, which the Sauk returned. After exchanging fire for an hour, the *Warrior* pulled anchor and continued to Prairie du Chien.

On the night of August 1, a few Indians succeeded in crossing the river, as Black Hawk, the Prophet, 10 warriors and 35 women and children escaped toward the Wisconsin Dells region, leaving the remaining disorganized Sauk to fend for themselves.

General Atkinson's army had caught up to within five miles of the Sauk by August 2, but his force of 400 regulars under Taylor and 900 volunteers of Posey's, Alexander's and a portion of Henry's brigades were decoyed north by a few Sauk to hide the main crossing at Bad Axe. Only that part of Henry's command bringing up the rear of the column discovered the real route. He soon found himself confronting a band of 300 warriors, nearly equal his own forces, in the only real "engagement" of the war.

As the fight progressed, General Atkinson and the rest of the troops returned to the battleground. The *Warrior* also arrived from Prairie du Chien, and aided the land forces in driving the Sauk across a slough of the Mississippi to an island. The battle turned into a massacre for the next three hours. Some 150 Indians, an equal number of both sexes, were killed by fire from the troops. Others drowned trying to escape or were caught and butchered. Many of the survivors died of wounds, hunger and exhaustion. A very few women and children were taken prisoner; more of them died in the massacre. American casualties were 17 killed and 12 wounded.

About 300 Sauk made it across the river to Iowa, where half of them were killed by Wabasha, the Sioux chief who was expecting them, as they made their way toward Keokuk's village. Of the 1,000 Sauk Indians who had crossed the river at Yellow Banks in April, fewer than 150 now remained alive.

Black Hawk's freedom did not last long. On August 7 he surrendered to a group of Winnebagoes, who took him to Fort Crawford and turned him over to Joseph M. Street, the Indian agent. After a short imprisonment, Black Hawk was taken on a tour of eastern cities, including Washington, D.C., where he met President Jackson. The purpose of this tour was to impress Black Hawk with the might of the United States and convince him of the uselessness of resistance — a purpose underscored in person by the President. Black Hawk understood, and broken in spirit, refused to permit his picture to be taken with a spear in his hand.

Seventy whites had been killed by the end of the war, but in mid-August, the war brought a far more deadly enemy than the Indian: cholera. Early in July of 1832, General Winfield Scott had been ordered west from Detroit to take charge of the Army of the Frontier from General Atkinson. Cholera broke out among Scott's troops as they were crossing Lake Michigan toward Chicago. Scott was detained at Fort Dearborn while the epidemic subsided, and he did not arrive at Fort Armstrong until the war was over. His orders now were to conclude the war and arrange the treaties.

Although the cholera among his troops had apparently run its course, Scott took the precaution of setting up headquarters on Rock Island away from the fort and from Atkinson's troops who were there to be mustered out. It did not work. By August 27 there were 145 cases of cholera at Fort Armstrong and 25 deaths. Between August 27 and September 2, about 150 new cases appeared. Many of Atkinson's soldiers who had survived the rigors of war now died or deserted.

By the middle of September the cholera had died down, and the treaty-making began. The treaty of September 21, 1832, arranged between General Scott and Governor Reynolds, and the Sauk and Mesquakie, now took much of the remaining tribal land. This time, in addition to the Illinois land, the

Indians ceded a strip of land 40 to 50 miles wide along the west bank of the Mississippi from the Missouri border north to the present Iowa-Minnesota border, except for a 400-square-mile reservation along both sides of the Iowa River, which included Keokuk's village.

The treaty also split up the British Band and ordered them to live in other Sauk villages. Black Hawk and his two sons, and the Prophet and his brother and two sons, were to be held as hostages to insure the good behavior of the tribes. Further, the United States agreed to pay George Davenport and Russell Farnham $40,000 to satisfy their claims against the Indians for goods received the previous seven years. Antoine Le Claire, the Indian interpreter, received two separate sections of land on the west bank of the Mississippi, one opposite the island of Rock Island, and one at the head of the Rock Island Rapids. This latter site became the town that today bears his name.

In return for their land, the Sauk and Mesquakie were to receive $20,000 paid over a period of 30 years. During the same 30 years, they were to receive annually 40 kegs of tobacco and 40 barrels of salt and the services of a blacksmith and gunsmith shop set up on the reservation. They were to receive additional presents should they point out to the United States the location of any new mine of a metal more valuable than lead or iron. Finally, the United States, "wishing to give a striking evidence of their mercy & liberality," agreed to give the Indians 35 beef cattle, 12 bushels of salt, 30 barrels of pork and 50 barrels of flour for use of the widows and children of warriors killed in the war.

The Sauk and Mesquakie were given until June 1, 1833, to move off of their ceded land. That year, George Davenport replaced his log home with a large two-story frame house on the same spot, a house which has been preserved and is still standing.

THE BLACK HAWK TREATY WAS SIGNED AT FORT ARMSTRONG ON SEPTEMBER 21, 1832. GENERAL WINFIELD SCOTT ARRIVED IN ILLINOIS TOO LATE TO PARTICIPATE IN THE WAR, BUT HE IS SHOWN HERE REPRESENTING THE UNITED STATES AT THE SIGNING, WITH THE OFFICIAL INTERPRETER, ANTOINE LE CLAIRE, AT HIS LEFT.

Black Hawk remained a prisoner for a year. On August 2, 1833, the anniversary of the Battle of Bad Axe, he was placed in Keokuk's custody in ceremonies at Fort Armstrong. He resented this, and in 1836, he and the remnants of his British Band attempted unsuccessfully to depose Keokuk as a principal Sauk chief. Defeated both in and out of his tribe, he lived with his wife and children along the Iowa River. In 1838 he and his family moved to the Des Moines River, where he died on October 3. He was buried sitting erect in a log tomb. After a grave robbery, his bones ended up in a museum in Burlington, Iowa, where they burned in a fire in 1855.

Fort Armstrong, its usefulness ended, fell into decay. It was evacuated on May 4, 1836, and its troops sent to Fort Snelling. All of the property was removed that November. From 1836 to 1838 the island and fort were under the charge of Joseph Street, the Indian agent. He was succeeded in 1838 by George Davenport. In 1840 several garrison buildings were repaired and an ordnance depot was established at the location, but was discontinued five years later. From then on, a series of custodians had charge of the fort, until part of it burned in 1855. The last of the original fort disappeared after the Civil War, when several of its beams were used in the construction of Storehouse A for the new Rock Island Arsenal.

After the Black Hawk War, white settlers moved quickly into Illinois and Iowa land, and just as quickly those landings, steamboat stops, posts and stores became villages — the nucleus of today's Quad-Cities. Of the Sauk and Mesquakie, there are left only legends, a park, a statue, a festival — and frequent arrowheads turned up by plow or rain. Of the steamboats, there are left only a bell, a wheel, a museum and postcards. Of the great log rafts, there are left only the mansions along the hill, and the wood in thousands of Quad-Cities houses. Only the river remains, joining the Quad-Cities, joining past and present. If this river and its valley were lovely for Black Hawk, it is haunting, too, for that old man standing along the river railing in Le Claire Park, for that traveler crossing the river high up on the I-80 bridge — and for us all.

BY KATHLEEN SEUSY

"Twas a hundred years or more, on the Mississippi shore
When a Farnhamsburg and Stevenson lie sleeping.
River towns of little fame unite and change the name,
For the spirit of the river came a creeping.
To the little isle of rocks,
Home of Indian Sacs and Fox,
With their wigwams of birches and the larch,
And when Black Hawk had to go at the cry of
Westward Ho!
Then Rock Island just started to march."
FROM *"THE SPIRIT OF THE RIVER"* BY WILLIAM LEVANDER

Rock Island County was formed by an act of the Illinois legislature in 1831. However, it was not until several months after the conclusion of the Black Hawk War in 1832 when the Indians had moved west to Iowa and Kansas that the county's boundaries were fixed. The first election, for the purpose of choosing three commissioners, was held at the house of John Barrel in Farnhamsburg on July 5, 1833. The Barrel home, a combination trading post, tavern, stage station and courthouse, stood some 450 feet to the north of present 28th Street and 5th Avenue.

Great excitement attended this first county election. There were two factions, one representing the Farnhamsburg or island people, and the other

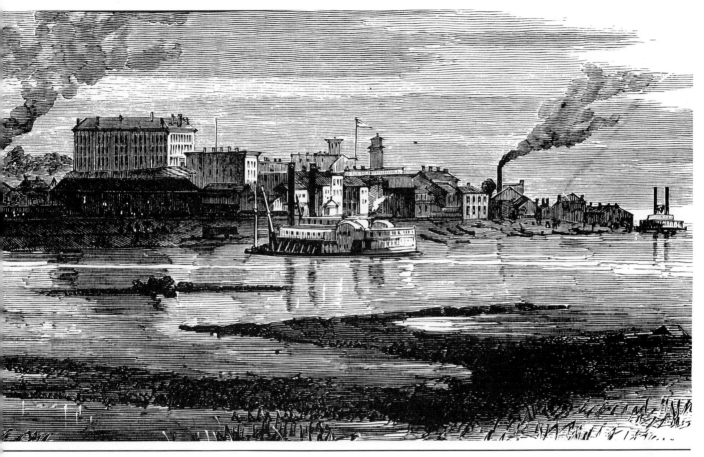

A VIEW OF ROCK ISLAND FROM THE ISLAND, PUBLISHED IN <u>PICTURESQUE AMERICA</u> IN 1874. SOME ARTISTIC LIBERTIES MAY HAVE BEEN TAKEN, BUT THE WAGON BRIDGE AND THE SPIRES OF ST. MARY'S AND TRINITY EPISCOPAL CHURCHES ARE EVIDENT.

the Hampton or mainland settlers. It had been arranged that Colonel George Davenport, an important citizen of the area and a leader of the Farnhamsburg ticket, would signal certain islanders if their votes were needed. The Hampton party caught the colonel in the act and fearing that he was summoning the soldiers from the fort, they determined to seize the poll book and stop the election. Warned in time, the two election clerks substituted a blank poll book for the real one. Once the Hampton men were chased out of sight by some of the island party, the regular poll book was produced. The election then continued with additional islanders arriving, casting their votes and electing their ticket of George Harlan, John Spencer and George Davenport. Sixty-five votes were cast.

As a final note to this election, Archie Allen of Hampton was fined $3 at the first court held at John Barrel's house. He was charged with the assault and battery of a Farnhamsburg voter.

Three days later on July 8, the commissioners-elect took their oaths which included swearing to never engage in a duel. They levied taxes of one-half percent on slaves and indentured or registered Negroes, on mulatto servants, carriages, carts, wagons, distilleries, furniture, clocks, and all livestock, and on town lots not already taxed by the township.

The commissioners also set tavern rates including the price of lodging, meals, and liquor, and granted a license to Jonah Case for $5 to keep a tavern at his house. The temporary seat of government having been established, the county was ready for business.

JOHN W. SPENCER WAS ONE OF
THE EARLY PIONEERS. IN 1827 HE
BEGAN CARRYING MAIL FROM
ROCK ISLAND TO GALENA. ON ONE
TRIP HE BROUGHT BACK THE
PRESIDENTIAL ELECTION
RESULTS. FOR THIS 200-MILE
ROUND TRIP, SOME OF WHICH HE
SKATED ON FROZEN RIVERS IN
WINTER, HE RECEIVED A SALARY
OF $5 PER TRIP. SPENCER WROTE A
BOOK, REMINISCENCES OF PIONEER
LIFE ON THE UPPER MISSISSIPPI,
DESCRIBING HIS LIFE IN A
WIGWAM AMONG THE INDIANS
AND HIS SERVICE AS A
LIEUTENANT IN THE ROCK RIVER
RANGERS DURING THE BLACK
HAWK WAR. HE HELD VARIOUS
OFFICES AND WAS THE FIRST
JUDGE OF ROCK ISLAND COUNTY.
HE HELPED BUILD THE FIRST DAM
IN MOLINE, AND IN 1852 HE
INHERITED, THROUGH HIS WIFE, A
CONTROLLING INTEREST IN THE
WILSON FERRY COMPANY. HE WAS
A STAUNCH MEMBER OF THE
METHODIST CHURCH. SPENCER
DIED IN 1878 IN ROCK ISLAND.

At later sessions, the commissioners discussed roads and selection of school lands, and chose the first grand jury. Licenses costing $3 each were granted to Joshua Vandruff and Rinah Wells to operate ferries across the Rock River, and to George Davenport to operate a ferry across the slough to Rock Island. Rates ranged from 12½ cents per person to $1 for a loaded two-horse cart. Additional licenses were approved the following year for Antoine Le Claire, William Brasher and Jonah Case for ferries across the Mississippi. Considerably higher rates were allowed, perhaps due to the width of the river.

Joseph Conway, the city clerk, was instructed to purchase two seals, one for the Circuit Court, and one for the commissioners. The design chosen was prophetic: a sheaf of wheat and a plow.

By now the growing settlement needed a better postal service. The only post office in the county was on Rock Island. Settlers had to pick up their own mail and as the alternative to fording the slough was to use the ferry, they claimed it to be inconvenient and costly. Since postage was 25 cents and a ferry trip 12½ cents each way, it was a reasonable argument, and the legislature granted their petition to move the post office to the mainland in 1834. The new office was housed in the log cabin of John Barrel. Occasionally, "a bad storm would require the postmaster to put his valuables between beds to keep them dry."

In 1835, the county purchased 61.95 acres from the government for the purpose of establishing a permanent seat of justice for Rock Island County. A town was platted on this lowland area between 10th and 17th Streets, and one third of the lots offered for sale, realizing nearly $4,000.

When the original town plot came before the Illinois legislature, it bore the name Davenport. However, one of the lawmakers, Colonel James M. Strode, felt that Colonel Davenport had made insulting remarks about his war record, and he objected so strenuously that the name Davenport was dropped. Instead, the legislature chose the name Stephenson in honor of Benjamin Stephenson, an early pioneer, whose son, James W. Stephenson, was a politician who had also fought in the Black Hawk War.

Only six years later the town became Rock Island at the insistence of a Dr. Silas Reed who came to Rock Island in 1838. Dr. Reed felt the name Stephenson inappropriate, and in 1841, he visited Springfield and persuaded the lawmakers to change the town's name to Rock Island. The city was then incorporated to include Farnhamsburg, Stephenson and three new additions.

Two years after Stephenson was plotted, speculators laid out another town at the south end of present Rock Island, beginning about where Black Hawk Park is located and extending some nine blocks west and 18 blocks north. On paper, it comprised more than 608 acres subdivided into 1,380 lots and was named Rock Island City. It attracted the attention of eastern investors who felt the site, with its natural advantages of position and water power, would become a major commercial artery. Among these investors was Daniel Webster who in 1837 purchased, sight unseen, a one-eighth interest in this paper city for $60,000.

The Illinois legislature had just embarked on a highly ambitious plan to improve the state's transport systems, and a canal was proposed to cut across Vandruff's Island allowing boats to bypass the lower Rock River Rapids. When the whole internal improvement plan collapsed in 1839 due to state bankruptcy, the canal was abandoned with only about one-fourth of a mile completed and Rock Island City was doomed. Webster and other investors sold out at a great loss and the city ceased to exist except in memory.

By contrast, the city of Rock Island was beginning to look more like a small town than a collection of log cabins. In the first issue of the *Rock Island Banner* in 1839, the editor said:

"Four years ago, there was but one house in the place. It now contains about 175 neatly built houses, and 600 inhabitants, seven stores, three taverns, three groceries, two saddle and harness shops, two cabinet shops, one cooper shop, one tinning shop, one watchmaker, one pottery, three physicians, and four lawyers and a beautiful court house, two stories high and about fifty feet square."

First courts had been held at the house of John Barrel, but as soon as the county seat was moved to Stephenson the commissioners began plans for a new courthouse and a jail. They purchased the block of ground where the present courthouse stands and after some problems with builders, the imposing brick edifice with its central cupola was finished in January of 1838. The first jail, a two-story log cabin, soon proved inadequate, and the city built a new one with a jailor's house attached in 1840.

Records show that the courthouse cost $12,100, but there was some question as to whether more than $3,000 had come from the estate of a certain Reverend John Brich. Brich, a Presbyterian missionary minister who rode all over the state, had frozen to death after being thrown from his horse on the night of March 9, 1837. He died in Henry County, but his saddlebags containing his unsigned will and personal fortune were found hanging from a tree just inside the Rock Island County line. The will was declared invalid by the town fathers, who claimed the estate, added the money to the city coffers, and perhaps used it to help finance their building plans.

At first the courthouse also served as a civic and social center with the sheriff opening the doors on Sundays for church services. Later, the courtroom could be rented by anyone for $1 per meeting.

More settlers were arriving. During 1840, steamboats alone deposited 183 new persons on Rock Island's shores. Money was scarce (the nearest bank was in Galena), forcing people to barter for their needs when they could not pay in coin. A claim of land might be traded for three yoke of oxen, saddles and harnesses for goods or several days' work. A tailor advertised tailoring done "in exchange for produce but money preferred."

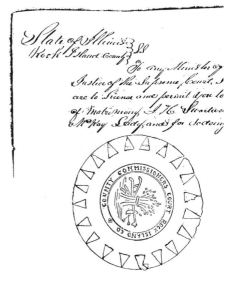

JOSEPH CONWAY PURCHASED THIS SEAL IN 1834 FOR USE BY THE COMMISSIONERS AND CIRCUIT COURT OF ROCK ISLAND COUNTY.

WHEN THE FIRST ROCK ISLAND COUNTY COURTHOUSE WAS ERECTED IN 1834, THE STAIRS WERE INSIDE THE BUILDING ON THE NORTH SIDE. IN LATER YEARS, THE COURTHOUSE WAS REMODELED, PILLARS WERE ADDED AND THE STAIRS WERE MOVED TO THE OUTSIDE. THIS COURTHOUSE WAS REPLACED BY THE PRESENT STRUCTURE, WHICH WAS DEDICATED IN 1897.

A newspaper article in 1841 showed the town now had 25 more buildings than in 1839, and also a more specialized work force. Included were tailors, shoe makers, gun smiths, carpenters, painters, printers, cabinet makers, a saddler, a cooper and a barber.

New land was added to Stephenson, one of the first parcels being the Spencer and Case Addition. When the plot was recorded, block eight was reserved for public use. By 1841, a wooden school had been built at its center thanks to voluntary labor and donations. For a while it was also used for religious services and political rallies. Three years later the Baptists bought the old school for $45.34½ cents, used it for the next seven years, and then sold it to the Upper School District.

It was understood that the area would be used for churches, schools and the public, and it was variously called Church, Public or Union Square. In 1855, Judge Spencer deeded the land to the city for certain financial considerations, and it became known as Spencer Square.

The small wooden school in the square was not the only early attempt at education. In 1839 a Mr. and Mrs. Joseph Gerrad opened a private school and offered to board a few out of town pupils. A year later Mr. Gerrad was found guilty of murder in a highly publicized trial (14 lawyers were present and 119 prospective jurors called) and the school closed. Mrs. Gerrad opened a new school in 1844.

By 1841 a Miss Adelia M. Lowell had arrived from Quincy and opened a school room furnished with "a stove, writing desks and comfortable seats." Rates were from 20-30 cents per week according to the needs of the pupil. That same year, the Rock Island Academical School opened. It offered a curriculum at three levels of education, but warned that "pupils who cannot read are not desired." Other private schools followed and many ran into financial problems. Salaries ranged from $14 per month for women to $30 a month for men. Students sometimes paid in kind bringing produce to the teacher or fuel for the stove.

Religious needs were taken care of with the various faiths meeting in private homes, the courthouse or school, and then building small churches as their membership increased. When the Presbyterians raised their house of worship in 1855, the pulpit was a remodeled dry goods box and their pews were boards laid across nail kegs. Sunday schools were founded by most of the denominations, and on July 4, 1845, a joint celebration picnic of all the county Sunday schools was held in Rock Island.

THE IOWA WAS ONE OF THE FIRST STEAM FERRIES ON THE UPPER MISSISSIPPI RIVER. JOHN WILSON, THE OWNER OF THE BOAT, IS STANDING ON THE GANGPLANK IN THIS PHOTO TAKEN ABOUT 1848.

Although the early pioneers worked hard, they also made time for
entertainment. House raisings, weddings, quilting bees, lectures, benevolent
society meetings and church suppers were all times of fellowship and fun. A
Lyceum opened in 1839 and by 1848 both the Masons and Odd Fellows had
founded lodges. A small theatre adjoined the Island City Hotel and
traveling stock companies could board at the hotel for $4 a week while
playing the town. Occasionally Shakespeare was performed, but more often
the plays were farces or musical comedies. In 1857 the Pioneer Company
presented *The Jealous Wife* and *The Married Rake* to enthusiastic
audiences.

Other visitors might stay at the Rock Island Hotel, conveniently located
near the ferry and steamboat landings. The hotel was a wooden two story
building that doubled as a stage station. Its gala opening was attended by
100 couples from as far away as Monmouth and Galena.

The hotel advertised clean and airy chambers, a bar room with the "choicest
of liquors" and "well attended stables." However, a Chicago newspaper
editor visiting Rock Island in 1853 described it as being "a full century
behind the time." Perhaps as a result, the hotel was enlarged to four stories
and served as a center for business transactions till it was razed in 1875 to
make way for a more modern brick building.

By 1848 the city had seen the beginning and end of various weekly
newspapers espousing the causes of both political parties. The editors kept
the townspeople up to date on world affairs and expounded at length on
local matters. Public service announcements included stage, boat and rail
schedules, current market prices, lost and found items including stray
animals, and lists of mail to be picked up or property taxes to be paid.

In 1851, *The Republican*, a weekly newspaper, began publication. Two years
later, under new ownership, it became the first daily paper in the county.
The new proprietor was Colonel J.B. Danforth, an energetic and forceful
editor and staunch Democrat who soon changed the paper's name to the
Rock Island Argus. This paper was the first to use steam power, to convert
to electric motors, and to use linotype. It outlasted 16 other city
newspapers.

A significant change in city organization occurred in 1849 when the citizens
of Rock Island voted 125-30 to obtain a charter. At the first council meeting
Benjamin Franklin Barret was elected mayor. His administration quickly
began to address some of the most pressing problems of the busy, expanding
community. Streets were resurveyed and livestock prohibited from running
at large, the graveyard situated on the knoll of Longview Park, then known
as Bailey's Pastures, was improved, and "groceries, ball alleys and billiard
rooms" were ordered to close at 11 o'clock at night and on Sundays. The
council also rented out storage space on the levee for 50 cents a month,
purchased a house for $20 in which to isolate smallpox patients, and bought
150 shares in the proposed Chicago and La Salle Railroad, later to be the
Chicago, Rock Island and Pacific.

Before the railroads came, rivers were the great transportation highways
to the new frontiers. The bulk of trade was from the industrial South to the
developing Northwest, and Rock Island's position was enhanced by the fact
it lay at the center of about 1,200 miles of navigable waterways. Goods could
be shipped directly to 15 states and three territories.

Furthermore, Rock Island was situated at the foot of a 14-mile stretch of
the Mississippi called the Rock Island Rapids. These rapids were difficult to
navigate because the river channel twisted and turned between chains of
rocks that protruded from each shore. To ensure safe passage, boats stopped
at Davenport, Le Claire or Rock Island and took on special river pilots if the
water was high enough to allow navigation, and then only in daylight hours.
If the river was low, the cargoes had to be unloaded into flatboats known as
lighters. On the up-river journey, the lighters were pulled over the rapids by

horses or oxen on shore. Sometimes the water was too low to allow any navigation and goods were temporarily stored or hauled around the rapids by wagon.

The costs for "lighterage," as this service was called, were high. The going rate for freight was 20-30 cents per bushel, but the owners of lighters often charged as much as $50 per trip. While this was a financial hardship for the steamboat owners, it aided the economic growth of Rock Island.

The river highway was not only expensive, it was often undependable. During the winter it might be closed for as long as five months due to ice, and in dry summers, the water level might be too low to allow any boat to navigate the Rapids safely. The alternatives were to load up a wagon or use the stagecoach. But roads were bad and it might take the stage up to 48 hours to travel from Rock Island to St. Louis, or a loaded wagon two weeks to make the round trip to Chicago.

To the citizens of Rock Island, the Mississippi and Rock Rivers presented other problems. In the winter people crossed on ice bridges, but there were frequent accidents when they tried to cross the ice too early or too late in the season. Sleigh fares were 5 cents in 1867 and 10 cents by 1879. Enterprising businessmen operated small concession stands along the bridges and sold hot drinks to passersby.

Once the ice bridges broke up the ferries took over. Although the Rock River could be forded safely, the Mississippi, with its greater width and stronger currents, was more easily crossed by boat.

Most of the ferrymen were notorious scoundrels, often charging double fare for strangers and refusing to carry anyone who could not afford the city regulated tarrifs. Joseph Vandruff, who operated a ferry across the Rock River, was described as "keeping something for the inner man," an allusion no doubt to the whiskey still he kept in his cellar.

John Wilson operated the ferry on the Mississippi between Rock Island and Davenport. He bought the ferry charter from Antoine Le Claire in 1837 for $1,000, $5 down and the rest on "easy terms," which included allowing Le Claire to cross "in ferry free of charge."

Wilson was a shrewd and aggressive business man who obtained a series of charters granting him a virtual ferry monopoly until his death in 1852. Citizens frequently complained about his rates, and in 1852 demanded to know why they paid 10 cents to get to Davenport whereas Davenport residents only paid 5 cents to reach Rock Island.

Sometimes would-be passengers had trouble raising the ferryman, especially if the boat was moored on the opposite bank. Take the case of Reverend Ithemer Pillsbury, who, having no horse, had walked 26 miles to Rock Island in order to cross on the ferry. Finding the boat on the Davenport side, he endeavored to attract the ferryman's attention by taking off his shirt and frantically waving it over his head. At the same time he began singing the doxology as loudly as possible. Eventually he succeeded in rousing the boatman.

Wilson solved this problem by introducing a ferry alarm. It was a triangle of metal that, when hit by a rod, could be heard for miles around. Later, Wilson installed a bell but citizens complained that when the bell rope broke, it was not "mended for months." Occasionally ferry services were halted due to bad weather or because the ferryman had been called to rescue other boats.

One of the earliest Wilson ferries was propelled by horses working a tread mill. This boat was followed by the *Rock Islander*, a locally built steam ferry. The first of its kind on the Mississippi above St. Louis, it proved to be less economical than horses and was soon withdrawn.

After Wilson's death, the business passed into the hands of three judges: John Spencer; Wilson's brother-in-law, Thomas Robinson; and James Grant. These men obtained another exclusive charter and renamed the venture The Spencer, Robinson and Company. They also introduced the *John Wilson* and *Davenport*, the first permanent steam ferries to ply

THE J.W. QUINLAN WAS BUILT IN THE KAHLKE BOAT YARDS IN 1904 AND PROVIDED FERRY SERVICE BETWEEN DAVENPORT AND ROCK ISLAND FOR MORE THAN 40 YEARS. ORIGINALLY CALLED THE DAVENPORT, SHE WAS BOUGHT IN 1925 BY J.W. QUINLAN, WHO REMODELED AND RENAMED HER. IN HER HEYDAY, IN THE 1930S, THE J.W. QUINLAN HAD DIXIELAND BANDS AND SLOT MACHINES ON HER TOP DECK. PASSENGERS MIGHT RIDE ALL DAY FOR A 5-CENT TICKET. TAKEN OUT OF SERVICE IN 1945, THE BOAT BURNED IN 1967.

between Rock Island and Davenport. The latter vessel became a
government transport ship during the Civil War.

Bigger and more elaborate boats followed, including the *Spencer, Augusta*
and another *Davenport*. When a new charter was granted in 1888, the
company changed its name to the Rock Island and Davenport Ferry
Company. The fare was only 5 cents, and boats ran every five minutes
between the two cities.

A new era arrived in 1904 when a third *Davenport* was launched with
nightly entertainment provided by bands. People began riding the ferries for
fun as well as necessity. On circus days, at the turn of the century, the nickel
fares were collected in nail kegs and rolled up the streets to the Rock Island
Bank for deposit. The *Davenport* was sold in 1925, remodeled, and renamed
the *J.W. Quinlan.*

Immigrants and settlers moving west often chose to cross the Mississippi at
Rock Island. Every new wave meant more ferry business, and a local
newspaper estimated that more than 100 teams had crossed the river by
1849. These numbers increased dramatically in the following years as more
land was opened up for settlement and prospectors seeking gold set off for
California. In order to guard against loss of revenue, ferry owners fought
every proposed bridge across the Mississippi, argued with the city fathers
over tariffs, and zealously protected the rights of their charters.

By 1850 it was apparent that it was only a question of time before the
railroads reached Rock Island. With its strategic location in relation to
markets and navigable waterways, the city was a logical choice for a
distribution center and railroad terminal. When the first train or "iron
horse" arrived from Chicago on February 22, 1854, there was a great
celebration with speeches and a lavish supper for about 1,500 people at the
Rock Island House. This and a later celebration, marking the historic link
up of the first railroad to reach the Mississippi, did much to publicize the
economic potential of Rock Island.

Further expansion west required the bridging of the Mississippi, especially
since Congress seemed unwilling to appropriate funds for the improvement
of the rapids. The railroad chose to span the river at Rock Island so it could
use the island as a convenient stepping stone. Work began in 1853. Despite
opposition from the steamboats and ferry companies which claimed the
bridge was both an infringement on their rights and a navigational hazard,
work was completed on April 21, 1856. The next day, the first passenger
train crossed the bridge to connect with a train bound for Iowa City.

*THE FIRST RAILROAD BRIDGE
ACROSS THE MISSISSIPPI RIVER,
BUILT IN 1856, HAD EIGHT FIXED
SPANS AND ONE SWING SPAN 286
FEET LONG – THE LONGEST SWING
SPAN IN THE UNITED STATES AT
THE TIME. IN 1860 OR '61,
SUSPENSION CORDS WERE ADDED,
AND IN 1866 NEW SPANS WERE
BUILT ON THE OLD PIERS IN AN
ATTEMPT TO STRENGTHEN THE
OLD BRIDGE AND ACCOMMODATE
HEAVIER TRAINS AND INCREASED
TRAFFIC.*

Two weeks later the steamer *Effie Afton* struck a pier causing considerable damage. Although the railroads, which were represented by Abraham Lincoln, won the ensuing court case, insurance companies believed the bridge to be a navigation hazard and charged double rates for boats passing between the piers.

The *Effie Afton* was the first in a long line of boats and log rafts that hit one or other of the bridge piers. In 1859 the *Aunt Letty* hit a span, and in 1861 another collision ended the careers of both the steamer *Grey Eagle*, and her captain, Daniel Smith Harris. The boat sank and Captain Harris, heart broken at the loss of seven lives, never piloted a boat again. Feelings against the bridge ran high and the Rock Island grand jury came within one vote of charging the railroad with murder. Accidents continued for years. Small wonder the riverboat men called the bridge "Hell's Gate" or the "invention of Satan."

Nevertheless, railroads succeeded, and increased use of the bridge combined with heavier trains made repairs necessary. With great skill and ingenuity, the spans were rebuilt in 1866 without any interruption of traffic. In 1868, an ice jam damaged two piers on the Davenport side and a windstorm struck the partially opened drawspan and dropped it into the river. The railroad immediately built temporary tracks to the river banks and transported passengers from the island to Davenport on special ferries. The first bridge was replaced in 1872 by a new iron and wood structure half a mile downstream.

The coming of the railroads changed the way of life in Rock Island. Although many immigrants passed through the city bound for new lands farther west, others saw opportunities in the community and settled. Between 1850 and 1855 the population more than doubled, and by 1860, the census recorded more than 5,000 people within the city limits. This growth was reflected in a newspaper editorial which suggested that street names be posted at intersections as the city was becoming so big it was difficult to find places of business.

One immediate result of growth was the jump in the price of real estate. A news editor reported that not one foot of vacant land remained in the city. Perhaps this was an exaggeration, but lots that had sold for 87½ cents per acre in 1852 were being sold for $5 to $10 per acre a year later. On Illinois Street, (now 2nd Avenue), land was offered for $75 per front foot. Shrewd business men invested in acreage and hung onto it knowing it would soon double in price. Such a man was Bailey Davenport, Colonel George's son, who at one time owned 2,500 acres in Rock Island and Moline.

This steady influx of immigrants created new markets for many products. Farmers began to realize the rich potential of the prairie lands, and between 1860 and 1890 more than 600,000 new farms were established in the states of Iowa, Kansas, Nebraska, Missouri, Minnesota and the Dakotas. Many of these farms were accessible by rail from Rock Island. Agricultural implements, lumber, household furnishings and certain foodstuffs were in great demand and the city was quick to exploit its favorable position.

In 1854, the first four-story brick building was erected in downtown Rock Island. Known as the Buford Block, it advertised a foundry, machine shop, a "store establishment," shoes and leather, and a grocery and iron store. Charles Buford, the owner of the block, had come to Rock Island from the South in 1852. He invested in real estate and built a Greek Revival mansion on a large lot on 7th Avenue (later the Tri-City Jewish Center) said to be worth $10,000. Interested in improving livestock, Burford was the first to introduce thoroughbred cattle into the area. His main enterprise, however, was the founding of the Buford Plow Company. Beginning with the manufacture of steel walking plows and Black Hawk Cultivators, the company kept adding different machinery until it had a general line of farm implements.

FOUR HIGH SCHOOLS HAVE BEEN BUILT ON THE LAND BETWEEN 6TH AND 7TH AVENUES AND 21ST AND 22ND STREETS. THE FIRST BURNED TO THE GROUND JULY 4, 1858, WITH THE LOSS FALLING ON THE CONTRACTOR SINCE THE SCHOOL WAS NOT FINISHED. A SECOND HIGH SCHOOL WAS BUILT IN 1859, AND A THIRD IN 1886. THAT SCHOOL, PICTURED, WAS ALSO DESTROYED BY FIRE, AND A NEW ONE WAS ERECTED AND DEDICATED IN 1902. IT BURNED IN 1949.

After a disastrous fire in 1880 caused heavy financial losses, followed by a severe flood that halted production of new farm equipment, the business was bought by several prominent citizens and renamed the Rock Island Plow Company. A new product, the Rock Island Hayloader, was introduced in 1889 and it became a national best seller. In 1937 the factory was purchased by the J.I. Case Company.

Other firms sprang up or enlarged their premises so quickly that by 1885 there were 435 business and professional establishments in Rock Island. "Rock Island," so a newspaper said in 1860, "is growing by leaps and bounds." With more than 5,000 people, the city ranked fifth largest in the state. In the navigable season, steamers and packet boats passed through the city daily bound for St. Louis, Galena and St. Paul. They carried an assortment of supplies for local stores, immigrants, livestock and special order items for the more wealthy citizens. Up river boats tended to be more crowded than those going downstream.

Between the 1850s and 1860s, when steamboating was at its peak, as many as 1,900 boats docked annually at Rock Island. When they used the city owned levees they paid a $1 wharf fee. Their arrivals and departures were published in the newspapers which also ran notices for local businesses advertising the arrival of such goods as "English and American calico, 12½ cents a yard," "Fancy spices" and the "latest fashions" from New York or Boston.

Passage from St. Louis without board cost as little as $1 in 1847, and many immigrants found boats the cheapest way to travel. But it was often a perilous journey. The average life of a steamboat was five years. Boats ran aground, hit rocks, log rafts and bridge piers, or got stuck in the ice. But the most feared disaster was the explosion of boilers.

Nevertheless, the boats continued to do good business despite the advent of the railroads. In 1888 the two major steamboat companies, the Diamond Jo, and St. Louis and St. Paul Packet and Freight Company, recorded 2,141 arrivals and departures at Rock Island. They also handled more than 1,000 tons of freight.

As the number of immigrants declined, the steamboats picked up trade by providing excursion trips. Visitors from New Orleans and St. Louis came north to seek the "shady retreats" of the river towns, and after 1860, Rock Island was considered quite a resort area. In 1901, Captain John Streckfus built the first steamboat designed exclusively for pleasure excursions. He called the boat the *J.S.* because he did not like long names.

Occasionally the steamers brought unwelcome immigrants. In 1854, the city charged that passengers afflicted with the dreaded disease of cholera had been dumped on the wharf. The ensuing epidemic caused more than 100 deaths. Mayor Ben Harper responded by buying four acres of land known as Sandy's Ford, and erecting a small hospital, all for the sum of $467.09.

The growth of the city was reflected in other ways. By 1852, the Rock Island Bank and that of Cook, Sargent and Parker had been founded. Two years later, Philemon Mitchell and Philander Cable arrived by train guarding their $80,000 in cash with shotguns. They bought out the Cook, Sargent and Parker concern. Theirs was the only bank in four to survive the financial depression of 1857. Mitchell and a new partner, Cornelius Lynde, bought the now defunct Rock Island Bank in 1861. After a series of mergers and additions, this bank became the First National Bank of Rock Island.

Until 1855 there was no formal cemetery. Many were buried in Bailey Davenport's pastures, now part of Longview Park. As the population increased, a need was felt for a more suitable resting place for the dead. The Chippianock Cemetery Association was formed, and its 11 charter members bought some 60 acres one mile south of town. Chippiannock, an Indian word meaning "City of the Dead," was especially appropriate since the cemetery lay on the old corn fields of the Sauk and Mesquakie.

OPENED IN 1878, THE HARPER OPERA HOUSE OFFERED A VARIETY OF ATTRACTIONS. MELODRAMAS, SUCH AS THE SILVER KING WITH ITS MODERN "REVOLVING SCENERY," WERE ESPECIALLY POPULAR.

Nine churches in 1861 advertised Sunday services, including one Swedish and two German speaking congregations, evidence of the growing number of foreign born residents in the city. The Germans especially wished to preserve some of their rich cultural heritage and a Turn Germeinde or Turner Society was begun in 1857. Its members believed in activities for both body and mind, and met regularly for debates, lectures, concerts and gymnastics.

Another organization that catered to the special interests of its members was the Rock Island Agricultural Society. It sponsored talks on farm management and held annual fairs. The first such event at City Hall was a great success. Cash prizes, premiums and books were awarded for the best livestock, handicrafts and farm implements. Competition was open to neighboring communities and the John Deere Company of Moline won $2 for the best center draft plow.

Nor was culture neglected. Noted lecturers and musicians were invited to perform by a group of young men who had founded the city's first public library, and called themselves the Young Men's Library Association. Both Wendell Phillips and Clara Barton accepted invitations to speak at Babcock Hall on 2nd Avenue. When Ralph Waldo Emerson visited the city in 1866, "his was the most scholarly lecture Rock Island has heard," but his speech was almost drowned out by the noises in the street below. This problem was rectified in 1867 when the hall was sold and renovated, and audiences could enjoy opera like *Faust* or modern plays like *Uncle Tom's Cabin* as well as famous speakers without annoying disturbances.

In the summer, July 4 was an eagerly awaited day. Fireworks were popular and in 1862, a local store advertised the arrival of 500 boxes of fire crackers. Accidents were common, especially when cannons were fired to better mark the day of independence. In 1872 two members of the Rock Island Light Artillery were seriously wounded and one man died when the guns accidentally discharged.

The Centennial Celebration of 1876 featured a large parade through the downtown streets that were decorated with arches of greens and flags. More than 25,000 people enjoyed the festivities but the *Argus* felt the bands and fireworks were "not up to expectations."

Another summer special was the arrival of the circus. Large advertisements appeared in the local newspapers, and local patrons were advised to buy advance admission so as to avoid pickpockets around the ticket wagon. The cost was 25 cents per person in 1855, and had risen to 50 cents by 1868.

Education took an important step forward in 1857. Prior to this date the city had been organized into five separate school districts, each of which had its own taxing power. Only three schools had been built and there was general disatisfaction with the whole system. Public meetings were held under the leadership of George Mixter, a local business man, and a special charter was obtained from the state legislature. The district was incorporated under one board of directors elected at large from the entire district. The first Board of Education determined to establish a system of thorough public instruction for all persons between the ages of 5 and 20. Tuition was to be provided for at least eight months in the year.

A survey of the district showed 835 prospective pupils, and the board immediately built an additional school. They also decided to finish the high school that the previous separate boards had agreed to fund. The building was erected at 21st Street and 7th Avenue. Unfortunately, it burned to the ground on July 4, 1858. Rebuilt the following year, it was known as the old white building although it was only painted white once. "A beam extended from a third floor window to hold a rope and pulley by which buckets of coal were pulled up for the stoking of the big stoves which stood in the corners of the class rooms," according to the *Argus*. "For water supply, the pupils had a bucket of water standing on a bench in the playground."

Younger children used the first two floors and the high school classes were held on the third. Until 1874 no one completed all the grades. Five women were graduated that year and were immediately employed in the primary schools. Two years later, the graduating class numbered 21, and by 1905 the number had increased to 39. This first high school was razed in 1892 to make way for the present Lincoln School.

In 1886, another high school, the pride of the community, was erected. It too suffered a mysterious fire in 1901. The wind carried the sparks as far as 17th Street and the heat was so intense that it cracked the windows at Lincoln School on the next block.

A third high school was constructed on the ruins of the second and dedicated in 1902. A large crowd toured the classrooms and the community was proud to have built the largest high school in the Tri-Cities.

As the town grew, it had to improve its roads and bridges. Due to its low position, downtown Rock Island was frequently flooded by the river. Between 4th and 8th Avenues lay a marshland known as Frog Pond where residents could actually go swimming and diving in wet weather. A dike erected by the city to protect 1st Avenue, then aptly called Water, Mississippi or Front Street, did little to stop the flooding. To make the roads more easily passable, they were frequently graded and sidewalks were laid on the main streets. The lack of funds for such improvements was partially offset by ordinances requiring all males between the ages of 21 and 50 to work on the roads three days a year without pay.

Business men were especially interested in promoting new roads to encourage customers to visit their stores. Realizing that expansion was blocked on the north and northwest by the Mississippi, and on the east by Moline, they were forced to look south for new areas of trade.

DUE TO ITS LOWLAND LOCATION, ROCK ISLAND WAS OFTEN FLOODED DURING THE 19TH CENTURY. SEVERE FLOODS OCCURRED IN 1868, 1880, 1881 AND 1892. IN 1880, THE NEWSPAPER REPORTED THAT 10 FEET OF WATER COVERED SOME DOWNTOWN AREAS, 125 HOUSES WERE SUBMERGED AND SOME EVEN FLOATED AWAY. THE WATER STAYED HIGH FOR MORE THAN A WEEK. IN THE PHOTO, BARRELS AND BOXES HAVE BEEN SET OUT TO DRY ON THE SIDEWALK ON THE WEST SIDE OF THE HARPER HOUSE. SPENCER SQUARE IS TO THE LEFT. THE DISTANT SPIRES BELONG TO THE METHODIST EPISCOPAL AND TRINITY EPISCOPAL CHURCHES.

IN 1903, THE FIRST HORSE-DRAWN STREET CAR CROSSED THE NEW TRACKS FROM SOUTH ROCK ISLAND TO MILAN. CITIZENS OF MILAN RANG THE FIRE BELL AND GATHERED ALONG THE STREETS TO GREET THE CAR'S ARRIVAL. THIS LINE WAS ELECTRIFIED SEVEN YEARS LATER. THE MILAN TOWN HALL IS ON THE RIGHT.

AN ARTIST'S CONCEPTION OF THE SEARS MILL ON THE ROCK RIVER IN 1868 SHOWS THE BRUSH AND STONE DAM DAVID SEARS BUILT UPSTREAM FROM THE MILL. MEASURING 650 FEET LONG AND 72 FEET HIGH, THE DAM PROVIDED POWER FOR SEVERAL MILLS. TO THE LEFT OF THE MILL IS THE PLANK BRIDGE THAT LINKED ROCK ISLAND AND CAMDEN, LATER RENAMED MILAN. THE RAILROAD BRIDGE ON THE FAR LEFT WAS BUILT BY THE ROCK ISLAND AND PEORIA RAILROAD TO CONNECT ROCK ISLAND WITH COAL VALLEY.

Their main obstacle was the Rock River. The Rock was considered navigable, and bridges were forbidden for fear they would interfere with water traffic. In 1843, the county was authorized to construct a bridge over the main channel. It was, in fact, the only contribution by the county to the city's bridge problems.

Money being scarce, corporations were formed to purchase land and build bridges and roads. Accordingly, in 1852, forty-two Rock Island citizens raised sufficient funds to construct a plank road from the downtown area to the Rock River. This road was the forerunner of 9th Street and was always called the Milan Road. This organization, known as the Plank Company, had soon bridged all the streams between Rock Island and Camden, as Milan was then called.

Upkeep was expensive so tolls were charged, but the Plank Company soon found that costs far exceeded income. They gladly transferred their stock to the city for $25,000 in 1859.

Despite the obvious advantage of better roads and bridges, farmers objected to the 10 cent fee saying they paid up to $200 in yearly tolls. Arguments continued until 1910 when a Big Island farmer crashed through the barrier at the bridge entrance declaring he would not pay another dime. Although arrested, he was never fined. Saying "Rock Island must wake up before it is bottled up," 55 local merchants convinced the city to abolish all tolls.

Although citizens devoted much time to problems, they also found time to get involved in state and national politics. They hosted conventions, held rallies and made their views known in letters to the newspapers. By the late 1850s the issue of slavery divided them and the nation. The Dred Scott Case, John Brown's raid on Harper's Ferry and the continued violence in "bleeding Kansas" could not be disregarded, and feelings ran high.

Many of the city's influential citizens had Southern roots and strongly supported the pro-slavery views of the Democratic party. Stephen Douglas had even come to Rock Island and delivered a fiery oration in the town square.

Anti-slavery groups included Northerners and many foreign-born residents who had come to America to escape oppression in their homelands. They supported the Republicans and Abraham Lincoln. The 1860 presidential election was essentially fought over the question of slavery, and when the city ballots were counted, Lincoln had been defeated by a margin of 20 votes.

With the secession of the Southern states, the threat of war became a keenly felt reality. On January 4, 1861, the people of Rock Island observed a day of prayer for peace. In April the dreaded news came and the *Argus* headlines for April 15, 1861, read: "CIVIL WAR COMMENCED. FORT SUMTER SURRENDERED." The newspaper, though staunchly Democratic, further declared "no patriot can hesitate to do his duty. He must sustain the administration in every proper effort to sustain the Stars and Stripes."

This feeling of patriotism was maintained in the city throughout the war. Bailey Davenport, the Democratic mayor, called for unity. He was re-elected five times during the Civil War, many said because he paid his large property taxes on time and kept the city solvent. A Democratic flag was raised on a Republican flagpole, and money was appropriated for the families of those who volunteered to fight. The ladies organized the Soldiers Aid Society and busied themselves with procuring blankets and other provisions that the soldiers might need.

Lincoln had issued a call for volunteers and the city responded enthusiastically. A basic training area called Black Hawk Camp was established on Big Island. Groups leaving on trains for Springfield were sent off with parades and speeches. The men received box lunches courtesy of the local hotels.

Some families had several men serving in the war. One of the more prominent was the Bufords. Although the family was from the South, two sons served as generals in the Union Army. Napoleon Buford, who had made the first survey of the Rock Island Rapids in 1829 before moving to the city, particularly distinguished himself at the battle of Belmont. His younger brother, John, became a hero at Gettysburg. He died of typhoid fever some months later.

Wire service had reached Rock Island with the railroad in 1852, and up to date reports on the war were transmitted via the telegraph to local newspapers. Soldiers' letters home were also widely reproduced.

When the South captured the United States Arsenal at Harper's Ferry, prominent citizens again pressed their case for the establishment of the new arsenal on Rock Island. Congress finally agreed in 1862 and the city was elated.

Work on the Arsenal had just begun when the government decided to erect a temporary prisoner of war camp on the island. The first batch of prisoners arrived in December 1863. Poor conditions at the camp were attacked by Colonel Danforth, Democratic editor of the *Argus*, who claimed men were dying unnecessarily because of disease, malnutrition and exposure to cold weather. These reports helped arouse the sympathies of various Rock Island ladies, especially those of Southern origin. The ladies visited the camp and distributed foodstuffs, particularly vegetables, and clothing and blankets to the Confederate prisoners. When plans were made to build a small hospital in an attempt to control the spread of smallpox, they donated $300 through the Soldiers Aid Society to help in the cost of construction. Perhaps these humanitarian actions partly accounted for the belief among the prisoners that Rock Island was a better city to escape to than Moline. In reality, escape was very difficult.

Rock Island businessmen soon realized that the camp offered opportunities for trade. They built a wooden bridge to the island to avoid the use of the ferry. Foodstuffs were especially welcomed and prisoners with money often bought provisions to augment their rather poor diets. One Rock Island merchant, A.C. Dart, was able to build a new three-story building on 2nd Avenue with profits from his visits to the camp.

When the war ended, the discharged regiments were welcomed back by parades and speeches, church bells and steamboat whistles.

In tribute to the soldiers of the Civil War, the community erected a handsome monument in Court House Square. Leonard Wells Volk, who had been a partner in a marble factory in Rock Island, was the sculptor. The monument cost $10,000, most of it raised by private subscription. An estimated 30,000 people turned out on dedication day to see what their money had bought. The ceremony took place on April 9, 1869, the fourth anniversary of the surrender of the Confederate Army at Appomattox.

THE MEAD, SMITH & MARSH MILL, AS IT APPEARED IN 1857. WEYERHAEUSER AND DENKMANN TOOK OVER THIS FINANCIALLY AILING MILL IN 1860, INCREASED ITS OUTPUT DRAMATICALLY AND MADE IT THE CORNERSTONE OF THEIR LOGGING EMPIRE.

With the coming of peace, the city entered a period of growth and consolidation. Trade was resumed with the South and goods could once more move freely on the railroads and rivers. Many businesses prospered, but none could match the rapid development of the lumber industry. Lumber was of prime importance in the settlement of America. As the Eastern forests became depleted, and expansion West created an even greater demand for good wood, lumbermen turned to the extensive pineries of Wisconsin and northern Minnesota for new supplies.

In Rock Island, several sawmills were in operation by 1854. They employed some 200 men and turned out about 2 million board feet of lumber annually. One of the earliest mills was owned by William Bailey and James Boyle. They used mostly local logs cut from the bluffs behind the town and transported to the mill by two-wheeled ox carts.

Apparently business was not profitable, for the sawmill changed hands three times in three years. In 1856 it belonged to Messrs. Mead, Smith and Marsh. These owners expanded and opened a lumber yard in Coal Valley, taking advantage of the new railroad spur opened to that village in 1857. As manager of their new branch, they chose a young German immigrant by the name of Frederick Weyerhaeuser.

Weyerhaeuser had come to Rock Island in 1856 to help lay track for the Rock Island and Peoria Railroad. He next worked for a brewery and then for the Mead, Smith and Marsh sawmill. He married and bought a lot on 10th Street on which he built a house for about $900. By the time he moved to Coal Valley, Weyerhaeuser had already shown his employers that he was an enterprising businessman. He was equally successful in the branch store where he adopted a barter system. Lumber was traded for livestock and produce, which was then exchanged for logs and converted into more lumber.

The mill in Rock Island began to flounder, partially a victim of the financial panic of 1857. In 1860 the property was seized by the sheriff and put up for sale. Weyerhaeuser convinced his brother-in-law, Frederick Denkmann, to go into partnership with him and the two men bought the business for $3,000, paying $500 down.

Denkmann, also from Germany, was some years older than Weyerhaeuser.

LOGS THAT WERE DRAGGED TO THE RIVER BANKS DURING THE WINTER WERE PILED UP, READY TO FLOAT DOWNSTREAM WITH THE SPRING THAW. MEN WITH LONG POLES HELPED KEEP THE LOGS MOVING AND BREAK UP ANY POTENTIAL LOG JAMS.

He worked for the Buford and Tate Foundry, and owned a small grocery store operated by his wife. A skilled machinist, he quickly improved production methods at the mill. By the end of the first season, daily output had doubled, and two years later, the mill had paid for itself. Many stories were told of Denkmann's devotion to the mill. He worked long hours, even on Sundays, to insure that the machinery was in proper order, and nothing kept him from his daily work. Once he nearly drowned while trying to save some logs that had escaped from the boom (a holding pen for logs along the river bank), and another time he lost two fingers in a planer. A worker at the mill reported that Denkmann "had his hand tied up and carried it in a sling and was back in the mill the next day."

Weyerhaeuser was a natural salesman and looked after the commercial side of the business. His nine years managing the lumber yard in Coal Valley taught him how to deal with people. When he moved his family to Rock Island in 1869 to escape a scarlet fever epidemic, he was ready to expand the lumber company.

Denkmann and Weyerhaeuser enlarged the original mill and added more machinery. They signed a lucrative contract with the Union Pacific Railroad for 950,000 board feet of lumber. Despite two financial failures, a flour mill in Coal Valley and a woolen mill in Rock Island, they bought into a second sawmill.

Now their most pressing problem was securing an adequate supply of logs. There were three main ways of acquiring logs legally: buying saw logs, purchasing stumpage (the land then reverted to its original owners once the trees were removed), and buying the timber lands outright. Weyerhaeuser and Denkmann used all three methods.

Some of the best timber was found in Wisconsin along the Chippewa River and its tributaries. Here grew the massive white pines whose soft, durable wood was much in demand. In winter the trees were felled, dragged to the river banks, and stacked in such a way that once the key logs were removed, the entire collection would start moving downriver with the spring thaw.

THE J.W. VAN SANT, AIDED BY A BOWBOAT IN FRONT, PUSHES A LOG RAFT DOWN THE MISSISSIPPI. SUCH RAFTS WERE MADE UP OF MANY SMALLER UNITS, MEASURING 16 FEET BY 32 FEET, LASHED TOGETHER. IT WAS NOT UNCOMMON FOR THEM TO EXCEED 300 FEET IN WIDTH AND 1,600 FEET IN LENGTH. BOATS WITH BOW-BOATS, SUCH AS THIS, BROUGHT THE RAFTS DOWNSTREAM IN THE LATER YEARS OF THE INDUSTRY. EARLY RAFTS HAD BEEN SIMPLY LOGS LASHED TOGETHER WITH A FEW OARS FOR STEERING. LATER, STERNWHEELERS PUSHED THE RAFTS, WITH OARSMEN GUIDING IN FRONT.

FREDERICK WEYERHAEUSER (TOP) AND F.C.A. DENKMANN (ABOVE) BUILT WHAT BECAME A LUMBER EMPIRE, BEGINNING WITH ONE STRUGGLING ROCK ISLAND SAWMILL.

Since many companies used the same waterways, each log was branded with the particular mark of the mill. The logs were caught in large pens or booms and sorted, but there were frequent complaints of delays and log rustling. Weyerhaeuser solved these problems by organizing the Mississippi River Logging Company in 1871. Several local mills — Dimock and Gould and Keator and Wilson of Moline, Schricker and Mueller of Davenport, and Weyerhaeuser and Denkmann — were among the 17 charter members. Weyerhaeuser was elected president of the company in 1872, and held that position for more than 35 years.

The Mississippi River Logging Company leased land at the mouth of the Chippewa River and built a huge holding pen, known as the Beef Slough Boom. During the busy season the company employed 1,200 to 1,500 men and kept 75 steamboats busy pushing log rafts on the upper Mississippi. In 1884, a record 741,837,000 logs were banked. Cooperation meant cheaper timber. By abandoning the branding of logs (with each mill contracting to take a certain number of logs out of the boom) they were able to speed delivery of lumber. In time they became the greatest logging power in the industry, controlling more than 300,000 acres of pine forests and employing 400 men in the rafting business alone.

Log rafts were assembled at the Beef Slough Boom and floated down river to the mills. The rafts of the early 60s were often more than 1,000 feet long. A crew of 20 to 35 men lived and worked on this log island, using sweep-like oars to help the pilot navigate the bends of the river and other natural obstacles such as sandbars and mud flats. Bridges were especially dangerous, and many rafts lost logs after a collision with one of the piers of the railroad bridge above Rock Island.

A major improvement in log transportation occurred in the 1870s. J.W. Van Sant and his son, Sam, built a sternwheeler during the winter of 1869 at their boatyard in Le Claire, Iowa. On its maiden voyage the *J.W. Van Sant* steered the Weyerhaeuser and Denkmann log raft down the Mississippi, under the Government Bridge and into the boom at the Rock Island sawmill. Within a few years, some 70 raft boats were operating on the Upper Mississippi. Smaller steamboats called bow-boats were tied sideways to the front of the increasingly larger rafts to help the sternwheelers maneuver. Raftboats speeded delivery of logs at a time when the demand for lumber was growing rapidly.

In 1896 a record 64 log rafts passed under the Government Bridge in one day. That same year, one of the longest lumber rafts came down the river powered by the *F.C.A. Denkmann*. The raft measured 1,560 feet by 296 feet and covered eight acres of water. It had to be split in two at Hampton to allow the logs to pass through the spans of the Government Bridge. Weyerhaeuser, always looking to the future, organized a second lumber company, bought timber lands in Minnesota and moved to St. Paul in 1892. The Rock Island mills ceased operation on November 18, 1905, when the final log was sawed. Denkmann died at the age of 81, six months before the mill closed, but Weyerhaeuser remained active in the logging industry and helped to run the newly formed Weyerhaeuser Timber Company in the Pacific Northwest. In 1915 the last log raft came down the Mississippi. How had this affected their holdings in Rock Island? Fire had destroyed their second mill, the Anawalt, Denkmann and Company, in 1876 with an estimated loss of $40,000. Despite the current slump in lumber prices, a new mill was built on the same site. Weyerhaeuser and Denkmann bought another firm, the financially troubled Keator mill on 24th Street, in 1878 and consolidated it with the Anwalt-Denkmann mill to form a new corporation, the Rock Island Lumber and Manufacturing Company. By 1888, the two companies employed 1,000 men and had annual sales of $175 million.

Further growth came with the purchase of an idle mill in Davenport, the old Renwick, Shaw and Crosset Company. Fire destroyed it in 1901. Denkmann

himself raced across the Government Bridge carrying extra fire hose from
another mill. Out of these ashes rose the White Lumber Company.
In order to expand out-of-state sales, this company purchased 40 retail
yards all over the Southwest and a lumber yard in St. Louis. A new
corporation, the Rock Island Sash and Door Works, was formed in 1897, but
it too was extensively burned in 1908. The conflagration destroyed 14 acres
of lumber and caused $750,000 of damage to both Rock Island mills, the
Rock Island and Burlington Railroad, and the Telephone and Telegraph
Companies. The blaze could be seen from 50 miles away. It was fought by
firemen from the surrounding communities. The main factory at the Rock
Island Sash and Door Works was saved, and insurance covered most of the
company losses.

The Weyerhaeuser and Denkmann partnership was dissolved in 1902 and
the business was incorporated with a capitol stock of $250,000. As the center
of the lumber industry moved west, local mills shut down, and the last
company owned firms closed in 1970. These were the East Moline Lumber
Store, the Moline Building Center, the White Lumber Company of
Davenport and the Rock Island Lumber Company.
Why had these men succeeded where others had failed? Weyerhaeuser
believed it was partly due to luck. He said, in an interview:

*"Whenever I've come to the forks in the road and I've been unable to choose, my
freedom has been taken away from me. Opportunity has knocked at my door
many times, but often I've been asleep, and then some other hand has lifted the
latch and let her in."*

Luck was aided by leadership, honesty, hard work and an almost fanatical
attention to detail. Nothing went to waste in their lumber business. The log
butts were made into shingles, the sawdust was burned in the boilers, and
the scrap wood was sold for fuel. They were never in debt, and, due to

*AFTER THE LOG RAFTS HAD
COMPLETED THEIR JOURNEY
DOWN THE MISSISSIPPI, THEY
WERE KEPT IN RIVERSIDE PENS
UNTIL LUMBER YARD WORKERS
COULD CUT THE LOGS INTO
BOARDS.*

others' failures, were able to buy bankrupt or financially troubled mills at low prices. A hard day's work was expected from their employees, but because they paid their men in full they had a loyal and skilled labor force who took pride in working for the company. Many family members, including six Weyerhaeuser and Denkmann sons, also worked in the business.

The three cities enjoyed excellent transportation and ample storage for lumber adjacent to both the river and the railroads. Some of the mills, especially those in Moline, had readily available water power. The other mills were operated by steam generated by coal dug along the bluffs on the Illinois side of the river and at Coal Valley. Both sources of power were relatively cheap.

Added to these advantages of location were the personalities of the men themselves. Their talents complemented each other. Weyerhaeuser achieved success through cooperation, not confrontation. He invited other firms to share in both the plans and profits of his ventures, and the logging companies he helped to found eventually controlled most of the pineries of Wisconsin and Minnesota, regulating the distribution of lumber throughout the Midwest.

The impact of the lumber industry on the area can be seen from the following figures. In 1860 the combined output of sawed lumber for the three cities was 22 million board feet. By 1890, the peak year, the output had risen to 213,629,000 board feet and the mills employed more than 2,000 men.

Lumber had made the Weyerhaeuser and Denkmann families wealthy, and they were generous to the city in many ways. They made contributions to worthy causes. The Rock Island Public Library and the Denkmann Memorial Library are living testimonials to this generosity. The West End Settlement and Longview and Lincoln Parks were made possible largely by their gifts of land and money. In 1954, the Weyerhaeuser family home at 3052 10th Avenue, and 26 acres of land that surrounded it were given to Augustana College. Students now live in the 32-room house called the House on the Hill, built by one of the lumber kings of America.

The busy sawmills encouraged the growth of other wood working industries. Companies that manufactured wagons, carriages, sashes, doors, barrels, matches and brooms developed, and found ready markets for their products. Boatyards, including those of Bailey and Boyle, and later Kahlke Brothers, built and repaired many of the sternwheelers and bow boats owned by the lumber mills.

Lumber was not the only industry to prosper after the close of the Civil War. By 1888 the Rock Island City Directory listed 26 major businesses and various smaller companies — including eight cigar factories. Three separate industrial cores had emerged. All were close to the banks of the Mississippi and within easy reach of the railroads.

The western area was composed of such companies as Weyerhaeuser and Denkmann, Rock Island Plow, Rock Island Glass Works, Rock Island Stove Company and the Rock Island Brewery. At the extreme western edge, where the river made a southward bend, was Kahlke's Boatyard.

On the east, the core was dominated by the Rock Island Lumber Company and Huber's Malt House.

Between the two areas, on the site of the original town, was a third commercial core. Here were found companies that manufactured wagons, children's carriages, leather goods, cigars and crackers. On 2nd and 3rd Avenues especially were smaller businesses engaging in wholesale and retail trade. Stores that sold foodstuffs, clothing, hardware, drugs and novelties jostled each other for space and customers. Close to both the railroad depots and boat landings, it was the best location for hotels, banks, public buildings and offices. The heart of the city, this area's only drawback in later years was lack of space.

As trade increased, some general stores became department stores with several floors and entrances. Such an establishment was L. S. McCabe and Company. It began as a small store in 1870 on 2nd Avenue. Business was good, and by 1900 it had expanded across the block with entrances on both 2nd and 3rd Avenues. McCabe was described as "a real merchandiser" who began the practice of semi-annual sales, widely advertised in the newspapers. Special discounts were offered on piece goods just before the "January and August sewings" when ladies selected materials for new clothing. An anniversary sale in October had the attraction of gifts and premiums. Customers then hired women to make their clothes. In 1905 there were more than 50 dressmakers to choose from.

Large stores such as McCabe's increased Rock Island's reputation as a shopping center, and much of the city's wealth came from substantial out-of-town trade. The Kimball Piano and Organ Company owned by Ray Bowlby, for instance, had 10 employees, six of whom were traveling salesmen.

Grocery stores relied on free home deliveries. The store owner or his employee spent half the day soliciting orders, and the other half delivering them. Grocers worked long hours, often from 6 a.m. to 10 p.m. Since nearly all foodstuffs were sold in bulk, the floor of the store was cluttered with barrels, baskets and boxes, and cats kept the shop clear of mice and rats. Vegetables and fruits were usually displayed outside on the sidewalks. Sugar came in 20-pound cones and had to be cut into chunks and then melted or crushed before being used. Customers brought their own containers for milk or syrups. In winter there might be a problem scooping out the molasses which had congealed in the cold weather. Eggs cost 9 cents a dozen, vegetables 24 cents a bushel. A dime bought three loaves of bread. Fresh fish was available at the fishermen's shanties on the river banks. Cash was still scarce so many stores adopted a credit system. Each family had a passbook in which its purchases were entered. The shop keeper kept a separate record and endeavored to see that the entries matched.

On the east of the city were two large breweries, both founded by German immigrants in the 1850s. The Atlantic Brewery was located close to the railroad tracks and shipped beer all over the Midwest in its own refrigerator cars. The other brewery was owned by the Huber family. In 1892, these two companies merged as the Rock Island Brewery with the joint output exceeding 100,000 barrels of beer a year.

The growth of industry was helped by the availability of lumber, clay, limestone and coal within a few miles of the city. Rock quarries were worked both in town and on the surrounding bluffs, and in south Rock Island there were brick factories that utilized the good clay of the area. As early as 1835, coal was being worked in Carbon Cliff, east of the town. Soon shafts were dug all along the bluffs. A local newspaper warned picnickers that there was "a danger of coal miners cutting away all of Black Hawk's Watch Tower." By 1876 forty-six mines were operating in the county. At $1.99 per ton, coal provided a cheap source of power to run machinery and an added incentive for businessmen to invest their capital in factories in Rock Island.

When the need for coal increased, it was shipped from Coal Valley on a specially constructed railroad spur. Many of these mines were owned by Philander Cable of Rock Island, a shrewd businessman who soon had almost a monopoly of the coal trade.

Rock Island's growth after the Civil War was largely the result of the lumber industry and the improvement of transport facilities. By 1876, three major railroads converged on the city. These were the Chicago, Rock Island and Pacific; the Chicago, Burlington and Quincy; and the Chicago, Burlington and St. Paul. Together, these companies provided a network of lines across middle America with direct routes to the Atlantic, Pacific and Gulf coasts. Other branch lines radiated out of Rock Island to Peoria, Coal Valley and Mercer County.

Competitive transportation was offered by the steamboats and packets that plied the Mississippi, helping to keep rail rates down. In 1866 the Corps of Engineers arrived at Rock Island to begin excavation of a 4-foot channel through the Rock Island Rapids. Congress authorized a 4½-foot channel in 1878 and a 6-foot channel in 1907. In 1930 work began on the locks and dams for the 9-foot channel, which is still maintained today on the upper Mississippi.

Two other waterways, the Rock River and the Illinois and Mississippi Canal (called Hennepin Canal by local residents) proved disappointing as transportation highways to the east. The Rock had rapids near its mouth. It was shallow, and it ended in southern Wisconsin. The canal was proposed as a short-cut between the Quad-Cities and Lake Michigan, cutting several hundred miles off the route down the Mississippi to the Illinois River, then up to Chicago. It was proposed as early as 1834. Work finally began in 1892, and after many delays it was finished in 1907. Schools in communities along its route were dismissed to allow the pupils a chance to see the first steamer, the *Marion*, pass. In Milan, several thousand people gathered to celebrate the opening of the new waterway.

Unfortunately, by the time the Hennepin was completed, river traffic had declined everywhere. Further, the canal was really too small for the large barges that then moved up and down the Mississippi, and by 1939, the canal had literally choked itself to death.

It was railroads, however, that made the greatest impact on the commercial growth of the city. By 1888 it was estimated that 36 passenger trains entered and left Rock Island daily, and in the same period more than 300 freight cars a day were loaded and assembled for shipping goods in all directions. Depots, machine shops, switching and side-track facilities were needed to handle all this traffic. The Chicago, Rock Island and Pacific roundhouse was said to be the largest in the world.

The first railroad bridge soon proved inadequate to handle the increasing number and weight of trains. In addition, its location caused a hazard to boat traffic, and it cut the growing Arsenal in two. For these reasons, the government agreed to share expenses with the railroad to build a new railroad and carriage bridge closer to the foot of the island.

Controversy surrounded the design and use of this new bridge. There were arguments as to whether the railroad track should be on the upper or lower level. The Chicago, Rock Island and Pacific Railroad was opposed to the use of the bridge by other railroads without a right-of-way fee. The ferry company saw the bridge as a serious threat to its monopoly, and tried to stop its use as a public thoroughfare.

To the relief of Rock Island, the bridge was opened to traffic in 1872. Regulations governing its use included the provisions that no livestock could be driven across, no one could fish from the structure, and "all drunken and disorderly persons and loiterers shall be kept off the bridge." A year later, a horse railway track was laid upon the bridge and several telephone companies were given permission to carry their wires across the structure.

THE GOVERNMENT BRIDGE LINKING DAVENPORT AND ARSENAL ISLAND WAS ERECTED IN 1872 WITH A WAGON ROAD BELOW THE RAILROAD TRACKS. THIS ORIGINAL CONSTRUCTION WAS REPLACED BEFORE THE TURN OF THE CENTURY WITH THE BASIC STRUCTURE THAT STILL IS IN USE.

In 1874, the first full year in which the bridge was in service, more than 330,000 people crossed on foot. There was also considerable wagon traffic. When the first electric street car crossed the span in 1894, it was forced to stop several times to reassure nervous teamsters and their horses. Speed limits were increased at that time from 6 to 12 m.p.h.

This double-decker wood and iron bridge, the first on the Mississippi for both railroad and wagon use, was remodeled in 1896. Heavier and larger locomotives required a more solid structure. Despite some problems with construction (ice had destroyed one nearly finished span that spring), the all-iron bridge was finished within a year. Built by Ralph Modjeski, a Polish immigrant, it was described as "unsurpassed by any other bridge in the world." Speed limits were lifted and horses could trot and cyclists pedal as fast as they wished.

The Government Bridge was joined in 1899 by the Crescent Bridge built by the Davenport, Rock Island and Northwestern Railroad. It crossed the Mississippi at 6th Street and entered Davenport close to Division.

The same era saw improvements in local and intercity transport. In the early days a two-horse omnibus ran between Rock Island and Moline. The trip took as long as an hour, provided the roads were passable. Fares were 15 cents each way, and in winter the floors of the vehicles were covered with straw to help keep the passengers' feet warm.

Travel became easier in 1868 when the Moline and Rock Island Horse Railroad Company was organized. Within two years, it had built tracks and was charging 5 cents for intracity travel and 10 cents for passage between towns. Cars were small and pulled by a single horse. Profits were substantial at first, but with the increased use of the telephone for business and the competition of another line, the company began to operate at a loss. In 1888 a Chicago syndicate bought all the existing lines in the Tri-Cities and began making extensive improvements in the system.

Eventually, Rock Island had tracks along all its major streets with lines to Milan, Davenport and Moline. The cars were pulled by horses in the downtown area and by steam engines or "dummies" up the hills to Chippiannock Cemetery, Black Hawk Park and the town of Sears on the banks of the Rock.

Electrical cars began to replace the horse-drawn cars in 1890. When the first electrified street car made a trial run over 30th Street hill, local residents lined the road and cheered enthusiastically. Once the line to Black Hawk's Watch Tower was electrified, trolley parties became fashionable. Prominent citizens would rent specially decorated open air cars and take their guests out to the park for the evening. The trip from downtown Rock Island took about 30 minutes and cost $3 if the cars were returned before midnight, $5 after that hour.

EMPLOYEES OF THE <u>MILAN INDEPENDENT</u> NEWSPAPER AND THEIR FAMILIES ENJOYED AN OUTING TO BLACK HAWK'S WATCH TOWER PARK IN 1910.

Black Hawk's Watch Tower originally belonged to Bailey Davenport, one of the earliest residents of the area. When he was 18, his father, Colonel George Davenport, gave him 9,500 acres of land in eastern Illinois. Bailey decided to deal in real estate. He sold property in eastern Illinois for whatever he could get, and was reported to have even traded 160 acres for a horse. Obviously a good businessman, he soon owned vast tracts of land in Rock Island and Moline, including coal mines and quarries. Real estate was not his only interest. He was president of a bank and the principal stock holder in the Rock Island and Milan Street Company.

His home was a magnificent 40-room frame house often referred to as "Bailey's Castle." It stood on a 500-acre estate that extended from 7th to 10th Avenue and from 15th to 17th Street. Bailey was described by some as a hermit, but "generous if properly approached." Others called him a land miser because he refused to sell certain lots considered necessary for city expansion. Whatever his reasons, he hung on to his lands, and at his death in 1890, most of his property was sold by his heirs to eager businessmen and developers.

Black Hawk's Watch Tower was one piece of land that Bailey had tried to sell. In 1873, he had offered 20 acres of the park to the United States government for a federal prison. The commander on Arsenal Island objected and the penitentiary was later established at Fort Leavenworth, Kansas. After this failure, Bailey continued to work the coal mines and quarries on the northern part of the property while developing a pleasure resort on the south. The chief attractions of this park were the view, lovely picnic areas, a summer house and the sparkling waters of its springs.

When Bailey died, the park was bought by the Rock Island and Davenport Railway Company, which developed the resort into a giant amusement park as a way of increasing the use of the street cars on Sundays and in the evenings. Attractions that would appeal to all levels of interest were booked throughout the summer. The public, caught up in the general craze for self improvement and the pursuit of culture, thronged to the park. Although the street car company also promoted recreational facilities at Prospect Park in Moline and on Campbell's Island, Black Hawk's Watch Tower was the most successful of the three.

Performing animals, vaudeville, concerts and light opera were booked, as well as special acts. The latter included a singing group called the Cherry Sisters who requested a "paeno and orchestry" to accompany them; a visit by the 89-year-old nephew of Black Hawk who brought 20 of his braves to play tom-toms and dance; and a daring young lady who ascended to 4,000 feet in a hot air balloon before leaping out and parachuting gracefully to the ground.

COAL WAS AN IMPORTANT SOURCE OF POWER FOR EARLY ROCK ISLAND INDUSTRIES. IN 1876, NEARLY 300,000 TONS OF COAL WERE PRODUCED BY 46 ACTIVE MINES IN ROCK ISLAND COUNTY. IN THIS 1886 PICTURE, BAILEY DAVENPORT, RIGHT, STANDS IN FRONT OF THE MINE HE OWNED IN BLACK HAWK PARK. THE OTHER TWO MEN WITH HIM IN FRONT OF CAR NO.2 OF THE ROCK ISLAND AND MILAN STREET CAR COMPANY ARE CLAUS H. LAMP, LEFT, THE CAR'S ENGINEER, AND CHARLES H. STODDARD, COUNTY SURVEYOR. AFTER THE COAL WAS DUG, IT WAS HAULED TO THE STREET CAR COMPANY'S YARD AT 10TH AVENUE AND 11TH STREET.

On opening night in 1892, some 100 prominent citizens of the Tri-Cities were invited to a banquet in the new Queen Anne-styled pavilion. Free transport was provided on special trains and street cars. The resulting publicity was a typical example of how the street car company used every means it could to promote the park. Two years later the pavilion was destroyed by fire. Nevertheless, the park was open the next day, and the newspapers reported that the performing elephants were the hit of the evening.

When plans were announced to construct a new pavilion, the town of Sears, within whose district the property lay, proposed to levy a tax on all concessions in the park. The street car company refused to consider rebuilding under such conditions, saying they had never been taxed before. After much politicking and publicity, punctuated by newspaper headlines that read "Sears is Sulking" or "Sears Blocks the Way," the street car company won and the new inn was completed in three months. Opening day was celebrated by 5,000 people who took advantage of free admission to the park and did not want to go home in the evening.

The new pavilion was much larger, with dining rooms, a ballroom and large porches on all sides to take advantage of the beautiful view. The building was surrounded by various concessions among which were a shooting gallery, roller skating rink, laughing gallery and a figure-8 roller coaster that rose 60 feet into the air and was called the first such "terror-maker west of Chicago." But the most popular ride was a toboggan slide that went down the cliff into the Rock River and was called "shoot the chutes."

Local people were not the only ones attracted to Black Hawk's Watch Tower. Many visitors came from out of town, and at the height of its popularity an estimated 50,000 people visited the park each summer.

In 1897, a group of local businessmen bought the Rock Island and Davenport Railway Company and the Moline street car lines and organized as the Tri-City Railway Company. They renovated the tracks and bought additional cars. More importantly, with control of the entire three-city transport system, they offered a free transfer plan. Until that time, passengers were required to buy a 5-cent ticket whenever they changed lines.

This monopoly was further extended in 1907 when Eastern financiers acquired Black Hawk's Watch Tower and the utility companies of all three cities. From this consolidation came the Iowa-Illinois Gas and Electric Company.

With the coming of bicycles and automobiles, the street cars were no longer profitable. Attendance at the amusement park declined and the Tri-City Railway put the property up for sale. Fearing that the land might be bought by real estate developers, a group of concerned citizens led by John Hauberg asked the state to buy the site for a public park. In 1927, the Illinois Legislature appropriated $200,000, and Black Hawk State Park became a reality.

J.P. NEWBERG BUILT HIS FIRST WATER SLIDE IN 1855, ABOUT ONE MILE EAST OF BLACK HAWK'S WATCH TOWER. LATER HE BUILT A SECOND SLIDE AT THE AMUSEMENT PARK. THE SLIDE RAN DOWN THE HILL INTO THE ROCK RIVER. CALLED "SHOOT-THE-CHUTES," IT WAS ONE OF THE MOST POPULAR ATTRACTIONS AT THE PARK. WHEN THE SQUARE-BOWED BOAT (THE STERN IS JUST VISIBLE IN THE LOWER RIGHT CORNER) WAS READY TO GO, A WARNING BELL WAS RUNG TO CLEAR THE TRACK. AFTER THE BOAT HIT THE WATER, IT WAS PADDLED BACK TO THE SLIDE, THE PASSENGERS GOT OUT AND WALKED UP THE STEPS WHILE THE BOAT WAS PULLED BACK UP THE TRACK. THE FASTEST RECORDED TRIP DOWN THE CHUTE WAS MADE BY A CLINTON MAN WHO RODE HIS BICYCLE DOWN IT IN 4 SECONDS. NEWBERG, THE RIDE'S INVENTOR, PATENTED HIS WATER TOBOGGAN AND WENT TO CHICAGO. HE RETURNED IN 1902 TO MANAGE THE INN AT THE PARK PAVILION.

The city continued to grow. The 1880 census showed 11,659 people living in Rock Island, with more than 19,000 in 1900. New residential areas were needed. By 1878, the original town of Stephenson had grown by 70 additions. Less than a decade later, the city encompassed four square miles and its boundaries extended to meet those of Moline. Finally, with the addition of Sears township in 1915, Rock Island stretched from river to river.

Sears, or Sears Town, was one of several settlements along the Rock River. Together with Lowell (on Vandruff's Island) and Camden (Milan) it was part of an ambitious scheme to harness the water power of the river and establish a large manufacturing center.

One of the earliest attempts to utilize this power was the erection of two piers jutting out from Vandruff's Island towards Black Hawk's Watch Tower. A saw and grist mill operated there for several years until destroyed by fire. This was followed by a stone and brush dam built from the south bank of the Rock to Big Island. It provided power for as many as six mills. Then in 1867 David Sears, an early pioneer who had constructed the first dam at Moline, bought extensive property near the foot of the Milan Bridge. He saw great possibilities for industry, and obtained a charter from the state granting him permission to build four new dams across the various branches of the Rock. In the following years, Sears also erected a large stone grist mill and two smaller ones along the banks of the river. None of the mills was as successful as Sears had hoped and all were closed by 1893. In the same year, the community incorporated under the name of its founder. Just a few years later, the water power at the Rock was bought by S.S. and T.B. Davis, pioneers in public utility systems in the Tri-Cities. New concrete dams replaced the old ones and a large hydroelectric plant was constructed to provide cheap electricity to the area.

Sears had also bought Vandruff's Island, which included the village of Lowell. Platted in 1841, Lowell's best known resident was Joshua Vandruff who operated a ferry across the river. Never much more than a few cabins and a short-lived store, Lowell really never got off the ground.

Camden, on the opposite bank of the Rock, had been laid out in 1843 by William Dickson. Cheap coal and abundant water power made it an attractive manufacturing site. By 1877 it was a thriving community with mills, shops, three churches, two hotels and a large distillery. The town changed its name in 1848 to Camden Mills to distinguish it from another Camden in Schuyler County, and to Milan in 1870 when a large three-story watch factory was built on Vandruff's Island. The company felt that Camden Mills was too long a name to fit on a watch face. No watches were ever made as the company had ordered the wrong machinery, and in 1906 the building was taken over by the Artista Piano Company.

By the late 1880s Milan had begun to decline as a manufacturing center. Water power, so important at the beginning, was not as reliable as steam power, and when a fire destroyed four mills and several warehouses in the town, they were not rebuilt.

Rock Island, meanwhile, continued to grow and on October 14, 1875, Augustana College was dedicated to "God and His Church." Founded in 1860 in Chicago by Scandinavian immigrants, it then moved to Paxton, Illinois. Lacking adequate financial support, the college decided to settle close to Rock Island and Moline where there were substantial Swedish populations.

The college bought 18 acres on the outskirts of Rock Island and erected the first brick building on a bluff known as Zion Hill. There were rooms for 100 students, apartments for four professors, a chapel, a library, classrooms, a dining room and a society hall.

The citizens of Rock Island helped the college survive the financial hardships of the early years. When construction on a stone building was halted due to lack of funds, Philander Cable, a retired banker and

businessman, gave the college $25,000. The beautiful domed structure was called Memorial Hall and later Old Main.

Augustana received another financial boost when it celebrated its 50th Jubilee Anniversary in 1910. More than $250,000 was pledged by loyal supporters creating a special endowment fund. The celebration also helped to publicize the needs of the college. One result was the gift of a new library by the Denkmann family.

A PHOTO OF AUGUSTANA COLLEGE ABOUT 1890 SHOWS THE ORIGINAL COLLEGE BUILDING AND THE LATER, DOMED STRUCTURE, NOW KNOWN AS OLD MAIN.

Originally a college for training Lutheran ministers, Augustana offered only classical courses for the first five years. After 1880, a broader curriculum was taught. By 1914 the curriculum included mathematics, science, classics, music, religion and art. The Swedish dream that began with only 21 students now had an enrollment of more than 650.

Many immigrants wanted their children taught by members of their own faith and they established parochial schools. The German Lutherans were the first, followed by the Swedish Lutherans and Catholics of many nations. Some classes were conducted in the mother tongue though this practice died out at the turn of the century. In 1901, the Villa De Chantal, a Catholic preparatory school for girls, opened on "Bald Bluffs" above 13th Avenue. Within 12 years it had 300 girls on its rolls.

Other changes had come to the city, most notably the improvement in public services. When the principal streets were first lit by gas lamps in 1855, there was a large celebration at the Island City Hotel. Electric light came in 1882, the same year that Thomas Edison opened Pearl Street Electric Station in New York City. Eleven 125-foot towers equipped with arc lights were erected at street intersections to illuminate the downtown area. From that height the bulbs were not very effective, and some residents thought the gas lamps did a superior job. The towers eventually were removed and lower lights on poles took their place.

In 1871, the city authorized the construction of a pumping station to pipe water out of the Mississippi. With the increase in population, this system soon became inadequate and the waterworks were enlarged. A $25,000 gift from the Cable family helped pay for the needed improvements. Later, reservoirs and a new pumping station were built on the bluffs, and the surrounding land became Reservoir Park.

The telegraph had come to the city with the first railroad in 1854.

*AFTER 14 YEARS OF DRAGGING
THEIR HAND ENGINE TO FIGHT
FIRES IN ROCK ISLAND, THE
VOLUNTEERS OF WESTERN
COMPANY NO. 1 WERE GIVEN A
STEAM ENGINE IN 1869. THEY
NAMED IT THE <u>WILLIAM
EGGLESTON</u> AFTER ITS DONOR.*

Telephones were in use by 1879, just three years after their invention by Alexander Graham Bell. A franchise was granted to the Western Telephone Company in 1881 and by the end of the year there were 100 phone subscribers in Rock Island. The two women employed at the company's switchboard were expected to handle all calls during their 12-hour shift. When the company allowed them a half-hour lunch break, there were so many complaints about the interruption in service that the lunch breaks were cancelled. For this 12-hour, 6-day work week, the women received $15 a month.

Mail services, which had begun in 1834 in John Barrel's house in Farnhamsburg, also improved. After the county seat was moved to Stephenson, the post office was housed in numerous buildings. In 1906, it moved into new quarters in the Federal Building on 2nd Avenue and 16th Street. When better facilities were needed, the old post office was enlarged and renovated and reopened in 1912 as the third largest post office in the state.

Posts did not come regularly until July 1862 when it was announced that "after this date, daily mail would come up the river by boat." Free delivery was provided to city residents in 1888 when 42 letter boxes were set out on the streets and five carriers were hired to deliver the mail. Rural districts did not get free home delivery of packages until 1913. When a small branch office called South Heights was established at 1815 17th Street in 1891, the salary of the postman was based on the number of letters he carried. For the first month his salary was only 33 cents so he quit.

One of the most welcome advances in public services was the beginning of a paid fire department in 1891. Before that, the city depended on volunteer groups for protection. The first volunteer company, Western No. 1, was formed in 1855 with 75 members and one fire engine. Response to fires was often slow because the men had trouble dragging the heavy engine over the unpaved roads. One mayor told residents it was their duty to help as often "the firemen arrived wearied out of all breath."

The extension of water mains to all parts of the city and the increase in tax revenues led to advances in fire fighting methods. New equipment was purchased in the following years, and by 1913 there were three two-horse hose wagons, one two-horse hook and ladder truck and one buggy for the chief. The five fire stations were manned by 19 full time firemen.

Law enforcement was originally the job of the sheriff and his deputies, assisted by local residents when needed. A police force of six men was organized by 1875, but uniforms were not provided until the 1890s. When automobiles became more common, the police department received a patrol car and an ambulance.

Many improvements were the results of effort by local businessmen and concerned citizens. In 1876, for example, several city aldermen visited the World's Fair in Philadelphia and were so impressed with the city's orderly system of street numbers that they got the Rock Island City Council to approve a similar plan. North-south roads were designated streets and east-west roads were called avenues. Rather than Mississippi or Front Street, it was now 1st Avenue; Eagle was renamed 17th Street.

This was just the beginning of a movement to enhance the looks of the city. A group of 100 influential businessmen formed The Citizens Improvement Association in 1888, and pressured the mayor and council into appropriating funds for the paving of roads, development of parks and the general cleanup of the town.

Their first project, the paving of 2nd Avenue, helped attract new stores to the street. It soon became the main thoroughfare in the city. Next they pushed for the complete renovation of the swampy, neglected land known as Spencer Square. For years there had been complaints about the condition of the square, which due to its lowland position flooded frequently until the grade was raised in 1880.

The mayor appointed a park commissioner who drew up plans, and a quarry was opened in the square itself to provide the necessary stone for sidewalks. Meanwhile, funds were solicited for benches, statues and other ornaments. By 1890, Spencer Square had been transformed into a beautiful park with a spectacular fountain at its center. Many citizens felt it was the handsomest square in the Northwest. Two years later, an impressive granite statue of Black Hawk was added, and a large crowd gathered to enjoy the dedication speeches and spectacular fireworks display. The statue was later moved to Black Hawk State Park when Spencer Square became the site of the new post office.

The success of Spencer Square marked the beginning of both a park system and a park board. Attention was then turned to the renovation of Garnsey, Court House and Denkmann squares. After much hard work, the park board members succeeded in raising sufficient funds to open a new park, Longview. The land had once belonged to Bailey Davenport. At his death, the property was bought by various businessmen who gave 40 acres to the city in 1897 for use by the public. It took 11 years to make the park a reality, but when it opened in 1908, it was the showplace of the city.

One last major park was added in 1909 when mass citizen meetings convinced the council to buy a 23 acre tract of land due east of Augustana College. This became Lincoln Park, so named because 1909 was the 100th anniversary of the birth of Abraham Lincoln.

One attempt at a park was not so successful. In 1892, the city of Chicago opened the Columbian World's Fair Exposition to mark the 400th anniversary of the discovery of America by Christopher Columbus. Caught up in the excitement of preparations for the anniversary, the citizens of Rock Island and Moline decided to buy property for a park and build their own world's fair. They proposed to buy 26 acres east of 38th Street and north of 7th Avenue and call it Twin-City or Columbia Park.

Each city pledged to raise $50,000 and committees were organized to solicit funds. The street car company, realizing that the park would increase business, immediately donated $5,000, but other organizations were not so generous. Finally, with less than half of the money raised, the cities began work on the park.

They hoped to have a grand opening in July but bad weather caused delays. Although the land was graded and the street paved, rain prevented the roofing of the grandstand and turned the race track into a sea of mud. On July 4, 1892, processions from both cities met at the park entrance. A flag was raised, more than 1,000 children sang patriotic songs and dedication speeches followed. The track was unfit for horses, but foot races were held on the saturated grass and winners were awarded cash prizes and medals. Baseball was next, and the Rock Island Arcades defeated the Athletics of Moline 10-8.

Although the afternoon fireworks were abandoned due to heavy rain, the weather cleared by evening and 15,000 people enjoyed the singing and fireworks display that was said to be "the crowning feature of the day's events." Gate receipts did not cover expenses, so though Exposition Park continued to be used for sports for some years, no further work was done on the fair. Eventually the land was sold and the first real joint venture of Moline and Rock Island ended in failure.

Despite this setback, the feelings of patriotism and civic pride that had given impetus to the creation of Columbia Park continued to flourish. The Rock Island Board of Trade and other businessmen's associations successfully advertised the advantages of the city and attracted new industries, and 1892 began a period of heavy investment in commercial and residential building. Stores were renovated, unsightly structures torn down and new ones erected "giving the appearance," said the *Tri-City Journal*, "of a modern looking city."

THE GRAND ARMY OF THE REPUBLIC PARADED DOWN 2ND AVENUE DURING ITS 1902 ENCAMPMENT IN ROCK ISLAND. THE LOCAL COMPANY, FORMED BY 32 FORMER UNION SOLDIERS IN 1883, TOOK THE NAME "BUFORD POST" TO HONOR THE BUFORD BROTHERS, HEROES OF THE CIVIL WAR. THE GROUP DISBANDED IN THE 1930S. THE G.A.R. BEGAN THE CUSTOM OF VISITING THE GRAVES OF WAR DEAD ON MAY 30, WHICH LED TO CREATION OF THE MEMORIAL DAY HOLIDAY.

At this time, a new tax for public improvements was levied. Sewers were laid, streets paved and work begun on improving the downtown sidewalks. Hitherto, the walks had been whatever width or height the property owner thought necessary. Now some of the tax monies were used to standardize and pave the walks so that pedestrians could negotiate the streets with relative ease.

Of the many new buildings, three especially were a source of civic pride. These were the Court House, the Library and the Y.M.C.A., each of which had outgrown previous premises. Residents had voted to replace the Court House in 1894, and two years later, one of the largest crowds to ever assemble in Rock Island witnessed the laying of the cornerstone by Benjamin Goble, oldest living resident of the city.

The library began in 1855 when a group of citizens formed the Rock Island City Library and Reading Room Association. Books were bought with the $500 raised by membership dues, and Library Hall was opened for public use. Taken over by the Young Men's Library Association in 1864, the library continued in operation until 1872. It then became a tax supported municipal institution, the third public library to be organized in Illinois. By 1895, the library had outgrown its rooms and desperately needed its own facilities. This became a reality in 1903 largely due to the generosity of Messrs. Weyerhaeuser and Denkmann. The opening of the beautiful classical building was the event of the year.

Public donations raised the money needed to build the first Y, which was completed in 1905. Seven years later, another campaign was launched to erect a new, larger building. Daily contributions were shown on a giant clock face lit by 125 incandescent bulbs and mounted on the pagoda in Market Square. When pledges exceeded the $125,000 goal in only seven days, the clock face was a blaze of lights.

It was a time of many social clubs, church groups and fraternal organizations. Some, like the Rock Island Club, had two main objectives: the entertainment of its members and the betterment of life in the town. Others were groups of businessmen who actively promoted the growth of capital and industry within the city. Ladies' societies, especially, continued to devote themselves to the care of the sick and less fortunate. They held charity balls, suppers, lectures and special meetings to help fund their various projects.

Sometimes collections were taken for the victims of disasters. In 1860, residents of Rock Island sent food, clothing and $3,425 to the survivors of a tornado at Camanche, Iowa. Money and provisions were also sent to the victims of the Chicago fire and the San Francisco earthquake. When severe floods partially submerged more than 125 houses in Rock Island in 1880, they raised $1,023 for relief work.

In 1897, the Associated Charities was formed to coordinate the work of the numerous benevolent organizations. Some institutions like the Bethany Home for orphans, also founded in 1897, augmented their funds with annual tag days. In 1912 more than $700 was raised in mostly nickel donations. This home was followed by the Association House and the West End Settlement which provided special services for disadvantaged families.

Diseases such as cholera, smallpox and malaria that regularly attacked the city began to be controlled through improved sanitation and advances in medical knowledge. When the need for a hospital arose, citizens opened St. Luke's in the west end of town. This 12-bed facility was replaced by a new hospital called St. Anthony's in 1892. In order to meet the needs of the community, St. Anthony's was rebuilt once, and enlarged 14 times before it closed in 1972. Two years later it re-opened as St. Anthony's Continuing Care Center.

Such improvements in the quality of life would not have been possible without the generosity and leadership of wealthy Rock Island families. They controlled the major industries, and as their fortunes grew they built palatial homes on the bluffs overlooking the Mississippi. No expense was spared to insure the comfort of the family members. The Cables, for example, even had their own railroad spur connecting their property on 5th Avenue with the main tracks of the Rock Island Lines.

The city offered many amusements. Roller skating, billiards, bowling and bicycling were popular sports at the turn of the century, and local baseball and football teams fought hotly contested games at Twin-City or Island City parks. Athletics had been part of school curricula since 1883, and the first high school football coach was hired in 1901. Perhaps this helped to account for the intense public interest in the annual student-alumni football match. In 1912, the newspaper reported that the alumni "relied on their beef rather than their strategy to win 6-0."

In winter, bobsledding was the rage for many years. Neighborhood clubs challenged each other to races down the bluffs and into town. Some toboggans had homemade horns, lights and brakes and were said to have reached speeds of up to 60 m.p.h. One club even claimed to have made the trip from the top of 17th Street to the fire station on 2nd Avenue in just over two minutes. Favorite hills were Greenbush (30th Street), Dock (22nd Street), and Flying Dutchman, Thunder and Lightning in Longview Park. Sometimes there were serious accidents, and as traffic increased and roads were paved, bobsledding lost some of its popularity.

Once regarded as an obstruction that had to be crossed, the Mississippi now became a source of pleasure. Skating carnivals were held in winter and steamboats offered inviting excursions during the summertime. A boat club was formed and its members participated in regattas and water carnivals. Bathing became so popular that the council was forced to prohibit swimmers from the shore between 18th and 19th Streets because they impeded the safe passage of the ferries.

Many of the clubs sponsored special events in addition to holding regular meetings. There were frequent picnics, festivals and suppers. But the greatest enthusiasm was reserved for parades. Civic and national events were celebrated by processions often followed by fireworks displays.

Several halls featured dramatic presentations, musical evenings, dancing and vaudeville for the price of 20-50 cents a person. The most famous of these was the Harper Opera House on the corner of 2nd Avenue and 16th Street. No expense was spared on its construction, and on opening night the 1,200 seats were filled with patrons who had each paid $2.50 (two days' pay for the average workman) to see the show. Performances continued at the opera house until the opening of the Illinois Theatre in 1901 took away most of its trade.

The opera house was only one of two showplaces built by Ben Harper who, it was said, "wanted to do something good for the city." Having made his fortune before coming to Rock Island in 1850, Harper proceeded to construct the finest hotel on the rail line between Chicago and the Pacific coast. When it opened in 1871, it was the first hotel in the West to boast a fire escape system and mercury alarms in every gas-lit room. In its prime, it attracted visitors from many states and played host to such celebrities as Sarah Bernhardt, Buffalo Bill and Tom Thumb. For many years the Harper buildings were considered "a better advertisement for Rock Island than any other business in the city."

With the beginning of the 20th century came the horseless carriage that changed the way of life all over America. Change was gradual with mud roads presenting a constant challenge to the automobile driver. When hard rubber tires succeeded the original steel-rimmed wheels, punctures and blow-outs were frequent. Onlookers laughed when cars broke down and had to be towed away by horses. One of the first cars, the Black Crow, described as just a buggy with a gasoline engine attached, sold for $1,500 in 1902. Ten years later, an automobile could be bought for only $1,000, and one

USING THIS COVER ON ITS PROGRAM, THE ATHLETIC CLUB OF ROCK ISLAND HELD ITS FIRST ANNUAL DINNER IN 1876. FORMED IN 1873, THE CLUB INCLUDED AMONG ITS MEMBERS MANY PROMINENT CITIZENS, WHO ENJOYED BOTH PHYSICAL ACTIVITIES AND SOCIAL EVENTS.

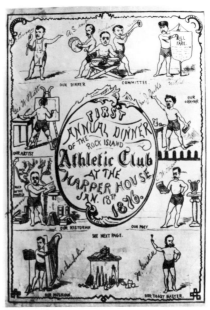

THE SINISTER FIGURE OF JOHN LOONEY CAST A SHADOW OVER ROCK ISLAND FOR MANY YEARS.

CIRCUSES PROVIDED A POPULAR FORM OF SUMMER ENTERTAIN-MENT. THE FIRST TROUPES ARRIVED BY STEAMER OR WAGON AND, AFTER 1854, IN SPECIAL RAIL CARS. A PARADE, SUCH AS THIS ONE ALONG ROCK ISLAND'S 2ND AVENUE, HELPED ATTRACT A CROWD.

enthusiastic car dealer declared that "cars were no longer the toy of the rich."

Speed limits were set at 10 m.p.h. within the city, with a $10-$50 fine for violations. This did not deter some joy-riders from becoming speed fiends, and when the first motorcycle patrolman went on duty in 1912, the newspaper warned, "Those who have been accustomed to making an Indianapolis speedway out of public thoroughfares will do well to keep an eye on the speedometer in the future."

Into this time of prosperity and civic pride came a man who was to bring Rock Island to the brink of anarchy. John P. Looney came to the city in 1887 to work for Western Union. Admitted to the bar in 1889, Looney had his first brush with the law in 1896 when he and two others were fined $2,000 on charges of conspiracy and fraud.

Four years later, Looney began publication of a newspaper called the *Rock Island News*. Billed as the only paper that dares "to publish all the news," it dealt in half-truths and innuendoes, and attacked the characters of many prominent citizens. Perhaps in retaliation, a bomb exploded in the newspaper building destroying the presses and suspending publication. Looney and his partner fought and the bitter feud ended in a pistol duel on 3rd Avenue, in which Looney was slightly wounded on one cheek.

Publication of *The News* began again and Looney continued to attack those with whom he disagreed. Things came to a head in March 1912 when Looney threatened to publish an article describing compromising events in the private life of Henry Schriver, mayor of Rock Island. The mayor retaliated by closing down the presses of *The News*, impounding the offending newspapers, and ordering the arrest of Looney. After his arrest, Looney was so badly beaten by police that hospitalization was required.

Events then moved swiftly. On March 25, two days after Looney's arrest, a large crowd gathered in Market Square to hear a speech by Harry McCaskrin, Republican candidate for state's attorney. At the end of his talk McCaskrin suggested that Looney had been unfairly treated, and that the Schriver story should be made public. Needing no further encouragement, the crowds rushed to the office of *The News* to obtain copies of the prohibited newspaper. They were met by the police and a battle ensued with the mob hurling stones and bricks at the police station. After several hours, the crowds dispersed and no one was arrested.

A second night of rioting left one man dead and 10 injured. Fearing more violence, the governor of Illinois put Rock Island under martial law and ordered the Sixth Regiment into the city. Conditions eased, and the last soldiers left on April 12. The mayor declared that the riot had been led by "riffraff and undesirables" and urged all citizens to help rebuild the shattered public image of the city. It was also pointed out with pride that the real spirit of Rock Island had been shown in the week after the riots when the campaign to build a new Y.M.C.A. had successfully topped its goal of $125,000.

Other communities were not so charitable. A Davenport paper suggested that the rioting was just the climax of several years of graft, greed, blackmail and inefficient law enforcement. "The real criminals," said the editor, "are the men higher up," and "when Rock Island gets rid of such men, better days will be in sight for the city."

Gradually the riots were forgotten and the damage to downtown buildings was repaired. Looney was tried in Peoria, found guilty of mailing obscene material, fined $5,000 and ordered to suspend publication of *The News*. A sick man, he left for Mexico and did not return to Rock Island until 1912. One humiliating footnote followed the March riots: President Woodrow Wilson, who had been scheduled to stop in Rock Island in April, decided not to test the city's recently enacted law against public gatherings (a direct result of the imposition of martial law) and gave his speech in Moline instead. Despite this setback, the Democrats won handily in the city elections in November, and held a triumphant celebration that ended with a giant bonfire at the levee.

Events abroad now began to catch the public's interest. Europe seemed poised on the brink of war and every new evidence of hostility was given front page coverage. Already in 1912, a group of 75 Greeks had left Rock Island to take up arms against the Turks, and many other foreign-born residents of the city waited anxiously as the crisis deepened.

Outwardly, life continued much as usual in Rock Island. On July 22, the long awaited Barnum and Bailey's Circus arrived on five special trains, and paraded to Exposition Park where the performances would take place. The last tent had barely been struck when residents learned that Austria had invaded Serbia and World War I had begun. The date was July 27, 1914.

Once again, newspapers covered the hostilities in detail, and the Red Cross made successful appeals for funds to help the suffering millions in Europe. With the sinking of the *Lusitania* in 1915, news became heavily slanted in favor of the Allies, and the idea of going to their aid gained in popularity. Finally, on April 7, the United States entered the war and the city was swept with recruiting fever. Displays, posters and speeches encouraged young men to go to the recruiting office in Spencer Square and help "beat back the Huns." The response was slow at first, but by April 12 Company A was moved from temporary quarters to Arsenal Island. One member of the group immediately came down with smallpox and all the men went into quarantine.

Although the Tri-City Federation of Labor sent a telegram to President Wilson stating its opposition to the war and to conscription, the majority of citizens supported America's decision. The whole city was touched by the patriotic example of 21 members of Augustana's band enlisting as a unit in the 6th Illinois Regiment on April 6.

A moving farewell was held in the Augustana Chapel with the band playing a final concert and leading a loyalty parade through downtown Rock Island. The next day the entire student body went to the railroad station to see the band depart. Olaf Cervin, architect and graduate of Augustana, spoke for the entire city when he said, "Every flag in Rock Island should fly today and honor those who march. Some, perhaps never to return, but all go forward to fight for their country's existence."

FOR MANY YEARS, SPENCER SQUARE WAS LITTLE MORE THAN A ROCKY, SWAMPY HOLLOW. DEEDED TO THE CITY IN 1855 "FOR USE BY THE PUBLIC" BY JUDGE JOHN W. SPENCER, IT WAS MADE INTO AN ATTRACTIVE PARK IN 1890. WHEN THE SQUARE BECAME THE SITE OF THE POST OFFICE IN 1954, THE GRANITE STATUE OF BLACK HAWK WAS MOVED TO BLACK HAWK STATE PARK.

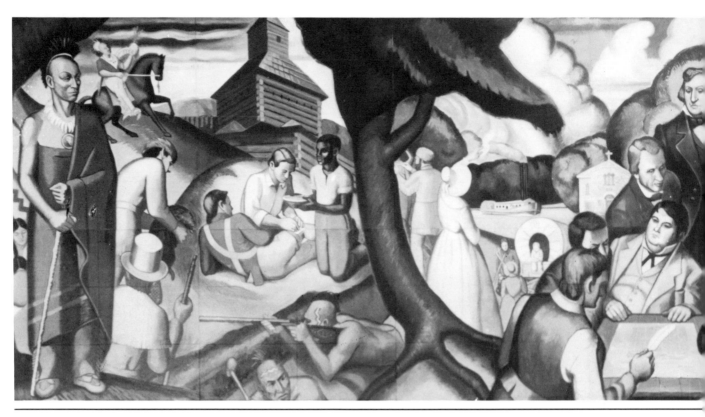

BY WILLIAM ROBA

COLONEL GEORGE DAVENPORT CAME TO PROVIDE SUPPLIES FOR SOLDIERS AT FORT ARMSTRONG AND STAYED TO FOUND A COMMUNITY.

While thousands of citizens of Davenport, Rock Island and Moline joined in celebration on July 4, 1845, three Rock Island residents passed up the event to take a cool, leisurely trip upstream in a skiff. By mid-afternoon, Benjamin Cole, F. A. Walker and his son, Earl, had rounded the north shore of the island of Rock Island when they heard cries for help. They landed the skiff and rushed into George Davenport's mansion on the island. They found him lying on a bed upstairs, splattered with blood but still alive. He described three gunmen who had shot him in the thigh, then beaten and choked him as they demanded money. All the thieves found were $700 from the safe and Davenport's watch, shotgun and pistol. Dr. H. Brown and Dr. P. P. Gregg soon arrived, but were unable to save him.

People throughout the Upper Mississippi River valley were outraged at the murder. Alfred Sanders, editor of the *Gazette*, called it "one of the most coldblooded and horrible atrocities which we recollect ever to have heard being committed in a civilized community, in broad daylight and for paltry plunder." Davenport's family had been at the general celebration on the Illinois shore. They were stricken with grief, offering a reward of $1,500 for apprehension of the murderers. Governor Ford of Illinois added $800 to the family's reward, as most able-bodied males began searching for the killers. Edward Bonney, a detective from Montrose, Iowa, systematically tracked down the gang and returned them to Rock Island.

The execution of John and Aaron Long and Granville Young became a major public event. Businesses closed as a large crowd gathered on October 29, 1845, even though the overcast sky promised rain. As the crowd watched, John Long's rope broke and he fell to the ground. Some people cried out for his release, interpreting the event as a sign from God to spare his life; others

UNVEILED IN 1936 DURING CEREMONIES MARKING DAVEN-PORT'S CENTENNIAL, THIS MURAL PAINTED BY LOCAL ARTIST HELEN J. HINRICHSEN FIRST HUNG ON THE SOUTH WALL OF WALGREEN DRUG STORE. IT IS NOW ON PERMANENT DISPLAY AT THE DAVENPORT ART GALLERY.

yelled to the hangman to do his duty. The crowd began to panic as a few noticed a group of strangers on horseback: was a rescue attempt unfolding? The hangman quickly executed Long and the other two. After the execution, three doctors got the bodies, purportedly for medical research. Dr. Patrick Gregg of Rock Island received John Long's body, Dr. Egbert S. Barrows of Davenport got Aaron Long's, and Dr. Ruben Knox got Granville Young's.

George Davenport's legacy included the frontier town named after him. On February 23, 1836, Antoine Le Claire, the former Indian interpreter at Fort Armstrong, had gathered together three other investors and two proxies to create a company. The aim was to develop land across the river into a town. The company paid Le Claire $1,750 for the site between present-day Harrison and Warren streets. Le Claire was land rich but lacked the money to develop his extensive holdings; in addition, he was half-Indian and a staunch Catholic, liabilities in attracting a large number of settlers. Davenport and the other incorporators had English names (Tom Smith, Philip Hambaugh), money to invest and government contacts. Historian George Wickstrom has suggested that they named the town after George Davenport because he had failed to attach his name to the town across the river. Within the next year, the town had attracted 90 settlers; by 1850 there were 1,848.

The topography of the site made it a natural location. An early settler recalled "a waving, irregular semicircle of bluffs, enclosing an amphitheater of some hundreds of yards in breadth, and two miles in length. The floor or 'bottom' of this amphitheater sloped gently from the water to the foot of the bluffs."

*THIS LITHOGRAPH OF DAVENPORT
IN THE EARLY 1840S WAS
PUBLISHED IN A GERMAN
COLLECTION, MEYER'S
UNIVERSUM, THAT PORTRAYED
MANY SCENES ALONG THE
MISSISSIPPI RIVER.*

Antoine Le Claire succeeded in making Davenport a frontier city. He was born in 1797, the son of a French-Canadian adventurer and a Potawatomi woman. He served as a government interpreter, earning the trust of Indians in the area because he was part Indian himself and because he could speak 14 Indian dialects, French and English. By the early 1830s, due to treaty provisions, Le Claire already owned significant amounts of land in advance of other settlers: 1,280 acres in Moline, a Lower Reserve of one section near the site of a Mesquakie (Fox) village along the western bank of the Mississippi River, and an equally large Upper Reserve, 14 miles upstream at the head of the Rock Island Rapids. Land ownership created his wealth, valued at almost $500,000 when he died.

Le Claire's vision of the city complemented the natural features. The 36 blocks followed an east-west axis parallel roughly to the river. The streets reflected the town site's Indian origins with the tribal names of Sauk, Fox, Chippewa and Potawatomi for the east-west streets. The riverfront area (or "levee") remained for public use. Unlike most other frontier towns subdivided for private houses, Le Claire also laid out four public squares that are still maintained for non-commercial use: Church Square, Bolivar Square (later used for the courthouse), La Fayette Square and Washington Square.

The Mississippi River stimulated the economic growth of the city. Ferryboats and skiffs connected Davenport to the Illinois shore. Steamboats were a seasonal activity, usually from March to November. Twenty boats of more than 150 tons cargo capacity were in regular service north of St. Louis by the late 1840s, stopping with goods and passengers at the Davenport levee.

Improvements on the Upper Mississippi began when Lieutenant Robert E. Lee. was assigned to St. Louis, arriving in August 1837. He and his surveying party traveled north from St. Louis to examine the channel's tendency to twist as it went through chains of rocks at the Rock Island Rapids. Lee and his men moved into an abandoned steamboat where they could fish for blue catfish over the side of the boat when the day's surveying was finished. His letters back to friends and supervisors indicated a greater degree of civilization in Davenport than he had expected.

A year before Lee, an early settler was as pleasantly surprised as he was. Clarissa Cook, who would later become a prominent philantrhopist could see the faint outlines of a future city. When she disembarked from the steamboat moored by the levee and walked four blocks north to Church Square, she found a wooden structure containing not only St. Anthony's

Catholic Church, but also a school and a court in session. She noticed other churches nearby: Presbyterian, Baptist, Congregational and Christian Disciple. She found that Andrew Logan had begun publishing a weekly paper, the *Iowa Sun*, the summer of her arrival. If she had wanted to, Mrs. Cook also could have noticed the smelly pork packing houses and bustling brick yards that flourished by the late 1830s.

In spite of competitors, Le Claire dominated the business activity of the fledgling city of Davenport. He owned a business block, theater, stone quarry and several farms. In 1843, he built the first "classy" hotel in the region. The Le Claire House was three stories tall with an observatory on the top floor. Downstairs were a reading room (supported by the Carey Library Association) and a restaurant. The outside suggested a classical style with a portico and four Corinthian columns.

CLARISSA COOK, AN EARLY SETTLER WHO GAINED PROMINENCE THROUGH HER PHILANTHROPY IN LATER YEARS.

Le Claire fostered the town's development with a mixture of civic participation and private enterprise. He served as Davenport's first postmaster and a partial term as alderman. A Catholic, Le Claire not only donated two city blocks of land to St. Anthony's Church, but received parish support in erecting a wooden church. He also donated Bolivar Square to the county. There the county built a jail and courthouse, which made Davenport a magnet for county residents needing to conduct public business such as land registration. Le Claire gave 13 lots to the trustees of Iowa College in 1847; the result was a private college, again attracting potential settlers.

Between 1837 and 1840, Le Claire and Davenport leaders such as James Thorington and Judge James Grant struggled to make their city the county seat. In 1837 the Territorial Legislature created the county boundaries, naming the county after General Winfield Scott, and designating Davenport as a "special charter city." Only one obstacle stopped Davenport from becoming the river city envisioned by Le Claire. That obstacle was the town of Rockingham.

Rockingham was settled opposite the mouth of the Rock River, one mile south of Davenport. On paper the town's location was superior; in reality, the town was situated on "bottom land" that flooded every spring. Each year, keelboats carried freight to the general store as the town became a virtual island for the population of several hundred. After three elections (and disputed results), Davenport became the county seat in 1840 by a vote of 318 to 221.

One of the first signs of Eastern refinement was a lecture society, begun in 1839. Davenport lawyers and doctors received public acclaim, and also got more clients and patients, because of their public speaking. The topics varied during a season defined by the opening and closing of the river with ice. During the November to March winter series, local speakers might talk on philosophical or political questions. On one cold winter night in the early 1840s, the Davenport Lyceum discussed the proposition, "Is love or revenge the stronger passion?" On another occasion, local lawyer John Morton advertised the debate topic, "Is the female endowed with the intellect equal with the male?" in the classified section of Davenport's new paper, the *Daily Gazette.*

Above Le Claire's Lower Reserve with its embryonic city lay the Iowa prairie. The bluffs above the river offered foliage and protection for all kinds of predators, including wolves, lynx and bears. The wildlife retreated during the 1840s as the pioneers improved and cultivated the rich prairie soil. The settlers' encounters with the other inhabitants of the grassland were not always peaceful. In 1846 John Humphrey killed a 600-pound bear that had strayed from the northern forest; the last recorded killing of a bear in Scott County was during the harvest of September 1849 when John Cooper killed a 400-pound bear in a field near Blue Grass.

In keeping with the urban aspirations of Davenporters, religious controversy was viewed with some concern. In the early 1840s, Mormons in the area settled five miles west of Davenport, near Buffalo. Meanwhile, a local Mormon leader, Mr. Hinkle, claimed the powers of prophecy, healing (he could cure the "itch" at public meetings), and inspiration to perform miracles. While Hinkle lived near Davenport before moving to Pittsburgh in 1845, he created a cult with his followers giving "the holy kiss" to each other and washing each other's feet. Davenporters breathed a sigh of relief when the Buffalo Mormons moved farther away, to Moscow — in rural Muscatine County.

As might be expected, the national movement for liquor control, called temperance, found supporters in Davenport. In 1842 the Davenport Temperance Society was formed. The society sponsored weekly meetings in St. Anthony's church, regular social functions and a "temperance band" to provide musical entertainment. Two other groups, the Scott County Temperance Society and the Washingtonians, publicized the names of those who had "taken the pledge" and stopped drinking.

By the 1840s the growing city of Davenport boasted of Iowa College. The "Iowa Band" of primarily Congregational missionaries to the frontier selected a site in 1846, after local money was pledged and Antoine Le Claire donated land. The trustees met and decided to build a one-story brick building near Western Avenue, between 6th and 7th streets. Still standing, the building measures 35 feet by 50 feet, with a chapel originally on one side and two recitation rooms on the other side. Thirty-three-year-old Reverend Erastus Ripley opened the doors of the college as a preparatory school on November 1, 1848. Within two years it had 34 students and its first college class of six freshmen.

The moving of the College of Physicians and Surgeons of the Upper Mississippi (1848-1850) to Davenport was another indication of growth. In the 1840s medical education used the "preceptor system" of apprenticeship. This meant that medical schools could be moved around quite easily, with a faculty of 10 or less that rented rooms and called itself a college. The Upper Mississippi school had originally begun in Rock Island. The medical school moved to the Forrest Block in Davenport, which contained an amphitheater, lecture rooms, and a sky-lighted room suitable for dissection. Altogether, 36 doctors graduated before the school moved to Keokuk. It eventually became the Medical Department of the University of Iowa.

EVEN BEFORE THE DECADE OF THE 1830S ENDED, A LITERARY SOCIETY HAD RENTED ROOMS ON THE THIRD FLOOR OF WITHER-WAX'S BLOCK. NINETEENTH CENTURY COMMERCIAL AND OFFICE BUILDINGS WERE KNOWN AS "BLOCKS."

In a frontier city, seasonal amusements were important. The circus was the biggest event of the year. In August 1838 the American Arena Company presented its "traveling world of wonders." The price was reasonable: 50 cents for admission to a managerie of horses and wild animals. With tent seating for up to 1,000 spectators, the circus featured Jack May the clown. Eight years later the Raymond and Waring Zoo arrived with unique animals including a "world famous sable elephant."

This, then, was the city developed by Antoine Le Claire. Addison Sanders has left us with a remembered vision of 1845, an urban vista bathed in sunset hues:

> *Strangely and singularly beautiful, the last rays of the setting sun streamed up the river in a golden pathway from an opening in the west range of bluffs, with but a glint of sunshine on the embracing shores, until the sun's rays rested on great cliffs of stone rising from the middle of the river, and on their heights rude log block houses, all now shining like burnished metal. But soon the shadows slowly climbed up the cliffs and then, for a brief time only, the log houses reflected the last rays of sunset.*

Davenport Grows in the Fabulous Fifties

In the 1850s, the city of Davenport gained a second generation of settlers. At times, the American-born residents felt threatened by new settlers, usually Europeans. But the coming of the railroad ended the earlier isolation of the river town and the unchallenged influence of the "first families."

Those families who settled in Davenport before 1846, when the Territory of Iowa became a state, were not landed aristocrats. But as the years went on, 1846 came to divide the old from the new in the collective consciousness of the city's dwellers. By the end of the century, those families who remained in Davenport were honored by being named on a bronze tablet in the third Scott County Courthouse.

The 1850s produced the first historical assessment of the "first families." A city directory in 1853 was an implicit statement that people did not know each other; they needed a list with addresses. Franc B. Wilkie's *Davenport, Past and Present* (1858) reveals a remarkably early self-perception of the achievements of the "first families." Not only are biographies of the elite of Davenport society told in detail; the statistics and chronology of city growth show even that early a realization of how Davenport was changing.

The economic growth of the city was phenomenal. Davenport grew from 1,848 people in 1850 to 11,267 just before the Civil War. To new arrivals at mid-decade, Davenport seemed to be a manufacturing center, similar to Rock Island and Moline. Davenport factory-owners had invested some $2 million in their businesses. A newcomer would notice the nearly 50 new commercial buildings: two iron foundries, two steam boiler plants, two agricultural implement firms, two carriage-making shops, six sawmills, four flour mills, three furniture factories, a plow business, seven wagon shops, a soap factory, a rope factory and 18 brickyards. The expansion of milling operations created new capital which was reinvested in related operations, such as 13 carpenter shops, eight lumber yards, two planing mills and five window factories by the end of the decade.

Nearby, a new settlement appeared. East Davenport was a small village, about one mile east of Brady Street. In 1852 William Hildreth and Dr. Witherwax laid out streets and lots in a broad ravine, on a bend of the river just below the chain of rocks at the foot of the Rock Island Rapids. An eddy in the Mississippi River provided a clear harbor at any river stage. Willard Barrows called it "a safe harbor for rafts where they may lay up in windy weather or when seeking a market at Davenport or Rock Island." Although later annexed to Davenport, this neighborhood retained a community sense of uniqueness into the 20th century.

ANTOINE LE CLAIRE, PIONEER AND KEY PERSONALITY IN THE EARLY DEVELOPMENT OF THE COMMUNITIES THAT WOULD BECOME THE QUAD-CITIES.

A MODERN ARTIST, PHILIPPE OSZUSCIK, RECONSTRUCTED WHAT H.H. SMITH'S OCTAGON HOUSE MUST HAVE LOOKED LIKE IN THE MID-1850S WHEN IT WAS NEW.

One other settlement within the county was Le Claire, a town in Antoine Le Claire's Upper Reserve. Several settlements appeared in the general vicinity of the tract, 15 miles upriver from East Davenport. By the 1850s they had all been merged into one town that prospered from the river trade. At one time, Le Claire was home to more steamboat captains per capita than any other place in America.

The look of Antoine Le Claire's 36-block Davenport changed as city life appeared. O. L. Burdick opened the first photography studio which now made daguerrotype available for the average citizen. The kinds of organizations usually found in Eastern cities cropped up in Davenport: the Young Men's Literary Association rented the third loft of Witherwax's office building (called "blocks" in the 1850s), transforming it into Literary Hall; the Masons, Odd Fellows, Sons of Temperance and Young Men's Christian Association rented rooms; a telegraph office opened; C. Parker founded the Commercial Writing Academy. The capstone to this development was the lighting of the downtown business district in 1857. Originally two Indian trails led out of the downtown: from the corner of 6th and Main along a ridge to the top of the bluffs and another up Le Claire Street along the eastern edge of the bluffs. Northwards from the downtown business district, following the old Indian trails, the first mansions appeared, built by businessmen who had succeeded and wanted to demonstrate their success. Antoine Le Claire built an Italianate house on a large estate north of the railroad bridge (corner of present 8th and Farnam); H. H. Smith built an octagon villa nearby (512 E. 6th); George B. Sargent constructed his mansion on the top of Brady Street Hill (where WOC is located, 805 Brady); farther west, J. M. D. Burrows erected a Greek Revival mansion, "Clifton," valued at $20,000 (1533 Clay Street).

Of these four buildings, the one that is most unusual from an architectural standpoint is the octagon house, which is still standing. Henry H. "Variety" Smith was a leading merchant and member of the city council whose downtown store was a stylish place for a "splendid stock of fancy goods from numerous buying trips to the East." He engaged the architect Willett L. Carroll to design a mansion for him. Carroll came up with a design that followed the basic recommendations of Orson Fowler, a leading phrenologist, who believed the octagon was the closest thing to the perfectly shaped circle and conducive to good health. The entrances conformed to the cardinal points of the compass. A carriage house, stable, grape vines and a picket fence, all now gone, once graced the large estate.

ANTOINE LE CLAIRE'S ITALIANATE STYLE MANSION DATES FROM 1855.

West of the downtown business area emerged a sprawling German neighborhood. The public square called Washington Park marked the beginning of an area which was flat and easily subdivided. Set off by language and customs, this neighborhood was a different development for Davenport.

Davenport contrasted with other cities of similar size in the Midwest partly because of the political beliefs of its German settlers. Other cities also grew in size with an influx of Germans, but after 1846 Davenport gained hundreds of political emigrants from Schleswig-Holstein on the border with Denmark. These Germans had strong political opinions which were transferred from their home German province to the city of Davenport. Most importantly, they controlled the cultural life of other Germans in the city by establishing their own schools and newspaper.

One of the Schleswig-Holsteiner opinions, quite unpopular in Germany, was that there should be no official, governmentally supported church. This anti-clerical attitude in Davenport blossomed into an aggressive type of "free thinking." Instead of parochial schools, a "Freie Deutsche Schule" opened in September 1852 near Washington Square on the corner of Western and Front (now River) streets. This privately operated school lasted for 35 years, indoctrinating the offspring of German families into a political stance of a separate German culture where secular concerns were paramount.

In perpetuating the revolutionary outlook of the 1840s, the school received large bequests. A good example of the Schleswig-Holsteiner attitude appeared in the life of Mathias Frahm. He became a successful brewer in Davenport after the Civil War. As a loyal member of many German organizations, he helped to continue a vigorous, German-speaking cultural life in Davenport. When the lawyers read his will, no one was surprised to learn of his intentions towards the "free school." He left the school $10,000 with the stipulation that his grandsons be educated there in its secular atmosphere. However, should a young Frahm ever become a minister or priest, he would be totally disinherited. This mental outlook was common in German families for generations to come.

According to some, *Der Demokrat* became an influential newspaper throughout eastern Iowa. Known as the "Low German Bible" of Scott County, its initially bipartisan politics influenced the Germans of Davenport. For a decade, Theodore Gulich edited the newspaper. He was also an alderman on the city council, and his political perspective combined with opportunities for real action molded opinion among the paper's German readers. Like other Davenport editors, he took a strong position against slavery, influencing public opinion to support John Brown and the abolitionist viewpoint.

Brown's ill-fated attack on Harper's Ferry in 1859 produced a howl of protest in Davenport. Anti-slavery sympathizers personally knew John Brown, who is said to have stopped off in Davenport to buy food at Burr and Swift's store en route to Kansas. Barclay Coppoc, Brown's assistant, was an Iowan, and abolitionists hid him in a downtown bookstore for several days before his arrest. Gulich's response to the execution of John Brown was a black-rimmed front page. The non-German community in Davenport was upset when leading German businessmen draped their stores with black bunting as if in mourning for John Brown.

As Germans became naturalized citizens, they emerged as a powerful voting bloc. As early as 1852 they were wooed by both the Whig and Democrat political parties. The Democrats were initially successful in staging a large mass meeting at the county courthouse. Handbills in German and English were supplemented by Strasser's Brass Band as a large crowd peaceably assembled. The rally began with Dr. Ernst Claussen speaking in German, followed by Judge Grant speaking in English about the future of railroads. The German vote helped put Democrats in office that year.

A TYPICAL PROGRAM PLAYED BY
TURN-OF-THE-CENTURY BANDS
INCLUDED MARCHES, WALTZES,
POPULAR AND CLASSICAL MUSIC.
THIS PROGRAM WAS PERFORMED
AT THE OPENING OF THE
PAVILION AT CENTRAL PARK,
LATER RENAMED VANDER VEER
PARK.

GRAND

CONCERT

OPENING OF PAVILION
CENTRAL PARK.

Wednesday Evening, Sept. 13, 1899,

GIVEN BY

OTTO'S ENTIRE
MILITARY BAND

PROGRAM.

1. a, March,   "Ocean Wave,"   P. F. Petersen
    b, Overture,   "William Tell,"   Rossini
2. Waltz,   "Beautiful Rhine,"   Keler-Bela
3. Fantasia,   "First Heart Throbs,"   Eilenberg
                As Introduced by Gilmore's Band.
4. Medley,   "Kentucky Airs,"   Boettger
5. Selection,   "El Capitan,"   Srusa
6. Cornet Solo,   "Remembrance of Switzerland,"   Liberati
                MR. P. F. PETERSEN.
7. Mazurka,   "La Czarine,"   Ganne
8. Descriptive,   "Hunting Scene,"   Bucalossi

P. F. PETERSEN,
'Phone 343.   Musical Director.

JACOB STRASSER'S BRASS BAND
WAS A POPULAR GROUP DURING
THE LATE 19TH CENTURY, PLAYING
FOR MANY SPECIAL OCCASIONS–
SUCH AS THIS JULY 4, 1890,
CONCERT AT THE SCHUTZEN PARK
BAND SHELL.

But within three years, antagonism had replaced agreement. An indigenous "Know Nothing" movement appeared in Davenport by 1855 with the goal of keeping politics for native-born citizens; the supporters claimed to "know nothing" about secret meetings or anti-German rallies. Early in 1855 a large rally was held to promote the mayoral and aldermanic candidates who ran on a Temperance label, candidates who had been selected secretly at a lodge meeting weeks before. Being against liquor was a subtle expression of anti-German sentiment. The Temperance candidates, Enos Tichenor for mayor, and three aldermen (out of six wards), won in a closely decided election.

For the remainder of the decade, a struggle between German immigrants and second generation Americans influenced the growth of Davenport. Anti-German sentiment was fuzzy and ill-defined. The continued use of the German language in a separate public lecture series and support for German plays annoyed many Americans. The separate social organizations such as the *Turnverein* with their physical training or the singing societies (*Liedertafel* for women and *Mannerchor* for men), were not so annoying. More controversial were customs such as their traditional "Continental Sunday" of dancing and drinking in beer halls, quite different from American practices.

The contradictory nature of anti-German sentiment can be traced in the Davenport career of George B. Sargent. He arrived in Rockingham at the age of 19, opened a general store, and after bankruptcy married a Blue Grass farmer's daughter in 1844. For a descendant of John Winthrop, Puritan governor of the Massachusetts Bay colony, this was an inauspicious beginning on the Iowa frontier.

He became a land speculator, joining forces with Ebeneezer Cook in 1847 to open the first bank in Davenport. He wrote *Notes on Iowa* (1848) as a promotional treatise, and served as surveyor general of Iowa from 1850 to 1853. The firm of Cook and Sargent platted the town of Walcott in nearby Cedar County and operated a branch bank in Rock Island. With the financial success of a decade behind them, the firm built a "marble bank" building with the first town clock at 2nd and Main, dedicated on September 28, 1857.

By this time, "General" Sargent had followed a common path by running for political office. He was elected on a platform of municipal improvements. In February 1858 he addressed the Boston Board of Trade on the business outlook, privately printed as "Lecture on the 'West'." He was a Whig who ran as an Independent; his administration received daily criticism from the *Davenport Democrat*, a newspaper owned by his competitor, the banker Austin Corbin. The newspaper was crudely partisan in its news stories, repeatedly attacking Sargent, the Republican party, German politicians and other "nigger loving abolitionists" to use one of its favorite phrases.

A different side of Mayor Sargent's nature appeared in his dealings with Iowa College. The school had expanded beyond its earlier prep school status by graduating the Windsor brothers with bachelor's degrees in 1854, and adding three new faculty members for the collegiate division. A new campus of 10 acres replaced the earlier land on the west bluffs after the city council extended Western Avenue through the acreage. Mayor Sargent's mansion was next to the new campus on Brady Street hill, and blended in with the new stone building and boarding house built in 1855 for $22,000. The mayor supported the city council when it voted to extend Main Street up the hill, through the middle of the campus. By the end of the 1858 school year, the trustees had had enough and voted to move to Grinnell, Iowa.

Sargent's treatment of Iowa College was connected to his support of vocational education. He was an honorary trustee of the new Davenport Commercial College in the downtown business district. It opened in 1856 with a full offering of business courses. As an acknowledgement of the large German population, William Riepe was hired as professor of German language. He proved to be a popular teacher who began the first *kindergarten* in the city by the end of the decade.

George Sargent aided the intellectual growth of Davenport in other ways, too. He embodied New England values in his support of the Young Men's Literary Association. Before the 1857 election he contributed $500 for the purchase of books "toward a public library accessible to every respectable resident of the city of Davenport or vicinity, at a charge not exceeding $3 yearly." For three years, the YMLA sponsored a lecture series, which brought famous speakers such as Ralph Waldo Emerson, Horace Mann and Horace Greeley to Davenport. Emerson recorded his impressions of the area by noting that in speaking the night before in Rock Island he was called a "Metaphysician," but in Davenport "the Essayist and Poet."

Sargent and other respectable citizens supported literature by encouraging young writers. They helped the first Iowa poet, Hiram Reid, to publish his poetry. Reid was interested in technology and phrenology, the "science of the head" taught by Orson Fowler. One of his poems, *Harp of the West* (1858), celebrates the opening of the Rock Island, Chicago and Pacific Railroad:

> With mighty snort the dragon loud responds,
> And shakes his heavy volumed mane aloft —
> Impatient fretting all his massive frame,
> In huge deposit of sinews iron-bound,
> And inward energies Herculean!
> He moves with giant pomp, in huge display.
> Of God like power trained to God like rise,
> Quadruple wings, forge-plated round, and ribbed
> For Godlike reaches of redolent flight.

Sargent's downfall and the end of the "Fabulous Fifties" came with the Panic of 1857. Cook and Sargent's bank honored notes issued from their branch bank in Florence, Nebraska, just beyond the Iowa border. There was no national standard for currency, and a bank could issue local currency beyond its gold reserves at any time. The national recession which was called the Panic of 1857 had an effect on Iowa's economy. Cook and Sargent

THE 1879 CHRISTMAS PROGRAM PRESENTED BY DAVENPORT'S GERMAN THEATER WAS PRINTED, AS WERE MANY PROGRAMS AND HANDBILLS, IN GERMAN.

FOR TWO DAYS, THE FIRST NATIONAL BANK OF DAVENPORT WAS THE NATION'S ONLY NATIONAL BANK.

issued too many bank notes, could not redeem them when depositors arrived at their bank, and suspended operations on December 16, 1859. Other businesses which had accepted Florence notes now found themselves without cash, and many went bankrupt. Some, such as Burrows and Prettyman, the wholesale grocery firm, were prominent.

Eventually Le Claire and other "capitalists," as they called themselves, stepped in to make partial repayments. Sargent's own household did not suffer; he retained three servants, but transferred $15,000 in real estate to his wife's name to protect it from creditors. Sargent moved his family to Durant in 1861, the same year that Antoine Le Claire died of a stroke. During the funeral procession for Le Claire, many citizens paused to look back at the accomplishments of the interpreter: from a few houses in 1836, the city of almost 12,000 now had a business district, beautiful mansions on the bluffs, and a growing German neighborhood on the west side.

The Victorian City Matures

In the 1860s, a new generation of Davenporters watched the outlines of a modern industrial city emerge beyond the original downtown area. This was largely the filling-in of residential areas on the bluffs and the west as the population almost doubled to 23,830 by 1885. It also meant the development of municipal services: paid firemen and policemen, street cars, sewers and water works.

In developing an industrial city, Davenport businessmen needed safe and reliable banks. George H. French became mayor in 1861, determined to create a sound financial structure for the city. After one term in city hall, French joined with others in opening the new First National Bank at the corner of 2nd and Main streets. On June 29, 1863, Henry Hess wrote a check for $12.60. It was the first to clear the new system of banking. For two days this bank was the only "national bank" in the country. As a national bank, it used a nationally uniform currency. Being national also facilitated the selling of war bonds.

Two blocks north and two blocks east of the bank was the Kimball House, which had replaced the Le Claire House as the finest hotel in the region. It was the focus of cultural life for the city, with national entertainment nightly in the adjacent Burtis Opera House. Plays, musicals and popular lectures were presented. For example, in 1869 Mark Twain lectured to a sold-out house on "The American Vandal Abroad," a humorous account of his travels in Italy. Serious topics were also presented at the Burtis. Susan B. Anthony lectured in March 1874 on the topic of women's right to vote. She argued that women should stop giving their wages to their husbands, be able to vote and "persist in the idea to become independent, rich like men. Then you can marry if you desire, and of your own free will."

Two blocks north and one block west of the hotel, the Academy of Science organized amateur scientists' efforts in a building on Brady Street hill. As tangible proof of science's importance, the museum provided educational programs and sponsored community involvement. An early example was the publishing in August 1869 of academy photographs of a solar eclipse, taken with the most advanced camera then available.

One block east and one block south of the academy was the new high school building. Only the children of the wealthy graduated from Davenport High School. In 1871 there were nine graduates in a total enrollment of 102 students. Students entered the high school only after passing an oral examination, personally conducted by the superintendent of schools. The Davenport Board of Education hired teachers, decided upon course offerings and defended the result — an educated elite. Public education remained a selective process of learning with a high school diploma the capstone of education.

ST. KATHARINE'S SCHOOL FOR GIRLS WAS OPERATED BY THE EPISCOPAL CHURCH.

The Board of Education under the direction of George French, longtime member, proved innovative in respecting the ability of women. In 1874 Miss Phoebe Sudlow became the first woman superintendent of schools in the brand new high school building. Offered the position at a salary less than most male superintendents in the state, she replied, "If you feel I am not the best person to qualify for the position, it is all right. But, if it is because I am a woman, I will not accept your offer." The school board agreed, raised their salary offering, and Miss Sudlow accepted.

Privately financed buildings also appeared through the generosity of Davenport benefactors. Before her death in 1879, Clarrisa Cook donated more than $200,000 to her favorite charities. As a loyal communicant of Trinity Episcopal Church, she advanced the bishop's plans to build a magnificent cathedral on Brady Street hill next to the college campus. Edward Potter, a New York architect, designed the Gothic Revival church as a memorial to her husband, Ebeneezer Cook. Her support of the Davenport Library Association helped build the Cook Memorial Library five blocks south on Brady Street hill in 1877. A major endowment expanded the services of a municipal home for the friendless and poor in the west end of Davenport.

Daniel and Patience Newcomb built two mansions on Brady Street hill after moving into the city in the 1850s. By 1866 a fine brick mansion (250,000 bricks were used) was built on the hill. Newcomb had been a farmer whose 1,200 acres in the county produced an unheard of 30,000 bushels of corn in 1842. After his death in 1870, Patience funded the Newcomb Presbyterian Memorial Chapel and donated the land for the Davenport Academy of Science, both buildings arising on Brady Street hill.

*IN MID-19TH CENTURY, COM-
MERECE WAS BRISK ALONG
DAVENPORT'S 2ND STREET
BETWEEN SCOTT AND RIPLEY
STREETS. BUSINESSES INCLUDED
BERWALD BOOKS AND STATIO-
NERY, THE PASSAGE AGENCY AND
PETER KLINDT'S GROCERY STORE.*

Nearby on top of the hill was Griswold College. In 1859 the Episcopalian Church purchased the former campus of Iowa College and began a new church-related institution of higher education. Bishop Perry kept adding to the college's library until a collection of 8,000 volumes made it the largest in the area. Community relations were good, with a Friday night lecture series, called the Griswold Athaneum, open to the public. The decision to reduce operations in the early 1880s, and offer only college preparatory courses, reflected years of low enrollment, although several hundred students had graduated with baccalaureates by 1885.

Instead of the earlier clash between Germans and Americans, the Civil War brought them together as their sons died on the same battlefields. This atmosphere of acceptance remained even though thousands of new German families moved to Davenport, increasing the number of singing societies, social clubs and fraternal organizations. They also began a *Schutzen Verein* (shooting club) which built a 20-acre park for Sunday family outings far away in the west end of the city. When it opened in 1870, the park realized the Victorian dream of romance with caves, ravines, dells, curving drives and cozy walks. Seven permanent buildings retained the amenities in the dream-like environment: dining hall, coffee house, lunch, shooting gallery, refreshment stand, music stand and awards hall.

At the same time, Davenporters supported public lectures, organizations and institutions separate from the German-speaking sector. The cultural assumptions behind this activity bordered on smugness in the middle of the Victorian period. The leaders of society applauded the notion of "progress" and pointed to the buildings on Brady Street hill. They stressed the tremendous strides made in education and pointed with pride to the regional settlers from New England.

The French family was an example of the "New England connection" with Davenport. George French migrated from Andover, Massachusetts, in 1855, and became an active citizen. He served as mayor, banker, trustee for the small Unitarian society and school board member. Before his death in 1888, he enjoyed the reflected fame from his daughter. Alice French (1850-1934) became the first Iowa author with a national reputation. Her first short story, "What Rang the Bell," appeared in 1871 in the Davenport *Gazette*. By the 1880s her short stories appeared in national magazines such as *Atlantic* and *Harper's* under her pen name of Octave Thanet.

In a series of short stories taking place in a "Western town," Thanet developed a fictional portrayal of Davenport (called Fairport in the stories). She followed the literary conventions of her day by blending realistic details and romantic ideals. She captured the surface details of speech by reproducing the language of German immigrants and the dialect of working class people in her fiction.

The industrial city that became the typical way of life for many Americans by the 1880s became one topic for Miss French to explore in a non-fiction work. Strikes were a new phenomenon. The most famous strike in this period took place in Davenport in November 1882. For several weeks, Local 172 of the Tobacco Workers struck Nicholaus Kuhnen's factory. More than 200 workers, primarily young German women, walked off the job. The work was tedious: rolling tobacco leaves into cigars for local consumption. Although known for high wages, Kuhnen had recently reduced wages from $2 to $1.50 for every thousand cigars rolled.

One part of Fairport not covered extensively was the under-class of day laborers living along the river front. Miss French stressed the charm of the river instead of the grinding reality of the river front dwellers. In squalid tenement houses and tar paper shacks lived casual laborers, transients, roustabouts and stevedores. It was here that most of the recorded crime was found, in pool halls where gambling, fights and shootings happened often. The city newspapers covered this "low life" with news accounts of arrested prostitutes (sometimes in the company of Moline aldermen), barroom fights and robberies. But aside from the sensational, the German leadership and the New England inspired elite, including the descendants of First Families, ignored this sub-culture along the river.

There was always the potential for violence in this transient world. For example, on July 29, 1869, the two-year-old steamboat *Dubuque* had on board a large group of raftsmen, four crews (120 men), returning to the pine forests of Wisconsin. The few deck passengers from St. Louis tried to steer clear of the drunken raftsmen. At Davenport, the raftsmen, who had been drinking whiskey, began attacking the black crew members. Eventually six were beaten to death or drowned as the boat headed upriver. "Pock-Marked" Lynch was the leader of the white mob, issuing orders and depositing freight at various points along the river's edge. Lynch was known as a card shark whose skill at Faro made him a "wanted" man. He escaped by slipping onto shore at Camanche, Iowa, before the steamboat landed at Clinton, Iowa, where the drunken raftsmen were met by a posse of deputies and a crowd of 5,000.

Alice French and her friends were horrified by the publicity, much preferring the refined atmosphere of boat races on the river. Municipal clubs appeared after the Civil War to provide training in nautical techniques. The Mississippi Valley Rowing Association was modeled after older clubs which were popular along the East Coast. Annual regattas drew entries from clubs from Clinton, Davenport, Muscatine and Burlington.

The river itself drew attention. In a negative sense, newspapers told of the recurring flooding. For example, on the cold winter night of February 12, 1869, massive ice chunks jammed the river, sinking two steamboats and flooding the first floor guests out of the St. James Hotel. In a more positive vein, the river attracted scientific attention in June 1880 when an Eastern newspaper began including Davenport in a chart listing the rise and fall of the Mississippi. On a lighter side, the river provided entertainment, as children rode velocipedes along the bank and saloon customers engaged in water fights.

Davenporters enjoyed their river and assumed that steamboat navigation would continue as the major form of transportation. But slowly a network of railroad lines appeared to compete with steamboats. In 1870 the Milwaukee and in 1879 the Burlington linked Davenport to the surrounding farms of eastern Iowa and western Illinois.

ALICE FRENCH, WHO WROTE UNDER THE PEN NAME "OCTAVE THANET."

THE RIOT ABOARD THE DUBUQUE WAS SENSATIONALIZED BY ILLUSTRATIONS IN MAGAZINES OF THE DAY.

ORIGINALLY DONE IN FULL COLOR, THIS 1891 POSTER ATTRACTED PEOPLE FROM 100 MILES AWAY TO THE GALA MISSISSIPPI RIVER CARNIVAL. ALTHOUGH THEY WERE NOT AS GRAND AS DEPICTED ON THE POSTER, COSTUMED CHARACTERS PORTRAYING "NEPTUNE AND VULCAN" ACTUALLY WERE PART OF THE EVENT.

THE DAVENPORT PUBLIC LIBRARY, BUILT IN 1904, USING SOME FUNDS FROM INDUSTRIALIST ANDREW CARNEGIE.

As Davenport matured during this period, 1860-1885, it followed the lead of much of the rest of America in imitating British culture during Queen Victoria's reign. Victorian style in Davenport flourished. Architects revived older house styles and wedded them to a new technology of iron and jigsaw. Many of those magnificent homes are still standing, mute reminders of Davenport's growth and developing industrial-based economy.

The Century Turns

An 1890s scene at the corner of Brady and 3rd Streets captures the flavor of a city different from others in the area. In that scene one sees representative types: the merchant, the professional, the loafer and the immigrant.

Many merchants passed by this corner six days a week. The biggest shopping day was Saturday, when all stores were at a merchandising peak. Davenport had become the commerical hub of the metropolitan area, its influence reaching far out into the rural countryside. Some merchants were most influential locally, mixing easily with the saloon-keepers and wholesalers. Others, such as the Hickey Brothers, attained national prominence. Their cigar stores stretched beyond the region by the 1920s with the slogan, "From Havana to St. Paul."

The central business district became physically defined in this period by the elevated railroad tracks that provided a visual cue as to the "downtown." Impressive buildings began to rise, such as the Richardsonian Romanesque Petersen's Department Store (1892).

Others found walking by the corner were the professionals: ministers, physicians, lawyers and school teachers. Dr. William Grant had his office at 223 Brady, and was one of many medical men in the business district. He moved to Davenport in 1871 and for almost 20 years was a medical innovator. His war record was forgiven (he had served for 16 months as a sergeant in the Confederate army) because of his technical brilliance. He was the first doctor in the city to perform an appendectomy.

The loafer could also be found downtown, chewing tobacco on his way to Bucktown, the center of nefarious and outright illegal activities. Three blocks east of Brady Street, Buckton was the site of Davenport's more than 150 illegal saloons. It was also the place for gambling, prostitution and criminal hangouts. The entrance way to the district was Brick Munro's dance hall. Other places to while away the day were the Senate Saloon, the Casino, East 3rd St. Bowling Alleys, Wiggles Theater, Pillon's Place and the Hotel Downs Saloon.

Finally, snatches of *platdeutsch*, or Low German, could be heard on the street corners downtown. In retaining this oral tradition the German-American community kept its identity. Most of the second and third generation families lived in the west end of the city, but maintained their connection to the central business district with the nearby Central Turner Hall and Turner Grand Opera House. In the fluid society of the late 19th century, leaders of the German community were accepted by the "first family" descendants who owned most of the choice land, influenced the spending of money and controlled access to political influence outside of the city.

The career of Charles August Ficke (1850-1932) is a success story of a German immigrant assimilated by American society. Born in Mecklenberg, Germany, he grew up on a farm about 20 miles from Davenport. As a teenager he dreamed of American success. He enrolled in Griswold College but his father felt he needed a practical education. He began as a clerk in a Davenport dry goods store, eventually becoming a teller in a bank. In 1876 he went to law school, returning to practice law. A leader of German voters, Ficke was elected mayor in 1890. Six years later he was chosen as an original member of the Contemporary Club, a select group of 33 gentlemen interested in preserving the essay as an art form.

The reorganization of the public library in 1905 reflects the acceptance of German immigrants by the New England elite. The only nativist trustee was Charles M. Waterman, attorney and member of the Contemporary Club. Heading the list of five German-American trustees were the Unitarian minister, Arthur M. Judy, and Frances Ficke, wife of C. A. Ficke. Dr. Alfons Hageboeck, medical doctor, was a member of the Contemporary Club and an 1881 graduate of Davenport High School. Two German businessmen were also selected, George Wolters, saloon owner, and Robert Schmidt, carpet shop owner. Edward Kaufmann was assistant cashier of the German Savings Bank. The remaining members represented the large number of Catholics in Davenport: Emma J. Richardson, principal of the diocesan school for girls, and the Reverend James P. Ryan, priest for St. Mary's parish. These trustees decided policy for the new library, built with the generous aid of Andrew Carnegie, a personal friend of Alice French. Higher education remained a matter of concern. Griswold College changed direction by reemphasizing its college preparatory department for Episcopalians. St. Katharine's school for girls opened in a beautiful mansion a mile east of the campus, while Kemper Hall for boys was built nearby. After 10 years, the boys' preparatory school and the collegiate department closed. The 8,000 library books were eventually transferred to the Davenport Free Library; Sheldon Hall reverted to private use. Another collegiate institution began in this period. In the early 1890s, D. D. Palmer, who practiced animal magnetism, rented the ninth floor of the Ryan Building at the corner of 2nd and Brady streets. On September 10, 1895, Palmer discovered chiropractic ("done by hand") as a healing technique, while working with a black janitor who could not hear. Within three years, his son, B. J. Palmer, had convinced his father that a school was needed for this new healing technique. The Palmer School of Chiropractic evolved during the first decade of the 20th century; B. J. Palmer purchased the mansions of J. C. Duncan, W. D. Petersen and Thomas Barron on the crest of Brady Street hill. Eventually a campus emerged with the addition of 360 feet of land one block south of the Trinity Cathedral area and the former Griswold College. B. J. Palmer was a great publicist and adorned the college buildings with sayings. This epigram above the entrance greeted students and Davenporters who came each day to eat in the cafeteria: "To eat is human — to digest divine."

THE BURTIS OPERA HOUSE, JUST NORTH OF 4TH STREET ON PERRY, WAS THE CENTER OF DAVENPORT CULTURE IN THE LATE 19TH AND EARLY 20TH CENTURY. NEXT DOOR WAS THE KIMBALL HOUSE HOTEL, WHERE RONALD REAGAN LIVED WHEN HE WORKED AS AN ANNOUNCER AT WOC RADIO. A 1920 FIRE DESTROYED THE BURTIS.

KIMBALL HOUSE
DAVENPORT, IOWA.
HOWARD BURTIS, Proprietor.

This Hotel is unquestionably the largest and best in Iowa. It is strictly first-class in all respects. Rates $2.50 and $3.00 per day. Theatrical and large parties liberally dealt with.

BURTIS OPERA HOUSE
Is connected with the KIMBALL. It has been refurnished, provided with new scenery, and thoroughly renovated during the last year.

The Catholic Diocese of Davenport was also interested in education. The Immaculate Conception Academy for girls had existed for 20 years before a Gothic Revival building was erected on Main, across the alley from the mansions which the Palmers would eventually buy. The Diocese also developed St. Ambrose Seminary, one mile northwest of the Academy, in the 1880s. Within a decade, a college preparatory department appeared in response to parish support for the idea. In 1908 a collegiate department began for boys who wanted higher education but did not aspire to the priesthood. A 1909 advertisement stated that the college offered "special inducements to boys and young men seeking a thorough mental and moral training."

The turn of the century also marked a blossoming of local writing. Four young Davenport writers enjoyed success as their short stories, poems and articles appeared in national magazines. They were influenced by the cosmopolitan nature of Davenport, which formed the background for much of their writing.

George Cram Cook was graduated from Kemper Hall in 1889, going on to study at the University of Iowa and Heidelberg. He was a dreamer and dilettante whose only novel, *The Chasm* (1911), showed his unfulfilled ambitions in writing. He moved to Chicago and eventually married Susan Glaspell, also from Davenport. Together they established the Provincetown Players in 1915. They discovered Eugene O'Neill and other promising new playwrights before moving to Greece.

Glaspell was Davenport's only Pulitzer prize-winning author. After graduating from Davenport High School in 1893, she worked as a reporter for two years before going to Drake University in Des Moines. In 1903, her first short story about a mythical city much like Davenport was published. Her later plays received wide acclaim; "The Inheritors" was hailed as her best work.

Floyd Dell dropped out of high school before graduating. He was a former *Davenport Times* reporter, who moved to Chicago in 1908 to become literary editor of the *Chicago Journal*. From 1912 to the end of the "Roaring '20s," Dell was a leader of the Greenwich Bohemians of New York. He was a close friend of the Socialist party martyr John Reed and the popular poet Edna St. Vincent Millay. His finest novel, *Mooncalf* (1920), takes place in Davenport in that period of time.

Harry Hansen graduated from high school in 1904 and immediately went to work for the *Davenport Times*. In 1909 he moved to Chicago, graduating from the University of Chicago and serving as a war-time correspondent for the *Chicago Daily News*. From 1926 to 1947 he was literary editor of the *New York World*. His only novel, *Your Life Lies Before You* (1935), was a nostalgic look at Davenport.

Meanwhile, Bix Beiderbecke was learning to play the coronet in a way that was to change American music, as he listened to ragtime music being played on excursion steamboats. In this way he learned the syncopated rhythms that became known as "jamming." In the 1920s he merged the syncopation of black musicians with his own version of lyrical inspiration from classical composers such as Claude Debussy. He became known in Chicago and eventually New York night clubs for his melancholy music.

BIX BIEDERBECKE PLAYED WITH THE WOLVERINE ORCHESTRA OF CHICAGO BEFORE MOVING ON TO OTHER JAZZ "GIGS."

Davenport's cosmopolitan population had more than doubled in size from 24,000 people in 1885 to 56,727 in 1920. The reason was increased employment possibilities. The formation of companies such as French & Hecht, and new firms such as the Voss Washing Machine Company increased the work force. The U. S. Census showed that, by 1910, Davenport had become the second richest city in America on the basis of per capita wealth.

It was about to become even richer. William Voss, a skilled wood carver, helped stimulate the city's economy. While at home recuperating from an injury, Bill Voss realized how hard it was for his mother to do the weekly wash. Using his inventive mind, he built a crude washing machine that cut the laundry time in half. Soon all his neighbors bought the hand-crafted washers and told their friends. After he formed a partnership with his brother, Voss sold washing machines nation-wide, primarily to farm women who did not have access to laundry service. The most popular model sold for the amazingly low price of $10. By 1912, Voss Brothers had become one of the five national companies which together did 60 percent of the business in washing machines.

Davenport expanded in this period, annexing the Village of East Davenport into its boundaries. Between the downtown and the village, a shantytown had grown up around the Weyerhaeuser Mill, the Lindsay & Phelps Mill, the Roberts wood yard and the Standard Oil storage tanks. The square mile of shingles, kindling, sawdust and 60-foot-high piles of lumber was a hangout for young boys. The sickening smell of drying timber and the scurrying of rats did not stop the gangs of boys from playing King of the Mountain, pretending to be lumber jacks, or jumping into rafts at the river's edge.

On July 24, 1901, Arsenal workers saw smoke as they trudged home in the 100 degree heat. Somehow a pile of kindling at the Rock Island Fuel Company had caught on fire. The fire spread quickly, threatening the downtown business district. The oil tanks seemed to be next. Davenport firemen and spectators were amazed as the path of fire miraculously stopped on Tremont Avenue hill, just below the bluff on which St. Katharine's Episcopalian School for Girls stood. Older residents remembered that, according to a local story, Reverend Charles Van Quickenborne in 1835 had blessed the hill for deliverance from natural disasters. The next day reporters tallied the damage: 20 acres of land smoldered, 250 people were homeless, businessmen suffered $1.25 million in losses. It took many years to replace the shanties with houses and factories.

IN THE 1890S, THE LINDSAY & PHELPS MILL OPERATED ONE OF THE LARGEST LUMBER YARDS IN DAVENPORT. THE 1901 FIRE THAT DESTROYED LINDSAY & PHELPS, ALONG WITH A LARGE AREA OF SOUTHEAST DAVENPORT, PRODUCED SUCH INTENSE HEAT THAT IT WARPED RAILS AND BUCKLED PAVEMENTS.

AFTER IOWA "WENT DRY" IN 1884, PHARMACISTS DISPENSED ALL ALCOHOL – "ONLY FOR THE ACTUAL NECESSITIES OF MEDICINE," AS THIS 1887 RECEIPT STIPULATED.

Davenport, Iowa, 24 Oct 188

To J. H. HARRISON, Registered Pharmacist, No. 469:

I am not a minor, am not in the habit of becoming intoxicated, and hereby apply for

AMOUNT   KIND OF LIQUOR.

1 pint Whisky

Which is to be used "only for the actual necessities of medicine."

Emma Adelia Rice
Purchaser.

Dispensed by *J H Hampton* Reg. Ph. No. 469

The civic strength of character needed to rebuild after disaster manifested itself in a political way in the response to the liquor question. In 1884 a new law made Iowa "crackerbarrel dry" on paper. An old river town stubbornness surfaced as the charter city of Davenport refused to comply. The mayor informed the governor that the administration of his city was autonomous in law enforcement, and as one wit put it, "the free and independent State of Scott County would brook no undue influence from anywhere outside its borders." Immediately the popular saloons began selling newly named intoxicating beverages such as Mum, Seafoam, Hop, Nectar and Kentucky Blue Grass.

For a generation, Davenport stood alone in the state with liquor flowing freely. In February 1918 the U. S. government issued the following order through the Secretary of the Army: "All saloons and bawdy houses within a half-mile of the Rock Island Arsenal must close within 36 hours." The order was intended to protect soldiers stationed on the military tract, who were found intoxicated while on duty. The order shut down 48 bars and 27 wholesalers in "Bucktown" on the riverfront.

The decline of Davenport's cultural mix accelerated during World War I.
As many Davenporters adopted the hyper-patriotic fervor of 1917, German-
Americans faced a dilemma. How could they remain loyal Americans while
being emotionally involved in the deaths of German relatives? One way was
to support American freedom of speech. Six prominent German businessmen
supported the public appearance of Daniel Wallace, a famous pacifist. In
July, Wallace appeared on the stage of the Turner Grand Opera House,
urging peaceful draft resistance. Soon he and the six businessmen were
indicted for treason. The "Davenport Seven" were convicted and their
businesses ruined, all because they exercised their constitutional right of
free speech.

Patriotic Davenporters were more interested in the news surrounding
Marion Crandall, the first American woman killed in active service, on
March 27, 1918. Born in Cedar Rapids, Miss Crandall had taught French at
St. Katharine's before enlisting through the YMCA only two months before.
A German bomb exploded in the village of St. Menehould, killing her as she
left the French soldiers' canteen. Three years later, trees were planted on
the grounds of the Statehouse in Des Moines to commemorate her and nine
other Iowa women killed in World War I.

Another part of the city's cosmopolitan nature was the existence of a
municipal Socialist party. By 1916, the Socialists began to win more seats on
the City Council. In 1920, a plurality of voters rejected a coalition of
Republicans-Democrats as a fusion political party. They chose a Socialist
mayor, five aldermen and a young police magistrate — Harold Metcalf. He
defined the Socialist party goal as wanting to "encourage and cultivate and
help develop the communal spirit of tolerance, brotherliness, without which
no form of socialism could ever succeed." But cooperation became
impossible for the party and they lost control of the City Council in 1922.

*GERMAN VETERANS OF THE
SCHLESWIG-HOLSTEIN STRUGGLE
FOR INDEPENDENCE IN 1848-50
GATHERED NEARLY HALF A
CENTURY LATER AT A MONUMENT
TO THEIR BRAVERY.*

On a sunny morning in 1907, a tremendous crowd gathered in Washington
Square Park to enjoy a large parade and dedicate a monument to German
soldiers who had died in fighting the Franco-Prussian War of 1871. On this
Sunday morning, the blend of German tradition and American dreams of
the good life worked. Many German and American organizations marched
together with representatives from Moline, Rock Island, Eldridge, Peoria,
Clinton and Durant. The gathering had speeches in both German and
English glorifying the American "open door" immigration policy. A former
mayor, Henry Vollmer, said in German, "This memorial stone shall teach
our children that we can be good American citizens without being ashamed
of the race from whence we have descended and its many thousand years of
glorious history." German descendants occupied high office, sat on powerful
boards of trustees, and participated in the cultural activities of the city.

BY BESS PIERCE

After the United States government survey of 1829, Joel Wells Sr., his sons, Levi and Huntington, and his son-in-law, Michael Bartlett, acquired land along the banks of the Mississippi in what later would become Moline. Almost simultaneously, the question of slavery arose. A squatter named Stevens took land near today's 48th Street along the riverfront and, according to early accounts "built two commodious log houses in which he kept 75 Negro slaves."

The statutes on slavery were muddied by a number of conflicting laws. But the issue was resolved, at least in the Walker's Station area of Moline, in October of 1829, when Joseph Danforth walked to the nearest justice of the peace in Galena, Illinois, and obtained a warrant for Stevens' arrest for holding slaves. George Goble, who lived in what would become Rock Island, warned Stevens, who immediately took his slaves and returned to the South.

In 1831 Farnhamsburg (near 30th Street and 4th Avenue, Rock Island) was the first recognized local settlement on the Illinois shore of the Mississippi. It soon was followed by a number of small unincorporated communities, among them Stephenson (Rock Island) and Rock Island Mills (Moline). After the official founding of Rock Island County, July 5, 1833, voters elected early Moline residents John W. Spencer as a county commissioner, Levi Wells as coroner, J. B. Patterson and Joel Wells Jr. as justices of the peace and Huntington Wells as one of the constables.

Very early the moral, conservative, religious bent of the emerging community took shape. In January 1834, the first religious services were held in the log cabin of Joel Wells. Only nine months later these Methodists organized a church under Reverend Thomas McMurty and a year later opened the first school. During this same period Sunday School classes were held regularly in a log home in what would become South Moline on the Rock River flats.

IN THE LATE 1840S JOHN DEERE MOVED TO MOLINE TO ESTABLISH HIS NEW "PLOUGH" FACTORY AND WHAT WAS TO BECOME THE WORLD-WIDE EMPIRE OF DEERE & COMPANY.

*MANY EARLY VIEWS OF MOLINE
EXIST, BUT ALL VARY SLIGHTLY IN
THE NUMBER AND PLACING OF
BUILDINGS ALONG THE RIVER-
FRONT AND ACROSS THE DAM.
THIS ARTIST'S CONCEPTION DONE
IN THE EARLY 1840S SHOWS THESE
BUILDINGS, FROM LEFT ACROSS
THE DAM AND DOWN THE RIVER-
FRONT: HARTZELL AND RUGGLES
MILL AT THE ISLAND END OF THE
DAM; CHAMBERLAIN AND DEAN
MILL MIDWAY ACROSS THE DAM;
FIRST SEARS MILL AT THE
ILLINOIS END OF THE DAM;
SECOND SEARS MILL NEXT ALONG
THE RIVERFRONT; THEN SEARS
AND FERGUS MACHINE SHOP AND
FOUNDRY. AFTER THIS VIEW WAS
DONE, THE PALMER CABINET SHOP
WAS BUILT BELOW SEARS AND
FERGUS, AND JUST BELOW THAT
JOHN DEERE BUILT HIS FIRST
FACTORY. THE LEFTMOST
BUILDING ON THE SHORE BEHIND
THE DAM IS THE JOEL WELLS
RESIDENCE. THE MOLINE HOUSE IS
THE LARGEST BUILDING IN THE
BACKGROUND, AND THE HUNTING-
TON WELLS HOUSE IS BARELY
VISIBLE AMONG THE TREES. THIS
PICTURE SHOWS THE VITAL
INFLUENCE EARLY WATER POWER
HAD ON THE DEVELOPMENT OF
MOLINE. THIS NARROW BACK-
WATER CHANNEL OF THE
MISSISSIPPI DICTATED THE
LOCATION OF THE TOWN, JUST AS
THE EARLY NEW ENGLAND
LEADERS LATER DICTATED THE
MORAL TONE OF THE COMMUNITY.*

In 1836, when David B. Sears, his family and household possessions arrived on a steamboat from Cairo, Illinois, there were three houses in Rock Island Mills. For $1,600 Sears bought a house and strip of land opposite the island of Rock Island beginning at what is today the Moline-Rock Island border and extending along the Mississippi to 15th Street. Decades later David B. Sears Jr., the first white child born in Moline, described in detail the second house his father built in 1837:

> *"This new house faced the river and was on the main stage road to Stephenson. It was of hewn logs, 20 feet by 30 feet and a story and a half high with a lean-to on the south. There were two rooms downstairs. The east one had an enormous fireplace. This house held the Sears family of nine, two hired men, and sometimes three or four transient families overnight, where they cooked their own provisions before the fireplace and slept on the floor."*

Although many area residents believe that John Deere founded the city, it was in reality David B. Sears and his vision of waterpower that brought about the city of Moline. All accounts give Sears credit for the original idea of building a brush and stone dam from the Illinois shore to the island of Rock Island. Some historians place the dam construction as late as 1841-42, but most place the beginning of the construction in 1836-37 before the state charter was granted. However, it is a matter of record that Sears' first mill was in operation on the Mississippi by 1838. This first mill was just a bit below where 15th Street would join the Mississippi River, and was a partnership undertaken by David B. Sears, Spencer H. White, and John W. Spencer. With the help of 40 volunteers they first built the 600-foot brush and stone dam across the narrow channel separating the Illinois shore from the island of Rock Island and then erected the mill. The main structure of this first water powered mill on the Mississippi had two floors and a north side lean-to. The power came from the water forced down the Moline side of the river by a millrace running east and west beside the mill. This mill sawed wood, ground wheat and corn and carded wool. White and burr oak were ripped for boat planks there.

Sears' big mill was built in 1846 and had a capacity of more than 20 bushels of wheat an hour and more than 30 bushels of coarse ground corn. At rush times the mill ran 24 hours a day. In A. C. Fulton's book, *Life's Voyage*, the early Sears mill was referred to as "Sears' little grist mill in the loft of his sawmill," but according to his son, that little mill provided the breadstuff for the populations of Scott and Rock Island Counties during the early years. Wood sawed by the Sears mills was used in the original Rock Island County Court House, and in the timbers of the first bridge to span the Mississippi.

The first Sears' mill stood at the southern end of the brush dam on the Illinois shore. Two other mills were on the dam and one eventually on the island of Rock Island at the north end of the dam. Controversy exists over whether this mill or the Sears mill built later on Rock Island was the one known as the "old red mill," a popular subject for early picture post cards and the mill referred to in the Laflin memoirs:

"There was a medical school in Rock Island and the students used to steal lots of bodies for dissection. One time they robbed a Negro's grave and took the body to the old mill, and some boys stole the body from the old mill and hid it in the old shoemaker's cave (This was the smaller of the two caves on the western point of the island, near the larger cave of Black Hawk's Great White Spirit. This cave was used both as a shop and residence by the shoemaker, and was filled in when the first pier for the railroad bridge was built). That old mill was a good place to hide bodies until it was safe to take them to the school."

The mill just north of the Sears mill belonged to Chamberlain and Dean, and had been built by Charles Atkinson in the mid-1840s. It was capable of sawing 4,000-5,000 board feet of pine logs and local timber in a 12-hour day. The log rafts for this mill were tied up at the Moline House, the city's first hotel. Next to that mill was the Spencer H. White Mill which had a sash saw, a lathe saw and a rotary saw.

Abraham Hartzel and a Mr. Ruggles owned the mill at the island end of the dam. Their power came from White's wheel. They manufactured buckets, household utensils and other small woodenware. Below the Sears mill on the Illinois shore Sears built his second mill. In the mid-1840s it was the largest north of St. Louis. Below the big mill was the Sears and Fergus Machine Shop, then a small factory run by a man named Palmer, who was a cabinet maker. When Deere moved to Moline, Sears is said to have offered him five years free power. Deere built his first shop just below the Palmer shop with a power shaft running from the Palmer shop to the new Deere shop.

The original village was platted by P. H. Ogilvie under the direction of David B. Sears, Spencer White, Joel and Huntington Wells, Charles Atkinson and Nathan Bass. The surveyor wrote Hesperia on one plat and Moline on the other. Asked the meaning of the names, he said the first meant "Star of the West," and the second was an adaptation of the French word for "milltown." Charles Atkinson is then supposed to have said, "Moline, let it be called."

This plat was acknowledged on June 6, 1843, before Justice of the Peace Nathanial Belcher and approved the same day by the County Commissioners. The records were destroyed by fire, however, and Moline was not legally incorporated until the spring of 1848.

THE "OLD RED MILL," AS THIS BECAME KNOWN, EXISTED LONG AFTER ITS USEFULNESS AND AFTER ALL PRIVATE INDUSTRY HAD BEEN MOVED OFF ROCK ISLAND. SEARS BUILT THIS MILL ON HIS SECOND DAM ON THE NORTH SIDE OF ROCK ISLAND AND BENHAM'S ISLAND. THIS IS UNDOUBTEDLY THE MILL REFERRED TO IN THE LAFLIN MEMOIRS AND ONE OF THE HIDING PLACES FOR BODIES STOLEN FOR USE BY THE STUDENTS OF THE MEDICAL SCHOOL IN ROCK ISLAND.

Moline sat on the sweep of the vast unconquered prairies of the Midwest. In the early 1830s prairie plows were huge chunked wooden things with wrought iron straps and sometimes metal points. According to the "Prairie Farmer" of the day, they were "little better than the 'hooked sticks' of the Egyptians." The prairie grass was thick, the alluvial soil almost impossible to break. Teams of eight to 18 oxen inched through only 1½-2 acres of the thick grasses and virgin soil in a day. The prairie lay waiting for the steel plow.

It was in 1836 at about the same time that Sears, Spencer and White began planning their brush dam across the Mississippi slough that John Deere left his native Vermont, traveling by canal, the Great Lakes and rutted roads to Grand de Tour, Illinois (later renamed Grand Detour). He left his wife, Damarius Lamb Deere, and children behind, but carried his blacksmith tools with him. His son, Charles, who became the moving force of Deere & Company after the death of John Deere, was born after his father left for Illinois.

In 1797 Charles Newbold of Burlington, New Jersey, had made a cast-iron plow share which was improved in 1819 by Jethrow Wood of New York who cast the plow in sections so worn-out parts could be replaced easily. For the lighter eastern soils these points worked well, but they would not scour in the thick prairie soil. Deere thought the answer was to make the moldboard of the plow of steel. There was no immediate source of steel in Grand de Tour and the first Deere moldboard was shaped over a log using a worn-out steel saw blade. Legend has it that the blade came from the Sears sawmill. However, since Sears was not in operation until 1838, it was unlikely that Sears and Deere could have possibly made contact during that year. Later, though, Deere did use blades from the Sears mills for his moldboards.

Not only did the steel plow stay clean, it polished brighter and became easier to pull with use. Deere's plow brought an end to the plowman's cleaning paddle and promised a new beginning for agriculture and the Midwest. In that first year John Deere made two or three plows at Grand de Tour and 10 the following year. Within 10 years Deere found it impossible to produce enough plows to meet the demand without a dependable source of steel. In 1846 he contracted to have Naylor & Company in England cast steel for him. To cut the cost he later went to Pittsburgh where, according to James Swank in his book, *History of the Manufacturing of Iron in All Ages,* "the first slab of cast plow steel ever rolled in the United States was made by William Woods at the steel works of Jones and Quigs for John Deere."

The national financial panic of the late 1830s had a serious impact on Illinois and the new state faced bankruptcy. Currency was scarce and wildcat bank notes doubtful. By 1841 the rate of immigration had declined by half and there were only about 450,000 people in the state. The rich land of Illinois went for a bargain price of $1.25 an acre. Despite the state's woes, Island City was platted on the island of Rock Island just east of the island end of the brush dam. Moline settlers and businesses, using the broad dam top as an access road, built homes and factories on the island as an extension of Moline, taking their Puritan values with them. Not only was the fledgling community growing on the island, it began spreading along the riverfront for manufacturing, and away from the river for its residences. Antoine Le Claire, the son of a French trader and the grandson of a Potawatomi Indian chief, was given 1,200 acres of land by local tribes. This was called the Le Claire reserve. Parts of this land and the four original farms belonging to Joel Wells, David B. Sears, Timothy Woods and a Mr. Edwards comprised the land where early Moline stood. The Le Claire name still shows on old plan and survey books and appears on many Moline property deeds. In the early 1840s the town ran all along the river almost to the Rock Island border, but the settled area was only from about the present 11th Street to 18th Street and from the riverfront to about 5th Avenue. The original plat contained only 78 acres. Had it not been for the willingness of Le Claire to sell his holdings so new manufacturers and settlers could find land, the village would not have grown.

The evolution of the community was well underway in 1842 when Dr. Henry F. Salter began his medical practice in the settlement. There were already at least two religious congregations when Reverend Woodruff began holding chapel in an old boardinghouse at 3rd Avenue and 15th Street. But for the future of Moline, probably the most significant religious gathering was held in December 1843 in the home of Charles Atkinson when the Congregational Church was established. Within a short time the Reverend A. B. Hitchcock became pastor of the congregation.

Early leaders decided the new community needed a school for all of its youngsters. In 1843 Moline's first public school was built on 16th Street near 4th Avenue by subscription. Records show 54 subscribers gave $457, almost entirely in work or material. Built of brick, the building also was

JOHN DEERE HAD THIS PHOTO TAKEN WHEN HE WAS IN HIS 40S ABOUT THE TIME HIS NEWLY ESTABLISHED BUSINESS WAS BEGINNING TO PROSPER IN MOLINE.

used by the Congregationalists and Methodists as a place of worship. Joseph Jackman, town clerk and justice of the peace, became the school's first teacher. He proposed a graded system, which the citizens rejected at first. In 1847 a portion of the original Sears dam was destroyed during a flood.

During its rebuilding, Spencer was swept through a hole, and his leg was broken. Later to save his life the leg had to be amputated.

John Deere was still in Grand Detour turning out almost 1,000 plows a year. But success created problems. His factory was remote, supplies were difficult to obtain, and transportation was bad. Coal had to be hauled 40 miles from LaSalle and the finished plows wagoned out, often in hub deep mud, to be shipped by canal and river to market. Deere with two of his employees, John M. Gould and Robert N. Tate, went looking for a better location. Moline seemed to have everything Deere wanted: the availability of river transportation, peripheral coal fields, a growing population of workers and founders like himself with strict, moral Northeastern backgrounds.

When Deere first moved to Moline he left his family in Grand Detour, and on visits there he talked Tate and Gould into joining him in partnership. The original Deere, Tate and Gould factory was housed in a three-story building with less than 3,600 square feet of floor space. This building stood until mid-June of 1930 when it was torn down to make way for a new Deere & Company building.

During this period the state of Illinois in error issued a permit for Sears to build a second dam from the island of Rock Island to a small island a bit off-shore on the north side, known as Benham's Island. Fort Armstrong had been abandoned, but the island itself had been retained as a government reserve. The state had no jurisdiction to issue a permit and so Sears had no right to build the dam. This small island is now regarded as the north side of the old Moline Lock near the mid-point of Arsenal Island, but in the mid-19th century Sears erected a grain mill, a steamboat landing and his own residence there. Other residences and businesses were set up on Benham's Island and on the opposing shore of the island of Rock Island to utilize the new power source. Among the new manufacturers was the wooden works of Dimock, Gould & Company. It was this dam with its group of manufacturers as well as the platted Island City that gave validity to later claims against the government by Moline residents when the island of Rock Island became a government arsenal.

THIS SHORT ARTICLE ABOUT JOHN DEERE'S PLOWS APPEARED IN AN 1859 ISSUE OF THE PRAIRIE FARMER. NOTE: THE NAME OF TATE IS MISSPELLED.

The Grand de Tour Plow. About ten years ago, a Mr. Deere commenced the making of a plow with the above name, which soon became celebrated in all the Rock River region, and for a considerable distance up and down the Mississippi. This plow, with improvements, is still manufactured by the original inventor, or one of the firm of Deere, Sate, & Gould, at Moline, the call for it having been greatly extended. Cast-steel mould-boards, made by Noyes & Co., of Sheffield, England, are now used. The implement is now named the "Moline Center Draft Plow."

JUDGE JOHN M. GOULD WAS A FORCE IN MOLINE CIVIC AFFAIRS FOR MANY YEARS.

DIMOCK, GOULD & COMPANY FIRST MANUFACTURED A FULL LINE OF WOODEN PRODUCTS, INCLUDING FURNITURE AND PRODUCTS FOR THE FARM AND HOME. AFTER THE ORIGINAL FACTORY BURNED, THEY MANUFACTURED ONLY SMALLER WOODEN PRODUCTS, AND IN THE LATE 19TH CENTURY DEVELOPED A FIBER PAIL THAT BECAME A NATIONAL "BEST SELLER."

Deere was 43 when he moved to Moline. There were no banks, and financing was impossible. Plows were traded to merchants in Davenport, Rock Island, Muscatine and other nearby communities who then gave supplies to Deere, Tate and Gould and their employees. Railroads had not yet reached the region, and the stage and river packets were the principal source of travel.

Meanwhile, Charles Atkinson and his brother made their way west from New England. On the trip they were threatened by a raging prairie fire, and in an attempt to backfire it, Atkinson's powder flask burst, burning and mutilating his hand. By the time the hand healed, he had little money. He took out a claim in Henry County, built a log cabin and lived there with his wife, Eliza Bates Atkinson, for seven years, becoming Henry County's first probate judge in 1837. In 1843 Atkinson moved to Moline. Within a few years he was an established businessman and leader. He decided the area needed better passenger transit. He first worked through the Frink and Walker Stage Coach Line of Chicago to bring a daily stage into Moline. When they refused he went to the Ohio Stage Company in Columbus and when they agreed Frink and Walker also instituted a daily stage to the area. But an even more important form of transportation was being planned.

In the mid-1840s a meeting was held in the home of Colonel George Davenport on the island of Rock Island to attempt to establish a railroad line for the developing communities. Atkinson attended the meeting along with the newly settled North Carolina lawyer, James Grant; A. S. Fulton; E. Cook; L. Andrews; P. A. Whittaker of Rock Island; Nelson Elwood, an engineer from Joliet; and the railroad surveyor, Richard Morgan.

As early as 1838 in a letter to John W. Spencer the Honorable John Buford had predicted that the first railroad bridge to span the Mississippi would be built here. It was the men and the meeting in the home of George Davenport on the island of Rock Island that brought it to reality. And, it was the stern New Englander, Charles Atkinson, by acting forcefully during the early planning of the road, who actually brought the line through the manufacturing area of Moline.

In the original plans the railroad was to run only from Chicago to LaSalle, but later consultants on the project proposed to build and equip it from Chicago to Rock Island, provided the charter could be amended and a local subscription of $600,000 in stock secured. Atkinson worked to meet those conditions and became a director of the road. He then convinced the railroad planners that the line should run through Moline rather than bypass the city by following the Rock River valley to the Mississippi and then going into Rock Island as first mapped. Because of Atkinson's determination the first train came through Moline's commercial district in February 1854 and the future of business and manufacturing growth was assured.

On April 21, 1848, Moline was incorporated as a town. Churches were founded to serve the new immigrant populations. In 1850 both the Swedish Evangelical Church, with Reverend Lars P. Esbjorn as pastor, and the Swedish Methodist Episcopal Church began. Founded in the home of Moline's first Swedish immigrants, Mr. and Mrs. Claus Bengston, this Methodist church retained Swedish in its services until the mid-1930s. Money from Eastern concerts given by Jenny Lind helped to build Moline's First Lutheran Church, which stands today as one of the city's landmarks.

In a newspaper ad of April 1852, John Deere informed everyone: "My factory is prepared to furnish plows to all, on reasonable notice and at rates suitable to the times. I can increase from 4,000 (the number now manufactured) to 10,000 annually." The company had already begun branching out into other plows with several varieties for different soils and purposes. In 1853, the year Moline got its first bank, Charles Deere turned 16 and became an employee of Deere & Company.

IN 1882, DEERE & COMPANY
WORKERS POSED FOR A PHOTO-
GRAPH WITH A LOAD OF THE
COMPANY'S FARM IMPLEMENTS ON
A CHICAGO, ROCK ISLAND AND
PACIFIC FLAT CAR EMBLAZONED
WITH THE COMPANY NAME.

A year earlier the partnership of Deere, Tate and Gould had dissolved. Tate
went into partnership with Buford in Buford and Tate at 2nd Street and
6th Avenue, Rock Island. In the mid-'60s the company became the B. D.
Buford Company. In 1880 it was destroyed by fire. After rebuilding, it
became the Rock Island Plow Company.

After the dissolution of the partnership, John M. Gould went into business
with D. C. Dimock as the first manufacturer of woodenware and furniture
west of Detroit. After their original factory burned in 1856 they
discontinued their line of furniture and made only small woodenware. By
1858 they incorporated as Dimock, Gould & Company, adding a sawmill
and lumber yard to the business. From the beginning Gould had been
president and managing director. In 1863 when the First National Bank of
Moline was organized, Gould became first its cashier and then in 1867 its
president.

At the time John Deere took sole control of Deere & Company, Moline
had 172 structures including businesses, residences, schools and churches. A
map prepared by M. A. Gould, surveyor, civil engineer, general contractor,
and friend of Deere (but not related to John M. Gould), included 20
factories, 14 or 15 stores, 2 packing houses, an office of a justice of the peace,
the Moline House, four churches, a school, several saloons, a groggery and
an ox parsonage (like a stable).

The great grandson of Gould, Gary Lovested of Moline, in a family
genealogy, relates his grandfather's childhood impression of John Deere:
"Our home was filled with the presence of John Deere who often visited us
on 7th Avenue to discuss engineering problems with my father, M. A. Gould.
John Deere rode in a surrey driven by a Negro coachman and he would
enter into the comfort of the kitchen where on an old table, M. A. and Deere
would wrestle with experimental problems. Lucinda (M. A.'s wife) would
swish the children into the backyard. 'Quick go out and play,' she would
whisper as the tall figure in a black suit descended from his surrey, but old
John Deere would always put a stop to that. 'Let them come in, I like
children,' he would admonish my mother." According to George M. Gould,
one of the children Deere allowed to stay in the kitchen, "He was plain as an
old shoe. He always wore sideburns and never a beard, and his suits were
always of a dark material."

AFTER A DEVASTATING FIRE IN 1856, DIMOCK, GOULD & COMPANY REBUILT AND MANUFACTURED TUBS AND PAILS ON ROCK ISLAND.

THE STEAM PUMPER <u>MISSISSIPPI</u> THAT MOLINE BOUGHT IN THE 1870S WAS ONE OF THE MOST ADVANCED FOR ITS DAY. VOLUN-TEERS PULLED IT UNTIL THE CITY ADDED A STABLE OF HORSES TO THE FIRE SERVICE. THE BOY LOOKING AT THE PUMPER IN THIS MID-1950S PHOTO, MICHAEL PIERCE, IS NOW THE FIRE MARSHAL OF THE MOLINE FIRE DEPARTMENT. THE <u>MISSISSIPPI</u> WAS GIVEN TO THE MUSEUM OF SCIENCE AND INDUSTRY IN CHICAGO.

After one of Deere's visits, Gould designed the first Deere & Company trademark of a deer leaping over a log. He cut the original brass stencil from his drawing and Deere gave it his official approval. According to the family history, though, the original deer had its antlers on backwards.

Just before the Civil War a growing number of firms moved into Moline. They like Deere were lured by the access to transportation, the waterpower, and a staunch church/community moralism. Among these were Alfred Williams, Bailey Williams, Charles Heald and Marvel White who formed the Williams, Heald and Company Moline Iron Works. They brought about a dozen men with them from Massachusetts to set up a jobbing machine shop and foundry located at the east end of what has become their present location on 3rd Avenue between 6th and 8th Streets. They first manufactured steam engines for the saw and grist mills of the area, some ornamental iron and eventually gears. In the early 1870s Henry Ainsworth joined the firm and shortly afterwards it was incorporated as Williams, White and Company.

In 1855 Moline was reincorporated by a special act of the legislature, and a very strict Maine liquor law was adopted almost unanimously. The reincorporation gave Moline official status and established annual elections for a president and five trustees. These officials were empowered to keep the streets, alleys and public roads in good condition. To do this they could require every able bodied male resident over 21 and under 50 to work on those projects up to three days annually. The new articles gave the city the right to control pets and farm animals within the limits, to prohibit gambling, indecent exposure of persons, to suppress and prohibit disorderly houses, groceries, tippling houses and houses of ill fame. They had licensing and policing powers over showmen, circuses and amusements. These 1855 statutes regulated not only the erection of wooden or unsafe buildings, but provided for fire prevention and control, the establishment of volunteer fire companies, and the responsibility to furnish water for firefighting. Under these articles a constable was appointed by the board. He was allowed to keep a percentage of all money collected, but he and his sureties were then held liable for all taxes that could have been collected. As the unidentified writer said in a handwritten diary dated April 17, 1857, "In Moline very little is left for chance or the devil." These statutes came too late for the fire that in May of 1855 broke out on the north side of Wells Street between Mill and Lynde Streets (today's 2nd Avenue and 16th Streets). It destroyed three stores and the offices of Chamberlin and Dean. According to an early newspaper account, "although the bucket brigade worked valiantly, nothing was saved." This loss was a serious financial blow to the businesses and the city. Within a few hours 13 citizens subscribed $950 of the $1,250 needed to buy a used fire engine from Chicago. The remaining money was raised. The newly established Rock Island Lines shipped the equipment free to Moline. By the time the pump *Metamora*, with its 2,000 feet of hose and hose cart arrived, a 50-member volunteer company wearing white pants and red shirts trimmed in blue was on hand.

Less than two weeks later smoke was sighted to the west. Pulling the *Metamora* and its hose cart, the fire brigade ran 30 minutes toward the fire, four miles away on the Rock Island riverfront. There they found the steamboats *Prairie State* and *Kentucky* blazing. Rock Island at that time had no organized fire companies.

Moline's first major fire after the acquisition of the *Metamora* occurred in October of 1856 when the Dimock, Gould Mill burned with a loss in excess of $30,000. In 1872 the *Mississippi* was purchased by the volunteers of Company B. This pumper was originally hand drawn, but in 1880 horses were added. The *Mississippi* was given to the Museum of Science and Industry in Chicago by the City of Moline for its fire exhibits in the late 1950s. During the late 19th century a number of volunteer fire companies evolved, including the A.O.T. (Always On Time), The Union Number One, the Onward Number Two, the Minnehaha Number Three, and the Dean Number Four, which met on 14th Avenue and 14th Street and eventually became the first fire station on the hill, the original Number Two Station. The Hook and Ladder Company which met on 16th Street between 4th and 5th Avenues became Central Station in the renovated and rebuilt old brick school house. Several manufacturers established hose companies including Deere & Company, Moline Plow, Barnard & Leas, and Deere & Mansur, who also assisted the city volunteers. The water to fight early fires came from the river and cisterns built by the city at various locations. Later in the century Dimock, Gould & Company and Deere & Company could lay line between the two factories and, with both of their pumps running, pump water under pressure to most of Moline's business area. The town's first fire alarm was located at the water works. Mutual fire aid from the organized fire companies in the surrounding areas was provided as early as 1881 when the Keator Mill burned and Moline's fire brigades were assisted by an engine from Rock Island Arsenal and others from Rock Island and Davenport.

BY THE LATE 1870S DEERE & COMPANY ADVERTISED IN PUBLICATIONS NATIONWIDE.

New Englanders Set the Moral Tone

Most of the early settlers and almost all of the city's leaders came from the Northeast. For this reason there was a heavy emphasis on religion, family life, law and order. There was a long period in the formation of Moline's business and manufacturing community when firms already established actively helped bring new ventures in if their proprietors stood up to the town's "puritan" values, while those with less desirable reputations were told to settle elsewhere. Even before the Civil War there was a marked difference in the people who settled in Moline and those of its neighbor, Rock Island. Monied persons of influence from the South had resettled in Rock Island, building large homes for their families, living in the elegance and tradition of the South. They brought with them a sympathy for their friends and relatives still in the South and, although they did not bring slaves into the Northern state, they retained a more pro-slavery attitude than most of the settlements in the area. Most of the residents of Moline were staunchly anti-slavery and the town and its inhabitants from very early times were referred to as abolitionists. In the 1860 elections almost a straight line was drawn between the cities. While the southern half of Rock Island County supported Douglas, Bell and Breckenridge with rallies and parades, the northern half of the county under the leadership of the Lincoln Wide-Awakes and most of the churches favored Lincoln and his anti-slavery slate.

DEERE & COMPANY CONTINUED TO GROW AFTER CHARLES DEERE TOOK OVER. HE EXERTED THE SAME SET OF ATTITUDES AND VALUES AS HIS FATHER IN BOTH THE COMPANY AND THE COMMUNITY.

The leading slavery opponent in Moline before the Civil War was the New England Congregational minister, Calvin Hitchcock. Weekly sermons thundered from his pulpit assaulting the system of slavery. A number of churches in Moline reflected this abolitionist attitude. But it was Hitchcock and the Congregational church, with a membership that included most of the influential families as well as many of its founders, that really gave backbone to the anti-slavery movement in Moline. A number of unsubstantiated stories tell of houses in Moline that supposedly had secret rooms, passages and entrances used as stations on the Underground Railroad, but no proof of these was ever found, and most of the houses have been torn down. Perhaps the best known of these houses was the one located near 22nd Street and 7th Avenue. During the late 1940s and 50s it was known as Johnson's Tea Rooms. According to several accounts, this home had a fireplace in the basement with an outside entrance leading to a hiding place in the basement where runaway slaves could be fed and warmed. The other home most often mentioned was the old Wilson home at about 6th Avenue and 21st Street where slaves were brought in wagons covered in hay.

DAVID B. SEARS POSED PROUDLY FOR THIS PHOTOGRAPH WITH A HOE MADE BY JOHN DEERE.

They were warmed and fed, then taken on by wagon or smuggled on foot to the next stop. John Deere was considered a strict abolitionist and is reported to have sent money directly to aid the Kansas movement.

Business prospered, along with religious and moral movements. The replacement of the original Sears dam in 1858 made more waterpower available. The new dam with a wooden frame and heavy stone fill meant not only more power, but a growing number of jobs and more people. Moline's first wave of immigrants had been pioneers from New England; the later waves were to change the city, sprinkling it with foreign languages, foreign sounding names and newspapers printed in foreign languages. These new immigrants — hardworking Germans, Swedes, Irish and Belgians — only ingrained more deeply the strict moral, family and religious values of Moline.

This growing population had an increasing need for commodities. Market Square was soon ringed with merchants, its center filled with farmers offering produce. Coal was available in the hills on both sides of the Rock River valley along with an abundance of timber. Early lumberyards used the available local lumber, but soon huge log rafts from the northern pine forests were a common sight on the Mississippi. Local hardwoods were used only for good furniture and the finest woodenware.

In these early years businesses located where land was available. Fortunately for Moline, during the period when firms were looking for riverfront sites, most of the desirable land in Rock Island was held in the grip of a few "land baron" families that refused to sell. The industrial section along the Moline riverfront stretched the city's full length. Although Davenport and Rock Island each had populations larger than Moline, it was Moline that employed a disproportionate number of workers. On April 21, 1856, when the first train of cars crossed the Mississippi on the new Railroad Bridge, a new era of manufacturing and growth began for Moline and all of the cities in the area. The opening of the West meant an almost insatiable need for the farm equipment manufactured here. Breaking the vast prairie expanses to agriculture also meant a growing need for lumber, furniture, woodenware and the day-to-day needs of the families moving with the railroad into the Western prairie states.

In the late 1850s and early '60s business interests across the country were trying to buy the island of Rock Island. The site had been considered for a national capital, or a university, and had been offered in St. Louis papers for bids. It faced an uncertain future. In 1861 Charles Atkinson headed a committee of Tri-City leaders to Washington, D.C., to urge the location of a general arsenal on the island. As late as 1859 factories and residences were built on the island, adding to the private investment already there. Other Moline residents and businessmen were afraid that if the government built an arsenal there, the city's waterpower might be threatened, so local backing for Atkinson and his committee was mixed. In Washington they found many of the opposing sites had better representation and some already had partisan congressional backing. Atkinson had a map prepared showing at a glance the advantages of the island and placed one on the desk of each member of Congress. On July 1, 1862, Congress appropriated $100,000 for the establishment of an arsenal on the island of Rock Island. Atkinson saw this as a financial asset for the growth of the area and its resources, but those persons living and working on the island knew it meant an end to their property rights.

The Civil War Disrupts City Plans

Just before the Civil War life in Moline had been built primarily around the lumber industry, the manufacture of agricultural machinery, the churches and the needs of the growing community. The city remained relatively free from the growing concern with war almost until the South seceded. Many young men of the area joined Company H of the 19th Illinois Infantry, listed in war records as the Moline Rifles of the 19th Illinois Volunteer Infantry. At the onset of the war, 57-year-old David B. Sears and his son, George, volunteered for the Union Army. The first Moline soldier to die in battle was Lieutenant Wellington Wood, killed December 31, 1862, at the Battle of Stone River.

During the war, the Union maintained a large prison on the island for captured Confederate soldiers. These men never seriously attempted to escape to the civilian settlement on the island or across the wide power dam, because the populations of the Island City and Moline were known as strict Northern abolitionists, firmly opposed to Southerners and their principles. In fact, when it was impossible to transport escaped slaves to the next stop on the Underground Railroad, personal diaries have suggested that they were hidden on the island under the noses of Union Army guards — and probably with their blessing.

DURING THE CIVIL WAR A PRISONER OF WAR CAMP WAS MAINTAINED ON ROCK ISLAND. A.C. DART WAS THE SUTLER COMMISSIONED TO SELL SUPPLIES TO THE PRISONERS UNTIL JUNE 1864. BEFORE THAT HE CAME TO THE CAMP ALMOST DAILY, BUT AFTERWARDS HIS VISITS WERE LIMITED TO HOLIDAYS SUCH AS CHRISTMAS EVE.

According to local legend, all the black squirrels in this area are descended from the two George Sears carried home from the South after the war and released near the Sears home on the eastern end of the island.

The Civil War postponed plans for the immediate construction of the general arsenal. After the war the plan was renewed. Before the new installation could be begun it was necessary to remove the squatters, the legitimate settlers and the businesses from the island and Island City, which was still a part of Moline. In October 1866 a board of commissioners met to recommend payments to island land holders, including $145,175 to David B. Sears for the dam, buildings on Benham's Island and on Rock Island and for about 31 acres of improved land; $40,740 to George and Bailey Davenport for 157 acres of improved land and residences; $28,270 to Stephens, Huntoon and Wood for their planing mill, paint shop and dwellings; and $1,100 to the town of Moline for its bridge and approach.

By war's end a well-established horse railway linked Moline and the Rock Island area and made possible a growing interaction between the two Illinois cities in trade, commerce and industrial workers. A philosophical difference remained between the populations. In a page one article in the *Davenport Democrat* for January 30, 1868, a Moline meeting was reviewed: "The Moline Literary Society had a discussion Tuesday night on the following question: 'Resolved, that the practice of dancing is an innocent amusement, and contributes to the morals and manners of society.' The question was decided in the affirmative." The town was growing in many ways: it was developing a new era of social groups, the old churches were flourishing, new churches were being formed, schools were being built, and the city was attempting to put the problems of the Civil War behind.

CHARLES ATKINSON WAS THE MOVING FORCE BEHIND MANY OF MOLINE'S EARLY ADVANCES. PERHAPS THE MOST IMPORTANT WAS THE GROWTH OF ITS WATER POWER DURING THE LATTER HALF OF THE 19TH CENTURY. THE GREAT WALL OF MOLINE, WHICH WAS MEANT TO SUPPLY THIS POWER, WAS A FIASCO. FIRST PROPOSED IN THE 1830S THIS MAN-MADE CANAL STRETCHED ALONG THE MOLINE RIVERFRONT AND WAS SUPPOSED TO SUPPLY ENOUGH POWER FOR CURRENT AND FUTURE BUSINESSES AND INDUSTRIES. EVEN WITH ALL OF THE FINANCIAL AND TECHNICAL BACKING OF THE FEDERAL GOVERNMENT, IT NEVER WORKED. AFTER MORE THAN 25 YEARS OF CONSTRUCTION, DESIGN AND REDESIGN, THE PROJECT WAS ABANDONED.

After the war, an elaborate plan was put in motion to assure Moline's riverfront industrial area of a continuous flow of water power. Charles Atkinson, as president of the Moline Water Power Company, which he had helped organize, secured a contract from the government to develop and maintain power giving the company one-fourth of the output free of rent, repairs or expenses in perpetuity. Histories disagree as to whether Atkinson instituted the arrangement, or whether government officials "used earnest solicitation" to strike the contract. But 30 years later, after hundreds of thousands of federal dollars had been spent on the power project, quotes such as "the Government has utterly failed to carry out its agreement" and "It is difficult to believe that the Government of this great country will continue to ignore its solemn obligations and withhold the justice so clearly due to its loyal citizens" continued to appear in print.

The water power plan was based on what journalists later dubbed the "great wall of Moline." Although government engineers developed the plan, the Honorable John Buford in an 1838 letter to John W. Spencer proposed a canal to supply the mills with power. The government plans called for the wall to be 20 feet high and almost a mile long. The first phase of the project began in 1868 and was completed in 1869. Although for its time it was a tremendous undertaking with almost all of the work done by men and horses, the first major stage was completed without incident, on time and within budget. Allegations from other industrial areas of the nation claimed the government was pouring millions into this project strictly for Moline industry. Actually the project was not a success. Moline industry did benefit from it, but the government never drew a watt of power from this fiasco.

Remnants of the wall can be seen today along the riverfront in Moline from about 14th Street to just east of the powerplant. According to the government agreement, the Water Power Company would cede its water power rights, and the dam from Moline to the island of Rock Island was torn out. Over the years this dam had served other than just the waterpower interests. It was a broad flat structure and could be used as a roadway access for wagons and pedestrians. The new lateral dam did not cross the slough. Instead, it began at the foot of 15th Street and followed the Moline shoreline, forming a canal to approximately the Rock Island city border. This produced a sluiceway for shoreline manufacturers to tap for waterpower. It provided power for the original industries which had used the old Sears dam, and additional land with waterpower potential to attract new industry. Moline Water Power probably quickly rallied round the new government power proposal because the old dam was wearing out. In addition, a number of residents were complaining that with the growing industry and urban population, that portion of the Mississippi shut off by the dam was becoming stagnant and a health hazard.

The lateral dam had a tailrace of varying width with 56 manually operated water gates along its course and a flume from the dam to each shoreline manufacturer. On the river side of the dam a seven-foot head of water (with the possibility that it could be increased to 11 feet) was to be maintained. This created enough power to turn the machines. The lower factories had flumes that carried the water back to the tailrace. Four years after the first construction, a canal was cut through a projection of Moline land, creating Sylvan Slough and cutting Sylvan Island from the mainland, in an effort to increase the effectiveness of the waterpower system.

Almost from the beginning the government and the Moline manufacturers disagreed on the use of the waterpower, and even on the terms of the agreement. The government wanted the gates closed on weekends and holidays so they could maintain the seven-foot head. Industries had always worked on weekends during rush times, and they continued to do so. With the gates open seven days a week, the head dropped and factories lost power. The controversy eventually led to the only protective military action in Moline's history. Soldiers were called out when, during low water, a mill owner opened his water gates without authority and stationed armed men along the shoreline threatening to shoot anyone attempting to close the gates and his operation.

Between the Civil War and the turn of the century the government built cofferdams, deepened and widened the channel, and spent more than $1.5 million on Moline's great wall before abandoning the project. The tailrace was filled in, the new government power plant was built on the north side of Sylvan Island and the city's power needs once more returned to private industry.

Moline officially incorporated as a city on April 10, 1872, a shaky year filled with ill omens. In a bitterly fought mayorial election that left bad feelings August 29, 1872, voters elected Daniel L. Wheelock over John Deere as the city's first mayor. (Deere won next time.) A tornado in June destroyed the bridge over Rock River and cut the city off from much of its local coal and lumber. In mid-September the Union schoolhouse burned, causing classes to be held for three years in churches and in an engine house. In the fall the Illinois State Legislature passed a law allowing cities to levy a library tax, and Moline became one of the first cities to adopt the tax. The following January Moline opened its first public library on the second floor above the post office. It contained 4,000 volumes. This building, known as Wheelock Library Hall, was deeded to the Library Board in March 1873. It still stands on 15th Street just south of 3rd Avenue.

A new moralism swept Moline with the return to peace and normality. Just as the fiery sermons of Calvin Hitchcock during the Civil War stirred

Moline abolitionists into action, so those of the Congregationalist minister
W.C. Barnard in the 1870s moved the moral conscience of his parishioners.
Perhaps his most famous sermon, "Work and Wages," indicated the tone of
the city during this post Civil War, pre-industrial boom. In it he said,

*"A good workman for one day is better than a bungler for two. A competent
teacher for three months is better than an incompetent for six. It is not easy then
to say a salary ought to be this or that. It will be this or that as people decide
what they want and must have. If a skilled workman is demanded, skill must be
paid for. All classes have the right to share in social prosperity, and they all have
the same right to share in its adversity."*

This sermon was delivered in a sanctuary where pew assignments belonged
to the political and social leaders of the community: Deere, Ainsworth,
Dimock, Gould, Wheelock, Huntoon, Cooper and Atkinson. The work week
was 65 hours and the pay between $1.25 and $3 a day.
Moline's first black church, St. Paul's African Methodist Episcopal, was
organized in April 1872 under the Reverend Joseph Perkins. During the
pastorate of Reverend W.W. Williams the old church was torn down and a
new one erected in 1895. Moline's first Catholic church was organized in
1875 and services were held in a frame building at 1624 9th Avenue. Before
that time the congregation of mostly Irish immigrants from the potato
famine had observed mass at St. Anthony's in Davenport. At times
traveling priests such as Father Alleman served mass in the home of W.E.
McEniry at 1412 6th Avenue. By 1878 the St. Anthonium congregation had
rebuilt the old Freja Hall, moved in and changed its name to St. Mary's. In
1884 they opened their first Catholic school in the church. It remained until
the brick school was erected in 1886. St. Mary's church today stands much
as it did when it was built. The early parishoners who sang hymns, carried
lanterns through the snow, and followed the railroad tracks to St. Mary's
Church in Rock Island for Christmas Mass built a close-knit congregation
that has endured as one of the strongest in the area.

*SMITH'S CONFECTIONERY WAS A
FIXTURE AT 23RD STREET AND 4TH
AVENUE BY 1912. IN THIS PHOTO,
LINNIE MABLE SMITH KOELZ
HOLDS STEPHEN ERNEST KOELZ,
AND HENRY WILLIAM KOELZ
STANDS IN FRONT OF HIS
UNIDENTIFIED BABYSITTER. AN
UNIDENTIFIED CUSTOMER STANDS
INSIDE THE SCREEN. THE FAMILY
LIVED OVER THE STORE.*

*THE CHRISTIAN MUELLER & SONS
LUMBER BUSINESS WAS ANOTHER
OF MOLINE'S EARLY FIRMS.
MUELLER BOUGHT INTO A LUMBER
FIRM IN THE LATE 1860S.
CHRISTIAN MUELLER & SONS DID
BUSINESS AT 2300 3RD AVENUE
UNITL APRIL 1, 1961. SHORTLY
AFTER THAT DATE THE BUILDINGS
WERE TORN DOWN TO MAKE WAY
FOR INTERSTATE 74.*

Education became a moving force in the city with the election of the first board in the 1870s. Central School (old Washington) was built at the cost of $25,000. West Ward (old Ericcson) cost $14,000. The teaching staff consisted of 16 women and a superintendent. Teachers' salaries ranged from $320-$480 annually; the high school principal earned $600, the superintendent $1,800. The schools had an enrollment of under 700 and the first graduating class in 1876 had five girls and one boy. The church and business leaders who had once held a tight rein on the town and its future through the statutes, the churches and employment, now began to use the schools as well. In 1879 a night school was organized for working men and boys. In 1880 art instruction was included in the curriculum and soon afterwards teachers for special reading and music were hired. The high school offered training for teachers. In 1881 the Unitarian Ladies Aid Society began a free cooking school for girls and within a short time they were joined in the project by women from several churches. Before long this program was also a part of the public school system. A kindergarten was established first by the churches, and then was incorporated into the system. By the 1890s there was an ungraded room for the slow learners.

The city had a succession of weekly newspapers from the middle of the century. On July 31, 1878, Oliver and Louise White published the first edition of the *Moline Daily Evening Dispatch*. A new era began but not without problems. In a few years the paper was in financial difficulty and it was turned over to creditors. Charles H. Deere bought out the others to keep the paper alive and then sold it on installments to McGlyn, Groom and Patterson. It had four pages, a daily circulation of about 500 and was printed on a Campbell cylinder press run by water power. The *Dispatch* has never missed a day of scheduled publication since.

On February 5, 1881, Deere & Company at the cost of $3,000 installed 16 electric lights in its blacksmith, grinding and wood shops and a rotating light on the bluff in Moline. The entire area turned out to see the switch thrown. At the time the membership in the Moline Athletic Club was growing, and boys could earn 15 cents a day making deliveries. Poetry and dramatic works were being read and performed at the new Wagner Opera House. Farm land in the county sold for $2.50 to $20 an acre. There were 61 telephones in the city, and McMaster and Browning had just incorporated to build an electric car line. Three years later the stores and business establishments in Moline had electricity. The 600-volt, 50-light arc machine installed in 1884 in the Water Works building was a master achievement for the company, and one of the largest in the United States at the time. Two years later 80 electric street lights were installed. Moline's conservative leaders moved decisively for industrial progress.

LIFE IN MOLINE IN THE DECADE AFTER THE CIVIL WAR WAS ONE OF PROGRESS AND A RESURGENCE OF RELIGIOUS DEDICATION. SUNDAY AFTERNOONS WERE SPENT AT THE WAGNER OPERA HOUSE, LEISURELY STROLLING OR WITH FRIENDS AND NEIGHBORS. THIS CROQUET GAME ON THE LAWN OF THE A. SINNETT HOME ON MOLINE AVENUE SHOWS THE ELABORATE DRESS OF THE PARTICIPANTS AT ALMOST ALL SOCIAL GATHERINGS.

Moline's power plants are thought to have been the first in the country to use engines and water wheels to operate the same dynamos and one of the earliest in the nation to interconnect power plants. Although the rest of the country was moving to fueled power plants, Moline retained its waterpower.

Although John Deere had always been known as a temperate man, when he became the city's second mayor, even he was pressured by the Woman's Temperance Crusade until he finally vetoed an ordinance to permit additional saloon licenses. Earlier, the Deere family influence had been felt in the industrial and moral directions of the city, but the new Deere generation's sphere of influence also moved into the cultural realm. Merton Yale Cady, the grandson of both Deere and the inventor of the Yale lock, designed the John Deere Block on the south perimeter of Market Square. In the late 1870s under the leadership of another Deere heir, Elizabeth Cady Stanton, the Moline Equal Suffrage Association was organized. This eventually became the Moline League of Women Voters.

Growing numbers of young women found employment in the Moline businesses. The Woman's Club opened a club room where these women could relax or get a hot noon meal at nominal prices. The Woman's Christian Temperance Union remained militant and progressively active against intemperance. They persuaded the state Legislature to pass a statute providing for scientific temperance instruction in all public schools in the state. It was also through the efforts of this group and Julia Mills Dunne that the statue of Frances Willard, president of the Woman's Christian Temperance Union and the founder of a world temperance union, was placed in Memorial Hall in Washington, D.C. She was the first woman honored in Statuary Hall.

In 1886 after some problems, the city took over full operation of the municipal pumping station at 17th Street and 1st Avenue. The bonds had been issued in June 1883 to finance the facility and extend fire protection to the entire manufacturing and business district. But the original $50,000 was $25,000 short of the actual cost of the construction, including boilers and intake, 50 hydrants and seven miles of watermains. Davis and Company filled the financing gap, constructed the facility and then operated it until the city could take over.

IN ITS EARLIEST DAYS, PROSPECT PARK WAS PRIVATELY OWNED AND OPERATED AS AN AMUSE-MENT PARK. IT EVENTUALLY BECAME A PART OF THE MOLINE PARK SYSTEM, THE RIDES WERE REMOVED AND PLAYGROUNDS AND PICNIC AREAS INSTALLED. THE PAVILION ON THE SOUTH HILL OVERLOOKING THE LAKE AND MOLINE'S ROCK RIVER VALLEY HAS BEEN USED FOR ORIGINAL DRAMAS, TRAVELING SHOWS AND CHAUTAUQUAS. IT IS NOW THE HOME OF THE QUAD-CITY MUSIC GUILD WHERE MUSICALS ARE PRESENTED EVERY SUMMER.

Moline's population grew through waves of immigrants. Early arrivals came from the Eastern states to set up businesses and build factories along the riverfront. Later, others came to fill the jobs in Moline industry or to farm the rich surrounding rural areas. Earliest records show that several Belgian families lived for a short time on the island of Rock Island before the Civil War, but moved to rural farmland in the area. While a few Belgians immigrated in the 1850s and '60s, it was during the 1880s and '90s that a steady stream of workers moved from Belgium to Moline. The men usually came first, found jobs, then sent for their families. This continued until about 1910 when a depression in Belgium reduced the number financially able to move. In 1906 the second Catholic church in Moline was founded to minister to Belgians. They first rented the second floor of the Turner Hall on Sunday for their mass and then during the Lenten season of 1907 they completed a combination church and school. The cornerstone of Sacred Heart Church was laid in 1919 and the old school that became a landmark in Moline was replaced by a new school in the 1950s. The Sacred Heart and St. Mary congregations have merged their schools into the new Seton School. Because of the number of Belgians that came to Moline, the first Flemish newspaper in the United States was founded in Moline by Father Culmans in 1907 and published until after World War I. The *Gazette Van Moline* merged with the *Gazette Van Detroit* to become the only Flemish paper in the United States. At one time in the early 20th century the area had the largest Belgian population in the nation. However, after World War I the flow of Belgians to Detroit and its auto industries increased substantially, and today the Belgian population here is second only to that of Detroit. A Belgian Consul operates in what has long been considered the Belgian part of the city, its west central hill section that for years had its own business district along 7th Street.

The city continued to prosper politically, socially and industrially, maintaining its high moral plane in spite of the fact that two of its leading families were often at cross purposes.

The Deere and Wheelock families were in competition not only politically within the city but on a larger scale too. In 1885 when Charles Deere was awarded the contract to furnish the post office for Moline for four years, it was considered a major victory. Up to that time Wheelock had, according to newspaper accounts, "manipulated his wires so that the postal service had been conducted through him by the Democratic administration." To get the bid Deere included carrying the mail from the post office to the depot and supplying free electricity for the building. This Deere post office was in the old stone building recently torn down to make way for one of the approaches of the new bridge to the Rock Island Arsenal.

Although most of the history of Moline shows almost constant progress, some improvements did not meet with immediate success. In May of 1890 in a stormy city council meeting several prominent citizens including Wheelock, Huntoon and a representative of Moline Water Power spoke vehemently against paving 3rd Avenue. A week later the same city council with approval of most of the prominent leaders of the city rejected a proposition to purchase Prospect Park.

Moline's Judge J. M. Gould drafted a bill to establish and maintain public hospitals through local tax levies which passed the state Legislature in 1891. Within weeks the city passed a two-mill tax referendum. The hospital opened in 1896 with one matron and two nurses on duty, and two student nurses in training. Three patients were admitted on opening day. An association of Moline women had formed a group to help furnish the hospital and to develop a school of nursing. At the dedication Judge Gould presented an elevator to the hospital and soon afterwards several businesses gave an ambulance to the facility.

In the mid-1890s Moline's Police Chief Kittelsen developed a garbage collection system for districts without sewers that reduced the bulk and weight so much that the residue of 8-15 loads could be moved by one team

THE OFFICIAL BELGIAN CONSULATE SHIELD HAS BEEN A FAMILIAR SIGHT TO THE RESIDENTS OF THE 7TH STREET HILL AREA. TODAY THE CONSULATE IS ON THE CORNER OF 18TH AVENUE AND 8TH STREET.

THE CITY'S FIRST STREETCARS WERE HORSEDRAWN, BUT WITH THE INTRODUCTION OF ELECTRICITY IN THE 1880S THE CITY'S TRANSPORTATION QUICKLY BECAME "ELECTRIFIED." MOLINE'S FIRST ELECTRIC STREETCARS TO CARRY PASSENGERS UP THE HILL WERE SOME OF THE EARLIEST IN THE NATION TO NEGOTIATE SUCH STEEP INCLINES.

of horses. It cost just over $6,000 annually to collect the city's garbage using four steel dump carts, nine horses and about a dozen men. Moline is believed to have been the only Illinois city owning its own garbage collection equipment at the time.

In 1896 eleven men, all of whom had been members of various volunteer companies, became Moline's first paid fire department.

In February 1900 Colonel Rider of the Central Union Telephone Company came to Moline to find quarters for the new "Central." In an interview with the *Dispatch*, Rider said, "When the new installation is made each current subscriber's instrument will be removed and replaced by new common battery bells and transmitters and bi-polar hand telephones. The subscriber no more will have to grind the crank to signal Central, but merely take the phone from the hook."

Increasing industrial growth brought the need for more workers. Although the Swedish immigration covered about the same period as that of the Belgians in the beginning, the Swedish immigrants kept coming in large numbers until well into the 20th century. They came looking for work with John Deere, but many of them also found employment in the various lumber industries and woodenware manufacturers. For the skilled immigrants there were always jobs at Moline Furniture Works and at Moline Organ.

Dr. F. M. Fryxell of Augustana College gives insight into the period in the biography of his father, John Fryxell, who came to Moline in an early wave of immigrants. The elder Fryxell arrived in Chicago by train after having spent two years on the east coast, the biography says.

> "I happened to get hold of a copy of Skandia, a Swedish newspaper published in Moline during the post Civil War period. I subscribed to the paper. I became attracted to Moline because of the work to be had there and on account of the Swedish associations and churches. I thought that if I should stay in America, Moline would be the place for me. John Deere was then the great magnet that drew Swedes to Moline, for it was well known that he gave preference to Swedish workmen. At nightfall on October 11, 1878, I arrived in Moline, got off the train, looked for someone who might be Swedish and, finding no one, set out to walk. I happened to hit 16th Street and walked north till stopped by the Mississippi. At 2nd Avenue between 15th and 16th Streets was a row of saloons and boarding houses. My first night in Moline was spent upstairs over a saloon."

Describing the struggles of his wife's family on their arrival, he said:

> "Families sold everything to go to America. Your grandmother's family arrived in America in 1869. Times were indescribably hard. Most of them went to Moline, some to Geneseo and other nearby places. Cholera, malaria, pneumonia and typhoid took a heavy toll. In Moline the immigrant families grouped together, several families living in a single home and all sleeping on the floors, many very poor. This is what your grandparents did with their little girl. As soon as they could they moved to a place of their own, a garret on Railroad Avenue furnished with second hand material."

It was during this heavy influx of immigrants that conductors stopped calling "Moline" on the immigrant-laden trains and instead called out "John Deere Town."

Along with Deere, Velie, Stephens or Gould, it was these hard working immigrants, the Germans, Belgians, Irish and Swedes — working in Moline factories and assimilating into the cultural, social and moral structure of the city — who continued to mold Moline. Industrial development in Moline was not symetrical because of its use of water power and the need for manufacturers to build in a line along the riverfront and even across the

MOLINE'S EVANGELICAL LUTHERAN CHURCH WAS A CENTER OF WORSHIP AND COMMUNITY SPIRIT FOR THE SWEDISH POPULATION.

first dam and onto Rock Island. The residential district grew first behind the industrial tracts staying on the flats below the river. The business section first was located between 15th and 17th Streets and from the riverfront to about 3rd Avenue. At about the turn of the century the business district began to move south of the railroad tracks, at first along 15th Street, then along 5th Avenue, until eventually the business community encompassed almost all the property from 12th Street to 19th Street and from the railroad tracks to 7th Avenue. The population began to move up the bluffs after the Civil War. Housing for the waves of immigrants remained largely in the flatland with the heaviest concentration of foreign born residents settling first west of the business district just south of the railroad tracks at the foot of the bluffs. However, the major reason for the denser expansion to the west was Bailey Davenport's extensive holdings in the eastern areas, which were not sold until after his death in 1890.

Moline Leads in Farm Machinery Industry

At about the turn of the century Moline was described by its leaders: "Moline never had a boom, but has had a steady growth, and today has about 22,000 inhabitants. In its factories there are 5,200 employed, Deere & Company, 1,699; Moline Plow, 1,200; Moline Wagon, 800; Sechler Carriage Company, 600; Wilson Carriage Company, 400; Malleable Iron Company, 400; and Moline Wheel Works, 200." This era was a part of the industrial growth of the city and the area. At the time Moline was the unchallenged agricultural center of the Midwest if not the world. The Deere plants were the largest of their kind in the country but the city boasted a number of other firms manufacturing agricultural equipment, forges, foundries, mills and other factories to make the machines that turned out the agricultural products.

EARLY FARM EQUIPMENT MANU- FACTURERS SHIPPED THEIR PRODUCTS ACROSS THE COUNTRY AND AROUND THE WORLD. BEFORE THE 20TH CENTURY THE AREA'S AGRICULTURAL FIRMS HAD DEALERS IN MUCH OF EUROPE AND THROUGHOUT SOUTH AMERICA.

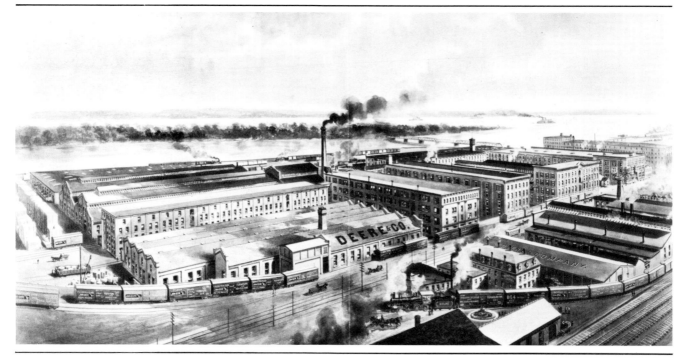

BY 1900 THE DEERE & COMPANY COMPLEX IN MOLINE ENCOMPASSED SEVERAL BLOCKS ALONG 3RD AVENUE AND MOST OF THE LAND TO THE RIVER. DEERE BECAME THE AREA'S LARGEST PRIVATE RAILROAD USER WITH SIDINGS, A SMALL SWITCH YARD AND JOHN DEERE RAILROAD CARS.

Rock Island Plow was probably the major agricultural manufacturing concern in the area outside of Moline before the turn of the century and during the expansion of the industry in the Tri-Cities. When Deere, Tate and Gould split in the 1850s, Tate went into partnership with B. D. Buford. As Buford and Tate they built a shop at 2nd Avenue and 6th Street, Rock Island, and began making steel plows. Their first product was a steel walking plow and within a few years they marketed the original Black Hawk split pole walking cultivator. In the mid-1860s the company became B. D. Buford and Company. The original plant was destroyed by fire in 1880 and rebuilt on a much larger scale. Branches were opened throughout the west. In 1884 the business incorporated as Rock Island Plow Company. It later marketed an entire agricultural line with products shipped worldwide. The company was sold to the Weyerhaeuser interests in 1908. The company grew with acquisitions and eventually was sold to J.I. Case, bringing to an end the home ownership of one of Rock Island's most profitable businesses. Moline Plow, another agricultural firm, was first organized in 1865 as Candee, Swan and Company. It initially manufactured fanning mills and hay rakes, beginning the production of plows in 1866 and incorporating in 1870 as Moline Plow. Innovations such as the Flying Dutchman sulky plow, the three-wheeled plow and the Moline Champion Corn Planter brought rapid growth to the company. By 1915 the firm had more than 200 traveling salesmen in the United States and abroad, and 3,000 employees in its numerous factories in Illinois, Wisconsin and Minnesota. This company later became Minneapolis Moline, which went out of business locally in the early 1950s leaving many long time employees and retirees without any benefits.

Deere & Mansur, established in 1877, was the third corn planter factory in the nation and soon became the largest manufacturer of corn planters and disc harrows in the world. Early in the 20th century the Deere Harvester Works in East Moline was constructed as a part of the operation. The 10-acre plant was extremely modern for its day. Its reinforced concrete buildings were fireproof and had an independent power plant for steam heat, total electric power, elevators, employee reading rooms, showers and their own firefighting equipment.

Other area manufacturers were a part of the overall agricultural industry: Moline Wheel, Sechler Carriage, Velie Carriage, Cooper Saddlery, Moline Wagon and countless small job shops.

The Illinois side of the Mississippi held the significant share of the area's farm equipment industry, at least in the early years. As early as 1846, W. Skinner and Company's Davenport Plow Factory was doing business at Rock Island (now Pershing) and 3rd streets in Davenport. This business begun by "Honest John" Bechtel was the largest agricultural firm in Iowa at about the time of the Civil War. It had $25,000 in capital and an annual production of 3,500 plows, 200 cultivators and 200 double and single plows. John Herman's Excelsior Agricultural Works and Machine Shop on Gaines Street between 3rd and 4th streets was a much smaller Davenport concern with a little over $1,000 in capital. It manufactured a smaller number of assorted agricultural machinery such as reapers and corn shellers. The foundries, the lumber, machinery and parts manufactured on the Iowa side of the Mississippi, and used in conjunction with the Illinois factories, made that part of the area a significant segment of the agricultural manufacturing complex beginning to grow by the mid-19th century.

In 1860 Scott and Rock Island counties were home to 10 factories that made agricultural implements. By 1870 the number grew to 12. Although by 1880 it dropped to only nine, the real growth lay not in the number of factories, but in the rise in capital, which went from $111,000 in 1860 to $1.53 million in 1880. The number of employees rose from 129 in 1860 to 1,481 in 1880. Deere & Company grew significantly in the early part of the 20th century with acquisition of the Van Brunt Manufacturing Company, the Dain Manufacturing Company, Kemp & Burpee, Syracuse Chilled Plow Company, Marseilles Manufacturing Company, the Moline Wagon Works and Deere and Mansur. As one company they could more economically and effectively sell and service products. This is the group that has become today's Deere & Company.

Agricultural manufacturers continued to move in as late as the mid-20th century. They were all branch plants of already established firms such as International Harvester which brought its Farmall Works to Rock Island and its general agricultural line to East Moline; J.I. Case to Bettendorf, and Caterpillar to Davenport and Bettendorf.

OVERHEAD BELTS TO DRIVE THE MACHINES CAN BE SEEN IN THIS INTERIOR VIEW OF A DEERE & COMPANY SHOP.

DEERE'S FORGE SHOP BECAME ONE OF THE LARGEST IN THE MIDWEST. THE BELT DRIVES COMING FROM A SINGLE SHAFT ARE EVIDENT.

THE GRINDING SHOP OF DEERE & COMPANY WAS ALMOST A BLOCK LONG AND STILL DEPENDED HEAVILY ON NATURAL LIGHT FILTERING IN FROM OVERHEAD AND SIDEWALL WINDOWS.

THE SUCCESS OF DEERE &
COMPANY AND THE CONTINUED
HARDWORKING MORAL TONE OF
MOLINE WERE DUE IN PART TO
THE ACTIVE RECRUITMENT OF
INDUSTRIOUS IMMIGRANTS FROM
GERMANY, BELGIUM AND SWEDEN.
THE COMPANY HELPED SUPPLY
INEXPENSIVE HOUSING AND
HOMESPUN ENTERTAINMENT FOR
THE MEN WHO CAME AND WORKED
TO BRING THEIR FAMILIES TO
"JOHN DEERE TOWN."

The Quad-Cities has become known as the farm implement capital of the world, and Moline is still often referred to as the Plow City. It was the Deere & Company empire that set work standards, improved the working conditions, first offered the $5 work day to agricultural employees, instituted benefits and became known as the fairest employer in the area. The Deere family broadened its industrial holdings when they opened the Sylvan Steel Mills in 1894, under the direction of Colonel G. Watson French. Basically a rolling and forging operation, the mill produced iron and steel bars, guides, plates and a variety of agricultural shapes. Just before 1900

Republic Iron and Steel of Chicago was formed; along with other small iron and steel firms, the Sylvan Steel Mills became a part of Republic. It remained in operation until the 1960s. During the later years it produced high carbon steel bars from rerolled old railroad rails. Sylvan was farther west than most other rerolling mills and had the pick of the rails from the Western lines. About the same time the machinery was becoming obsolete steel rails were becoming hard to get, so production ended and the company moved out leaving the remnants on Sylvan Island of what had once been a vital Moline industry.

FROM THE 1880S TO THE EARLY 1900S MOLINE BUILT LARGE TWO-STORY ELEMENTARY SCHOOLS THAT WERE ALL SIMILAR IN DESIGN. MOST HAD THE FIRST TWO OR THREE GRADES AND AN AUDITORIUM ON THE FIRST FLOOR WITH THE REMAINING GRADES ON THE SECOND FLOOR. THIS EARLY 20TH CENTURY CLASSROOM WAS TYPICAL.

Moline Comes of Age

As business and industry matured, education kept pace. From the first brick schoolhouse built in the early 1840s, Moline's educational system was a source of pride and a measure of the success of the city. Just before the turn of the century the district built a grand high school on 16th Street just north of 11th Avenue which, because of its configuration, became known as the "castle." Of this building a Brazilian visitor said,

> *"A person who goes from the island of Rock Island to Moline, either by street car, carriage or afoot along the picturesque avenue, will see a mansion at the foot of a hill as he enters Moline. This is the nicest structure in that city, elegant, but not luxurious, surrounded by a large and nice lawn, dominated by the sight of the Mississippi. This mansion does not belong to any nabob as one would easily presume, less still a baron or prince — it is only Moline's school. This school is attended by the sons of factory workers as well as by sons of rich businessmen and industrialists. Thus, children get accustomed to equality when still young, learning to respect others for their moral and intellectual qualities. There they are taught the true principles of freedom, independence of character, love of their country and work, acquiring the sense of duty and true respect of the laws which will never mean subservience to anybody. There in Moline's school lies the largest secret of the United States."*

MOLINE'S FIRST HIGH SCHOOL WAS OFTEN REFERRED TO AS THE "CASTLE." THE BUILDING SERVED LATER AS CENTRAL GRAMMAR, AN ANNEX TO BOTH THE NEW HIGH SCHOOL AND MOLINE COMMUNITY COLLEGE. IT WAS TORN DOWN TO MAKE A PARKING LOT FOR MOLINE COMMUNITY COLLEGE.

Early in the 20th century with the help of Andrew Carnegie, Moline's new library was built on the corner of 17th Street and 5th Avenue. With the erection a few years later of the new City Hall on 16th Street and 7th Avenue, the business community was firmly established on the south side of the railroad tracks. In 1903 the city engineer reported that the city had made its biggest annual improvements. By then there were 2,180 acres within the city limits, 53 miles of city streets, 11 miles of alleys and 33 miles of sidewalks.

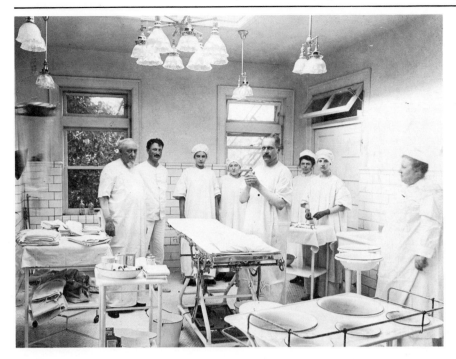

In 1906 Moline's second black church, the Tabernacle Baptist Church of Moline, was organized. The congregation's first church was at 8th Street and 16th Avenue, but in 1912 they moved to 26th Avenue and 15th Street where their sanctuary stands today.

With a prospering City Hospital on the hill, in 1910 the notorious Freeman Cancer Institute opened. It was operated by J.F. Freeman, who arrived in Moline in 1880 and worked as a carpenter for Deere & Mansur for several years and then was employed by Moline Plow. He quit to spend all of his time treating cancer patients. His first patient, "cured" in 1887, reportedly lived 30 more years, according to the *Swedish Element in Illinois*. By 1917 Freeman had treated more than 2,500 cases and, according to the written reports and records of the time, claimed to have cured 90 percent of them without a knife. When the Institute opened at 1330-1334 7th Avenue, Freeman's son, Dr. D.B. Freeman, a graduate of the University of Iowa, worked with him.

The early industrialization of the waterfront and the subsequent growth of manufacturing increased the city's problems caused by the Rock Island Rapids. The business leaders became more vocal in their demands for river access and a guaranteed channel.

Early river surveys made by Robert E. Lee and subsequent government engineers recommended a number of ways to alleviate the navigation bottleneck through the Rock Island Rapids. A lateral dam of stone, sand and rock was designed, and work was begun at several locations along the length of the dam site. Parts of the channel were dredged, but the action of the river filled these in again. By the early 1900s the first lateral dams had been joined into one long dam that extended from the east border of Moline to about 23rd Street where a break was left for navigation. Then the dam began again joining the east end of Benham's Island near Arsenal Island. Portions of this look now like a narrow island along the edge of the old Arsenal Canal, and other portions of it are barely visible as rocks during low water. Locally it is known as the "wing dam." In 1907 when the Moline Lock was opened, giving Moline a navigable harbor for the first time, the wing dam was important. The remains of the old lock are standing along the northeast end of Arsenal Island to Benham's Island at just about the place where Sears built his last mill. In addition to improving access to Moline and giving its manufacturers river transportation facilities, this lock was intended to improve three miles of the rapids. River shipping from Moline never caught on, and after 1909 use declined.

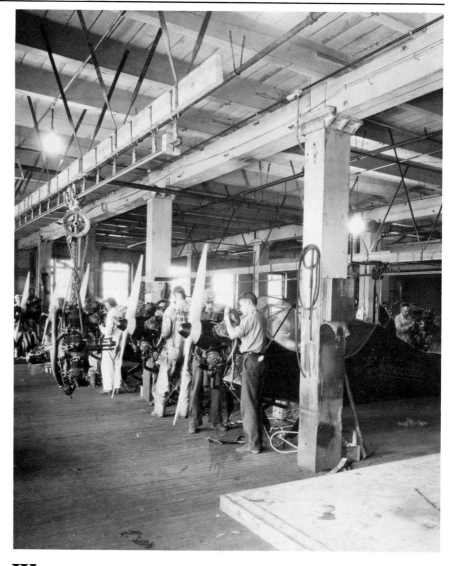

With a well established agricultural industry, some manufacturers became intrigued with the new automobiles, and in the early 1900s several models were manufactured in Moline. Perhaps the least known was the Midland which before 1910 was said to have been driven from Moline to San Francisco and back. The Deere-Clark was in production in 1906, and the Moline-Knight from 1917-1921. As early as 1911, the Drednought manufactured by Moline Automobile Company had a self-starter and a presto-lite tank for lights. It sold for $1,700. However, it was the Velie, advertised as having airplane-type motors, that became the best known automobile made in Moline. Willard Lamb Velie, the grandson of John Deere, founded the Velie Carriage Company and developed the first Velie automobile as early as 1907. He began production in 1908. The ad for the Velie Six asked the question,

"How much of the money you put into your motor car do you take out in actual service and satisfaction? For years automobile manufacturers have been trying to develop a 'Six' that would operate at low cost. Until the appearance of the new Velie 'Six' (1,000 pounds lighter), not one manufacturer touched the real vital spot. Weight is the big factor that governs expense. Cut down weight, and the properly built 'Six' costs no more to run than the average four-cylinder car."

The first Velie car, "Olde Maude" had "Made in Moline" on its nameplate, and "the name insures quality" stamped on every instruction book. Other Velie cars gained national attention and Moline was considered in contention to become the center of auto production. The car companies employed 1,500 men in their 3rd Avenue factories with estimates that between 75,000 -100,000 Velies alone were made here in 20 years.

Like the car, the Velie Monocoupe airplane was built in Moline. Willard Velie with his son in 1919, through the Velie Motor Corporation, designed and built the first six-cylinder valve-in-head airplane motor. They later developed the famous five-cylinder radial aircraft engine which powered their renowned two-place monocoupe. The early motors were rated at 62 horsepower at 2,000 rpm and were for their time true pioneers of the air age. The most successful of the early Velie planes was designed with a closed cabin body and instrumentation developed by Don Luscombe and Clayton Folkerts in Bettendorf in 1926 and powered by the famous Velie engine. This resulted in the founding of Mono Aircraft, Inc., a subsidiary of the Velie Motor Corporation. Within months a newer Velie engine was introduced featuring aluminum cylinder heads and sodium valves. In the 1928 National Air Races in Los Angeles the Velie Monocoupe scored its first victory in close-course racing, winning a number of events, averaging just over 100 miles per hour against competition flying aircraft with far greater horsepower. The Velie car and the Velie Monocoupe were setting national standards when the untimely death of both Velies, father and son, within a few months brought the car and airplane to an end in Moline.

But the age of flight had come to town. Charles Deere became a member of the Aero Club of America and a licensed pilot in 1916, and in 1919 Rusty Campbell and Roy McElvain brought two planes to Moline and sold rides from a pasture on the old Midvale Farm. In the early '20s Campbell took over the operation of the newly established Franning Field in association with Gustaf DeSchepper, Moline's first civilian pilot, Floyd Kenner and Dr. C. Sloan. In the '20s Franning Field hosted army squadrons and the National Air Races. It became one of the nation's first airports to handle airmail and then passengers.

World War I and the flu epidemic afterward had changed life in Moline. Its young men were fighting on foreign soil and the industries suffered without the younger workers. The Woman's Christian Temperance Union had for two decades or more been influencing the political direction of the city. Mayoral candidates of the same party ran in the primaries on who was the most temperate. With the end of the war came a changing populace. There was peace, the soldiers were home, money was more plentiful, manufacturing and the economy were returning to normal. But the "boys" who came back to Moline were not quite so sure they wanted prohibition, absolute church doctrine and living by the staid rules of yesterday. They had seen the world.

A morality gap was brought on in part by the war, and in part by the changing lifestyles. A growing number of amusements, new theatres, bowling alleys, pool parlors and soda shops sprang up. But even though the strings of austerity might have frayed a bit in Moline, by the mid-'20s when the "boys" became family men and members of the social order, the city began again to slip back into the staid personality it had held for almost a hundred years. In the words of Silas Leas,

"Moline was a very moral and temperate place in comparison with frontier towns generally. It had a population of about three thousand before any liquor was legally sold. This was due in some great measure to the influence of the first arrivals. They chose from among those who sought new homes and business opportunities here, men of character and principal. They aided them to get started in the community, while the other element were encouraged to go elsewhere."

Once again Moline was becoming the moral and temperate place of the Quad-Cities.

THE VELIE MANSION WAS THE LARGEST AND MOST PALATIAL OF ITS TIME IN THE AREA. IT WAS RESPLENDENT IN AN ERA OF AFFLUENCE AND ELEGANCE. IT BECAME THE PLANTATION RESTAURANT.

FIFTH AVENUE MOLINE WELCOMED HOME THE MEN RETURNING FROM THE WAR. OF ALL THE BUSINESSES IN THIS PHOTOGRAPH ONLY JOSEPHSON'S REMAINS IN THE EARLY 1980S.

ARSENAL

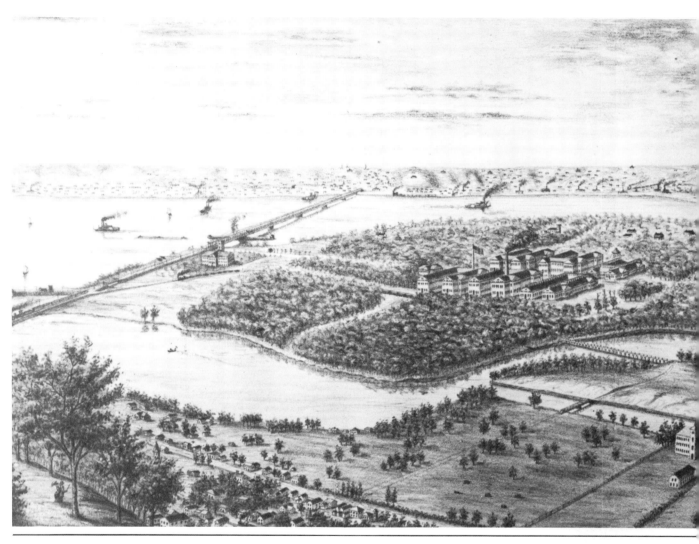

BY ROBERT BOUILLY

Three days after Confederate troops fired on Fort Sumter on April 12, 1861, President Lincoln asked for 75,000 ninety-day volunteers for the Army. In both Iowa and Illinois volunteers quickly responded to the state calls for troops. Within days the Davenport German community furnished a company in the first Iowa regiment, led by August Wentz. They soon departed for Missouri, clothed in uniforms sewn by the ladies of the town and armed with an assortment of guns scavenged from various state armories. In the zeal so typical early in the war, they stayed in southwestern Missouri a whole month beyond the expiration of their enlistments to participate in the first western battle, at Wilson's Creek, on August 10, 1861. Rock Island was just as eager to support the war and sent its first company off under a flag made from bunting used at a Senator Stephen A. Douglas speech. The first casualty from Rock Island was not even an American citizen but an Irishman in the Irish, or Mulligan, Regiment who died in the Battle of Belmont.

Unlike the conduct of more recent wars which found the national government organizing and directing the fight, the Civil War was fought

ISLAND

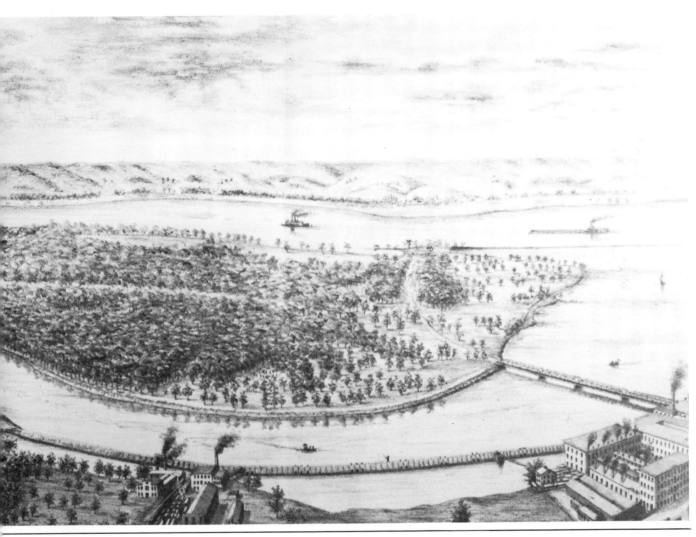

largely by the states. It was the states which raised the troops and initially supported them. Most troops fought in companies made up of local men, in regiments made up exclusively from state companies. This pattern of military organization, combined with the accidents of geography, made the local Civil War experience of Scott and Rock Island counties quite different in several respects.

Davenport became the largest Iowa collection center for troops. The heavy concentration of population in eastern Iowa and the availability of transportation on the Mississippi River made such river cities as Dubuque, Davenport and Keokuk the military collection and training points. Because the telegraph went no further west than Davenport, Governor Kirkwood of Iowa had to shift portions of his administration from Iowa City (then the state capitol) to Davenport in order to keep abreast of the news. His adjutant general, Nathaniel Baker, for example, conducted the war effort from a popular Davenport hotel, the Burtis House. Moreover, both Army Brigadier General B.S. Roberts, in command of the Military District of Iowa, and the provost marshal for the Second District of Iowa made their headquarters in Davenport.

COLONEL W.D. FLAGLER COMMISSIONED THIS 1876 DRAWING OF THE ROCK ISLAND ARSENAL TO ILLUSTRATE HIS PUBLISHED ACCOUNT OF THE PROGRESS HE HAD MADE. THE TAILRACE IN THE FOREGROUND, WHICH WAS FILLED IN AT THE TURN OF THE CENTURY, IS CLEARLY VISIBLE.

Over the course of the war the military established five military camps, one of which was later split into two camps, on the outskirts of the city. The best known was Camp McClellan located on what is now the McClellan Heights area. It was used mostly during the navigation seasons as a gathering place for the troops. By the end of the war 40,000 of the 80,000 troops from Iowa passed through its gates. In April 1863 the military authorities isolated a section of the camp by building a wall and renaming it Camp Kearney. Here the government deposited one Winnebago and 277 Sioux Indian braves, 16 squaws and two children for the duration of the war. All the warriors had been convicted of crimes in a bloody uprising in southern Minnesota which took the lives of about 750 people. Military authorities hanged 38 Indians at Mankato, Minnesota, and only President Lincoln's personal intervention saved these Indians from a similar fate. Nearly 100 died at the camp before they joined remnants of their tribe in the Dakotas in 1866.

Camp Hendershott was a cavalry camp established in October 1862 just southeast of the present location of St. Ambrose College. Daily the cavalry rode through town to water the horses at the river and, almost as frequently, they agitated the townspeople with their obstreperous and disorderly behavior. Eventually several members of the cavalry broke up Conrad Ascherman's bar and escaped legal retribution. Under pressure from the city, the adjutant general abandoned the camp and established a new one in July 1863 further from town, south of Duck Creek and west of what is now the Oakdale cemetery. At first called Camp Roberts and later Camp Kinsman, the site eventually became the Iowa Soldiers' Orphans' Home.

Two other military camps existed briefly. Camp Joe Holt, bounded by 13th and Locust, and Pershing and Perry streets, was laid out in September 1861 and flourished for only a few months. Similarly, Camp Herron existed only briefly on top of the hill around Farnam Street where it was laid out in October 1862.

In all, Davenport was a military entrepot. It trained, equipped and housed thousands of soldiers while it also served as a government horse-buying center. Moreover, Camp McClellan possessed one of the state's few military hospitals.

*THE BOARD AND BATTEN CON-
STRUCTION OF THE HOSPITAL
BUILDING AT CAMP MCCLELLAN
WAS TYPICAL OF TEMPORARY
MILITARY CONSTRUCTION DURING
THE CIVIL WAR.*

In contrast, Rock Island and Moline had no military camps. Briefly Rock Island housed some of the troops destined for Arsenal Island, and only with the ice bridge in winter did the Illinois side have to endure the ill-mannered soldiers from the Iowa camps. Unlike Davenport, Rock Island County was on the periphery of the war effort. Its volunteers went off to the likes of Ft. Douglas in Chicago, Camp Yates in Springfield or Camp Long in Dixon.

In the fall of 1863, not the state, but the federal government brought something of a military presence to the Illinois side in the shape of a prison camp on the island. Ultimately 12,000 Confederate prisoners passed through its gates. Almost 2,000 of them died and are buried in both the Confederate and National Cemeteries on the island. Margaret Mitchell in her famous novel, *Gone with the Wind*, characterized the prison as the "Andersonville of the North." In reality the Rock Island Barracks, as it was officially called, was an average prison. A prisoner's chance for survival was considerably less, for example, in the prison at Alton, Illinois.

Volunteers were the backbone of the Army, and over the course of the war Scott County provided 4,000 and Rock Island County 2,299. Two hundred and twenty-two from Scott County and 226 from Rock Island County never came home again, including General John Buford, the cavalry officer who initiated the Battle of Gettysburg. The volunteers fought mainly in the western armies. They kept Missouri in the Union at Wilson's Creek and opened the Mississippi River at Belmont, Island No. 10, Fort Donaldson and Vicksburg; they held the Confederate armies at bay at Shiloh, Murfreesboro and Chickamauga; they dismembered the Confederacy at Chattanooga, Kenesaw Mountain and Atlanta.

Relief efforts were quite similar on both sides of the river in contrast to the marked difference in military presences. Volunteerism and aid supplied at the county level were the two major forms of relief. Without the substantial federal relief structure we are used to today, Americans during the Civil War had to provide double relief — financial assistance to families who sent their men off to the war and both medical aid and sundry supplies to the troops in the field. Neither task was easy. The counties helped the families at home and local ladies' soldiers' aid societies headed much of the voluntary aid effort for the troops.

Soldiers were expected to use their small salaries to support both themselves and their families. A private who made a grand total of $11 a month was expected to resist the temptation of the sutlers who followed the armies offering small amenities such as tobacco and extra clothing. Instead, the soldiers were supposed to send money home through private parties. In February 1862 Henry Dart & Sons, the large Rock Island grocer, for example, received $1,310 from members of Company D of the 12th Illinois Volunteers stationed at Paducah, Kentucky, with a list that detailed how the money should be distributed.

The Rock Island County Board of Supervisors appropriated $3,000 to aid the families of soldiers in the field soon after war broke out. With limited resources and a feeling that soldiers were not sending enough money home to their families, the board announced in February 1862 that it would discontinue the aid. Amid great protest the board reconsidered its stand, and beginning in June paid each wife or widow of a soldier $4 and each child $1 per month until the end of the war. Scott County provided aid in much the same way to its citizens.

Congress attempted to aid the troops with legislation which set up a national voluntary organization known as the Sanitary Commission. Through regional offices like the one in Chicago, the commission tried to provide creature comforts and medical aid to the soldiers as supplements to the inadequate services provided by the Army. Local ladies' aid societies formed under its auspices but they usually worked as local entities sending aid directly to the hometown soldiers. In a typical request after the Union victory at Fort Donaldson, Governor Yates of Illinois wired the local societies with a simple request. "Send surgeons, friends and clothing for the wounded." Rock Island responded by sending Dr. Truesdale, Mr. Swiller and Mr. Steel as well as clothing and hospital supplies. Davenport also responded. Days later the Davenport delegation returned in boxcars filled with the wounded and the dead. As the war dragged on, the communities sent out similar delegations to the battlefield.

CONFEDERATE ARMY PRISONERS LINED UP FOR A REVIEW AT THE ROCK ISLAND BARRACKS. IN THE FOREGROUND IS A SPINDLY WOODEN HORSE WITH ITS HEAD ARCHED OVER THE CULVERT. PRISONERS WHO WERE PUNISHED FOR BREACHES OF CAMP DISCIPLINE WERE FORCED TO SIT ASTRIDE THE HORSE FOR AN EXTENDED PERIOD.

*ANNIE WITTENMYER, WHOSE
CONCERN FOR THE WELFARE OF
CIVIL WAR ORPHANS LED HER TO
FOUND THE HOME THAT BEARS
HER NAME.*

The ladies raised money at concerts, socials, sanitary fairs (now we would call them flea markets) and by solicitations door to door. They sent forth to the soldiers bed ticking, preserves, newspapers, whiskey, shirts and socks and packages of lint for bandages. They helped supplement aid to soldiers' families in the counties and even provided supplies to the Confederate Prison Camp on Rock Island.

As the war relentlessly produced casualties the relief effort had to address the postwar wreckage of broken homes. In Davenport Annie Wittenmyer from Keokuk established the Iowa Soldiers' Orphans' Home. In 1864 she traveled to Washington, D.C., and persuaded the federal government to donate both the land and buildings at Camp Kinsman for the home. In 1866 she returned to Davenport from Keokuk to head the home for two years as matron. The institution still stands, now an administration center for problem children, and Davenport has come to claim Annie Wittenmyer as its own. With the end of the war Illinois established its orphans' home at Normal and in September 1867 Rock Island County sent its first 20 orphans there.

Little is left now to remind us of the war — a cemetery for prisoners on Arsenal Island, a center for problem children and two monuments — one on the lawn of the Rock Island courthouse, the other in the middle of Main Street east of Central High School in Davenport.

The Development and Growth of Rock Island Arsenal

Rock Island Arsenal sits in the Mississippi River surrounded by the Quad-Cities. It is the product of military interest in the area since at least 1825. Before there was any thought of an arsenal the Army built Fort Armstrong on the western tip of Rock Island, which it abandoned in 1836 after the Indians moved out of the area. The fort served as an Indian agency for a few years. Then in 1840 the Army reoccupied it for use as a depot. This renewed activity did not last long because in 1845 relations with Mexico deteriorated to the point that the Army withdrew all its stores to St. Louis in preparation for the coming war. Thereafter the island became simply a playground as Fort Armstrong fell into ruin. Boys often went over to play "soldier" around the fort and picnickers frequented the island. In 1859, for instance, the Rock Island high school had its spring picnic there and crowned Miss Susan Buford queen of the May.

As often happens to abandoned structures, arson took its toll on the old fort. In 1855 and again in 1859 parts of the fort burned. Finally in 1864 workmen dismantled the remaining portions of the fort for construction materials. The Army had only a passive interest in the future of the island. Local citizens were much more actively interested. Near Moline several manufacturing enterprises developed on the island in the 1850s. They manufactured such items as shingles and paper pails. They sawed lumber and quarried stone. The railroad cut down almost all the trees for ties and squatters spotted the landscape with small farms.

The Civil War was to change all this. When confederate forces destroyed the Harper's Ferry Armory in April 1861 Congress and the Army suddenly had to find a replacement. Ultimately that replacement became Rock Island Arsenal.

*THIS FIRST PERMANENT BUILDING
AT THE SOLDIERS' ORPHANS'
HOME, FOUNDED BY ANNIE
WITTENMYER, BURNED IN 1889.*

The Arsenal developed most of its current functions and capacity in the period from 1862 through the end of World War I in 1918. The only major changes since 1918 have been the placement of a command headquarters at the arsenal after the Korean War, the demise of harnessmaking and the removal of tank production to Michigan on the eve of World War II.

Today the arsenal functions as a depot through the storage and distribution of Army supplies. More importantly, the Rock Island Arsenal manufactures

war materiel in two broad areas. Its primary function today is to
manufacture a great variety of small job lot components or assemblies
which private industry cannot supply at economical prices. The arsenal also
performs a number of highly specialized manufacturing processes such as
the assembly and repair of machine guns and towed artillery gun carriages
as well as the production of artillery mounts and recoil mechanisms.
The command located at Rock Island is called the U.S. Army Armament
Materiel Readiness Command — ARRCOM for short. The command
procures and distributes guns to the Army and to foreign customers.
Similarly it procures and distributes ammunition to all the American armed
services and to foreign customers. It is a subordinate command of
DARCOM (the U.S. Army Materiel Development and Readiness
Command) which does all the buying, selling and distributing of materiel for
the Army. The U.S. Army Armament Materiel Readiness Command
employs more than 4,000 people and is essentially an indirect successor of
the old Ordnance Corps. A good share of the command employees work in
the Headquarters at the Rock Island Arsenal. The arsenal itself currently
employs about 2,500 people.
Over the years the development of the Rock Island Arsenal has been largely
due to the political exploitation of its location and facilities. The
development of the arsenal involved both decisions made by Congress and a
number of internal Ordnance Corps decisions as to the location of various
manufacturing functions within the arsenal system. In virtually all these
decisions the local communities played a contributing role.
During the Civil War Bailey Davenport, the son of George Davenport, was
mayor of Rock Island. He led local interests as they began to orchestrate
support for a congressional choice of Rock Island as an arsenal site. Bailey
Davenport had extensive real estate interest in the area and prompted a
local newspaper, the Rock Island *Argus*, to publish a series of long articles
advocating the use of the island as an arsenal. Davenport induced the City
Council to appropriate $1,600 for the publication of a promotional pamphlet
and for other expenses. The pamphlet amplified an earlier citizens'
memorial and argued that the armory should be located in the upper
Mississippi Valley at Rock Island. Here it would be centrally located with
access to good river and railroad transportation and safe from invasion and
destruction in urban riots. Rock Island, the pamphlet argued, was free of
disease and could provide cheap labor, cheap food and lots of coal.
Moreover, the Mississippi River provided a vast potential for water power,
and the initial cost of establishing the arsenal would be cheap since the
government already owned the island.
Bailey Davenport became a member of a committee of 10 who conducted
the campaign. Half the committee members came from Rock Island and the
rest represented Davenport and Moline. One member, Major H.C. Connelly
of Rock Island, went on a tour of every leading city in Missouri, Wisconsin,
Minnesota, Iowa and Illinois to promote republication of the *Argus* articles
in the local newspapers. In 1861 and 1862 several committee members spent
considerable time in Washington, D.C., lobbying for the adoption of bills
introduced by Senator James W. Grimes of Iowa.

The arsenal promoters used a simple legislative strategy to get a bill
enacted which would establish an arsenal at Rock Island. The local
committee realized that neither Illinois senator was particularly interested
in Rock Island. The senators acted true to form in the final debate when
both supported other arsenal locations, and one — Senator Orville H.
Browning from Quincy — refused to vote for Rock Island when it was the
only choice left. Instead, the committee chose to work with Iowa's Senator
Grimes. A House bill presented local interests with a wide-open opportunity
to promote the location of an arsenal virtually anywhere in the Old
Northwest. Consequently, the committee believed that it would be virtually
impossible to get a bill out of the House of Representatives that would
name Rock Island as the arsenal site. Furthermore, they knew that a

number of Illinois congressmen clearly favored the location of an arsenal in Chicago. The committee believed that if they could get a bill passed in the Senate which named Rock Island, they could then get passed in the House. Their strategy worked with only slight modification. Senator Grimes' bill originally called for the building of an arsenal for the construction, repair and deposit of arms at Rock Island. But in order to gain enough support for passage the committee supported changes to the bill which called on the Army to establish three lesser arsenals at Indianapolis, Indiana; Columbus, Ohio; and Rock Island. These arsenals would be for repair and deposit only — not manufacturing. The bill passed first the Senate and then the House, and became law on July 11, 1862. The law did not solve the pressing problem of the moment because it did not provide a successor to the Harper's Ferry Armory.

Creation of even a small arsenal of deposit and repair at Rock Island presented a formidable task. Over the years the lack of a military presence on the island had led to ambiguity as to ownership of the land. A number of legal and quasi-legal claims to the land left only 702 of the Island's 947 acres clearly in the hands of the War Department by 1862. The first Arsenal commander, Major Charles P. Kingsbury, had constant problems with land ownership and prevailed upon the chief of ordnance to support legislation which would secure for the Army clear ownership of the whole island. Consequently, in the next session of Congress, Representative Elihu B. Washburn from Illinois introduced legislation authorizing the Army to take possession of the whole island and settle all legal claims to the land. The wording of the bill was much stronger than the 1862 bill because it described the arsenal as one of construction, deposit and repair. When the bill became law April 19, 1864, the arsenal finally possessed the potential to succeed the Harper's Ferry Armory as a major manufacturing establishment.

Fortunately for Rock Island, the Army Ordnance Department favored the development of a major arsenal on the island. As early as December 1860 the Department publicly recommended a reduction in the number of arsenals of construction to four — one each in the East, the South, the West and the Pacific. When Congress designated Rock Island — in the West — as an arsenal of construction the Army chose to honor its intent. On June 3, 1864, the chief of ordnance, Brigadier General George D. Ramsay, reviewed the qualifications of Rock Island as a replacement for Harper's Ferry in a letter to Secretary of War Edwin Stanton. He concluded that "after a careful study of this question of location, there is no position which to my mind affords so many advantages and at the same time presents so few objections as Rock Island, in the Mississippi River." His reasons for recommending Rock Island were essentially the same as those put forth in the promotional pamphlet sponsored by Bailey Davenport. Ramsay went on to urge that the plans for an armory that had been developed at Springfield in the winter of 1863 should be applied immediately to Rock Island. Years later in 1871 General A.B. Dyer, chief of ordnance, elaborated on his predecessor's view of Rock Island:

> It seems manifest that Congress intended that...[Rock Island Arsenal] should be made the great arsenal of deposit and construction for the Mississippi Valley, and that it should possess the manufacturing capacities of the national armory at Springfield, Massachusetts, and of one of our largest arsenals of construction, and it was planned with that end in view, and has been so built.

After the Civil War the Ordnance Department continued to consolidate the arsenal system along the lines of its 1860 pronouncement. It developed a plan to build a major arsenal of construction outside of New York City to complement the development of the Rock Island Arsenal in the West and Benecia Arsenal on San Francisco Bay. After the Civil War the Ordnance Corps had no interest in placing a construction arsenal in the South.

A DRAWING OF THE ARSENAL PRINTED IN 1888 REFLECTS THE EARLY PLANS BEFORE 1875, WITH SMOKESTACKS FOR EACH BUILDING, THE STOREHOUSES BEHIND EACH WORKSHOP AND THE ROOFLESS WATER RESERVOIR ON THE EXTREME LEFT.

Congress never approved the great New York City arsenal but continued to pump construction money into Rock Island for the next 25 years. Meanwhile, from 1861 to 1879, the Ordnance Corps reduced its arsenal system by disposing of 12 smaller arsenals. Clearly the Corps expected the Rock Island Arsenal to be an important part of the post-Civil War arsenal system.

Actual construction of the arsenal began in September 1863 on the large storehouse which was to be one of three buildings. This became what is now known as the Clock Tower and is currently occupied by the Rock Island District Corps of Engineers.

Work on the building proceeded by fits and starts. Major Kingsbury supervised the project and encountered numerous difficulties. He ran into constant jurisdictional disputes with the officials of the Confederate Prison Camp who also occupied the island and into a seemingly endless series of contractual and financial problems. When no one in the area would honor the government's St. Louis bank drafts, he had to return them to Washington. When the stone contractor held up deliveries because he wanted more money, Kingsbury facilitated a renegotiation of the contract, only to see the contractor abscond with the money, leaving the government with additional obligations. At about the same time news came that Congress had approved the larger construction arsenal and all work on the clock tower building ground to a halt. With only a basement and part of the first floor completed, Kingsbury gave up in frustration. In 1865 he asked to be relieved from command at Rock Island and was replaced by Brevet Brigadier General Thomas J. Rodman.

THOMAS JACKSON RODMAN, COMMANDING OFFICER AND DESIGNER OF ROCK ISLAND ARSENAL, 1865-1871.

The choice of Rodman to plan and supervise the construction of the arsenal was fortuitous. Rodman was a man of grand architectural plans. Previously he had come under congressional fire for his lavish construction of an officers' quarters at Watertown Arsenal in Massachusetts. At Rock Island, he planned even more grandly. Rodman designed a manufacturing complex of 10 large shops in the middle of the island rather than at the western end as the previous plans had called for. The shop complex in the middle of the island allowed for expansion of the shops and placed them within reach of a dam designed to provide waterpower. These 10 shops and the dam became the core of the arsenal. They still stand today. The shops face each other in two rows. The northern five shops were designated for use as an armory, the southern shops as an arsenal. The middle shop in each row is one story and the rest are three stories tall. All have the same "U" shaped floor plan with 300-foot by 60-foot wings jutting back from a 210-foot by 60-

foot base. The two-story shops also have full basements. Each covers more than an acre, and all are alike with their limestone facades of pillowed blocks. They are the core of a national historic site and constitute one of the largest single American construction projects in the last half of the 19th century.

The other buildings and structures from the original plan match the core shops in design and grandeur. The limestone quarters for the commanding officer has more than 19,000 square feet of floor space, which makes it second in size only to the White House as a government residence. The power dam, too, which lies unobtrusively in the backwater of Sylvan Slough, was once grand. It stood upon its completion in 1891 as the second most powerful dam in the United States next to Niagara Falls.

General Rodman conceived the broad outline of the arsenal and began vigorously to execute it. He finished the Clock Tower begun by Kingsbury, built a new railroad and vehicle bridge to Davenport on the site of the present swing bridge and began to build the first of the great stone shops. In anticipation of their completion, he built the first government dam for waterpower and built a very long tailrace along the Moline waterfront to provide adequate power for a string of private manufacturers including the John Deere and Williams, White Companies. As a part of the tailrace project he created Sylvan Island by cutting a channel for the river through solid limestone across a neck of land. Finally, he almost completed the magnificent Quarters One which meant so much to him. Tragically, he died in 1871 having only begun the arsenal which was to be the capstone of his career.

Contrary to popular belief he never got a chance to live in his new quarters. He probably would be pleased to know now that so much of his construction work is considered historically significant. Besides Rock Island Arsenal both the quarters he built in Watertown, Massachusetts, and the home he purchased in Rock Island are on the National Register of Historic Places. He had style.

CONSTRUCTION OF THE 10 STONE SHOPS AT THE ARSENAL BEGAN IN 1867 AND CONTINUED UNTIL 1890. THIS PHOTO WAS TAKEN ABOUT 1878 FROM ONE OF THE WATER POWER TOWERS.

ROOF CONSTRUCTION ON A STONE
SHOP. THIS IS PROBABLY SHOP I IN
1889. THE IRON GIRDERS ARE SET
IN PLACE ON ONE WALL AND RIDE
ON BEARINGS IN THE OPPOSITE
WALL TO ALLOW FOR EXPANSION.

Rodman's untimely death left development of his grand plan to his
successor, Major D.W. Flagler. The execution of the final designs for the
buildings and construction of much of the arsenal were Flagler's work. Over
15 years from 1871 to 1876 Flagler vigorously constructed the buildings and
promoted their use. He did so in the face of peculiar labor and funding
constraints. Congress in those days stipulated that all appropriations had to
be spent in the fiscal year they were appropriated for. Money could not be
carried over from year to year. This led to a curious construction cycle.
Appropriations would be approved by Congress some time in March or April
for the fiscal year beginning in July. There would be a massive hiring of
stonecutters and laborers in midsummer and frantic activity on the
buildings until just before Christmas when virtually all the men would get
laid off until the next summer when the infusion of money for the next fiscal
year would trigger a repeat of the cycle.
The stone for the buildings came from the Midwest. Much of it came from
Joliet, some from Grafton, Illinois, and Berea, Ohio, a suburb of Cleveland.
Several buildings are constructed of stone from the Anamosa, Iowa, prison
quarries.

Much of the manufacturing effort at the arsenal before the Spanish-
American War concentrated on construction of the buildings. The rolling
mill produced most of the roof trusses and machinery shafting from 1878 to
1900. The foundry and machine shop made much of the machinery and
building hardware such as the locks and stairways. The carpenter shop
made the window frames. Contract labor did some of the work while civilian
employees and soldiers did other portions of the job. In the construction
period the arsenal was virtually a self-contained manufactory. Even with all
the work done by the workers employed at the arsenal, the government still
spent about $12 million in its construction and on manufacturing equipment
for the shops by the turn of the century.
At first the arsenal acted as a depot. As early as 1869 the arsenal reported
that it had cleaned and packed 55,361 pieces of infantry accouterments,
36,340 pieces of horse equipment and 503 sets of artillery during the year.
This was strictly hand work and typically a depot function which required
little if any machinery.
The depot function at Rock Island increased in the next several years as the
Ordnance Department closed several depots. In September 1873 the depot
at Omaha, Nebraska, closed and in May of 1874 the Ordnance Department
broke up the Leavenworth, Kansas, depot. Subsequently the commander of
the Rock Island Arsenal noted that in 1875 Rock Island supplied nearly all
the ordnance stores required for the Army in the "Indian Country."
Manufacturing began slowly, in July 1875. In May the chief of ordnance,
Stephen V. Benet, had visited Rock Island. Soon thereafter he gave Major

LIEUTENANT COLONEL D.W.
FLAGLER, COMMANDER OF THE
ARSENAL, 1871-1886. FLAGLER
TRANSLATED GENERAL RODMAN'S
PLANS INTO BRICK AND MORTAR.
IN LATER YEARS, HE BECAME
CHIEF OF THE ARMY'S ORDINANCE
CORPS.

Flagler the go-ahead to begin the manufacture of infantry and cavalry equipment. Only a few months earlier he had ordered the arsenal to begin breaking up obsolete Civil War ammunition. Later a newspaper article noted:

> Some 50 or 60 men are employed at Rock Island Arsenal manufacturing infantry equipments, covering saddles and doing miscellaneous leather work for the cavalry arm of the service. This is the first manufacturing ever done in the way of equipments for the Army at this arsenal.

Four years later, in April 1879, the same paper reported that 280 men were employed on the island and in the shops. By 1897, the Army employed 484.

POWER FOR THE ARSENAL CAME FROM A DAM IN SYLVAN SLOUGH. A FLOOD IN 1888 DESTROYED THE FIRST GOVERNMENT DAM. HERE FOREMAN ROBERT MCFARLAND SURVEYS HIS CONSTRUCTION CREW IN LATE 1889. TYPICAL OF THE GOVERNMENT'S FRUGALITY ARE THE ARTILLERY CARTRIDGES USED AS COUNTERWEIGHTS ON THE CRANES.

In the 1880s the government made a key decision which had considerable indirect impact on the arsenal at Rock Island. The decision affected the Watervliet Arsenal in New York directly. Rapid post-Civil War developments in steel cannon technology eventually forced the War Department and Congress to realize that its Civil War-era heavy weapons had become obsolete and that the Army and Navy would have to begin a rearmament program. The naval appropriations bill of March 3, 1883, directed that an Army-Navy Gun Foundry Board be established to determine which of the government navy yards or arsenals could best be "adapted for the establishment of a Government foundry." A couple of boards and several recommendations later the Navy decided to build a gunyard at the Washington Navy Yard: the Army chose Watervliet Arsenal.

Rock Island was not even considered as a possible location. When local interests suggested that the Ordnance Department should locate the gun tube foundry at Rock Island, the chief of ordnance described the arsenal as too remote from the seaboard and the proving grounds. For once Rock Island's location proved to be a detriment to its expansion. The chief of ordnance believed further that the buildings at Rock Island were not sturdy enough for heavy gun work and lacked adequate light for precision lathe work.

The new gun tube facility at Watervliet forced a reorganization of functions at the Watervliet Arsenal. As a result, in 1891 the Army transferred its manufacture of equipment for soldiers and horses to Rock Island. This transfer gave no new function to Rock Island but it did substantially increase the harness work and light equipment production that had begun in 1875.

BEFORE 1902, WHEN THE ARSENAL SWITCHED TO ELECTRIC POWER, WIRE CABLES, SUSPENDED FROM A SERIES OF TOWERS, MECHANICALLY TRANSMITTED ABOUT 300 HORSEPOWER TO THE MACHINERY IN THE SHOPS. THE GUN CARRIAGE AND LIMBER IN THE FOREGROUND WERE PRODUCTS OF THE ARSENAL DURING THE LATE 19TH CENTURY.

The new gun tube foundry was designed to produce large caliber seacoast defense guns and this meant that the Watertown Arsenal in Massachussetts would make the new, heavier gun carriages. As Watertown began to work on the heavy gun carriages, Rock Island Arsenal began to inherit from Watertown the job of making lighter carriages for guns up to seven inches in caliber. This was a new function for the Arsenal. The transfer of these functions from Watervliet and Watertown gave Rock Island its first significant role as a manufacturing arsenal. The arsenal completed its first gun carriage in 1894 but never produced more than 50 in a year before World War I. On the eve of the Spanish-American War the manufacturing activity at Rock Island Arsenal occupied only one of the 10 shops and a portion of another. The rest were used for storage.

The war with Spain brought a tremendous spurt of activity to the Arsenal. Employment reached a peak of 2,900 only to fall off to 1,200-1,500 in the immediate post-war years. During the war the arsenal gained no new functions. The war, however, did reveal that the Army's standard rifle was inadequate and prompted the War Department to choose a new rifle design. The department realized that the Springfield Armory could not provide the weapons fast enough, so the chief of ordnance recommended that the Rock Island Arsenal be equipped with a rifle-making capability as a supplement to Springfield Armory's production.

Local businessmen took their cue from the recommendation of the chief of ordnance. Quite suddenly they rediscovered that the community had a substantial stake in keeping up employment at the arsenal. Local business clubs individually and in concert began to actively lobby for the arsenal. Both the Davenport Business Men's Association and the Rock Island Club began efforts which resulted in their sending three lobbyists to Washington, D.C. The War Department and the businessmen met with success in 1899 when Congress appropriated money for a small arms factory. Forty-three years after the destruction of Harper's Ferry the Ordnance Department finally got the chance to realize its early goal of building an armory at Rock Island. After the Arsenal extensively refurbished three shops and furnished them with $800,000 worth of machine tools it assembled its first model 1903 Springfield rifle on December 20, 1904. Over the next 9½ years it turned out more than 234,000 rifles.

TURN-OF-THE-CENTURY RESIDENTS OF THE QUAD-CITY AREA VIEWED THE ARSENAL AS A SCENIC PARK. WITH WOODED ROADS THAT HAD NAMES LIKE BO PEEP LANE, THE ARSENAL HOSTED MANY A SUNDAY AFTERNOON TOUR IN A SURREY. THESE THREE LADIES HAD THEIR PICTURE TAKEN IN THE GUNYARD.

After the Spanish-American War the workforce at the arsenal seldom dipped below 1,200 people, but local businessmen feared the Ordnance Corps would pursue policies which would lead to its closing. In 1905 the Tri-Cities Press Club and the Davenport Business Men's Club importuned Chief of Ordnance William Crozier not to allow further cutbacks in the arsenal work force than had already taken place. They attributed the cutbacks to an unfortunate Ordnance Department policy of emphasizing procurement of munitions from private contractors rather than through government manufacture. General Crozier, in reply, blamed the reductions on the fact that the Army had finally begun to fill its wartime reserves.

Crozier was correct, but he failed to convince Clyde H. Tavenner, a young reporter for the Rock Island *Argus*. Seven years later Tavenner became the congressional representative from the 14th District in Illinois (Rock Island). Tavenner was an ideologue who elevated local support for the arsenal to the level of broad national legislation. With messianic zeal he entered Congress in 1913 determined to defeat Crozier's efforts to foster a private munitions production capability in the United States.

INTERIOR OF THE BLACKSMITH SHOP IN SHOP E IN MAY 1904.

TIN CUPS AND SADDLES, HARNESSES AND CANTEENS WERE SOME OF THE ITEMS MANU- FACTURED AT ROCK ISLAND ARSENAL ON THE EVE OF THE SPANISH-AMERICAN WAR IN 1898. CHILDREN WORKED ALONGSIDE THE MEN.

Tavenner believed that the private munitions manufacturers systematically gouged the War Department through collusion on contract bids and that government production was more efficient than private manufacture. He firmly believed that much of the government ammunition production could be accomplished at Rock Island Arsenal. He initiated an amendment to the 1914 military appropriations bill which forced the government to limit private contracts to 10 percent of the procurement budget. Subsequently, in January 1915, fellow Illinois Congressman Charles McKenzie called for the erection of gun and ammunition plants at Rock Island Arsenal to replace private munitions production.

In the hope of securing more work for the Arsenal, the Davenport Commercial Club arranged for a dinner in September 1915, with all the local business clubs in attendance. The object of the dinner was to plan and coordinate a lobbying effort. The businessmen at the meeting set up a committee of 15 people headed by ex-congressman A.F. Dawson and decided to sponsor a preparedness conference for Midwestern congressmen and government officials. By all accounts the conference was a success. Nine senators and a number of congressmen attended and toured the arsenal. The arsenal commander pointedly reminded the visitors that only seven of the 10 shops were used for the manufacturing role they had been designed for. It did not matter that these same businessmen had turned down a government offer to build a plant on Arsenal Island in 1907. Now the businessmen at the preparedness conference and in Washington stressed the location of Rock Island as the primary reason for building an ammunition plant there. In the face of the German submarine offensive, the coastal munitions factories at Picatinny Arsenal at Dover, New Jersey, Frankford Arsenal in Philadelphia and the DuPont complex at Wilmington, Delaware, appeared vulnerable. In contrast, a munitions plant in the heartland of America appeared invulnerable. The Army appeared to agree when two years later Rock Island was the only arsenal which did not have aircraft defense batteries.

Less than a month after the conference General Crozier indicated that he favored a government ammunition factory in the Midwest — probably at the Rock Island Arsenal. In the spring of 1916 Congress passed the sundry appropriations bill which included Iowa congressman John Hull's bill for a $1.25 million appropriation to build a load, assembly and pack artillery shell plant at the arsenal. As a result the arsenal assembled 167,000 155-mm artillery shells during World War I, but with the close of the war the Army shut down the plant and converted it into a machine tool shop.

Probably the Ordnance Corps closed the facility because it had more than enough artillery already available and because it was considered too dangerous an activity for a populated area except in wartime. Essentially the ammunition loading program at the arsenal was an aberration. It appears that congressional criticism (led by Tavenner) and strictures on munitions procurement forced the Ordnance Department to give preference in 1916 and 1917 to the development of government munitions plants over private firms. The Republican administrations of the 1920s clearly favored a return to the private production of munitions.

The local business organizations also supported a number of other proposals which would expand the functions of the arsenal or at least use some of its land. Their campaign to locate an armor plate factory on the arsenal or in the Rock River Valley foundered on the Navy's insistence that Rock Island was too near the Great Lakes to be safe from invasion and too close to an Army facility. Similarly the local businessmen tried to get a $20 million nitrate plant placed on the island or in the vicinity as they stressed the great water power potential at the arsenal dam. This too came to nothing.

Three functions which greatly expanded during the war were small arms manufacturing, field gun carriage production and the depot activity. As war became imminent the Ordnance Department reopened the small arms plant which had closed in 1913. With an eye to the post war period it also moved to expand the arsenal's storage facilities. The arsenal built a huge five-story warehouse and a whole series of one-story sheds from 1918 through 1920. The arsenal's most significant expansion of facilities and of function came with the decision in 1917 to build a huge 600-foot-long field and siege gun carriage factory capable of handling up to 16-inch guns. This building, known as Shop M, effectively doubled the size of the arsenal's gun carriage manufacturing capability. The new facility, combined with the machine tools and machinist expertise that had accumulated at the arsenal since the early 1890s, enabled it to become the only successful American producer of the French style recoil mechanism for its 75-mm guns. The arsenal has made recoil mechanisms ever since. Even today with widespread use of numerical control machinery, very few private firms are willing and able to make these types of mechanisms. The required machining tolerances are much more fine than in normal industrial practices so the Rock Island Arsenal continues to make the mechanisms in quantity.

Employment at the Rock Island Arsenal reached 13,400 at the end of World War I. Manufacturing and storage activities crammed the buildings so that for the first time since 1865, when General Rodman and the chief of ordnance laid out the plans for the arsenal, it operated at full capacity. But war has not been a full-time activity. With the close of this "war to end all wars" the future existence of the Rock Island Arsenal became problematical. Again the local business clubs sent delegations and petitions to Washington in support of their arsenal. Again, in a sense, they succeeded. The Army transferred the harness makers to Jeffersonville, Indiana, in a postwar adjustment, and finally decided in 1920 to retain — but greatly cut back — activity at the arsenal. The first to go were women. The *Argus* headline read "Arsenal Offers Women Workers to Local Firms." Single men followed — then men with families. Finally it shut down most manufacturing activities and pared the workforce to a mere 225 in 1924. Political instability in Europe and Southeast Asia in the late 1930s prompted renewed activity at the island. At its peak in World War II it employed more than 23,000 people. With the subsequent "Cold War," the Korean conflict and Vietnam, the arsenal never again dipped to the nadir it experienced in the 1920s.

SHORTLY BEFORE THE UNITED STATES ENTERED WORLD WAR I, AND THE ARSENAL BEGAN SUPPLYING WAR MATERIEL, RESIDENTS OF THE TRI-CITIES MARKED THE CENTENNIAL OF FORT ARMSTRONG. POSTERS SUCH AS THIS PUBLICIZED THE EVENT THROUGHOUT THE CITIES. A HIGHLIGHT OF THE CELEBRATION WAS A REENACTMENT OF THE SIGNING OF THE TREATY ENDING THE BLACK HAWK WAR.

Fort Armstrong Centennial Celebration

Moline · Rock-Island · Davenport

1816   1916

EVERY MEMORIAL DAY, CONFEDERATE FLAGS ADORN THE GRAVES OF SOLDIERS BURIED IN THE CONFEDERATE CEMETERY ON ARSENAL ISLAND. THIS CUSTOM IS UNIQUE AMONG CONFEDERATE CEMETERIES IN THE NORTH.

BETTE

BY JON RYAN

DRED SCOTT'S OWNER, DR. JOHN EMERSON, CLAIMED A LARGE PIECE OF LAND WHICH EVENTUALLY BECAME THE SITE OF BETTENDORF. LOCAL LEGEND PLACES THE FAMOUS SLAVE IN A RUSTIC CABIN AT THE APPROXIMATE SITE OF THE TWIN BRIDGES APPROACH.

With the official opening of the Black Hawk Purchase in June of 1833 came the first white settlers to lay claim to what would, 70 years later, become Bettendorf. In December of that year, or perhaps early in 1834, the Fort Armstrong post surgeon, Dr. John Emerson, laid claim to a 320-acre parcel of ground and began a legend which endures to this day. The legend centers upon Dred Scott, the slave whose bid for freedom before the United States Supreme Court so aroused abolitionist feelings before the Civil War. Dr. Emerson's claim stretched eastward from roughly the present-day Davenport-Bettendorf city limits to 14th Street, from the river north to the bluffs. Legend claims that Emerson built a cabin near the present site of the twin bridges, cleared an area and placed his manservant, Dred Scott, in the cabin to prove his claim.

Emerson had brought Scott to the island with him from St. Louis. They made the acquaintance of Major Lawrence Taliaferro and his slave, Harriet. In 1835 Taliaferro was transferred to Fort Snelling, at what is now St. Paul, Minnesota, and in the spring of 1836, when Fort Armstrong was abandoned, Emerson was also sent to Fort Snelling. Later that year, at Fort Snelling, Dred Scott and Harriet were married.

In his absence, Emerson left Antoine Le Claire the right to rent and maintain the Iowa claim as he, Le Claire, saw fit. It was not until 1841 that Emerson actually purchased the ground from the federal government and received his deed. Emerson left the Army in 1842 and returned to this area intent on establishing a private medical practice. He left Dred Scott in St. Louis, never to return to Scott County. Emerson purchased some additional land in Davenport and began to build a brick home on 2nd Street, between Perry and Rock Island streets (now Pershing). A plaque on the building

EMPLOYEES OF THE BETTENDORF COMPANY LINED UP FOR THIS PORTRAIT DURING THEIR ANNUAL PICNIC IN 1921.

there indicates that this spot was the home of Dr. Emerson, though he died December 29, 1843, in the Le Claire House Hotel, before his home was completed.

The essential question of the legend — did Dred Scott really *live* in a cabin in what is now Bettendorf? — is probably never fully answerable. But perhaps Emerson did clear an area and tramp his claim in the company of Dred Scott.

That plot of land where Emerson and Dred Scott's rustic cabin perhaps stood is a geographical focal point for much of the history of what follows, as wilderness gives way to villages and finally to the emergence of Bettendorf as a city.

Up the Mississippi from Emerson's claim another early settler crossed the river from Hampton and built a cabin in the fall of 1833. Roswell Spencer, a veteran of the Black Hawk War, later built a sawmill on Spencer Creek, farmed extensively, developed other businesses and was responsible for platting Valley City, now known as Pleasant Valley. The Indians had named that creek Wau-pe-me-sepo or White Pigeon Creek.

Between Spencer Creek and the Emerson land another major creek entered the Mississippi. Duck Creek, known to the Indians as Si-Ka-Ma-Que-Sepo, Gar Creek, was the site where Captain Benjamin Clark began operating a sawmill in 1835. He floated lumber downriver to build the town of Buffalo. In the mid-1850s a county fair was held near there. It flourished for seven years, complete with a race track and tavern and exhibition halls. Land was donated for a county courthouse at the site, but the anticipated growth of a town never occurred.

THE MAN WHO WOULD BECOME "BUFFALO BILL" SPENT THE FIRST EIGHT YEARS OF HIS LIFE IN SCOTT COUNTY. WILLIAM FREDERICK CODY WAS BORN FEBRUARY 26, 1846, IN A FOUR-ROOM LOG CABIN WEST OF LE CLAIRE. CODY'S FATHER, ISAAC, BRIEFLY MANAGED A FARM ALONG THE WAPSIPINICON RIVER, RAN A WEEKLY STAGE BETWEEN DAVENPORT AND CHICAGO FOR SEVERAL YEARS, THEN MANAGED ANOTHER FARM, NEAR LONG GROVE. HIS WIFE, MARY, AND THE FOUR CODY CHILDREN MOVED WITH EACH JOB CHANGE. IN THE FALL OF 1853, CODY'S OLDER BROTHER, SAMUEL, DIED. THE DEATH TRIGGERED ISAAC'S WANDERLUST, AND WITHIN A YEAR THE FAMILY MOVED TO KANSAS. ISAAC CODY DIED IN 1857. WILLIAM FILLED THE NEXT QUARTER-CENTURY WITH HIS LEGENDARY EXPLOITS: PONY EXPRESS RIDER, CIVIL WAR SCOUT, BUFFALO HUNTER FOR A RAIL-ROAD, INDIAN WAR SCOUT, RANCHER, BUSINESSMAN AND NEBRASKA LEGISLATOR. IN 1883, HE FORMED HIS "WILD WEST SHOW," WHICH TOURED THE UNITED STATES AND EUROPE FOR MORE THAN 25 YEARS. IN ONE OF HIS "FAREWELL" SHOWS – WHICH STRETCHED OVER SEVERAL YEARS – CODY LAST PLAYED DAVENPORT AUGUST 3, 1911. AFTER HIS DEATH IN 1917, HE WAS BURIED ON LOOKOUT MOUNTAIN, COLORADO.

Fenno Cemetery, on Belmont Road near Valley Drive, holds the remains of Samuel Hedges, another miller who located on another of the numerous creeks which roll down to the Mississippi. According to an early history:

> "In 1835 Samuel Hedges built a mill on Crow Creek, where that stream is crossed by Middle Road. Crow Creek was more of a stream than now, now that farm improvements and removal of woodland have sapped its sources. The mill did a fair business for sometime, but not bringing promised success, was abandoned; not, however, before the despondent owner had suspended his body from one of its roughly hewn beams."

During the winter of 1835-36, in a log cabin located on the upper side of today's Valley Drive, a block and a half southwest of Pigeon Creek, the first school opened in Scott County. The school teacher was Simon Craigin, a former soldier in the War of 1812 and a native of Bangor, Maine. Craigin claimed to have discovered the Wapsipinicon River, held numerous land claims in the area and was the first recorded death in Le Claire township. Little else is known of him.

It is known, however, that he was a plain-speaking man who could act and talk in the tradition of Davy Crockett and Mike Fink. He was described in a local history as "one of those unceremonious, backwoods, frontier, half-civilized persons that lurk around the border settlements."
In September of 1837 Craigin attended a meeting of area inhabitants who had gathered to discuss "the peace and good order of the community."
As the meeting began to adjourn, a young newcomer from Hennepin, Illinois, assumed an arrogant air and suggested no one should be allowed to hold more than one land claim and then only if he lived on the claim.
That was more than Craigin could quietly swallow. He approached the young stranger and, according to an 1882 history of the county, voiced a "Mike Fink challenge"

> "My name, sir, is Simon Craigin. I own 14 claims and if any man jumps one of them I will shoot him down at once, sir. I am a gentleman, sir, and a scholar. I was educated in Bangor; have been in the United States Army and served my country faithfully; I am the discoverer of the 'Wopsy'; I can ride a grizzly bear, or whip any human that ever crossed the Mississippi; and if you dare to jump one of my claims, die you must.
> "My name is Simon Craigin, sir, all the way from Bangor, Maine, and you must leave these diggin's with but few remarks."

The young stranger left.

The colorful pioneers who clustered in this area in the 1830s include Sir Isaac Hawley, father of the onion-growing industry which dominated agriculture in these black river bottoms for nearly 100 years. Born a Vermonter, veteran of the War of 1812, Hawley headed west in 1820. While traveling he "was lost nine days and the only food they had was a 'possom, which was relished by all with the exception of Mrs. Hawley, who could not eat it." The Hawleys settled in Illinois until the spring of 1837 when they moved to Scott County where "he bought a claim of Buck Spencer, paying $1,400, there being a log cabin and a few acres broken. At this time there were but six buildings in Davenport."
He brought with him a packet of onion seeds, the first man to grow onions in the state. He and his sons, George and Daniel, developed the onion-growing industry, spreading their ideas and pungent vegetables across the creeks and river bottoms. They transported their onion crop, plus a few head of hogs and any extra saleable chickens, to St. Louis each year on a flatboat. Following common practice, in the city they sold their produce and animals, knocked apart the flatboat and sold it for lumber.
The Emerson land, by the 1840s, was being broken up. A deed recorded on

the day of Emerson's death, December 29, 1843, transferred 25 acres of the claim to Calvin A. Tuttle. This acreage is the area at approximately the bridge ramps today.

The remainder of the claim was sold by Emerson's widow in 1848 to an Alfred Churchill for $2,400 and was long known as Churchill's Farm. The land east of 14th Street was deeded in 1840 to William Benham who has disappeared into history without further notice. His ground was also broken into smaller lots and in 1850 a newly arrived easterner, Elias S. Gilbert, built a home on former Benham land, the present site of Our Lady of Lourdes Church. Gilbert erected a large home and barn, grew corn and experimented with growing tobacco on the river bottoms. In later years he constructed a large brick building at the foot of 14th Street near the river and attempted a starch factory, earning the nickname Starch Street for what is now 14th. The factory was less than successful, however, and he eventually concentrated most of his efforts on tobacco.

Some few hundred yards downriver, near the present-day boat landing, a German immigrant named Henry Kuehl began in 1850 a limestone kiln. Burning local stone, he created a substance which, when pulverized to fine grains, became lime for plaster. Some of that plaster was probably used in the large home constructed by Austrian immigrants, the Borneman family, in about 1852. Their home served as a tavern and dance hall and post office.

As the Gilbert farms and business enterprises developed, there was a need for housing for local laborers. From 10th to 14th Streets, along both sides of today's State Street, Elias Gilbert platted 29 lots. The residents, primarily German immigrants, were farmers and skilled laborers and small business operators. On lot 21 the Lillienthal family built a tavern and dance hall and, by virtue of their business establishment, lent their name to the tiny village. Never incorporated, Lillienthal was made a part of Gilbert, a town officially platted June 30, 1858, under authority of the county surveyor by Elias Gilbert. Gilbert never incorporated either, but Lillienthal eventually became known as the Lillienthal addition.

The Lillienthal population included a list of notables. One was Oscar Kobs, town drummer and town crier during the Civil War, who called the residents to meetings on the "commons," approximately where Volunteer Park is now.

William Holmes, brother-in-law of Gilbert, for whom Holmes Street is named, was a construction engineer for the railroads who dabbled in growing fruits of all kinds, including attempts at bananas and other tropical varieties, along the river. Legend reports that his daughter, Clara, met a dynamic young man in her travels and he followed her home to Lillienthal. He proposed, but she refused him on the grounds that he could not support the wealthy lifestyle she preferred and thus refused as husband Andrew Carnegie.

AN EARLY RESIDENT OF WHAT WOULD BECOME BETTENDORF SHOWED OFF HIS SULKY BEFORE A TRIP.

WILLIAM BETTENDORF (TOP) IS GENERALLY CREDITED WITH THE INVENTIVE ABILITIES, AND JOSEPH (ABOVE) IS ACKNOWL-EDGED AS THE FINANCIAL AND MANAGERIAL LEADER. THE TWO COMBINED THEIR INDIVIDUAL TALENTS WITH EXTRAORDINARY HARMONY.

Other residents included James Kuehl, who earned a living hunting deer and ducks and geese, selling them in town. A gentleman named Greve resided there, rumored to have been a coachman for Napolean, and a Kroeger who raised broom corn, made brooms, and sold them.

Gilbert and Lillienthal continued for 45 years as a rural village. In 1893 Gilbert sold his mansion and 70 acres to Frank W. Downs who raised shetland ponies. In turn, however, he sold the property to the Seibengartner family who subdivided the acreage into lots and sold them. Eventually the home itself was sold to Our Lady of Lourdes Catholic Church and was used as the church school until demolished in the 1950s when the present church was built on the site.

The Bettendorfs Transform Gilbert

In 1902 the sleepy village of Gilbert was invaded, and an early 20th century historian of Scott County remarked about the change:

> *"The steady people of Gilbert raised onions and cultivated flower beds, kept early hours and good habits and were content with a quiet life in the eastern suburbs of Davenport, when all of a sudden they awoke in a whirl of industry, with chimneys that smoke and wheels that hum, mammoth hydraulic presses that make steel cars and shears that chew up boiler plate. The necromancer, W.P. Bettendorf, and his associates have worked the transformation."*

William P. Bettendorf and his brother, Joseph, were the "necromancers" who catapulted the rural town into the 20th century with the construction of their plant on the current site of J.I. Case Company.

Sons of a German immigrant, William and Joseph had followed their father as he searched for roots in the new world, teaching school in Mendota, Illinois, conducting a grocery business and general store in Missouri, and serving as a government clerk in Fort Leavenworth, Kansas. Both boys received only what rural education was available to them during these years.

William, the older brother, was born in 1857. He struck off on his own in 1870 and provided his own support at the age of 13 by working as a messenger boy in Humbolt, Kansas, and later as a store clerk in Peru, Illinois. By the time he was 17 he was serving an apprenticeship in the machinist's trade with the Peru Plow Co. Moving from job to job and from city to city, Bettendorf amassed a wealth of experience for a young man, experience which would aid in his own inventions and manufacturing projects.

In 1878 he invented the first power lift sulky plow. Though it is hard to imagine now, in earlier days farmers were forced to lift the blade of the plow out of the ground at the end of each furrow. By the simple device of a gear apparatus, Bettendorf's invention allowed the farmer to remain seated on his horse-drawn plow and raise the blade out of the ground by pressing his foot on a lever. William's next invention was the "Bettendorf metal wheel," another innovation in the farm implement industry. He allowed the Peru Plow Co. to manufacture his wheel, but when they failed to keep up with the demand, he began a search for a manufacturing site which he could operate himself. Bettendorf met E.P. Lynch, the president of the Eagle Manufacturing Co., and was induced to locate in Davenport in 1886, sponsored by a group of local industrialists and bankers. At this time, Joseph Bettendorf joined his brother.

Seven years younger than William, Joseph had also severed home ties early in his life and struck off on his own, working at a variety of jobs. In the years between 1886 and 1895 the brothers invented and manufactured many new metal wagon parts and the machinery to make them, and eventually an all-metal farm wagon. In 1895, the brothers formed their own company, the Bettendorf Axle Co., with William serving as president. The brothers continued to "work together in utmost harmony," and by 1902 had greatly expanded their manufacturing site, which was located on 1st Street in Davenport, between Ripley and Scott Streets. On January 28, 1902, they suffered heavy losses in a fire and in May a second fire destroyed their plant.

A fund-raising drive among area residents and businessmen led by Clarence Brown netted $15,000 to purchase the remaining portion of the old Gilbert farm which stretched along the Mississippi. The offer of free land for his new plant brought Bettendorf to Gilbert and construction began in 1902 along the Davenport, Rock Island and Northwestern tracks, just east of the depot which had been built in 1899 near the present site of Volunteer Park. By early the following year local residents and Bettendorf Company employees filed a petition for incorporation of the town of Bettendorf, and on April 28, 1903, at a general election the proposal was approved by 69 votes for and 26 against. Bettendorf officially existed. The name, naturally, was chosen to honor the Bettendorf brothers; an additional advantage was that a second Gilbert in Iowa had created confusion in mail delivery, which was now ended.

The original shops were built to construct steel wagon gears and various other metal parts for the agricultural trade. In 1903, however, William Bettendorf invented the truck side frame for railroad cars, insuring his fortune and the continued growth of his firm.

The truck frame, which held the wheels to the railroad car and supported the weight of the car, had originally been made of several pieces of steel bolted together. As the railroad cars rocked along on the railbed these bolts often worked loose, delaying trains and on occasion causing derailments. The new Bettendorf design enabled this frame to be cast in a single piece and revolutionized the railroad industry. A "B" in a small circle was the symbol of this improved truck frame, cast in steel, and it is still possible to find such frames bearing the mark of the Bettendorfs.

THE BETTENDORF PLANT MADE CONSTRUCTION OF A COMPLETE RAILROAD CAR POSSIBLE UNDER ONE ROOF IN A CONTINUOUS FABRICATION PROCESS.

Within a few years the Bettendorfs were building railroad cars on their own frames and marketing them across the United States. From 300 employees in 1902 the firm had expanded to 800 by 1910. With the development of new inventions and the acquisition of other firms it had increased to 3,000 employees by 1920, greater than the total population of the town. Plant size was tripled in 1909 and a foundry was completed which was 436 feet by 440 feet in size. Two open-hearth steel furnaces daily produced about 100 tons of steel casting. The entire plant stretched nearly a full mile along the tracks and river and included a separate building with lockers and lavatories for employees, a power plant and an office facility. The plant erected a completed railroad car, from the basic raw materials to the finished product, in a continuous process from one end to the other. At the far eastern end, the foundry produced the basic steel. There, according to a 1910 history,

> "shop locomotive cranes carry the material to the east end of the shop, where other traveling cranes reach down powerful magnets, take up the immense bars that would defy the lifting strength of many men, and carry them to various machines, until they issue from the west end of the shop in the Bettendorf steel cars, underframes and trucks, which have been pronounced by railroad men generally as the finest cars of the kind ever produced."

Much of the equipment used in the car works, as well as that used in the manufacture of other Bettendorf inventions and acquisitions, was designed by William. From the gear assembly to lift a plow from the ground to the machinery to slice bread to a new way to build railroad truck frames, William's fruitful mind was the creative inspiration of the Bettendorf enterprises. Brother Joseph is generally credited with the business sense which continued the expansion and financial growth of the Bettendorf Company.

Together, they were a complementary team and "functioned so well together that the first team of horses used at the Bettendorf Axle Co. were named Billy and Joe."
Their efforts created an international reputation for Bettendorf. A 1910 historian related a popular anecdote of the time which still has a nice ring to it:

"Something of the extent and prominence of the Bettendorf business is indicated in a humorous reply recently made to a Davenport man in Pittsburgh. When asked where he was from and telling the city of his residence, the inquirer said, 'Oh yes, Davenport. That is near Bettendorf, isn't it?' This indicates how widely the town of Bettendorf — and the town is practically the great Bettendorf works — is known."

In addition to the great physical changes wrought by the manufacturing facilities, the Bettendorf brothers constructed two mansions which dominated the bluffs overlooking the plant and river valley. Each was a showplace of turn-of-the-century opulence. What is now the Iowa Masonic Nursing Home — at 26th and State Streets — was built for William and designed to be the most lavish home in the area, where visiting railroad executives could be entertained in grand style. Built in the Spanish-style on a 22-acre plot, the house was surrounded by oak and maple trees. There were large porches, a grand fountain and a carriage house large enough to hold six cars. Total cost of construction for the estate was more than $150,000.

Inside there were linen tapestry wallhangings, oak stairways and hand-carved oak woodwork, mural ceilings and a fireplace in nearly every room. Artisans from Europe were brought to Bettendorf to complete the detail work and returned home when the work was finished. Whole trees were brought to the construction site and sawn for paneling, allowing an entire room to be paneled with exactly matching pieces from the same tree. During construction the family lived in a bungalow adjacent to their home. Ironically, William never lived in his mansion. In June of 1910, a stomach ailment bothered William. He delayed treatment, due to the press of business, until a true emergency developed. A surgeon was summoned from Chicago; he traveled by specially chartered train from Chicago to Clinton, then down the Inter Urban. Unfortunately, he arrived too late; William Bettendorf died June 3, 1910.

Upon completion of the mansion in the fall, Bettendorf's widow and stepson moved into the home. They lived there until 1926, when it was sold to the Grand Lodge of Iowa, AF & AM. The Masons immediately added a 50-room wing to convert it to a nursing home, for which it is still used today. The other Bettendorf mansion — now St. Katharine's/St. Mark's School at 1821 Sunset Drive — was built in 1914-15 for Joseph W. Bettendorf. Originally a 28-room mansion, the grounds and support building covered 17 acres. A winding driveway led off Mississippi Boulevard up a south terrace to the glass roofed marquee which covered the main entrance on the north side of the building. A grand staircase, flanked by a pair of statuary guard dogs, led through a terraced, landscaped garden on the south side of the house.

THE JOSEPH BETTENDORF MANSION INCLUDED EXTRAORDINARY GARDENS AND SUPERIOR CRAFTMANSHIP IN CONSTRUCTION.

East of the main building was a large bath house and swimming pool. The pool has been filled in and the bath house is now a private home. A formal garden on the north side of the property surrounded a central pond, with fountain, a large rose trellis and a wide variety of flowers. Nearby were tennis courts, stables, a greenhouse, a chicken yard and a carriage house. Again, craftsmen imported from Europe built much of the home, hand-carving matching patterns in the woodwork, doors and main staircase. Throughout the home there were marble fireplaces, marble floors, ornate ceiling decorations, paneling of various kinds of wood, crystal chandeliers and leaded glass windows. The basement contained two bowling alleys, a cardroom, gymnasium and billiard room. A huge ballroom occupied the entire third floor.

At approximately the same time that Joseph Bettendorf was building his mansion, a third magnificent building was being constructed at the corner of 14th Street and Central Avenue — the former Carmelite Monastery, built in 1915-17.

THE BETTENDORF COMPANY ADOPTED THE BEAR AS ITS SYMBOL AND USED IT EXTENSIVELY – FROM BASEBALL TEAMS TO ADVERTISING ITEMS. IT WAS EVEN USED TO DECORATE LIGHTING FIXTURES IN THE BETTENDORF OFFICE BUILDING.

Bettendorf old-timers remember watching the construction in what was then an undeveloped portion of the city. Fourteenth Street hill was a favorite winter sledding area, as a clear run at the foot of the hill allowed sledders to nearly reach the Mississippi before trudging to the top of the bluff for another run.

Formally named The Queen of Heaven Monastery, the facility held 20 small cells, or rooms, on the third floor. Original furniture included only "a wooden chair, wooden chest of drawers and wooden bed with straw mattress." The order observed strict rules of silence and fasting and discouraged face-to-face meetings with outsiders.

With the eruption of war in Europe in the teens the growing Bettendorf manufacturing complex ran into labor shortages; Armenian and Greek immigrants had provided much of the work force. As plant operations began to be affected, recruiters were sent to Mexico.

The result was a village within a village — Holy City. Located east of the Bettendorf Company and stretching from the river to State Street, where the tank farms are now located, Holy City was home for some 600 Mexican workers and their families.

A Bettendorf representative began recruitment in Juarez, Mexico, and signed 150 Mexican peasants to come north and work. The workers arrived in Bettendorf in five railroad cars pulled by a steam engine, and local eyewitnesses reported the new arrivals "streamed out of the doors and windows" when the train arrived.

The wives and children of many of the workers came north later and settled into a series of one-room cottages which had been built in two straight rows by the Bettendorf Company. There were also several two-story, frame "apartment" buildings where the unmarried laborers lived. Later, several boxcars were also used for housing. The cottages were heated by a single wood-burning stove in the center of the single room. On cold winter nights, like all good farm people, many Holy City residents would add their chickens and goats to what must have been extraordinarily cramped quarters.

A Bettendorf resident who grew up in Holy City reports that generally it was a clean, well-organized community. Local legends of shoot-outs in the streets and knife-wielding brawlers are based, not on fact, but probably on a few random Friday night fracases which grew in magnitude with years of retelling.

HOLY CITY, HOME FOR THE MEXICAN WORKERS WHO CONTRIBUTED SO MUCH TO THE GROWTH OF THE BETTENDORF WORKS, WAS INUNDATED BY THE FLOOD OF 1926.

Cold weather forced many of the immigrants to return home and the "Great Flood of 1926" created havoc and drove some families away, but most of the Mexicans remained. Their numbers grew with the years, but gradual assimilation into the general population of Bettendorf reduced the size of Holy City over the years. The last remnants were demolished in the 1940s. Perhaps because of language difficulties between English-speaking supervisors and Spanish-speaking laborers, most of the men were recorded on the company books as having the first name of "Jesus." Thus, according to legend, the name "Holy City."

Many also said they were named "George Washington" and the most common birth date given was July 4th. Even though considered aliens, the Mexicans were forced to register for the draft in World War I. Literally corraled in groups of 20 to 30 surrounded by a walking rope picket, they were marched down State Street by an insensitive local police force to be registered at the town hall.

These Mexicans, with the Greeks and Irish and Armenians, coupled with the Germans, who had also immigrated here a generation or two earlier, made the Bettendorf Company a success. They were piece workers and day laborers with salaries of $40 to $50 per week. A work week included six 10-hour days, from 7 a.m. to 6 p.m., with an hour off for lunch. Many of the laborers walked across State Street to a small amusement park to buy their lunch — a small loaf of bread and a nickel bucket of beer.

With Industry Comes Government

In addition to creating a town, then populating it, the Bettendorfs, directly and indirectly, were responsible for the organization and development of a town government.

Formal incorporation in April 1903 was followed by the election of a council and mayor and the establishment of appropriate ordinances during that summer. E.W. Robeson was the first mayor, incidentally an employee of the Bettendorf Company and a $400 contributer to the fund-raising which had purchased the ground for the Bettendorfs.

The first ordinances included specifications for building wooden sidewalks, rules for riding bicycles on the streets only, never sidewalks, and a prohibition against allowing livestock to roam loose, complete with appropriate fines and punishments.

By 1908 a permanent new City Hall was built at a cost of $12,000. The fire station and city offices occupied the main floor, a dance hall was on the second floor, and a cupola with fire bell topped the structure. City Hall was located at the existing foot of the bridges. It was moved 30 feet east of its original location in 1935 when the first span was built and razed in 1958 for construction of the second span.

In 1909 the City Council leased space in City Hall's first floor for the establishment of the Bettendorf Savings Bank and even agreed to place steel bars on a back window. They tacked an extra 25 cents per month onto the $15 per month rent for the improvement, however. This was a wise decision. Throughout much of those early years, city financial records show continuing overdrafts and deficit fund balances. The town marshal was even instructed to actively seek out violators of the new 50 cent dog tax when only two residents came in for licenses. A major squabble over screen doors lasted several meetings as discussion covered the need for them, which sections should have them, and whether the upstairs dance hall proprietor, the volunteer fire department or the city would pay for them.

When a resident fell into a culvert along State Street, he presented a bill to the City Council for $23 — a $5 doctor's bill and $18 in lost wages. The council offered $10 for settlement in full.

Similarly, when offered a used fire pump for $100, the council offered $75 and asked the sellers, West Liberty, to deliver. The Bettendorf Fire Department, then as now, depended upon volunteers. When the bell in City Hall was rung, volunteers would race to the fire, pulling hose reels by hand. In 1912 the first motorized fire truck was built when the volunteers converted a Meteor automobile in their own garages and blacksmith shop.

City services came to Bettendorf in 1909 with the establishment of the Bettendorf Water Company and the Bettendorf Light and Power Company. The water company holding tank was near the old high school at the top of the bluffs and water was carried originally in wooden mains. The municipal code stipulated water costs for various uses, including $3.50 per year for each horse and $2.25 per year for each cow. Livestock continued to be a problem; a petition was received requesting the council to forbid residents from tying their cows so they stood on the public sidewalks. The council directed the town marshal to investigate.

Much of life in Bettendorf from the beginnings through the Depression centered around the massive car works or the related interests of the Bettendorfs. City government was dominated for more than 30 years by the Bettendorfs' employees. Homes were constructed by the Bettendorf Improvement Company and sold on favorable terms to employees. Street cars to Davenport were initiated at the request of the company. Public services were supplied by the franchised Bettendorf companies; even gifts of hoses and nozzles and other equipment aided the volunteer fire department. Company loyalty was standard procedure for employees and The Bettendorf Loyalty Club boasted hundreds of members with the minimum requirement of 15 years of service.

The company adopted the bear as its corporate symbol in 1908 and bears began to appear on advertising, in children's books for employees, and on company calendars. Joseph Bettendorf's home included bears on the interior door key guards and on a fireplace. Company-sponsored baseball, bowling and football teams were known as the Bears.

During those "boom years," 1903 to 1933, the Bettendorfs acquired interests in many other businesses, offering sometimes a loan or other helping hand, sometimes simply taking over a faltering business. In 1914 the Zimmerman steel plant, with a large cash advance from the Bettendorfs, constructed its factory on the far east end of the Bettendorf plant. One of its fabrications was the Monarch Stump Puller, an item designed to help clear stumps from farm ground after trees were cleared.

Other Bettendorf acquisitions included the Dooler Oil Company, eventually known at the Bettendorf Oil Burner, "Buddy L" toys, Chippewa Pump, water pumps, Slice Master bread and cake slicers and others. Micro and Westco were corporate holding companies and into these were merged many other acquired lines, eventually becoming Micro-Westco. Other company lines included a hand dolly to move railroad cars, a table-top cigar lighter, ice crushers and a machine to compress and bundle wastepaper. An old-timer reports that at one time the Bettendorf Company and its divisions made 29 separate types of machinery or tools.

Other firms and businesses developed in Bettendorf during those three boom decades, including a huge greenhouse complex along the river at the foot of Devil's Glen Road. A large quarry at the site of present-day Meier Park supplied gravel for Scott County roads. About 1908, the Meteor automobile was being manufactured at a site south of the current Volunteer Park area by Arnold Peterson. It was "a seven-passenger, 50 horse-power auto, with four forward speeds and two reverse speeds." Manufacture of the auto ended about 1912.

In October 1926, Don Luscombe of Davenport and Bettendorfer Frank Wallace, who owned a hangar and flying field near the corner of today's 18th Street and Spruce Hills, joined to form Central States Aero Company. They began building monocoupe airplanes — the first in April 1927 — and located at a converted tabernacle on State and 15th Streets. The company was sold in 1928 to the Velie Company which continued to manufacture the monocoupes.

Numbers of grocery stores and taverns developed to serve local needs. Hotels were built, including The Bettendorf Hotel, located across from the Bettendorf's corporate headquarters. Originally named Mechanic's Hotel, the facility served as a home for many of the company's employees.

Motor companies and service stations opened to serve the new means of transportation. A local ordinance, however, maintained a speed limit of 8 miles per hour within the city limits. Subdivisions began to sprout around the already developed section. In 1910 and 1911 State Street was paved, but the job was less than perfect and the street was dubbed "Washboard Avenue." A grass boulevard served for a few brief years as decoration, then held street car tracks for a half dozen years.

As the population grew, the need for larger schools became apparent. In 1870, a school was built near State Street at the foot of 21st Street. Gilbert School, often referred to as the "old stone schoolhouse," was eventually abandoned for public use and became a restaurant and tavern, a frequent gathering place for Armenian immigrants who worked in the car shops.

In 1908 a bond issue was passed for the construction of the Bettendorf School, now the Bettendorf Museum on 16th Street. In 1914 Bellevue School was built on Central Avenue where it doubled as a church school on Sundays. Both were modernized and added on to in 1923. In 1927 they were renamed Washington School and Lincoln School.

FALL HARVESTING OF THE ONION FIELDS FILLED SCORES OF RAILROAD CARS THROUGHOUT THE VALLEY.

Onion Industry Flourished

While the Bettendorfs were creating their industrial empire in central Bettendorf, the rural Germans along the up-river farms were developing the onion industry. Selective breeding, careful attention to crop rotation and natural fertilization — and plain hard work — had made the area "noted for raising the greatest variety and finest quality onions in the state." Though much of the work from sowing to setting to weeding to topping was done by hand, the patenting in 1916 of an onion set planter by Fred Schutter and William Hartz revolutionized onion planting by saving the work of 20 men. Onion seed planters were also invented during this time, led by Russel Rice, and speeded the work of planting for those growers who preferred seed. It was not unusual for an acre of the rich bottomlands to produce 500 or 600 bushels of onions. The record was achieved on a 12-acre plot which averaged more than 940 bushels per acre in 1912. In fall, the Inter Urban railway and the main railway would be filled with carloads of onions.

But this flourishing industry suffered three major setbacks beginning in the 1920s.

In 1923 onion farmers formed a co-op — The United Onion Growers of Pleasant Valley — to market their produce. M.W. Lorch of Chicago was retained to handle sales in 1925. Lorch's local representative was Milton C. "Speed" Coggins, who operated out of his Buick and his residence in Davenport's Blackhawk Hotel. In 1926 Lorch disappeared. His car and clothing were found near the Chicago River, but his body was never found.

A YOUNGSTER IS ALMOST HIDDEN AMONG THE TOPS OF MATURE ONIONS. THEIR PUNGENT SMELL FILLED THE VALLEY ON WARM SUMMER DAYS.

For seven years his estate was in litigation, and he was finally declared legally dead. Unfortunately, his disappearance had left 55 train carloads of local growers' onions unaccounted for. They were included in Lorch's business assets and the local farmers received nothing for their produce for the seven years after his disappearance. The final accounting allowed a pro-rata award of $11 per carload — a tremendous financial blow in 1933.
Also in the late 1920s "Yellow Dwarf" — a fungus which destroyed onions — infested the area. Professors from Iowa State and private researchers were imported, funded by a self-imposed assessment on all onions grown in the valley. Local farmers, attempting to secure "clean" growing land free of the disease, rented acreages as far away as Milan. Onions grown on the clean areas were free of the disease, but many of the local planters turned to other crops on thier own fields and never returned to onions.
The Great Depression only provided the death blow to an industry already crippled.

The Depression also ruined the mighty Bettendorf Car Works. By 1932 the plant was shut, the state was demanding back taxes and threatening a sale of the property, and in May of 1933, Joseph Bettendorf died. The plant became the site of a tank arsenal during World War II, then was sold to J.I. Case after the war.
The Bettendorf Water Company was merged with the Davenport Water Company and the Bettendorf Light and Power Company was absorbed by Iowa-Illinois Gas and Electric. At the height of the Depression, even the street lights were turned off from 11 p.m. to 5 a.m. to save money. By March of 1933 the City Council had lowered the salaries of city employees, arranged for vacant lots to be used for gardens and considered offering an extra half-day's work to men on relief at 25 cents per hour. The Bettendorf Savings Bank had closed, freezing $13,000 of city funds. The budget for 1934 was less than $30,000 and a close reading of city proceedings indicates the monetary strain city officials labored under. The only bright spot of 1933 was the issuance of a beer permit to W.T. Glynn who founded a local pub which lasted nearly 50 years and became a Bettendorf landmark.
The Depression marked an ending of many things — from onions to railroad cars — but also a new beginning. The land at the foot of 14th Street, along State and to the River, had been center stage for a host of special Bettendorf activities. John Emerson claimed this land and tobacco was grown on it by Elias Gilbert. Civil War musters were held here on the grass of Gilbert's town commons and the railroad depot was built here. The first City Hall was built on the site and the Meteor automobile's short-lived manufacture took place close by. The Inter Urban swept by this spot and onion farmers drove by with wagonloads of produce on their way to the Davenport markets. Only a stone's throw away loomed the gigantic Bettendorf Car Works. It is somehow appropriate that this pariculatly historic spot was the site of a new bridge across the Mississippi.
Dedicated November 18, 1935, the first span was commemorated with speeches by the governors of Iowa and Illinois and local officials, complete with a horse show and fair. The bridge, dedicated to the U.S. soldiers and sailors of World War I and named the Iowa-Illinois Memorial Bridge, cost $1.5 million. The first, western section was originally a two-way bridge with two lanes. Tolls were collected to pay for it. When traffic needs grew, rather than widen or replace the existing bridge, a second span was added to the east and completed in 1960.
The original bridge placed its feet in an Iowa plot rich with local history — from Emerson to Lillienthal to Gilbert to Bettendorf — and there must have been a fascinated and fascinating gallery of ghosts at the dedication.

BETTENDORF TAKES CREDIT AS THE "HOME OF SLICED BREAD"! IN THE EARLY 1930S BREAD WAS STILL SOLD UNSLICED. MORE THAN ONE DAVENPORTER TAKES CREDIT FOR INVENTING THE BASIC BREAD-SLICER CONCEPT, WHICH WAS EXPANDED UPON BY A LOCAL BAKER WHO BEGAN TO DEVELOP IT FOR THE RETAIL BAKING TRADE. SURVIVING RESIDENTS STILL ARGUE ABOUT WHO REALLY "INVENTED" THE IDEA, BUT IT WAS A DIVISION OF THE BETTENDORF COMPANY, THE MICRO COMPANY, THAT POPU-LARIZED THE CONCEPT WHEN IT DEVELOPED AND SOLD COMMER-CIAL BREAD SLICERS. ORIGINALLY DESIGNED TO BE USED ON THE COUNTER OF THE NEIGHBORHOOD BAKERY BY THE BAKER HIMSELF, THE SLICER EVENTUALLY WAS SOLD TO MAJOR BAKERIES THROUGHOUT THE WORLD. THE MICRO COMPANY ALSO DEVELOPED AND SOLD CAKE SLICERS, MACHINERY TO SHARPEN THE BLADES USED IN THE SLICERS, THE BLADES THEM-SELVES AND WRAPPING EQUIPMENT. WHEN FIRST USED, THE SLICER PROVED UNPOPULAR BECAUSE SLICED BREAD DRIED OUT TOO QUICKLY AND MUCH WAS WASTED. WHEN MICRO ADDED AN AUTOMATIC WRAPPER, THE SLICED BREAD BEGAN TO CATCH ON AND BY THE END OF THE '30S SLICED BREAD HAD BECOME A STANDARD OF THE BAKING INDUSTRY.

E A S T   M

BY LADONNA BREIDFJORD
BACKMEYER

Born in eastern Canada on July 15, 1811, Henry McNeal ran away from home as a boy and made his way west. He spent some time working on the Great Lakes, and in the leac mines near Galena. Then he moved down the Mississippi and settled at the site that one day would be part of the village of Hampton. After locating a suitable section of land, Henry began to cut and furnish wood for the river's steamboats as he cleared the property for farming and settlement. The forest that surrounded his log cabin, located on a bluff above the wide, white sand and gravel beach, was rich with towering oaks, elm trees, maples, hickory trees and wild plum bushes. The year was 1828 and Henry was 17.

Although Hampton was first known as McNeal's Landing, Henry was not the first settler of the township. Martin Culver had arrived in 1827, and the Reverend John Kinney, with two of his brothers, arrived a short time after Culver. Four other settlers located within the township in 1828: Joel Thompson, Michael Bartlett, Asaph Wells and Joel Wells Jr. Every year brought new pioneers to the area, and Henry McNeal rode out to meet each stranger with his hand held out in friendship and welcome. The settlement continued to grow, and by 1833 the people had need of a school. Classes, taught by Lucius Wells, were held in a log cabin throughout the first years. Lucius, a native of Ohio and one of the many sons of Nancy and Rinnah Wells Sr., was to become one of the leading citizens of the community.

Along with Henry McNeal, Michael Bartlett, John Kinney, Samuel Kinney, Joel Thompson, Joel Wells Jr. and John, Asaph, Eri and Ira Wells, all from

THE FIRST CHICAGO AND ROCK ISLAND ROCKET TRAVELED FROM CHICAGO TO JOLIET IN 1852. TWO YEARS LATER THE ROCKET REACHED ROCK ISLAND. "DESCENDANTS" OF THIS TRAIN MADE THE SILVIS YARDS OF THE ROCK ISLAND LINES BUSTLE YEARS LATER.

Hampton Township, he joined the Rock River Rangers in 1831. He was elected county commissioner in 1836 and sheriff of Rock Island County in 1839. Lucius was a religious man as well as a political leader and teacher, so when the Reverend John Kinney needed a home in which he could hold Methodist services, the Wells family graciously offered their cabin.

The place name of this river location, McNeal's Landing, became a part of the past when the villages of Milan (not the present Milan) and Hampton were laid out and platted in 1837 and 1838. Located next to one another, the two communities became thriving business centers. There were pottery shops and blacksmith shops, general stores and saloons, dance halls and churches, drug stores, carpentry shops, coopers and meat markets. A.W. Hayward crafted skiffs, canoes, bows and arrows, and Charles G. Thomas ran a ferry across the Mississippi. The ferry, propelled by horse power, could transport two teams and wagons on each run. Lucius Wells built and operated the first sawmill in the vicinity, and Joel Thompson became the first postmaster. The village of Hampton (including the village of Milan) eventually boasted four steamboat wharves and at least two hotels, the first being opened in 1838 by James P. Harvey. This was a growing community, and had there not been so much game-playing in Rock Island County's pioneer politics Hampton might have continued to expand, probably evolving far beyond the pleasant, sleepy river community it is today.

A 19TH CENTURY WOOD-CHOPPER'S CABIN ON THE BLUFF ABOVE HAMPTON. PICTURED, FROM LEFT, ARE JOHN EDELMAN, GUS HAYWARD, CARROL VINCENT AND MANIEL SMITH.

HENRY MCNEAL'S HOME IN WATERTOWN AND THE VILLAGE'S FIRST POSTOFFICE (THE SMALL BUILDING ON THE RIGHT) WERE RAZED WHEN THE WATERTOWN BAPTIST CHURCH EXPANDED IN 1967.

On July 5, 1833, an election was held between the rival strengths of Hampton and Farnhamsburg (now Rock Island), in which 65 ballots were cast, electing to office three men who would determine the future location of the Rock Island County Courthouse. However, the men of Farnhamsburg had already decided which community would house this significant building. They made an arrangement with Colonel George Davenport in which the colonel would signal certain persons on the island should the votes of island men be needed to swing the election to Farnhamsburg's favor. Later in the day, Colonel Davenport lifted his handkerchief and made the required signal.

The Hampton men saw Colonel Davenport's move. They knew the outcome of the election was being rigged, so they seized the poll book, sprang to their horses and galloped away. But, because the wise clerks had anticipated the actions of the Hampton party, the book the galloping horsemen carried off was a blank. The Farnhamsburg men who chased after the Hampton clan probably did so to add a touch of realism to the farce, and to make sure the island men had enough time to vote before the citizens of Hampton discovered that, due to trickery, they did not have the poll book after all. After the horsemen had disappeared, the real poll book was reintroduced and the island populace voted for the candidates from Farnhamsburg. In 1936 Morris S. Heagy, a Hampton historian and Rock Island banker, noted, "Politics is (and was) a game of wits."

Campaigns and election days throughout the 19th century were spirited, argumentative and dramatic events that included speeches, flag raising and torch light parades. Men hurried to the polls early on election morning, and they stayed all day, usually arriving home late that night. The drum, the fife and the flag were as prominent as the garrulous and powerful politicians, and many of the women contributed to the holiday spirit by serving dinner and coffee to the voters who would stop throughout election day.

Water, Rails, Coal and Timber, but no City

Henry McNeal had moved to the future village of Watertown by 1839 and in 1857 the Warsaw and Rockford Railroad stretched up the river and past his farm. Henry, Alonzo Nourse and Alfred Sanders platted the village, then Henry and Alonzo began to advertise the advantages of their Mississippi River location. In circulars sent to Eastern cities they attempted to sketch the potential future of Watertown to manufacturers who might wish to relocate in the West. The village had a superior harbor, the circulars noted, and the river at this point offered the best location for a dam that would span the breadth of the Mississippi. Watertown could be a rival to its neighboring city, Moline. The great coal fields of Illinois were in the immediate vicinity, and the land surrounding the townsite was well timbered. Thus, Watertown offered a rare opportunity for investors. However, the dam was never built and the manufacturing city never materialized. By 1874 Watertown, which had served as a stage stop before 1857, was still a small village, its only buildings a boxcar depot, an engine house, a turntable, a watertank, a few homes, one church and a small, wooden school house. Lucius Curtis, the first postmaster, opened a general store in 1857, which he sold to Dan McNeal in 1860. Other than farming, the coal mines located near the village provided the only additional source of industry for the 300 citizens of the community.

Happy Hollow, a nearby mining town with a population of 1,000, shipped about 40 cars of coal daily over five miles of spur track to the railroad station at Watertown. The spur track was built by the Western Union Railroad Company, as were other tracks to various mines in the area, and most of the coal was sold directly to the railroads.

Happy Hollow was not so pleasant a town as its name implies, not after the coal mining companies destroyed the natural beauty of the land in their search for underground mineral deposits. This was a mining town in a very real sense, complete with a company store, which encouraged the workers to exist on credit, and numerous unpainted and temporary homes. Mining towns were not built for beauty, and the men who ran the companies seldom wasted money on paint.

Although Charles Ames mined and marketed the first coal in Hampton Township in 1838, mining did not become one of the main enterprises in the area until 1870. Once established, this industry brought a people to the neighborhood who were very different from the farmers, storekeepers and craftsmen who had settled earlier. According to historian Morris Heagy, the miners were a rough breed. They were always ready for a good fight, though in most cases no one was badly hurt, as the men tended to fight with their fists rather than with guns or knives. And the women who married these men tended to be lusty scrappers, too. Whether Yankee, Irish, English or Welsh, the mining people had two realities in common: they were all poor and they were all tough.

On January 12, 1880, a riot broke out at Happy Hollow, ending a miners' strike that had lasted for many weeks. Five women and two men, all of whom had been armed with clubs at the time of the riot, were arrested two days later for having threatened workers who had refused to strike for higher wages. There were few tears when the posse and Sheriff Perkins made the arrest, and one of the female prisoners danced a jig before boarding the train that would transport the crew, along with eight children who would otherwise be uncared for, to the jail in Rock Island. The train left Happy Hollow amid a party atmosphere, as most of the citizens of the village had turned out to watch the captured rioters depart. The prisoners, who had worked hard while living in near poverty conditions, joked about the bill of fare at the Perkins House (the jail), sang songs and discussed their new quarters while riding the rails to the county jail.

BUILT ABOUT 1873 ON LAND DONATED BY WILLIAM COOK, THE ONE-ROOM COOK SCHOOL SERVED THE MINING AND FARMING FAMILIES OF THE HAPPY HOLLOW AREA FOR NEARLY 90 YEARS. THE BASKETBALL COURT SHOWN IN THIS PAINTING BY FRANK ROSS WAS CREATED WITH LIMITED FUNDS. TWO USED TELEPHONE POLES WERE DONATED BY THE PHONE COMPANY, AND EVELYN KUEHL, A TEACHER FROM 1932-1948, BOUGHT THE RIMS. THE CHILDREN AND THEIR TEACHER MADE THE NETS FROM BINDER TWINE. COOK SCHOOL DISTRICT CONSOLIDATED WITH SILVIS AND HAMPTON IN 1960. IT WAS THE LAST ONE-ROOM SCHOOL HOUSE IN ROCK ISLAND COUNTY.

LOCATED IN HAMPTON, THE NORTHERN MINING COMPANY STORE (HEAGY'S) SOLD SUPPLIES TO THE COMPANY'S EMPLOYEES AT HAPPY HOLLOW. IN THE PICTURE, FROM LEFT, ARE JOHN EDELMAN, JIM WINANS (POSTMASTER), GEORGE MCNABNEY, JOHN HERMES, G.D. TOOTHAKER, FRED ROBINSON AND AN UNIDENTIFIED BOY.

EDWARD HOLMES GUYER PLAYED A HUGE ROLE IN DEVELOPMENT OF UPPER ROCK ISLAND COUNTY.

Later that same week the miners and the women were fined $50 each for intimidation, $10 each for rioting, and costs for both charges, though collection of the fines was suspended as long as the people involved exhibited good behavior. Also, the families had to sign an agreement stating they would vacate their homes by the first of February. According to the *Rock Island Argus*, the rioters had learned a valuable lesson: "The law does not allow people to interfere with the legitimate business or property of others." The *Argus* also reported that 500 additional miners were expected in the area within a few days to replace the strikers at the Hampton and Rapid City mines.

Happy Hollow is gone now; it has been gone for nearly 100 years. The mines in that vicinity closed in the 1880s, and by the turn of the century the lively little village that had once been home to an isolated group of people, a community of laborers who had loved life and laughter while knowing poverty and misery, had decayed to a ghost town. Nothing remains of that ghost town today, not a scrap of wood or a piece of metal, and nature has erased from sight the scars that were made upon the land. Along with the wind and the rain and the passage of time, peace has come again to Happy Hollow.

Boom Town Rises from Slough and Swamp

Although East Moline's official history dates back to 1857 and the platting of Watertown, the actual village of East Moline did not exist until 1903, eight years after E.H. Guyer of Rock Island had hired Henry G. Paddock to survey and plat the 2,500 acres of land on which Guyer and his associates held options. Guyer was a land speculator and a dreamer of cities, and he definitely had dreams for the land east of Moline. At the onset of his fantasy in 1895, the location he envisioned as an industrial city of great magnitude was merely a swamp with frog ponds, grasslands and a railroad shanty called Port Byron Junction. Many cows grazed upon the grasslands, and only one house, the home of the railroad inspector, was situated close by the shanty.

The options, held by Guyer, S.H. Velie, C.H. Deere, George W. Walker and C.H. Pope, had to be exercised by the spring of 1896. Thus, 1895 was a busy year for Guyer. Deals had to be made for the location of factories and interest had to be instilled within the people of Moline and Rock Island.

THE CORNERSTONE LAYING CEREMONY AT ILLINOIS WESTERN HOSPITAL FOR THE INSANE, LATER KNOWN AS WATERTOWN STATE HOSPITAL, THEN EAST MOLINE STATE HOSPITAL. THE BUILDINGS NOW HOUSE THE EAST MOLINE CORRECTIONAL CENTER.

With the help of R.R. Bemis of Chicago, a professional promoter, Guyer and
his associates planned a spectacular barbecue and auction sale for
September 12. The sale was extensively advertised and an auctioneer, one of
the best, was brought in from Kentucky. The men involved were sure that
this potentially historic auction would be a success. If it was, they would
raise enough money on the sale of lots to exercise the options, thus gaining
actual title to the land.

The barbecue was a huge success. Thousands of people, possibly as many as
six or seven thousand, gathered in the grove on the north side of the tracks
to have a good time and to consume the enormous amounts of food that had
been prepared. Beef and mutton halves were roasted on live coals in
trenches. There were several refreshment stands, and a brass band had been
hired for the day. Bemis, the promoter, finally mounted the auction block
and a crowd of 800 or more surrounded him. He portrayed the city-to-be in
glowing, colorful words, and he congratulated the people who were present
for having had the key to opportunity presented to them. The auctioneer
asked for the first bid, but the crowd was reluctant. After a time one man
came forward and hesitated before he offered a bid of $75 on the lot
presented. The auctioneer waited for someone to raise the bid, but no one
did. Once again Bemis painted an unblemished word-picture of the
future industrial city. Still, no one offered a higher bid. Five lots were sold
that day, none for more than $75. The potentially historic auction had
become a historic flop and East Moline was allowed to progress at a more
normal pace.

The atmosphere was gloomy in Guyer's office after the sale, but the gloom
lifted when the aged and trembling Jeremiah Keator, a pioneer lumberman
from Moline, entered the building with frail but determined steps and
offered to give the men all that he had left to spare, $600, so that they could
build the city that he, too, believed in. A short time later Charles Deere
came forward with enough money to extend the options on the land. Guyer
was in business once again.

Guyer continued to lead the development of East Moline. In 1896 he
persuaded Daniel McNeal, the son of Henry McNeal, to give an option on
his bluff property in Watertown so that he, Guyer, might sell the property
to the Illinois State Welfare Department. Daniel willingly gave the option,
and the cornerstone for the Western Illinois Hospital for the Insane was laid
in September of that same year on land that Henry McNeal had once
owned. This sale eliminated 900 acres of valuable land from the market,
land that might have competed with the East Moline project. The East
Moline Land Company, an organization belonging to E.H. Guyer, C.D.
White and C.H. Pope, was now able to purchase the entire townsite of the
envisioned city at a low price, and by the end of 1900 three industrial
corporations, the Root and VanderVoort Engineering Company, the
Marseilles Company and the Union Malleable Iron Works, had located
within the boundries of their land. Houses began to appear on the ridges
below the bluff. Dimock & Gould, realizing that a building boom was about
to begin, bought 13 lots on which they would later build a branch lumber
yard.

In December of 1902 an election was held to incorporate the village of East
Moline. According to legend, the votes had all been cast by noon and two of
the three judges became tired and fell asleep. One of the napping judges
moved in his slumber, upsetting an ink bottle into the ballot box and
causing the judge on watch to panic. The startled man feared that the ink-
smeared ballots would be declared invalid and he knew that the citizens
would object to the expense of another election. After a bit of quiet
deliberation this cautious mender-of-fate unlocked the box and marked a
new set of tickets to replace those that were damaged. The story, kept secret
for many years, claims that the judge did not have to look at the old, ink-
stained tickets as he marked the new ones; he knew the opinion of every
voter.

BUILT IN THE 1880S TO CARRY HORSE-DRAWN COAL CARS FROM THE TINKERVILLE MINES TO PORT BYRON JUNCTION, THIS TRESTLE RAN FROM THE BLUFF ABOVE PRESENT DAY EAST MOLINE AND EXTENDED OVER WHAT IS NOW THE CITY'S BUSINESS DISTRICT.

East Moline was incorporated as a village on December 23, 1902, and Walter Ammerman, the first village president, was elected to office on January 17, 1903. Thomas Caverly was elected village clerk. In December 1903, Caverly published the first edition of the *East Moline Enterprise*, a newspaper that later became the *East Moline Herald* (final edition: February 1970).

By December 1903, the infant city was bursting with activity. Village crews had laid plank and cement sidewalks and a drainage system was under way. Street cars passed through East Moline every 15 minutes. Businesses were built or were being built in every direction. A city was rising from the swamps and sloughs, and the East Moline Land Company hired George W. Ross, a Chicago lawyer who had been involved with the promotion of Chicago Heights, to promote the city's development. Ross placed ads in the *Enterprise* that encouraged people to buy property in the village while lots were cheap. This land, Ross claimed, would triple in value over the next three years.

The *Enterprise*, too, was attempting to lure people to East Moline. The December 18, 1903, edition of the paper gave an extensive account of the businesses existing in the growing village at that time. T.J. Gorman was managing the East Moline Mercantile Company, P.J. Sunberg had opened a hardware store, and there were three hotels in town: the East Moline Hotel, managed by Fred Hocall; the Malleable Hotel, managed by William Titue; and the City Hotel, managed by Wallace W. Gates. Fred Schlueter's market was open, Lindrall and Edlund were general blacksmiths, and the East Moline Liquor Company was operating. Shirley, the chef at Roy Ausbury's Artisian Restaurant, guaranteed "a good meal and a clean one." Four bars — The Farmers Home, Peter Auer's, A. VanderBeke's and Leon Callewaert's — had opened their doors to the thirsty.

Guyer's dream was beginning to materialize. Two clothing stores, the Famous Store of Moline and William Janen's, were open for business. C. Lundquist was managing Dimock & Gould, and Mr. Buckly was managing the Mueller Lumber Company. East Moline had lured three doctors and one dentist to the village. The New Process Steam Laundry was enjoying a wonderful success. F. J. Clendenin and P.V. Dumbeck had opened drug stores, the Moline Coal Company had established a yard under the charge of J. Clark Lloyd, and the East Moline Fuel Company was managed by P. V. Clark. J. Frankel had opened a pool hall and billiard parlor. Peter Huey opened a grocery store that also did a general business, and P. B. Fisk was operating a grocery store that had evolved from a pop stand opened by Fisk's son and one of the Skinner boys.

THIS EARLY PHOTO OF ONE OF EAST MOLINE'S FIRST BUSINESSES WAS TAKEN BY C.R. REDFIELD OF EAST MOLINE. THE YOUNG MEN IN THE PICTURE ARE PAUL OLSON AND ARTHUR BISHOP.

Although the Mississippi Valley Traction Company bought historic Campbell's Island in 1902 with the intention of building a summer resort covering the whole of the island, construction of the resort had been delayed because the former owner had stipulated that Nels Olaf Bergstrom, an immigrant watchmaker from Sweden, could continue to live out his life on the 12 acres of land he occupied at the time of the sale. Nels Bergstrom died on February 6, 1904, and after his death the company announced the completion of a street car bridge to the proposed recreational site. By August of that year crowded interurban cars were crossing a narrow trestle to the island every half hour. People came to swim, dine, dance, picnic, take hikes, or to be entertained by the various orchestras that performed at the band stand. Sunday school picnics, company picnics and lodge outings were held on the grounds. On September 10, 1904, the descendents of Joseph and Mary Cox, pioneers of 1836, met on Campbell's Island for a reunion.

East Moline became a city in January of 1907 and Dr. G. F. Johnson became the city's first mayor. According to F. O. Lovins, a newspaper man and an early East Moline historian, Dr. Johnson designed a political machine that kept him in office for nearly a generation. Knowing the value of publicity, the new mayor organized a corporation, purchased the *East Moline Enterprise* and changed the name of the paper to the *East Moline Herald.* "Doc belonged to the Southern school of journalists," Lovins wrote. "He attacked his political enemies with brimstone and sulfuric acid."

The new mayor's first war is said to have been with the street car company. Shortly after being elected, the mayor wanted the company to sign a new agreement with the city that would lower fares. When the company refused to comply, the doctor demanded that the cars stop running. The railway company would not submit to Doc's pressure and one car came through. The crew was jailed and Dr. Johnson sent "Big Ted" Anderson, an East Moline policeman, to halt any additional cars that might attempt to pass through the city. The huge officer sat down on the track and defied the company men to run over him. Not wanting to commit homicide, the street car company agreed to sign a truce.

By 1910 the population of the city had reached 2,665, and there were 18 saloons in town. In that year, too, the volunteer fire department, organized in 1905, ceased to exist. The city needed fire fighters, but not a full time department. Louis Bornhoeft, East Moline's chief of police, was given the added responsibility of fire chief. The three patrolmen, Schlueter, Glasgow and VanNeste, doubled their duties as fire fighters.

After reorganizing its fire-police department, the city purchased a "one horse power" fire truck and an iron-grey fire horse named Broncho. Broncho was speedy, but he was hard to steer and he tended to backfire, throwing his rear hoofs high into the air. The city was without a siren at that time, but when a fire did occur the R&V Motor Company would blow its whistle. After the "siren's" initial scream the citizens would stampede to the city streets and Broncho would emerge from the truck house, straining on the reins under the control of Chief Bornhoeft. The chief's coattails flew flag-like under the force of the mighty wind and the firemen held to the sides of the truck as the entire mob rumbled, rolled and clattered its way to the fire. Broncho was later replaced by a team of black and prancing steeds, and the team was replaced by a motor-driven truck in 1916.

East Moline's early days were high-spirited, as wages were good and business opportunities were plentiful. Then, too, many of the citizens were immigrants, passionately proud to be Americans. They left their native homes in Belgium, Greece, Germany, Sweden and Ireland for economic reasons, and because they were people with dreams of a better future for themselves and their children. Some of the names on the city's small business establishments, names such as the Kandis and Mihael confectionery and Kero's pantatorium, reflected the heritage of the owners.

THE FIRST STREET CAR BRIDGE TO CAMPBELL'S ISLAND WAS BUILT ON TOP OF AN OLD CLOSING DAM BUILT BY THE GOVERNMENT ENGINEERS IN 1899.

A WOMAN ENJOYS THE SECLUDED SHORE OF CAMPBELL'S ISLAND IN THE 1910S.

THE PEOPLE ALONG THE RIVER CALLED HIM "CRAZY GEORGE," BUT GEORGE COATS WAS MERELY STRANGE. HE AND HIS FIVE DONKEYS ROAMED THE RIVER TOWNS FROM CORDOVA TO ROCK ISLAND FOR MANY YEARS. GEORGE WAS A NATURAL COMEDIAN, WHO BROUGHT LAUGHTER AND JOY TO THE PEOPLE THROUGH DANCE AND SONG, THOUGH HE COULD NEITHER DANCE NOR SING. HE PASSED HIS HAT FOR PENNIES, WORE CAST-OFF CLOTHES AND SLEPT AND ATE WHEREVER HOSPITALITY WAS OFFERED. ALTHOUGH THIS PHOTO WAS TAKEN ON THE MOLINE STREETS IN THE 1890S, COATS WAS VERY MUCH PART OF EAST MOLINE. HE DIED AT AGE 63 AFTER BEING HIT BY AN AUTOMOBILE IN 1913. AFTER HIS DEATH THE EAST MOLINE HERALD PRINTED A LENGTHY ARTICLE HONORING THIS "KINDLY AND CHEERFUL" MAN WHO THREW KISSES TO THE GIRLS FOR SMILES. "GEORGE'S DEPARTURE FROM LIFE HAS LEFT THE STREETS LONE-SOME AND THE DAYS A LITTLE DULL," THE HERALD SAID.

The Belgian immigrants organized St. Mary's Catholic Church, the Greeks worshiped at the Orthodox Church and the Germans worshiped at St. John's. Job opportunities brought black Americans to East Moline during World War I, and they, too, built and maintained their own church, the African Methodist Mission.

The early years were the "good old days." The days were filled with bits of news about some murder that took place at Leon Callewaert's saloon, the attempted robbery at the East Moline State Bank, or about the huge Fourth of July celebration, rained on but not rained out. People were enjoying picnics at Campbell's Island, *Why Women Sin* was playing at the Wagner Opera House in Moline, the men were discussing politics or the housing shortage at Salzman's cigar shop or Clendenin's drugs, and one poor woman was held for "wickedly contriving and intending" to poison her husband.

There were social hops at the Woodmen Hall, box socials at the Bliss Building, and on one Sunday afternoon Benjamin Mitchell drove his automobile all the way to Port Byron.

This was also a time of giving. Ernest Cox donated a building site to the Ridgeview Congregational Church, and J. S. Bailey donated his services as a plasterer for the new Plymouth Congregational Church — should they decide to build.

In 1912 East Moline graduated its first high school class, a class of one — Verna Parrott Koster. Floyd E. Thompson arrived in town wearing "a derby hat and an air of confidence," bought the *East Moline Herald*, ran for state's attorney and won.

The girls were playing baseball, as were the boys, and "the last sad rites were performed over the dead aspirations of the married men's baseball team (the Benedicts) at the feed (banquet) to the victorious Bachelors in the I.O.O.F. Hall."

Typhoid fever made the news, as did smallpox and the "Do you Tango" craze. One article in the *Herald* claimed that "when a man has chickens and lets them run at large in this day and age he is liable to become entangled with the law."

In 1917 the black population of East Moline, according to the *Herald*, put a
petition before the city for their own school and their own teachers. But the
Moline Daily Dispatch cried out that the petition did not reflect the
interests of the black people. Some of the new citizens had signed, but they
had not understood the nature of the petition. J. W. Whitfield of the
N.A.A.C.P. met with the board and it was decided there would be no
segregation. The East Moline School Board changed the school boundry
lines, thus placing the black children within a newly created district.
World War I interrupted the growth of the city and changed the lives of
many people. East Moline's long-time mayor, Doc, received a demand to
defend the freedom of his country — and his city. Lamb, Hanson and Van
Rissegham died in action. Others brought home scars.

Steamboat Kings and Railroad Empires: Cultures Conflict

At 5 p.m. February 22, 1854, a festively decorated locomotive belonging to
the Chicago and Rock Island Railroad Company steamed into the first
passenger house in the city of Rock Island. Swarms of local residents
scrambled into the six brightly painted yellow coaches as quickly as visitors
descended, and some of the men swaggered and threw their weight to the
roof of the train as the crowd below cheered and waved handkerchiefs or
flags in honor of the historic moment. This was a twofold holiday, the
birthday of the father of our country, and the day in which the Atlantic
Ocean was finally wedded to the Mississippi by bands of iron. The city
shuddered from the triumphant detonation of artillery and lamps were lit in
the public houses of Rock Island and Davenport. That evening a great
number of citizens from both sides of the river continued the festivities with
speeches, fireworks, supper at the Rock Island House, and, for many, a ball
at the Le Claire House in Davenport. Henry Farnham told the people they
could now travel from New York to Rock Island in 42 hours. That was quite
an improvement over the stage, which could travel about eight miles an
hour on a good road.

However, even as Farnham spoke that evening, he and his partner, Joseph
Sheffield, knew the railroad was in trouble. They had accomplished a great
deal by building the Chicago and Rock Island to this point, but to continue
expansion the company needed to attract the interest of additional
investors. One could be sure to draw attention if one could bait the leading
Eastern journalists to the area, so on May 1, 1854, Sheffield sent invitations
to stockholders, bondholders and prominent citizens throughout the
Eastern states, including the leading journalists and politicians of the day.
These people were to be guests of the railroad at a "formal celebration" of
its opening on June 5, 1854. The guests gathered at the Tremont House in
Chicago, and on the day the festivities were to begin they left Chicago in
two trains, each of which had eight coaches.

STREET CAR LINES LINKED EAST
MOLINE TO MOLINE, ROCK ISLAND
AND DAVENPORT AS EARLY AS
1903. BY 1907 SILVIS, TOO, WAS
LINKED TO THE TRI-CITIES. THIS
PHOTO SHOWS EAST MOLINE'S
18TH AVENUE, LOOKING TOWARD
SILVIS. ED TOBIN, THE CON-
DUCTOR, WAS ON BOARD THE
FIRST STREET CAR TO CROSS THE
BOUNDRY BETWEEN THE TWO
VILLAGES.

AN ICE GORGE DISPLACED A SPAN OF THE RAILROAD BRIDGE ACROSS THE MISSISSIPPI RIVER IN THE SPRING OF 1868. SHORTLY AFTER-WARD, A TORNADO PUSHED THE SWING SPAN OF THIS FIRST BRIDGE ACROSS THE MISSISSIPPI INTO THE WATER.

At 4 p.m. that same day, the 1,200 distinguished Easterners, including the 13th president of the United States, Millard Fillmore, were greeted at the Rock Island depot by cheering citizens, flags, bands, fireworks, steamboat whistles, rain and mud. After a small amount of hesitation, the ladies and gentlemen descended from the train. This was the West, the point at which the legendary land began. They could see Fort Armstrong crowning the island, a symbol of the red man's sorrow and the white man's progress. Five elegant steamboats, *Golden Era, Sparhawk, Lady Franklin, Galena* and *War Eagle*, were waiting at anchor in the Missisippi. On board these boats the visitors would journey to Fort Snelling and St. Paul in Minnesota Territory. The strangers were struck by the beauty and the glory of what they saw before them and they broke into a mighty cheer. Overnight, the Chicago and Rock Island became the best known railroad west of the Alleghenies.

Although tension had been building between the railroad men and the steamboat men for some time, the cooperation shown at the time of the much celebrated rail and water tour led some to believe that the two opposing forces might be able to work together. However, this did not prove true. The steamboat men watched with growing concern as the railroad continued to build up river, down river and to the West. And they watched with an even greater concern as the bridge that would link Rock Island and Davenport, the first bridge over the Mississippi, neared completion. So, when the church bells of the Twin-Cities rang out the news that the first passenger train had crossed the river on April 22, 1856, the joy of the bells must have sounded like a death knell to the river men. Two weeks later, on May 6, the *Effie Afton*, a fine and newly painted steamboat from St. Louis, rammed a pier, burst into flames and ignited a span of the bridge. After the span fell, the other steamboats on the river sounded a long and loud note of what seemed to be delight; however, some who watched from the banks of the Mississippi said the whistles were meant to be warnings, attempts to steer other boats clear of the floating wreck. This explanation was weakened after Mr. Webster of Port Byron reported that he had seen the steamboat *Hamburg* carrying a banner that bore these words: "Mississippi Bridge Destroyed — Let All Rejoice."

The case of river versus rail went to court in September 1857, after Captain J. S. Hurd, one of the owners of the *Effie Afton*, filed suit against the Railroad Bridge Company in an attempt to have bridges prohibited for all time from navigable rivers. Norman Judd of Chicago, George E. Hubbell of Davenport and Abraham Lincoln of Springfield were attorneys for the railroad. Lincoln was appointed principal attorney, but even he could not prove beyond all doubt that the wreck of the *Effie Afton* was an unintentional disaster. John MacLean, the presiding judge, decided the whole case came down to one question, whether the bridge was a material obstruction to navigation; however, the jury could not agree upon an answer. A rescheduled trial was later dismissed by Captain Hurd, and the bridge, which linked the Chicago and Rock Island Railroad to Iowa's Mississippi and Missouri Railroad, was allowed to stand because of indecision.

On May 7, 1858, James Ward, a steamboat leader from St. Louis, filed suit against the Mississippi and Missouri in the Iowa courts, hoping the court would find the bridge a nuisance. After reviewing a great deal of evidence, including a damaging statement against the structure prepared by the Corps of Topographical Engineers, the presiding judge, John M. Love, agreed with the steamboat interests and ordered the railroad company to remove the Iowa portion of the bridge and its piers. The railroad company appealed to the Supreme Court of the United States. The Supreme Court, probably because it was concerned with problems relating to the Civil War at that time (1862), reversed Love's decision without taking the danger of the bridge into consideration. The judges ruled the Iowa court had no right to order removal of the structure, and they established for all time the right to bridge navigable streams.

The first bridge at Rock Island came to be called the "gate of death" by river men, probably a title with more than one meaning. Although many steamboats and lumber rafts were thrown against the structure and damaged, one accident is more symbolic of the title than the others.

On May 9, 1861, *Grey Eagle*, a steamboat piloted by Captain Smith Harris, was thrown against a pier while going through the opened bridge. The boat sank to the upper deck and 117 persons jumped to the river. These were saved, but seven others, including a mental patient who was chained to the lower deck, were drowned. The *Rock Island Argus*, among others, cried out that the bridge should be indicted and tried for murder. The Rock Island County grand jurors did vote on the matter, not once, but twice. The first count of their vote was 13 to 10 in favor of indicting the bridge officials. Recess was called and a new vote was taken the next morning. The new count was 11 to 9, one short of the majority of 12. The bridge officials escaped trial for murder by a single vote.

The Chicago and Rock Island merged with the Mississippi and Missouri in 1865 to form the Chicago, Rock Island and Pacific Railroad Company. A new bridge was constructed between Rock Island and Davenport in 1872, and the old, badly constructed bridge was removed after a mere 16 years of service.

Easterners Settle in Pleasant Valley

John Silvis, along with his wife, Elizabeth, four sons and one daughter, left Harrisburg, Pennsylvania, in 1854. The family traveled by covered wagon to Rock Island County and settled at Pleasant Valley, a small community of farmers and coal miners on the stage line that ran from Rock Island to Chicago. The Pleasant Valley House, a hotel built in 1835, served as stage stop. Most of the homes were log cabins.

According to a story handed down within the Silvis family, John soon grew lonely and wanted to go back to his family and friends in the East, but Elizabeth would not hear of it. Angered, John left without her, though he soon returned. He built a home large enough to house all those people who might come through Pleasant Valley as they traveled west from Pennsylvania. Strangers, friends and relatives: many came and all were welcome.

Pleasant Valley continued to be a rural community of truck farms, orchards and dairies throughout the 19th century, though there were two other industries in the valley. Thomas and Richard Silvis, sons of John and Elizabeth, owned the Silvis Mining Company, and F. J. Robinson, Franklin

Rhodes and Fred Titterington of Rock Island owned and ran the Argillo Pottery Works. The Chicago and Rock Island Railroad, which Titterington rode to work every morning and home every night, ran through the farm land of the valley and made the community a distant satellite of the Twin-Cities.

One Town, One Industry, One People

Since E. H. Guyer, the father of East Moline, had made previous land dealings for the Chicago, Rock Island and Pacific Railroad, that company contacted him once again when it needed a man to buy land at Pleasant Valley. The year was 1902. Guyer proceeded to purchase land belonging to Richard Shippen Silvis, then hired Silvis to secure the additional 800 or more acres the railroad needed. However, no one was to know the railroad was involved in the purchases, so Guyer was to hold all options in his name. But secrets could not be kept. Although the Tri-City communities were growing, they continued to be small-town in matters of gossip. It was not long before news about the mysterious happenings at Pleasant Valley could be read about in various area newspapers.

On January 1, 1903, the *Moline Dispatch* began to run daily reports of land deals in Pleasant Valley. There had been rumors for quite some time, tales that told of huge buildings being planned and a boom that would create a new city with a population of nearly 10,000. It was reported that the Skinner family had sold a great deal of land west of Pleasant Valley, and that W. H. Gulley of the Rock Island Railroad's construction department

THE ARGILLO POTTERY WORKS EMPLOYED MANY MEN FROM PLEASANT VALLEY, AND FROM 1860-1885 THE CHILDREN OF PLEASANT VALLEY ATTENDED SCHOOL IN ONE OF THE COMPANY BUILDINGS.

had bought a house in the valley for $1,200. Farm land, the newspaper reported, was selling for $400 an acre.

The news became official on January 28 when the Rock Island Railroad announced it was holding options on 800 or 900 acres of land in Pleasant Valley, and that the company intended to build a complex of shops on the land that would employ 2,000 (the *Argus* said 3,000) men at its commencement. On the following day it was announced that the road extending from Rock Island through Pleasant Valley was to be moved a bit to the south as it ran through the valley. The new section of road would be 100 feet wide.

However, there were problems. Susan Schrumm and Susan Griffith, two land owners in Pleasant Valley, refused to agree upon a selling price until the Rock Island Railroad began a condemnation suit against their property. Also, Pleasant Valley School, built in 1885, had to be moved, but the school board could not agree with the railroad's choice for a new location. According to legend, the dispute ended when the railroad out-maneuvered the board by moving the school secretly one February night in 1903. The cemetery, too, had to be relocated, as did some human bones uncovered during the grading of the new road. The cemetery was removed to Hampton, and the bones were reburied with respect at a site higher on the hill. The historic Pleasant Valley House was sold to Chris Gueldenpfennig, who transported it to Cleveland Ferry in Henry County.

Pleasant Valley ceased to exist, as did Skinnerville (located on land that is now the west end of Silvis). First referred to as the land east of East Moline, the property the railroad owned and its surrounding area was later called Vulcan, then New Shops.

RICHARD SHIPPEN SILVIS. SILVIS SOLD NEARLY 58 ACRES OF LAND TO THE RAILROAD, THEN HELPED THE RAILROAD BUY LAND.

SILVIS IN 1912. NOTE THE ROUND-
HOUSE IN THE BACKGROUND.

SOME SAY THE CHICAGO, ROCK
ISLAND AND PACIFIC SHOPS IN
SILVIS WERE THE LARGEST
LOCOMOTIVE REPAIR SHOPS IN
THIS COUNTRY. OTHERS SAY THEY
WERE THE LARGEST IN THE
WORLD.

On January 28, 1904, the *East Moline Enterprise* reported that 1,000 men would begin work at New Shops on February 1, and that until the men could find homes, street cars and work trains would make special trips to transport workers between Davenport, Rock Island, Moline and New Shops. However, the *Enterprise* continued, this arrangement was to be temporary, and the men had been told they would have to move to East Moline if they wanted to keep their jobs. Since East Moline was still basically an industrial area having few homes, this stipulation must have been difficult for the shop employees to understand. It takes time and money to build houses, and many years would pass before the problem of housing in Silvis (and in East Moline) could be solved.

The settlement was platted in 1905, the same year the shop officials decided they wanted to name their newly platted townsite after the sturdy and energetic Richard Shippen Silvis. Silvis agreed, but only after being approached three times. The lively and good natured land dealer, who loved to tease and rode a good horse, had resisted the honor due to his understanding that places were named after people only after the name-lending person was dead, which he was not.

The village of Silvis was incorporated in 1907 and Richard Walsh, the operator of a brake shoe foundry, was elected president of the village board. Willis Hopson, the village marshal, kept order in the community and lit and tended the gas lamps along the cinder path. V.H. Dumbeck served as postmaster and William Downing was appointed village clerk. The first village hall was housed in a boxcar, as was the fire department, a bucket brigade organized by Morton Penell.

According to Earl "Pappy" Hall (retired from the shops and a current Silvis poet), in 1906 Silvis consisted of about 12 houses, Leekley's store and John Soey's pool hall, but by 1907 the population of the community was more than 300. Nearly 1,200 men were employed at the Rock Island Railroad shops, and businessmen were being attracted to the townsite from outside the boundaries of its platted land.

OUR LADY OF GUADALUPE CATHOLIC CHURCH SILVIS ILL

George Nichol, an immigrant from Northumberland, Scotland, bought the first lot sold in Silvis and founded a coal and express company. Ben Erzinger opened a bakery, R.B. Cox was a grocer, and the Downing brothers owned a clothing and shoe store. John Groom was the first barber in the village and George Newton operated the first meat market. Charles Swanson made cement blocks and Ole Lindquist opened a blacksmith and wagon shop. Herman Kuehne opened a tavern, as did Hanson and Warner, and Walter Lyood operated the first hotel. W.D. Chapman was the village doctor and L.T. Outen was the dentist. H.J. Crowder founded the first banking business, but was later beaten and robbed. Crowder died; the robbers were captured and given long prison terms.

By 1908 the railroad-centered community had established a public park with a bandstand. The business district was furnished with hitching posts and water troughs, and a large fire bell was located near 12th Street and First Avenue. A third school was built, ready for occupancy in January of that year. One month later, Sixth Street School, completed two years earlier, was destroyed by fire. Many students finished the year in classes held on the second floor of the old post office, or in the flat above Leekleys store. The school (renamed McKinley) was rebuilt at the same site by the next season.

The Silvis Women's Club, organized in 1910 under the leadership of Mrs. John Pike, and the Needlework Club, founded in 1912, were moving forces behind the formation of the community library, which found its first home in Dumbeck's drugstore and its second home in the Keystone drugstore. In addition, these same clubs were active in the formation of community parks, social work and educational programs.

Silvis was a tightly centered and well run village, but it continued to have a housing problem for many years. A large number of Mexican workers came to the shops in 1917, probably to strengthen a work force diminished by World War I. The Mexican immigrants could not find homes, so the families moved into deserted boxcars north of the tracks. The men, like Silvis men of all backgrounds, put on the uniform of their trade: blue denim overalls, a striped railroad cap and a gaudy bandanna. The women, like Silvis women of all backgrounds, fought with coal dust from the Chicago, Rock Island and Pacific engines.

Thus, "born as a child of the iron horse and reared in the atmosphere of puffing engines," Silvis and the railroad shops became synonymous. The Chicago, Rock Island and Pacific Railroad Company, because of financial difficulties, closed its shops in Silvis on April 1, 1980. But the demise of the shops did not erase the spirit of the railroad from the minds and the hearts of the Silvis people, nor will it in the generations to come. Stories and histories will be passed down from one generation to another and the legend of the shops, the town and the people will continue.

THE CONGREGATION OF OUR LADY OF GUADALUPE CATHOLIC CHURCH WORSHIPED IN TWO BOX-CARS FROM 1927-1930. THEN THE RAILROAD RECLAIMED ITS CARS AND ITS LAND, SO MANY OF THE MEXICAN-AMERICAN PEOPLE IN SILVIS HAD TO LEAVE THEIR HOMES AS WELL AS THEIR HOUSE OF WORSHIP. THE PEOPLE BUILT HOMES FOR THEMSELVES, A NECESSITY, BUT THEY COULD NOT FIND FUNDS FOR THEIR NEW CHURCH, LARGELY BECAUSE OF THE DEPRESSION. THE CHURCH, DEDICATED ON DECEMBER 14, 1930, WAS CONTRIBUTED BY THE DIOCESE OF PEORIA. OUR LADY OF GUADALUPE WAS A MEXICAN NATIONAL PARISH FROM 1930-1962, BUT TODAY IT IS A TERRITORIAL PARISH. THE CHURCH HAS ENTERED THE MAINSTREAM OF AMERICAN LIFE (30 PERCENT OF THE MEMBERS HAVE MEXICAN-AMERICAN NAMES, WHILE 50 PERCENT HAVE NAMES DERIVED FROM A BELGIAN-AMERICAN BACKGROUND), BUT THE PEOPLE OF THE CONGREGATION CONTINUE TO CELEBRATE THE MEXICAN ROOTS THAT ESTABLISHED THEIR CHURCH. THEY HAVE HELD A YEARLY FESTIVAL IN HONOR OF THOSE ROOTS FOR 31 YEARS. DUE TO A GROWING CONGREGATION, A LARGER HOUSE OF WORSHIP WAS CONSTRUCTED IN 1968.

BY JIM ARPY

TRI-CITY AREA MEN LEAVING TO SERVE IN WORLD WAR I WERE GIVEN A WARM SEND-OFF BY MEMBERS OF THE RED CROSS CANTEEN COMMITTEE. DURING 1917-1918, THE CANTEEN WOMEN PROVIDED ARTICLES THE MILITARY MEN MIGHT NEED ON LONG JOURNIES TO TRAINING CAMPS AND PORTS OF DEPARTURE. THIS PHOTO WAS TAKEN AT ROCK ISLAND'S 31ST STREET STATION.

The World War I song, "How Ya Gonna Keep 'Em Down On The Farm After They've Seen Paree?" symbolized the far-reaching changes that began to transform the Quad-Cities, or the "Tri-Cities" as the area was known until after World War II, shortly after the conclusion of "the war to end all wars." The tempo of this transition would begin slowly but would gain momentum with each succeeding decade and affect almost every aspect of life in the areas joined by the Mississippi River.

A provincialism that was a natural result of its middle-of-the-nation isolation would begin to erode before the tides of new methods of communication and transportation, far-reaching technological advances and an influx of new people with fresh ideas, including those military veterans who had, indeed, seen "Paree" and brought back to their hometowns an expanded world view.

The journey from the "Roaring '20s" to the threshhold of the Space Age would offer challenges and rewards to the Tri-City area, as well as turbulent and often trying times. The way would, on occasion, be led by villains, as well as by persons of vision and a sense of civic responsibility. With the rest of the nation, the area would experience the heady, euphoric, take-a-chance-mood of the post-World War I era, with all of its glitter and promise, and the bleak bursting of the bubble as the stock market crashed in 1929.

Area residents, enjoying the fruits of the good times — more money, better housing, good jobs, automobiles and that new miracle, radio — would see many of their gains swept away in the long Great Depression days, a period of trial that would end only when they geared up their factories once more for another world war.

Times of war, periods of peace, eras of prosperity and years of joblessness and uncertainty brought with them their own particular brands of change that irrevocably altered the area cities to which the doughboys of World

War I had returned. Bound to the rest of the nation through commerce and communication, and to the world through the age of flight and an emerging electronic age, the Quad-Cities, as it would later come to be known, expanded its horizons and continued to grow.

Two events that would affect the area occurred practically within a year of one another.

Passage of the Volstead Act on July 1, 1919, would have far-reaching effects. It brought nationwide Prohibition, or, as some called it, "the great drought."

Ratification of the 19th Amendment to the U.S. Constitution on August 26, 1920, gave women the right to vote. For the first time, they could express their preferences in local, state and national elections.

Iowa had voted on the issue of women's suffrage as early as 1916, but Davenport and Scott County voters, all males, had turned out in record numbers to defeat the proposal by a two-to-one margin. In fact, the measure won approval in only two of the county's precincts.

By contrast, Iowa had voted Prohibition into effect as early as December 31, 1915, nearly four years before the entire nation went dry. Illinois remained "wet" for two more years, creating quite a trek of thirsty Davenporters to the less parched side of the Mississippi.

Violence Scars Tri-Cities

Prohibition would trigger an era of lawlessness of a type never seen before or since, and for years area newspapers would carry almost daily stories of bootlegging, raids by federal agents on homes, clubs, warehouses and other so-called "dens of iniquity," along with other seamy tales of official graft and conspiracy, gangsterism, murder and indictments.

DAVENPORT'S RIVERFRONT IN THE EARLY 1930S HOSTED FEW PARKED AUTOMOBILES, BUT DID PROVIDE DOCKING FOR LUXURIOUS EXCURSION BOATS. THERE WAS NO SEAWALL THEN AND THE BIG CRAFT COULD MOOR RIGHT NEXT TO THE SHORELINE, JUST AS THEY HAD DECADES EARLIER WHEN STEAMBOATS MADE THE CITY A REGULAR PORT OF CALL.

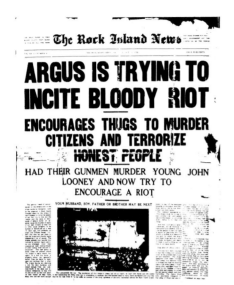

JOHN LOONEY WAS AN ENIGMATIC FIGURE WHO CAST A DARK SHADOW OVER ROCK ISLAND FOR ALMOST TWO DECADES IN THE EARLY 1900S. HE PUBLISHED A BLACKMAILING SCANDAL SHEET AND ESTABLISHED HIMSELF AS THE OVERLORD OF VICE UNTIL A MURDER CONVICTION ENDED HIS REIGN. THE HEADLINES ON HIS ROCK ISLAND NEWS WERE AS FLAMBOYANT AS HE WAS.

One figure whose corruptive presence had blighted the Tri-City area and particularly Rock Island for two decades earlier, before he fled to escape prosecution, returned from exile in New Mexico to reestablish control of the major illegal enterprises. He was a criminal genius named John Looney who, as he had earlier, soon gave Rock Island a reputation for wide-open sin and lawlessness that the city did not easily live down.

Looney's flourishing criminal empire could not have existed, though, without the devil-may-care mood of the Roaring '20s and the willingness of many citizens to flout provisions of the Volstead Act, even though it meant committing criminal acts.

Looney, as he had earlier, once again ruled with pen and gun as undisputed king of the Rock Island underworld. He slandered, he ruined, he inspired fear and, until the citizenry finally had enough, he killed with impunity.

In addition to publishing the infamous *Rock Island News*, a scandal sheet whose lurid pages were used for blackmail and extortion, Looney kept an iron grip on gambling, prostitution and large-scale bootlegging. A curious mixture of evil and intelligence, Looney proclaimed to intimates that he could never be killed because "the devil protects me."

During his almost 30-year reign (1892-1922), broken only by occasional brief exiles, he plundered the pocketbooks and the reputations of upstanding citizens and criminals with equal zeal. When he was finally toppled, Looney took with him not only his own shady cohorts, but also many hopelessly ensnared and dishonored public officials, among them a former mayor, the chief of police, police magistrate, city attorney and numerous lawyers. So bold was Looney that he even controlled, behind the scenes, the Rock Island Police Department, using it for his own profit and vengeance. He shared the power of the force jealously with a crooked chief and Helen Van Dale, a mink-draped madam known as "the queen of the Rock Island underworld," who was the female counterpart of Looney's own ruthlessness.

Looney, who pretended to war on vice and crime and railed against "corruption" in his *Rock Island News* scandal sheet, schooled his only son, John Connor Looney Jr., in crime. He saw the 22-year-old young man gunned down by a rival gang in a Market Square shootout in 1922. The attack upon Looney and his son was in retaliation for Looney's earlier slaying of Rock Island tavern owner Bill Gabel. Later testimony in Looney's trial for the murder of Gabel would disclose that young Connor, as he was called, had driven the car from which the fatal shots were fired. Gabel was assassinated because he was about to present evidence against Looney to federal authorities.

The elder Looney escaped the hail of bullets on Market Square. As he knelt over his dying son, the youth told him that his gun had jammed. Connor's death did not halt Looney's lawless activities. During the '20s, he and his many cohorts extended their activities into neighboring Illinois cities and across the river into Davenport. Gambling houses ran wide open, prostitutes were hauled from city to city on both sides of the Mississippi, and police and other city officials, some bribed and others blackmailed or frightened by threats, looked the other way.

The cadaverous-looking Looney fled Rock Island in December 1922 to avoid prosecution for Gabel's murder. Three years later, he was captured in New Mexico and returned to stand trial in a Galesburg, Illinois, courtroom. There, with his former henchmen seeking to save themselves by testifying against him, Looney was convicted of murder and found his former kingdom reduced to the size of a cell in Joliet Penitentiary. Released after serving about nine years, Looney is believed to have died shortly thereafter of tuberculosis.

If Looney cast a dark shadow on the area in the early '20s there were still plenty of bright spots, and popular songs like "Look for the Silver Lining," "Ain't We Got Fun?" and "It Ain't Gonna Rain No Mo" seemed to epitomize the energetic, optimistic mood of the Tri-Cities.

Lawlessness and Prohibition seemed an integral part of that mood, and Davenport, though less under the thumb of one individual, was also experiencing its own crime wave. In fact, Iowa's 1915 Prohibition Act had been in effect only 10 days when the first charges of illegal liquor sales were filed in Davenport. And that was only the beginning. There were more and more arrests for the sales of "home-made hooch" like bathtub gin, made from distilled water, grain alcohol and a few drops of essence of juniper, some more toxic potions that blinded or killed, and so-called "home brew" beer, or "near-beer" spiked with alcohol.

Bootlegging flourished with such intensity in the Tri-Cities that Prohibition agents made the area their base of operations for a wide district. Almost daily, newspapers carried stories of raids and arrests. The bootleggers, many of them first-time lawbreakers, devised ingenious ways to thwart Prohibition agents. On some houseboats, jugs of booze were strung on wires that had been staked out in the harbors. When lookout men spotted raiders in the vicinity, the jugs were released to slide down the wires and crash into conveniently placed rocks, an effective way to get rid of the evidence. In the basement of one camouflaged Davenport house, agents uncovered the biggest stills found in Iowa up to that time. One was of 100-gallon capacity, and the other of 75 gallons. Also seized were 40 gallons of hooch and 100 gallons of rye mash. On November 30, 1928, agents raided the East Davenport Turner Hall, and in the basement confiscated 4,185 bottles of home brew. Hundreds more were taken from the Davenport Eagles' clubrooms.

THE REV. BILLY SUNDAY DREW HUGE CROWDS TO A SPECIALLY BUILT TABERNACLE IN ROCK ISLAND IN 1914 WHEN HE CRUSADED AGAINST SIN.

As Prohibition continued, so did violence. On May 25, 1932 (the same year a young Eureka [Illinois] College graduate named Ronald Reagan went to work as a part-time sports announcer for WOC-Radio in Davenport), one-time bootleg king Nick Coin was gunned down in front of his Davenport residence. Two assassins in a big, black sedan were spotted, but were never caught. Just a year earlier, Coin's good friend, Angelo Kaloudis, had been found shot to death in the blood-drenched rear seat of his car, on a lonely country road not far from Durant, Iowa. That case also remained unsolved. Years earlier, the renowned pulpit-pounding evangelist William A. (Billy) Sunday had sought to set the Tri-Cities on the path of righteousness with a seven-week revivalist campaign. He chose Rock Island, where the infamous Looney held sway, blasting it as a "citadel of sin." A central committee representing area churches had planned four years for Sunday's crusade, and had built, at the corner of 24th Street and 5th Avenue a sprawling tabernacle capable of seating 8,000. It had cost $15,000. Lighting, heat, transportation and staff expenses took thousands more, but the $50,000 raised through donations more than paid for everything.

THE ROARING '20S SAW AMERICA RELAXING AND ENJOYING ITSELF AFTER THE RIGORS OF WORLD WAR I. IT WAS THE ERA OF THE BOBBED-HAIRED FLAPPER, STUTZ BEARCATS, RACCOON COATS AND PARTIES, PARTIES, PARTIES. THIS GALA OCCASION WAS THE TRI-CITY FLORISTS' DANCE AT DANCELAND BALLROOM, DAVENPORT.

The crusade began in September 1914 and drew huge crowds. Few escaped the evangelist's ire. He lambasted the German-born in Davenport for their batches of home brew, and took particular aim against a product of the Roaring '20s — the flapper, with her short skirt, boyish form, bobbed hair, lipstick and artificial eyelashes. "Cigarette-sucking women!" Sunday roared from the pulpit.

Thousands were turned away from the evangelist's opening service, so two additional ones were held the same day, for a total of 20,000. For the entire length of the crusade, the tabernacle, with four inches of sawdust on the floor, was filled nightly to capacity. Special separate programs were held for men and women only. By the time the crusade ended, Sunday claimed to have made 10,612 converts among Illinois and Iowa residents.

More than 12,000 jammed into the tabernacle for Sunday's final sermon. Those who could not find seats sat in the aisles. Sunday's only salary was the collection taken on his final day in any city. From it, he paid one-third of his staff's salary. The sponsoring committee of local citizens paid the rest.

Sunday was no stranger to the area. His penniless mother, widowed during the Civil War, had put him and his brother, Ed, into the Iowa Soldiers' Orphans' Home in Davenport 45 years earlier. Billy Sunday had remained there for three years.

Typical of the towers of words he would build and topple onto sinners were these he launched against the nation's beer brewers: "I've fought those damnable, infamous, vile, rotten, beetle-brow, hog-jowled, black-hearted, white-livered, good-for-nothing dirty imps of hell and damnation, and I will fight them to hell and back again!"

Despite Sunday's efforts, though, a lot of area residents continued to support the sin he railed against, and a thorough cleanup was years away. The more mobile type of crime was only one of the transitions through which the area passed as it put World War I behind it and roared into the 20th century.

Better Roads Ease Travel

There would also be many credits in its ledgers, and improved roads were among the more important achievements. Nationwide, better highways ended the relative isolation of places like the Tri-Cities, attracting not only tourists and businessmen, but also persons who found the area an attractive and promising locale in which to settle.

There was a national clamor for better roads after World War I, and the Tri-Cities was no exception. At that time, most of the country's three million miles of rural roads were little better than dirt trails. Travel anywhere outside of the city limits was hazardous and the chances of an auto becoming bogged down to the running boards were excellent.

The experience of a Davenport physician, Dr. Walter Matthey, was typical. The doctor, in his Will-St. Clair coupe, was returning from Iowa City on November 12, 1922, after watching the State University of Iowa's Hawkeyes drub the Minnesota Gophers in football. Dr. Matthey had turned off the unpaved River-to-River Road, (later U.S. Route 6) to travel toward Muscatine. As cold rain poured down, Dr. Matthey was unable to prevent his car from sliding into a ditch full of sticky mud so deep that the car doors were jammed and he was trapped until Oscar Staby of Bettendorf came plowing through the mire in his car and freed him. Farmers in the area had a profitable day charging other stuck-in-the-mud motorists from $2 to $10 to pull their autos out.

In June 1919, the issue of hard surfacing of primary roads was carried by 1,100 votes in Scott County. More than 73 miles of road were improved in the next few years. However, in Illinois, hard surfacing of major roads did not get underway until 1924, and until then a trip from the Tri-Cities to

Chicago involved all of the planning and pitfalls of a major expedition. Nationwide, during the '20s and '30s, more than 45,000 miles of highways were surfaced each year.

To accommodate a growing number of travelers, service stations sprouted all over. Before the '20s, a motorist usually serviced and repaired his own car, carrying tools and gear with him.

Aside from convenience, another reason for the demand for better roads was that closed cars were replacing the open-air models and motorists dared to venture greater distances in all kinds of weather.

As the flamboyant decade of the Roaring '20s dawned, most residents still depended on the Tri-City Railway's trolleys for intercity transportation, but a time came when some owners of cars saw a way to turn a fast dollar. They were abetted by a prolonged trolley strike that began in 1919. Drivers turned their personal autos into "jitney buses," driving passengers around the area at fares ranging from a nickel on up. As the strike dragged on, more jitneys appeared on the streets. In Rock Island and Moline, free jitney licenses were issued, and by mid-August at least 200 cars were operating as four-wheeled, rubber-tired trolleys in all of the area cities.

The licenses were withdrawn in Rock Island and Moline only when jitneys continued to make their runs after settlement of the strike. Officials of the Tri-City Railway protested that they were ruining business. Several more years elapsed, though, before Davenport banned jitneys.

As an early and growing industrial center, the Tri-Cities had been a major rail crossroads since the late 1850s. By 1886 seventy-two passenger trains departed from and arrived at the area every day.

As the area continued to undergo changes and moved toward the nuclear energy age in the mid-1950s, it was still served by four railroads, with Davenport receiving 40 freight and passenger trains daily. The area was on the main line of the Rock Island Lines between Chicago on the east, Denver and Colorado Springs on the west, Kansas City to the south, and the Pacific Coast transcontinentally.

During that period, the Chicago-Milwaukee and the St. Paul & Pacific connected Davenport with Milwaukee to the northeast and Kansas City to the south, on freight routes. The Chicago, Burlington & Quincy linked Davenport with Minneapolis to the north and St. Louis to the south, for freight shipments. Each line had connections to other major cities.

PEOPLE LINED THE STREETS OF DAVENPORT IN THE LATE 1920S TO SEE THE DAVENPORT GAS-ELECTRIC LOCOMOTIVE. IT WAS BILLED AS "THE MOST POWERFUL LOCOMOTIVE OF ITS SIZE EVER MADE." IT WEIGHED 10 TONS AND HAD NO TRANSMISSION OR CLUTCH.

THE TREACHEROUS ROCK ISLAND RAPIDS, EXTENDING FROM ARSENAL ISLAND TO NEAR LE CLAIRE, WERE A MENACE TO NAVIGATION AND ONLY A SKILLED RIVER PILOT COULD LEAD A BOAT SAFELY THROUGH THEM. EFFORTS TO ELIMINATE THEM BY BLASTING AND DREDGING WERE LARGELY UNSUCCESSFUL, BUT LATER A SERIES OF LOCKS AND DAMS PROVIDED DEEPER WATER, AND THE RAPIDS CEASED TO BE A PROBLEM.

COFFER DAMS HELD BACK THE MISSISSIPPI RIVER WHILE CONSTRUCTION OF LOCKS AND DAM 15 WAS UNDERWAY IN 1931. LARGE CROWDS WATCHED THE MASSIVE ENGINEERING PROJECT DURING THE SUMMER MONTHS. DAM 15, COMPOSED OF 11 GATES, AND THE MAIN AND AUXILIARY LOCKS, WAS OFFICIALLY OPENED TO TRAFFIC IN THE SPRING OF 1934.

By the early 1930s, many new steam locomotives and trains had replaced the square bulky look with sleek streamlining, and in 1934 the lightweight diesel-electric passenger train made its first appearance in the Tri-Cities. Neither the steam engine nor airfields managed to kill one of the oldest transportation systems, the ferry. Ferryboat service linking the Iowa and Illinois cities literally went into operation with the first settlers. By 1886, two steamboat lines and several independently owned boats, in addition to the ferry *J.W. Spencer*, were engaged in carrying passengers and freight to and from Davenport and its Illinois neighbors.

Even after the establishment of airfields in Moline and Davenport during the '20s, the ferry continued to be a viable and nostalgically romantic means of river transportation. In 1925, the *Spencer's* business was taken over by William J. Quinlan, who became operator of the large *W.J. Quinlan*. That craft continued to ply between the Iowa and Illinois shores into the late 1950s, as did Fred Kahlke's gas-powered ferry, *Transit*. Its river days over, the *W.J. Quinlan* went into permanent drydock in the Kahlke Boatyards at the foot of Mill Street, Rock Island. In 1967, a fire apparently set by an arsonist destroyed the old paddlewheeler.

Locks, Dams Ease River Transportation

There have long been efforts to improve transportation on the Upper Mississippi River. The Rock Island Rapids, a treacherous, rock-strewn, boat-eating stretch of water that extended from Arsenal Island to near Le Claire, had long been a menace to navigation. Efforts to eliminate the rapids by blasting and dredging had been largely unsuccessful.

The subsequent Corps of Engineers' survey of the river between St. Louis and Minneapolis, authorized in the 1927 Rivers and Harbors Bill, resulted in a decision to provide, through a series of locks and dams, a nine-foot channel that would ensure deep water navigation. Because the Rock Island Rapids were considered the most serious navigation hazard, Locks and Dam 15, between Rock Island and Davenport, at the foot of Arsenal Island, became the first of 26 similar installations authorized by Congress. The main and auxiliary locks opened August 16, 1933, twenty-seven months after the project was begun. In addition to improving navigation, it provided many much-needed jobs during the Depression. It was a massive engineering project that was eagerly watched during the warm weather months by large crowds.

With the locks finally operational, construction of a series of roller dams began. These dams had to be designed to be functional under the special conditions the area imposed. The Mississippi at the Rock Island location was too shallow for the type of submersible gates in use on the Ohio River. The Mississippi often rose to flood stage in the spring, exerting tremendous force, so engineers installed moveable gates that could be raised completely out of the water when the river was on one of its frequent rampages. Gates in the main channel also had to be exceptionally strong to resist the pressures of ice floes and jams. The roller gate design was adopted because it allowed water to pass under rather than over the dam, thus permitting the migration of fish, stabilizing water levels above the dams, aereating water passing under the rollers, and allowing silt and debris to pass without backing up behind the dams. Dam 15, composed of 11 gates, and the main and auxiliary locks were officially opened to traffic in the spring of 1934. Total cost of the project was about $7.5 million. With the nine-foot channel established, Rock Island became the most important river port city in Illinois.

Even earlier, in 1927, the federal government had launched the Inland Waterways Corporation to operate the Federal Barge Lines. Rock Island was considered the logical site for the Tri-Cities' terminal. That city's voters approved a $300,000 bond issue for construction of the terminal, which was built in 1931. A floating wharf barge 230 feet long and 40 feet wide was installed at the terminal after being towed from Jeffersonville, Indiana, where it was built.

LOCKS AND DAM 15, BETWEEN DAVENPORT AND ROCK ISLAND, BECAME THE FIRST OF 26 SIMILAR OPERATIONS APPROVED BY CONGRESS. IN ADDITION TO PROVIDING A DEEPER MISSISSIPPI RIVER CHANNEL, THE PROJECT PROVIDED MANY MUCH-NEEDED JOBS DURING THE DEPRESSION OF THE 1930S. LOCKS AND DAM 15 WERE NEARING COMPLETION IN THIS PHOTO, AND THE ROLLERS WERE IN PLACE.

The first actual barge service on the Upper Mississippi had been inaugurated in the area when the *S.S. Thorpe*, a recently completed towboat, docked at the Municipal Levee in Rock Island on August 19, 1927, after a two-week trip from St. Louis. It arrived with three barges and added a 500-ton barge loaded with agricultural implements after making port in Rock Island.

The inauguration of barge service would have tremendous impact, extending to the present, on the Tri-Cities, and completion of the nine-foot channel added impetus to a rebirth of river commerce that would, in succeeding years, see new tonnage records consistently set.

At the time the Inland Waterways Corporation was formed, and the first of the 26 locks and dams that would extend over 663 miles of river was completed, Mississippi River shipping had slipped from several million tons annually to a mere 500,000 tons a year.

The Federal Barge Lines operated until 1953 when the government disposed of it to avoid competition with private shipping lines.

Another factor that opened the Tri-Cities to outside influences and eventually had an effect on life and business was the coming of the air age. Early in the 1920s there were several small flying fields on both sides of the river. The Iowa side boasted the Frank Wallace field in Bettendorf and another on Credit Island. For a short time, there was also a field at the rear of Davenport's National Guard armory building on Brady Street.

In Rock Island County, early airports included one east of downtown Moline on 23rd Avenue and another located in a pasture and known initially as Franning Field. This site would be known eventually as the area's major field, the Quad-City Airport.

On November 12, 1928, a landing site on Division Street officially became Davenport's airport and was dedicated as "Cram Field," in honor of Ralph Cram, editor and publisher of *The Democrat* newspaper. Cram's tremendous enthusiasm for flying won him the nickname of "the flying editor." As the field was dedicated, a squadron of Army planes flew over in review. During the next 10 years the city took steps to acquire the field as a municipal property. It had been under lease previously.

THE MOLINE AIRPORT WAS STILL A MODEST VENTURE WHEN THIS PHOTO WAS TAKEN IN 1935. IT WAS SURROUNDED BY CORNFIELDS AND SERVED ONLY A SMALL NUMBER OF PLANES. THE HANGAR WAS CLOSE TO THE JUNCTION OF AIRPORT ROAD AND ROUTE 150. THIS PHOTO WAS TAKEN JUST AFTER FIRE DESTROYED ONE OF THE SMALLER AIRPORT BUILDINGS, JUST TO THE RIGHT OF THE CENTER OF THE PICTURE.

The present multi-million dollar Quad-City Airport south of Moline grew out of this early area interest in aviation. In the 1920s, the *Daily Times* was one of the few newspapers in the country to utilize its own airplane in its daily operations. Davenporters were among the earliest pioneers in aviation. On November 14, 1910, a Davenporter, Lieutenant Eugene Ely, made flying history when he made the world's first flight from the deck of a ship, the *Birmingham*. During that same year, Oscar Solbrig, a pioneer Davenport aviator, thrilled thousands in Iowa and Illinois as he gave them their first view of a plane in flight.

The Moline Airport, as it was first known, observed the beginning of regularly scheduled air service on May 12, 1926, when National Air Transport inaugurated regular mail flights between Chicago, Kansas City and Dallas, with one stop in Moline. The next year saw the addition of east-west service at the Moline field. It was begun by Boeing Transport. In 1931, National Air Transport, Boeing and two other carriers were merged to form United Air Lines.

The day that Colonel Charles Lindbergh flew his famed *Spirit of St. Louis* into the Moline Airport brought cheers from an enthusiastic crowd of 10,000. "Lucky Lindy" had very recently electrified the nation by flying his frail craft non-stop to Paris. Lindbergh circled the Tri-Cities, dipping his plane's wings in salute. Greeted with roaring acclaim after landing, Lindbergh waved from an auto parade that wound through East Moline, Moline, Rock Island and Davenport.

The conqueror of the Atlantic was not the only renowned pilot to visit the Moline Airport. Famed woman flier Amelia Earhart once put her plane down there, and another woman flier, Phoebe Omlie, established an altitude record for women while soaring over that field in 1929, quite appropriately in a plane manufactured by a Moline firm, the Velie Motors Corporation. Nothing that flew, though, could have provided Davenporters with a bigger thrill than the day the great *Graf Zeppelin* soared above their city. The date was August 28, 1929, and the *Graf* was on an around-the-world flight. Davenport was not on her list of places to visit, at least not until the big ship's commander, Dr. Hugo Eckener, received a telegram from former Davenport mayor John Barewald. He pointed out the number of former German citizens living in Davenport and asked Dr. Eckener to make an aerial detour to fly over his city.

Dr. Eckener agreed and at 2 p.m. the huge craft, cruising at an altitude of about 1,000 feet, slowly circled the city while below thousands waved and cheered. It was a sight that those who saw it never forgot.

By 1939, passenger airplanes were making five daily stops at the Moline Airport, and 24 private planes were based there. Approval of a $175,000 bond issue resulted in construction of a large hangar that included a ticket station and offices for United Air Lines, the Civil Aeronautics Administration staff, and the U.S. Weather Bureau. A year later, a four-lane highway opened from Moline's 23rd Avenue to the airport.

When World War II began, the Moline field was closed to private fliers. During the conflict, nearly 1,000 Air Corps men received their first flight training there, and wounded servicemen returned from battlefronts in hospital planes to land there for transport to Army hospitals in Clinton, Iowa, and Galesburg, Illinois. Under an Army contract in 1944-45, almost 600 medium aircraft engines were rebuilt at the Moline Airport.

By the mid-1940s, a struggle over air transportation facilities for the metropolitan area triggered some bitterness among the Iowa and Illinois neighbors. Though Davenport had the oldest field, Moline's had far outstripped any in the area. Through the Illinois Airport Act of 1945, which created local airport authorities with taxing and bonding powers, and later through a 1947 referendum vote, the citizens of Rock Island County had bought the Moline Airport. Developed and maintained through the Quad-

City Metropolitan Airport Authority, it became known as the Quad-City Airport. This identification gave strong impetus to the area becoming widely known as the "Quad-Cities," though the "Tri-City" designation did not easily or quickly fade away. Within five years, more than $3 million had been spent modernizing runways and taxi strips and making other improvements at the airport.

The disappointment of Davenporters over loss of the major airport to Rock Island County was understandable. They had made an early start in aviation and were proud of their first facility, Cram Field. The arrival of the first airmail plane there on February 19, 1934, drew more than 2,000 shivering persons. A powerful beam from an Army Air Corps 800,000-candlepower searchlight lit the way for the pilot of the Curtis-Shrike A-12 attack plane, which arrived at 8:09 p.m., after making the flight from Chicago in one hour and nine minutes.

This was a big moment in the history of Davenport aviation. Davenporters had reason to be proud of their field with its new runways, and green and red lighted markers to facilitate night flying. The former cow pasture had developed into one of the best-equipped airports in the Midwest. Cram Field was supplanted in time by the Davenport Municipal Airport at Mount Joy, which continues to serve many industries and individuals with private planes. For a rather brief period, it offered regularly scheduled airline services.

Entertainment Fills Leisure Hours

To return to earlier times, the post-World War I boom in the Tri-Cities, as elsewhere in the nation, triggered shortages and high prices. It was during this period that a phrase that would haunt future generations was first coined: "The high cost of living."

Still, it was an age of optimism and tremendous growth and change. Area residents, along with the rest of the country, hummed "Tea for Two" and "Rhapsody in Blue," and savored their new prosperity. They were saddened, too, when fire on April 26, 1921, destroyed an area institution, the 54-year-old Burtis Opera House in Davenport. Flames shot 50 feet into the air after an arsonist put the torch to the theater where thousands had laughed and cried at the best entertainers in show business.

There was other entertainment, though. The new $300,000 fairgrounds opened on West Locust Street in Davenport on August 16, 1920. More than 60,000 jammed the grounds on opening day to inspect livestock farmers brought for judging, and to gape at a woman that a farm implement firm, foreseeing a strong trend in future American advertising, had hired to demonstrate tractors. The fairgrounds offered everything from auto to bicycle racing and fun on the midway, and by the end of the opening week attendance totaled 115,262.

One embarrassing incident slightly marred the fair's opening activities. Suspicious of melons being sold on the midway, Davenport police raided the stand and found, in each hollowed-out watermelon, a half-pint of bootleg whiskey.

The Mississippi River has always played an important role in the area's lifestyle, and in the 1920s riverboat excursions were a popular form of recreation. Former owners of steamers and packets transformed their craft into posh floating palaces, augmenting elegant surroundings with attractive dance halls and high-class orchestras. The captivating notes of a calliope inevitably signaled the arrival of the latest excursion boat. Still welcomed, too, were the lushly fitted-out showboats that brought a variety of live entertainment to the area's doorstep.

Movies also became a popular form of entertainment in the Tri-Cities during that period. It was like Broadway around the Capitol Theater in Davenport on the night of November 28, 1921, when *The Sheik* starring Latin lover Rudolph Valentino opened there.

Soon, some area theaters were equipped with pipe organs as well as smaller organs and pianos as musicians provided musical accompaniment to the silent movies. In 1921, admission to the Capitol was 20 cents on the main floor and 15 cents in the balcony.

The Capitol, which opened Dec. 25, 1920, was one of the most elegant theaters of its day. It featured, in addition to a giant pipe organ, an orchestra pit that could be raised or lowered and a section of what soon came to be known as "lovers' chairs." Of these, *The Democrat* newspaper observed: "The swains from Blue Grass or Buffalo may sit there and hold hands." The Capitol's first show, *The Man Who Lost Himself*, drew 10,000 persons to its opening. In 1921, it offered Douglas Fairbanks and Mary Pickford in *The Three Musketeers*; Harold Lloyd in *Safety Last*, in 1923; and Fairbanks and Pickford again in another silent film, *Little Annie Rooney*, in 1925.

The Capitol, then the second largest theater in Iowa, seated 2,000, followed by the Columbia, with 1,300. The Capitol was operated by the RKO Corporation, and the Columbia by Paramount-Publix. The Garden was the other large downtown Davenport theater during this time.

The 1920s brought the world into area living rooms through the magic of a new medium — radio. The frontiers it opened had a profound effect on the Tri-Cities, as well as the rest of the nation, but the impact was especially felt in the area because Radio Station WOC in Davenport was the first station west of the Mississippi River and the second licensed radio station in the entire United States. Listeners all over the country fiddled with their sets as they sought its frequency.

In 1922, Dr. B.J. Palmer, who headed the Palmer School of Chiropractic in Davenport and was an avowed showman and publicist for the chiropractic methods of healing, purchased the fledgling radio staion and moved it from Rock Island to a studio atop Brady Street Hill. Radio was then in its infancy and WOC's first studio looked more like a comfortable parlor in someone's home than a broadcasting center. The first program, aired in 1922, was an all music show with live musicians, and included Davenport's mayor, Alfred Mueller, playing a cello solo. A nationwide audience tuned to WOC for such programs as "Radio Rex" reading test recipes over the air, and B.J. Palmer discussing chiropractic cures and his world travels in hour-long talks.

Radio was then so new that few firms were manufacturing sets, so enterprising listeners made their own by winding wire around a round cereal box, adding a loop, sliding tuners and a so-called "cat's whisker" to scratch a crystal. The homemade device was then hooked up to batteries and an earphone. The sound was often thin and the signal unsteady, but the nation's love affair with radio was instant and lasting.

One program in particular captured the attention of the whole country for years, and the Tri-City area was no exception. Every week-day night around dinnertime everything stopped for *Amos 'n' Andy*. In some area theaters, the projectors would be halted while the 15-minute program was aired, and many factories set up radios so their workers would not miss a single episode. Charles Correll, who played Andy on the program, had lived in Rock Island for several years and had been a member of a popular vocal trio made up of Morgan Sexton and Charles Paridon, also Rock Island residents. Area residents then, as now, loved good music. The Tri-City Symphony Orchestra, 12th oldest in the United States, founded by Ludwig Becker in 1914, enjoyed strong attendance throughout the decades, never missing a season despite war, depression and assorted disasters. There were 88 members in the orchestra, considered to be one of the finest in the Midwest. In the years from its founding and on through the end of the 1950s, the orchestra had only six directors.

Later, the Civic Music Association, founded in 1949, added to the cultural life of the community by presenting full seasons of high-caliber musical shows, utilizing the abundant talents available in the area. Quad-City Music

THE PALMER COLLEGE OF CHIROPRACTIC, ATOP BRADY STREET HILL IN DAVENPORT, LOOKED LIKE THIS IN THE LATE 1930S. EVEN THEN IT WAS DRAWING STUDENTS FROM THROUGHOUT THE WORLD AND WAS KNOWN AS THE "FOUNTAIN-HEAD" OF THE CHIROPRACTIC PROFESSION. "A LITTLE BIT O' HEAVEN," WHICH CONTAINS ARTIFACTS GATHERED FROM MANY EXOTIC PLACES, IS AT THE EXTREME LEFT OF THE BUILDING IN THE FOREGROUND.

THE ORIGINAL STUDIOS OF WOC RADIO IN DAVENPORT LOOKED MORE LIKE A COMFORTABLE PARLOR IN SOMEONE'S HOME THAN A BROADCASTING CENTER. THE STATION WAS THE FIRST WEST OF THE MISSISSIPPI RIVER AND THE SECOND LICENSED RADIO STATION IN THE ENTIRE UNITED STATES. IT USED TO FEATURE BROADCASTS OF LIVE MUSIC, AS WELL AS TRAVEL TALKS BY B.J. PALMER. THIS PHOTO WAS TAKEN IN THE 1920S.

Guild, established in Moline, brought a musical theater and its productions utilized the singing, dancing and orchestra talents of area performers.

From its early days, the area had been considered a good place for touring theater groups to play, and a procession of glittering stars trod the boards at the two principal theaters, the Burtis Opera House and the Grand Opera House, both in Davenport. Audiences saw the celebrated English actress, Ellen Terry, and thrilled to the voice of Jenny Lind, the "Swedish Nightingale." Other notables who appeared in those theaters included Sarah Bernhardt, Lily Langtry, Joe Jefferson, Otis Skinner, Maurice Barrymore, Edwin Booth, Eddie Foy, Eleanor Duse and many others. A host of 1920s vaudeville stars would entertain later audiences.

A significant indicator of the vitality of the theater in the Tri-Cities was the presence of a large and healthy family of amateur groups, descended from such organizations as the German Theater Society, whose members performed in the new Davenport Turner Hall when it opened in 1887. Other amateur groups included the Emerald Dramatic Club, the Friendly House Players and Masquers, Inc. Later, a large tent on the grounds of a Moline restaurant provided a theater-in-the-round setting for the Tent At The Tower players. Another amateur little theater group, the Playcrafters, in 1959 acquired and remodeled an enormous barn off Coaltown Road in Moline, its first permanent home. They had been itinerant performers since the 1930s. Smaller groups worked in more specialized areas, such as Genesius Guild, presenting classical Greek plays in Rock Island.

Area persons acquired an early interest in theater, both as players and spectators, through the Park Board-sponsored Children's Theater, the only program of its kind in the Midwest, in which casts were entirely composed of youngsters.

Other forms of culture have long been nourished in the area. In 1925, the Davenport Art Gallery was founded and located in the city-owned armory building at 120 West 5th Street. Special enabling legislation was needed to allow the city to operate the municipal gallery, the first of its type in Iowa. But as early as the late 1880s, members of the Art Association of Davenport were holding exhibits and displaying artworks in the Davenport Academy of Sciences building. Increasing travels abroad by Scott County citizens resulted in fine examples of French and German art being brought back and donated. One of those who did that was C.A. Ficke, a Davenport attorney. He was so attracted by the works of the old masters that he acquired several hundred of them and gave the gallery 334 of them, then valued at $225,000. This formed the nucleus of the new gallery's collection. Another large donation of artworks was made by Dr. C.T. Londley of Davenport.

The Tri-City Art League was founded in 1910 as an outgrowth of the Davenport Art Association and successive groups and flourished for several years, operating in rented rooms, engaging art teachers and becoming a cultural asset in the process.

The Tri-City area in the 1920s and 1930s made important literary contributions, too. The roster of novelists and poets was brightened by the names of such persons as Octave Thanet, Arthur Davison Ficke, Susan Glaspell, George Cram Cook and Floyd Dell.

Dell turned out a number of literary works, including the prize-winning novel *Moon Calf*, published in 1920. Alice French wrote as Octave Thanet and several of her works were well-received nationwide. She began to write fiction in the 1880s, and later used Iowa as a background for her book, *Stories of a Western Town*.

Susan Glaspell and her husband, George Cram Cook, both called Davenport home though they met and married in Provincetown, Rhode Island, where they founded the Provincetown Players and drew around them a number of talented artists and writers, including the playwright Eugene O'Neill. Susan Glaspell's first novel, *Glory of the Conquered*, was published in 1909. In

1931, she won the Pulitzer Prize for drama with *Allison's House*. Her husband wrote novels and plays.

Arthur Davison Ficke was a Davenporter, who quit the practice of law to become a writer, lecturer and world traveler. He wrote 15 books of poetry and several novels under his own name.

The area joined by the Mississippi River was always sports-minded, too, and in the late 1920s, Wharton Field House was built in Moline through the sale of bonds, on land donated by J.T. Browning in 1910. Though the fieldhouse was built primarily for basketball, it hosted many other forms of indoor athletics and served also as a place for political rallies and high school graduation exercises, since it had one of the area's largest seating capacities. When its indebtedness was paid off, Wharton was deeded to the Moline Board of Education.

Mood Changes in the '20s

The decade that followed World War I brought to the Tri-Cities the same change in mood and moral codes that was sweeping the nation. In the years before the onset of the Roaring '20s, an area resident seeking diversion might take the trolley out to Watch Tower Park in Black Hawk State Park, Rock Island, to sample various amusement rides, or he might hitch up old Dobbin for a buggy trip to the West Davenport fairgrounds to take in the wonders of such things as the Sells-Floto Circus.

The 1920s, though, ushered in an era of a more frantic pursuit of entertainment, the "eat-drink-and-be-merry" Jazz Age of all-night auto rides, cigarettes, gin and some sin, and "23 Skidoo." A revolution in morals and manners was underway. Nice girls smoked cigarettes and drank openly. Clothes were looser, dancing sensuous. It was a time of girls in rolled stockings, collegiate males with patent leather hair, students wearing raccoon coats and young men tearing around in Stutz Bearcats.

Movies, considered lurid by the standards of the times, made their first appearance, as did confession magazines and "sexy" picture books. The new freedom of the automobile and the excesses generated by Prohibition quickened the pace of living.

The cocktail hour was born as the well-to-do began to serve drinks before dinner. There were mixed parties in Rock Island speakeasies where women stood alongside men with one foot on the bar rail. Reformers, aghast at the goings-on, attacked the new closed cars as, "nothing but love nests on wheels," and agitated for a return to less tempting, open-air models.

In those years, B.J. Palmer's "A Little Bit O' Heaven," a shrine-like collection of memorabilia from his world travels, drew hundreds to be married in "Heaven's" tiny chapel. Some even repeated their vows over the Palmer-owned WOC Radio station.

It was a restless, self-seeking time, as men perched atop flagpoles in Rock Island, seeking to set endurance records, and the same goal was pursued by weary couples on the dance floor at the Exhibition Hall at the Davenport fairgrounds, as they staggered through marathon dances, in which one or both partners would often collapse from exhaustion.

It was a time of miniature golf, chain letters, Mah Jong and crossword puzzles. Fashionable folks danced to "Kitten on the Keys" or "Always," but the real sports swung to the Charleston, which better expressed the age's constant desire to be in motion, going somewhere, doing something.

One who typified that frantic, fast-paced age was Davenport-born Leon (Bix) Beiderbecke, creator of a musical legend and world-wide fame that has grown steadily since his death in New York at the age of 28. Bix was born in 1903 and died August 6, 1931, of pneumonia and the complications of excessive drinking. Yet, in that short period of time, he created musical history with his cornet and his piano melodies.

Just before his 16th birthday, Bix bought a second-hand cornet for $8 and was soon playing simple melodies. Blessed with perfect pitch and an unerring ear, he could, before he was five, instantly repeat passages he heard played on the piano.

Bix made his first public appearance at a high school vaudeville show, improvising on the cornet for a tap dance routine. In 1920, he made his first semi-professional appearance, working weekends with a four-piece band in Delavan, Wisconsin. His first fulltime professional playing job was with the Wolverines Band, which he joined in 1923.

At that time, Bix began to develop and refine his clear, pure tone that would continue to captivate listeners many generations later. His interest, however, extended beyond jazz to include the music of Debussy, Ravel, Stravinsky and Tchaikovsky, perhaps a reflection of his family's preference for classical music.

Bix achieved fame in 1926 and 1927 with the Jean Goldkette Band, and assured his legend when, along with Frankie Trombauer, he joined Paul Whiteman's world-renowned band. From 1924 to 1930, Bix traveled the United States with Goldkette, Whiteman and other bands, winning growing respect, and even awe, from his colleagues as his genius and style developed. He was a product of the Roaring '20s and its insatiable demands took their toll. Keeping irregular hours, never turning down a request to play some more, drinking to excess, Bix died at the zenith of his career. When news of his death went out, it brought accolades from musicians whose names were known around the world.

Since his death, Bix Beiderbecke has been the subject of a motion picture, numerous nationally circulated books, newspaper and magazine articles and a documentary movie of his life. In 1972, a tradition to honor him was begun in his hometown — the annual Bix Fest on the Davenport levee, an event always attended by many thousands.

ALTHOUGH BIX BIEDERBECKE USUALLY PLAYED CORNET, IN THIS RECORDING STUDIO JAM SESSION HE PLAYED TRUMPET. OTHER MUSICIANS INCLUDE TOMMY DORSEY ON TROMBONE AND PAUL MERTZ ON PIANO.

Darker forces were present, too, in the general gaiety of the 1920s. A few came who sought to sow seeds of hate and dissent. On December 17, 1922, five figures in white robes and with pillow slips over their heads suddenly glided down the aisle at St. John's Methodist Church in Davenport. While the congregation watched in wonder, one of the hooded men handed the pastor an envelope. Then the group filed out silently. When the pastor opened the envelope, he found a donation of $25, and a letter explaining that it was "for charity." The letter was signed by "The Davenport Klan, Knights of the Ku Klux Klan, Realm of Iowa."

That same day a similar letter was delivered to the Salvation Army chapter in Davenport. The Klan, avowed harbingers of hate and racial bigotry, had chosen to make its area debut in the guise of a philanthropic organization. Unlike some other cities in Iowa, Davenport never welcomed the Klan, though a few members were initiated as the robed night-riders burned crosses on properties, held rallies and staged a Saturday night march. The Klan's real purpose was soon clear as it demonstrated against a Roman Catholic Church in what is now the Glen Armil addition (near North Division and 35th streets). On another occasion, Klansmen, mounted on snow-white horses, paraded from the Davenport business district all the way to the west edge of the city for a cross-burning ceremony and initiation of new members.

The presence of the Klan and the evils it represented were strongly blasted in area newspaper editorials and in public speeches. But despite the fact that the Klan clearly was unwelcome, it managed to get three of its members nominated as candidates for the Davenport Board of Education, though on election day all were soundly defeated.

Though the Klan never secured a foothold or posed a serious threat to the peace and order of the Tri-City area, it was a different story in some towns and cities in Iowa where businessmen almost had to belong to the Klan in order to keep their doors open.

THE STREETCAR WAS STILL AN IMPORTANT MEANS OF TRANSPORTATION IN DAVENPORT WHEN THIS PHOTO WAS TAKEN ON WEST 2ND STREET IN THE 1920S, BUT THE GROWING NUMBER OF CARS ON THE STREETS WERE ALREADY SOUNDING ITS DEATH KNELL. BUSES BEGAN TO APPEAR IN THE CITY AS EARLY AS 1926 AND IN THE NEXT DECADE IT WAS EVIDENT THAT THE DAYS OF THE TROLLEY WERE ALMOST OVER.

Davenport received national attention in 1921 when voters elected a Socialist administration. The Socialists swept into office with a landslide victory on a ticket headed by Dr. C.L. Barewald for mayor. The vote was unprecedented in a city that usually voted heavily Republican, but that time Republicans managed to snare only three aldermanic seats. In interviews, Dr. Barewald attributed his party's victory to "a general discontent against high prices and high taxes, and a protest against un-American methods of speech, opinion and personal liberty."

But the Socialist administration was plagued from its onset with intra-party bickering and feuding, so much so that before he had completed a year in office, Dr. Barewald stepped down as mayor. The Socialist aldermen, he said of his colleagues, refused to cooperate in any way in putting through conservative measures.

During his first few months in office, Dr. Barewald and his council had argued bitterly over a number of issues, including proposals for lower streetcar fares and one-man trolleys. The mayor had also waged a vigorous campaign against vice, personally led raids and once suspended the chief of police for 10 days.

It was this dissent that led to an event very similar to one that would occur more than 50 years in the future, would be known as "Watergate," and would topple a president and many of his top aides. The mayor's office was bugged!

When a hidden recording device was found in a light fixture in his office, Dr. Barewald charged that his colleagues were trying to get something on him. An investigation disclosed that the bugging device, crude by present standards, had been installed by the city electrician on orders of three Socialist aldermen. Many threats and counterthreats followed the incident, but no charges were filed.

At the next election, Davenport voters soundly repudiated the Socialist administration and elected an all-Republican ticket, except for two Democratic aldermen and a Socialist police magistrate, Harold Metcalf.

Post-War Boom, Then Crash

The 1920s might be thought of as a time of "clang, clang, clang, went the trolley," in the words of a song, but as early as 1926, buses, a forerunner of future transportation, had begun to appear on area streets. In the next 10 years it was evident that the electric trolley's days were numbered. The end of the line for them came on April 16, 1940, with the final run of the last trolley, the Bridge Line car operated by the Tri-City Railway Co. A jingle-jangle era had ended and motor buses, less romantic, perhaps, but more efficient, took over.

The decade after World War I saw much construction of new buildings and residences in all the cities in the area. Many new downtown structures housed financial institutions or provided office space for business and professional people. Demands of expanding industries for workers kept residential building moving briskly.

Tri-City residents from early days were aware of their responsibilities to their less fortunate citizens, and had long supported charitable institutions. The Davenport Associated Charities, for example, was an organization established in 1886. It preceded by one year the first Community Chest federation formed in Denver, Colorado. The organization functioned until 1896 when 22 separate agencies came under the blanket of Community Chest, and considerably later, United Fund organizations.

MANY BUSINESSMEN'S ORGANIZATIONS PRECEDED THE PRESENT DAVENPORT CHAMBER OF COMMERCE, WHOSE BUILDING HAS BEEN AT THE SAME LOCATION SINCE 1920. THE ADVANCE CLUB AND THE BOARD OF TRADE WERE BOTH ACTIVE IN DAVENPORT IN THE MID-1880S. THE DAVENPORT BUSINESSMEN'S ASSOCIATION, FORMED IN 1888, BECAME THE DAVENPORT COMMERCIAL CLUB IN 1905, AND THE DAVENPORT CHAMBER OF COMMERCE IN 1920. THEN, AS NOW, ITS HEADQUARTERS WERE AT 404 MAIN STREET.

Businessmen, too, had early banded together to promote their communities. The Advance Club was active in Davenport in 1886, as was the Board of Trade. In 1888, another group, the Davenport Businessmen's Association, with 150 members, was formed "to protect the rights and advance of the mercantile, manufacturing and other interests of the community." Soon, the Association had more or less replaced the Advance Club.

In 1905, the Association expanded to become the Davenport Commercial Club, and finally the Davenport Chamber of Commerce was born as the Commercial Club amended its charter in 1920. The new organization's headquarters were established at 404 Main Street. The Davenport Junior Chamber of Commerce, and later the Scott County Junior Achievement program, emerged under the auspices of the Chamber of Commerce. Similar organizations were formed in the other area cities. For example, the Bettendorf Chamber of Commerce was organized in 1928, and by the end of the 1950s it had 300 members.

Another factor that improved the quality of life in the Tri-Cities in the late 1920s was the installation of gas heating in many homes, freeing householders from the messiness and inconvenience of coal-heating. By this time, too, the area had become the largest electrical consumer between Chicago and Omaha, St. Louis and St. Paul.

That decade also brought a change in leadership to one of the area's largest industries. In 1928, Charles Deere Wiman, great-grandson of the founder, John Deere, took over as president of Deere & Company.

The year 1929 began as one of continued prosperity, with speculation at fever pitch and many Tri-Citians recklessly gambling on Wall Street. But, the Roaring '20s were about to end with a whimper.

Tuesday, October 29, 1929, saw 16,310,030 shares traded on the New York Stock Exchange, the peak trading of all time. Prices crashed and bewildered investors wondered what was happening to them.

THE AMERICAN RESCUE MISSION IN ROCK ISLAND COLLECTED FOOD TO DISTRIBUTE TO THE NEEDY AT CHRISTMASTIME.

MORE AND MORE WOMEN JOINED THE WORK FORCE IN THE TRI-CITIES, A PHENOMENON THAT BEGAN DURING WORLD WAR I WHEN WOMEN REPLACED MANY MEN IN FACTORIES. AT THE TIME THIS PHOTO WAS TAKEN AT DAVENSHIRE MANUFACTURING CO. IN DAVENPORT IN THE LATE 1920S, THEY WERE STILL PERFORMING MANY TASKS CONSIDERED LARGELY FEMININE IN NATURE. THESE WOMEN WERE OPERATING SEWING MACHINES FOR CLOTHING MANUFACTURE.

The full impact of the crash was not felt immediately in the area. On October 1, 1930, bank deposits in Davenport's six lending institutions, for example, totaled $65,441,141, the greatest number of deposits ever shown in a consolidated statement of banking interests to that date.

The banks included the American Commercial & Savings Bank; the Union Savings Bank & Trust Co.; the First National Bank; the Northwest Davenport Savings Bank, and the Home Savings Bank. In addition, there were 12 banks in the county outside of Davenport. The city also boasted many important bond houses, and was called "the financial center of the State of Iowa." The city's first bank had been formed in 1847, by Cook and Sargent.

Strong as they were then, within a very brief time most of the banks would fail. By September 1931 depositers were hounding the banks for hard cash. The first run was on the American Bank, the largest banking institution in Iowa, with deposits of $40 million. Withdrawals were so great that the Davenport institution was quickly in trouble. A 60-day notice for withdrawals was posted. Almost at once, there was a run on the Union Bank, with $25 million in deposits. Four abreast, depositers surged into the bank, demanding their money.

Something had to be done to avoid financial disaster. While depositers continued to jam the lobby, an orchestra played on the mezzanine and entertainers sang. E.P. Adler, publisher of the *Daily Times* and a director of the bank, moved up and down the milling lines, assuring everyone of his confidence in the bank. When all persuasion would fail, Adler would take a depositor's passbook and write into it his personal guarantee of the amount on deposit. Meanwhile, commercial deposits of the *Daily Times* and *The Democrat* newspapers were left in the bank. In a move to save it, Adler prevailed upon the State of Iowa to transfer $407,000 to the institution as a mark of confidence. The run on the bank was stemmed — at least temporarily.

Adler was then drafted to reorganize the by-then-defunct American Bank. He called a mass meeting of depositors to wage a campaign for establishment of a new bank. Those who had lost funds in the American Bank were brought face-to-face with the reorganizing committee. On a November night in 1931, some 5,000 persons filled the Masonic Temple as Adler outlined plans for reorganization. He called for subscription of $1.5 million in new capital stock, which would make 60 cents immediately available on every dollar to depositors. The rest would be in the bonds of a liquidation corporation. When a final campaign report was received, the bank goal had been over-subscribed. The new institution was named the Davenport Bank & Trust Company. While banks were crashing in cities throughout the nation, Davenport was opening a new one. The new bank initially went through some anxious and trying periods of financial uncertainty, but survived. The Union Bank, though, tottered, and on December 26, 1932, closed its doors for good.

The hardships of the depression were being felt in the Tri-Cities in 1931, and grew worse as the winter of 1932 approached. As the banks closed, so did many factories, and many persons were umemployed. On WOC Radio, crooners sang a bittersweet hit song that reflected the calamity that had overtaken the nation: "Buddy, Can You Spare A Dime?"

By mid-December of 1932, all six plants of Deere & Company on the Illinois side of the river were employing only 716, although by 1937, with the depression in full swing, the firm's gross receipts would still total a respectable $100 million.

Thirty-eight suicides, twice the normal number, were recorded in Scott County in 1932, and the increase was attributed to stress over the economic conditions. Area cities were on the verge of bankruptcy, and in Davenport, city finances were so bad that Ralph Graham, superintendent of public works, was re-cooking old discarded asphalt for street repairs.

Those who did not lose their jobs were forced to take pay cuts. All Davenport city employees in 1932 took 15 percent salary reductions. In Moline, some banks closed and city employees were paid in scrip. Similar situations were experienced in Rock Island. Some unemployed workers began to labor in government-funded WPA projects. In Davenport, those so employed lengthened runways at Cram Field, repaired county roads and city streets, dug a lake at Credit Island, extended the levee seawall and redecorated City Hall. College graduates with a flair for writing undertook compilations of area histories and were paid by the federal government. As the Depression weighed ever more heavily, relief rolls soared. By 1932, the number receiving relief in Scott County averaged more than 7,000 a month. Surplus foods — simple staples like beans, potatoes and flour — were distributed by the tons.

Soup kitchens for the jobless and hungry were set up in Rock Island. F.W. Donaway and a corps of assistants with the American Rescue Mission fed 150 persons a day. Usually the fare was something like bowls of potato soup swimming with chunks of bacon ends. Donaway's helpers also delivered many baskets of food to poor families and held Christmas parties for underprivileged children.

A dollar was hard to come by, but went a long way in the depression years. One could buy two packs of Camel cigarettes for a quarter at any of the Hickey Bros. cigar stores in the Tri-Cities, and a new Ford car sold for less than $400.

For just 60 cents, a family of four could go to the Capitol Theater in Davenport to see a movie like *20,000 Years in Sing-Sing*. Dancing to the music of Dan Russo and His Orioles at the Davenport Coliseum cost a mere 35 cents, while those who swayed to the tunes of Emil Klindt and his Varsity Band at the Moonlight Gardens out on Brady Street in Davenport paid only a quarter.

In 1932, the bonus army of disgruntled veterans of World War I marched on Washington, D.C., and Tri-Citians were reading Erskine Caldwell's popular new novel, *Tobacco Road*.

In hand with the depression, the excesses of Prohibition plagued the area. Finally, on December 5, 1933, it ended. In Rock Island and Moline, liquor sales became legal on that date, but Iowa, dry since 1915, did not legalize sales of liquor until the middle of 1934, though beer went on sale during 1933. The vote in Scott County during a national referendum on the repeal of Prohibition was 17,806 to 2,374 for repeal. The first state-owned liquor store opened in Davenport, at 411 Harrison Street, on July 2, 1934, but there was no big crush of customers on the first day.

THE GRAF ZEPPELIN OVER DAVENPORT AUGUST 28, 1929
PHOTO BY A.E. WILLIAMS DAVENPORT TIMES STAFF PHOTOGRAPHER

THERE WAS GREAT EXCITEMENT IN DAVENPORT ON AUGUST 28, 1929, WHEN THE FAMED GRAF ZEPPELIN MADE A SPECIAL, LOW-FLYING TRIP OVER THE CITY, AS A SALUTE TO ITS LARGE GERMAN POPULATION. PHOTOS, LIKE THIS ONE TAKEN BY A.E. WILLIAMS, DAVENPORT DAILY TIMES STAFF PHOTOGRAPHER, LATER APPEARED ON MANY CALENDARS AND SOUVENIRS.

DURING THE DEPRESSION, IMPROVEMENTS WERE MADE AT MOLINE'S AIRPORT, THANKS TO THE WORKS PROGRESS ADMINISTRATION.

THE YEAR 1936 WALLOPED RESIDENTS OF THE AREA WITH BITTER COLD WEATHER AND TOWERING SNOW DRIFTS, AND THE SUMMER WAS JUST AS BAD. JULY OF THAT YEAR SHATTERED ALL RECORDS FOR ABSENCE OF RAINFALL AND INTENSITY OF HEAT. THERE WERE 11 CONSECU-TIVE DAYS OF TEMPERATURES ABOVE THE 100-DEGREES MARK. THIS THERMOMETER REGISTERS 111.3 DEGRESS ABOVE ZERO, STILL A RECORD FOR THE QUAD-CITY AREA.

The awful winter of 1936 would add severe weather woes to Tri-Citians, already staggering under the hardships of the depression. It was a winter that shattered all records for cold, just as its summer would break all previous heat and drought records. That winter, for three consecutive weeks, the mercury did not rise above zero, and the average reading was a chilling 10 below zero. Howling winds whipped drifts as high as telephone poles in many rural areas, marooning entire communities. July of that quixotic year shattered all records for absence of rainfall and intensity of heat. July 14 set the Tri-Cities' mark of 111.3 degrees above zero, some 133 degrees higher than the coldest reading of six months earlier. There were 11 consecutive days of temperatures above the 100-degree mark. These were days before widespread air conditioning, and the death toll soared. That September was the wettest on record to that time, with more than nine inches of rainfall recorded during the month, and 16 inches from August 16 to November 2.

Some improvement had been noted in the Tri-Cities by 1934, though it would be short-lived. That year grocery sales were up by 15 percent, and new car registrations by 34 percent. Employment climbed slowly, too, with 2,200 at work in the Deere & Company plants. Farmers in Scott County received a much-needed boost in the form of $300,000 in government funds under the corn-hog program.

In Moline, where the population stood at just over 32,000 in 1936, the power company was paying average wages of $38 a week, while salaries at trucking companies averaged $12 a week. Gas supplied by the power firm cost 20 cents a month for the first 25 therms.

Ethnic Groups Find a Home in Quad-Cities

By the years of the Great Depression, the community that would be known as the Quad-Cities had become the home of many ethnic groups. By that time, the Germans in Davenport and Moline's Swedes and Belgians had settled comfortably. At the same time, nearly every group retained elements of its homeland culture, making the community something of an ethnic "patchwork quilt."

Other large ethnic groups — blacks, Jews, Hispanics — had also been present in the community for some time.

By the Depression, many blacks — a large number of whom had migrated from the deep South — already were living in central Davenport, Rock Island's west end, near the river in Moline and the area of East Moline that had been Watertown. Blacks first began moving to the community during the Civil War and for a few years after hostilities ended. After the turn of the century, blacks again headed north in large numbers, and many settled in the community where jobs could be found with the railroads or the farm implement industry. That period of migration continued into the Roaring '20s.

The Depression and World War II saw little increase in the black population – or any other groups – due to migration. After the war, as farm industry production picked up, blacks again were attracted to jobs in the Quad-Cities. Many came as the result of less than honorable recruiting efforts by some industrial employers who were looking for inexpensive labor. Lured by the promise of wages that were higher than what they could earn in the South, blacks came north, worked until they were eligible for union membership — and paychecks — and then found themselves laid off, replaced by new recruits from the South. Abandoned by their employer, the black workers and their families faced a bleak situation. In most cases, they did not have enough money to return to their homes in the South, so they had little choice but to take whatever work they could find — often at wages little different from what they had left.

Although that one experience caused much bitterness, Quad-City blacks have generally put such experiences behind them. Black churches have been an integral part of the community since the 1870s. Black social awareness organizations had their origins between the world wars and flourished in the 1960s. Blacks, once exploited and relegated to the lower end of the wage scale, now can be found at all levels of the community's industrial, service and professional sectors.

Though fewer in numbers, Jews have also been a significant part of the Quad-Cities for much of its history. In the 1840s, '50s and '60s, peddling was the easiest and most common way for newly immigrated European Jews to make a living on the frontier. Although physically demanding, peddling solved the problems they faced of cultural differences, limited opportunities and religious prejudice. At the same time, it allowed those men to save enough money to bring their families over from Europe and make the transition from traveling peddler to settled shopkeeper.

Early worship occurred mostly in the homes. The first congregation was B'nai Israel of Davenport (after 1886 called Temple Emanuel), which was begun as an Orthodox synagogue in 1861. It served Jews from throughout the Tri-Cities. One of its first needs was the establishment of a cemetery.

Jewish settlement centered in Rock Island, in the area bounded by 2nd and 6th avenues, 2nd and 18th streets, with a concentration in eight blocks near the center of that neighborhood. In the 1880s and '90s, many refugees from religious and political persecution in Europe moved into that area. Their presence probably influenced the description of the area by Rabbi Simon Glazer in his 1904 book, *Jews of Iowa*, as "a ghetto in the full meaning of the word. All keep Sabbath. Friday evening puts a holy garb over that part of Rock Island. Through every window of a Jewish habitation lurk the Sabbath candles."

By the turn of the century, Temple Emanuel had evolved into a Reform congregation. B'nai Emes, an Orthodox congregation, was formed in 1894. Kosher butcher shops, bakeries, Jewish benevolent organizations and social groups flourished. Because the Rock Island ghetto had more European traits, most newcomers settled there. Its Jewish community was more than twice the size of Davenport's, and more traditional.

Throughout its development in the community, the Jewish population contributed prominent citizens. For example, Berthold Lowenthal was elected to a two-year term on the Rock Island City Council in 1856. Others served in all the cities' governments in the 1860s, '70s and '80s. Morris Gismar was elected a director of Moline's First National Bank in 1898. Many other Jews served as bank directors. In 1899 Emanuel Phillip Adler at age 27 moved to Davenport from Ottumwa, Iowa, to become publisher of the *Davenport Times*. For the rest of his life, he was a pillar of the community: director of the Lee Syndicate (later Lee Enterprises, Incorporated); vice president of the Associated Press and officer of other news groups; president of Temple Emanual; president of a bank; and president, chairman, director or trustee of every major civic organizion from the Art Gallery to the YMCA.

As the Jewish population grew, so too did the number of Jewish organizations in the community. B'nai Brith Lodge No. 174, the first in Iowa, was chartered in Davenport in 1872. A Young Men's Hebrew Literary Society was begun in 1857 in Rock Island. The Tri-City Zionist Organization was formed in 1920, and Hadassah was begun three years later.

Although later in arriving in the community than either blacks or Jews, Hispanics — predominatly Mexicans — also have enriched Quad-City culture. They came in the early years of the 20th century to work at the Silvis Yards of the Chicago, Rock Island and Pacific Railroad and for the Bettendorf Company.

Other peoples have come from Europe and Asia. Mid-19th century saw an influx of immigrants from the British Isles. English, Welsh and Scots

THE TRI-CITY JEWISH CENTER IN THE BUFORD MANSION WAS ONE FOCUS OF THE JEWISH FAITH IN THE QUAD-CITIES FROM ITS DEDICATION ON DECEMBER 16, 1936, UNTIL A NEW CENTER WAS BUILT IN 1981.

clustered in Coal Valley, Cable and Sherrard where they found jobs working in the coal mines. Although not an area resident, one son of Britain, John Armstrong, was secretary of war during the War of 1812 and gave his name to Fort Armstrong, a focal point of early community settlement; his great-great-great-great-great granddaughter is Mary Jane Pearson of Moline. Fleeing famine and English oppression in the 1860s and '70s, the Irish settled predominantly in Davenport and the Greenbush area of Rock Island. Many Irish men, whose homes were clustered between 5th and 9th avenues, 24th and 30th streets, worked for the railroad. Sacred Heart Catholic Church had a decided Irish accent.

At the end of the 19th century and into the 1920s, many other Europeans came to the community. Enough Greeks lived here, mostly in the Illinois cities, to form St. George Greek Orthodox Church in 1910 in Moline. The congregation later split, St. George Church moved to Rock Island, and Assumption Church was built in East Moline. Davenport also had a sizeable Greek population by those years.

Before World War I, Poles, Serbs, Croatians and Italians all were well established. At Holy Trinity Catholic Church, established in 1914, priests heard confession in Polish, and sermons were delivered in both Polish and English for many years. St. Luke Lodge of the National Serbian Federation, begun in 1914, and the more recent Croatian Crest Club help the peoples of segments of Yugoslavia carry on their ethnic traditions. Since the turn of the century, Italians have lived in Davenport, East Moline and other communities; a Sons of Italy chapter was founded in 1928.

Improvements Bring Optimism

Further impetus for a common identity for the Iowa and Illinois communities came during the 1930s and 1940s with the completion of the Centennial Bridge, linking Davenport and Rock Island, and the Iowa-Illinois Memorial Bridge that joined Moline and Bettendorf. The latter, the area's first toll span, was completed in 1935.

By the end of the 1950s three new bridges and the old 1872 Arsenal Bridge spanned the Mississippi River in the Tri-Cities. They carried the weight, in an average year, of 85 million motor vehicles and 20,000 trains.

The Crescent Railroad Bridge, between Rock Island and Davenport, featured a swing-span to allow boats to pass under it, and was completed in 1900 at a cost of $950,000.

With completion of the locks and dams in the Tri-Cities and the creation of massive pools between the series of Mississippi River locks, new sources of water recreation were created. The area behind Locks and Dam No. 15 became known as "Lake Davenport." In 1936, two years after completion of the dam, the Lindsay Park Boat Club was established, and the activity there earned the area the title of "Sailboat Capital of the Upper Mississippi."

Private boating facilities sprang up on both sides of the river to take advantage of new "Lake Davenport" whose depth could be controlled. Later, a new breakwater, constructed with federal assistance at Lindsay Park, helped to provide a marina for 200 boats, many of them quite large. Rock Island District Corps of Engineers' statistics at the close of the 1950s showed that 48,204 pleasure craft, double the total of five years earlier, had passed through the district's locks. The number of passengers recorded was 128,301.

Spectator sports were always popular in the area. Davenport was a member of the first professional league of organized baseball in the Midwest, as early as 1879. The league included Rockford, Dubuque and Omaha. However, it folded that same year.

In 1888, an Interstate League of eight cities was formed, but it, too, collapsed in mid-season, though Davenport finished out the year in the Western Association, replacing Minneapolis.

By 1889, baseball was ready for another try in the Tri-Cities. The Interstate League was revived, with Burlington, Peoria, Quincy, Springfield, Evansville, Terre Haute, Danville and Davenport as members. Because they were locked in a hot pennant race, Davenport and Quincy enjoyed success, but the other teams suffered from a lack of support and the league, by August 15, had failed again.

Another attempt to revive area baseball came in 1891 when the Two-Eye League (Iowa and Illinois) was organized, but it, too, soon fizzled out. It was not until 1901, with the birth of the Three-I League, that baseball, played in Davenport, drew respectable crowds. The league flourished until 1906 when lagging attendance caused it to be disbanded.

The so-called "golden era" of baseball in the Tri-Cities occurred from 1910 to 1916 when Dan O'Leary took over the managerial reins, winning Davenport's first pennant in 1914. That league was discontinued after 1916, and from then until 1929 the area was without organized baseball, though there were some semi-pro leagues.

The Mississippi Valley League was formed in 1929. Two years later, Davenport's Municipal Stadium (later John O'Donnell Stadium) opened at the foot of Gaines Street. The Mississippi Valley League was closed out in 1933, but a year later Davenport was in the Western League, playing there for the next four seasons.

After the 1937 season until the close of World War II, the Tri-City area was out of organized baseball, and after that baseball's fortunes went up and down. The city of Davenport was in the Three-I League from 1946 through 1952, at which time the club failed. The Chicago White Sox made Davenport their farm team in 1957-58, but then dropped the affiliation. There was another absence of baseball in the area until 1960 when Davenport got a berth in the Class D Midwest League, with a tie-up with the Milwaukee Braves. There would be other affiliations in subsequent years.

FROM THE EARLY DAYS, QUAD-CITIANS WERE AVID BASEBALL FANS AND A GREAT NUMBER OF LEAGUES AND TEAMS CAME AND WENT OVER THE YEARS. DAVENPORT WAS A MEMBER OF THE FIRST PROFESSIONAL LEAGUE OF ORGANIZED BASEBALL IN THE MIDWEST AS EARLY AS 1879. THE DAVENPORT BLUE SOX, A SEMI-PRO TEAM, WERE READY TO TAKE THE FIELD IN 1933 WHEN THIS PHOTO WAS TAKEN.

DAVENPORT BLUE SOX, 1933

The 1930 census showed Davenport with a population of about 62,000. Moline numbered 32,000 and Rock Island 41,000. Scott county as a whole had 16,417 children in schools. Davenport factories, just before the depression took its toll, were creating $54 million in wealth annually, and the value of the city's manufacturing products had almost doubled over the previous four years. There were 150 major diversified industries manufacturing a total of 218 different products.

One key event focused attention on the Tri-Cities on October 30, 1940, when 133,000 persons crowded onto the Henry Keppy farm in Scott County for the National Corn Husking Contest. A total of 180 acres had been set aside for cars, band concerts, a parade and the huge numbers of visitors. Airplanes and a blimp circled overhead as political leaders and other celebrities took part in the festivities. All four winners set national records for picking corn the fastest.

A more efficient supply of power for the area was assured in 1942 when the Iowa-Illinois Gas & Electric Company was organized with the consolidation of six area power, gas and transportation firms, including four companies from outside the Tri-City area. Later, the transportation business was disposed of by the new company. The Tri-City Railway and the Clinton, Davenport & Muscatine interurban had been part of the utility's transportation system.

Though conditions were improving somewhat, the lingering depression still held the area in its grip in 1939, but a drastic change was just over the horizon. In that year, World War II started as Hitler marched into Austria and the bombing of Great Britain began. The dictator's conquests continued the following year as Congress passed the Selective Service Act and area young men began registering for the draft.

Tri-Cities Go to War

When Pearl Harbor was bombed on December 7, 1941, the Tri-Cities, in step with the rest of the nation, went to war. Soon its factories, many idled by the prolonged depression, were busily turning out materials for that effort. Production had hit a massive scale by 1943, the year that Mussolini resigned as Duce in Italy, and the Women's Army Corps came into being in America. Young men from the Tri-City area went off to fight for their country.

As the area tooled up for war production, both output and prices of consumer products soared giddily. Suddenly more people had purchasing power and inflation resulted. When production was at its peak in 1944, between 90,000 and 100,000 persons were working on both sides of the river. By the end of the war, they had turned out $2 billion worth of defense materiel, from armor-piercing shells to 500-pound bombs, and countless other defense items. Thousands of area women donned slacks to work alongside men in the war plants.

The Rock Island Arsenal, with 18,675 employees, was virtually a city in itself. The work force had jumped from a total of 2,735 in 1939 to the war-time high. Not only did the arsenal manufacture the materials of war, but eight major schools held classes there to provide skilled technicians for ordnance posts in the United States and overseas.

During four years, all production marks in the arsenal's history were broken. Working virtually around the clock, employees manufactured 7,000 artillery carriages, 25,000 gun mounts, 85,000 machine guns and 715,000 machine gun barrels, in addition to immense amounts of all types of artillery and small arms equipment. This included machines for the Navy, and vast numbers of spare parts for all types of military equipment.

In order to obtain the skilled workers the arsenal needed, special recruiters traveled through Kansas, Oklahoma and Arkansas. Many of these people and their families remained in the area after the war, adding to the population and affecting change with new ideas and customs.

AS THE QUAD-CITIES TOOLED UP FOR WORLD WAR II, VAST AMOUNTS OF WAR MATERIEL, INCLUDING THESE TANKS BEING FABRICATED AT SHOP M AT ROCK ISLAND ARSENAL, ROLLED OFF ASSEMBLY LINES. THE ARSENAL, EMPLOYING 18,675, WAS VIRTUALLY A CITY IN ITSELF. THE WORK FORCE INCLUDED MANY WOMEN. THIS PHOTO WAS TAKEN IN 1942.

Area plants that in peacetime produced farm equipment converted to war production. The government bought the Bettendorf Company, a Bettendorf firm that had been producing railroad car underframes and trucks. The plant with sprawling factories spread over 250 acres became the Quad-City Tank Arsenal, and its foundry, the Ordnance Steel Foundry. Later, the site would be occupied by the J.I. Case Company for the manufacture of farm equipment. Other area plants aided the war effort through sub-contracts with the arsenal, the tank arsenal, the Chicago Ordnance District and others.

By this time, the area came to be known more as the "Quad-Cities," though the "Tri-City" identity was slow to disappear. With the rest of the nation, the area experienced rationing of such items as sugar, meat, coffee, butter, gasoline, automobiles, tires and such other items as rubber boots and typewriters. In the latter months of the war, Tuesdays and Fridays were observed as meatless days.

With gasoline strictly rationed, the area's bus business boomed, and in a typical day buses might transport from 125,000 to 130,000 passengers. Rent control offices were set up in the Quad-Cities to prevent spiraling housing costs, and throughout the area the real estate business prospered. Two million dollars worth of homes changed hands in Davenport alone in 1943, and bank clearings in the area reached all-time highs.

Living space was desperately needed for all of the new war workers pouring into the area. The rambling Arsenal Courts were erected in Rock Island by the federal government at a cost of $1.26 million. On the Iowa side, Davenport Garden Homes developed the Keota Avenue housing project and three other Garden residential areas. In Bettendorf, Valley Village, a $150,000 private project, was completed in 1944.

The Quad-Cities responded enthusiastically to numerous drives for scrap material to be used in the war effort. Newspapers printed during World War II frequently picture vast piles of discarded metal and tires awaiting collection.

TANKS MANUFACTURED AT ROCK ISLAND ARSENAL SERVED ON ALL MAJOR BATTLEFRONTS OF THE WAR. THE ARSENAL'S WORK FORCE JUMPED FROM 2,735 IN 1939 TO THE WARTIME HIGH OF MORE THAN 18,000. DURING THE FOUR YEARS OF WAR, ALL PRODUCTION MARKS IN THE ARSENAL'S HISTORY WERE BROKEN.

MANY ITALIAN PRISONERS OF WAR WERE INTERNED IN THE QUAD-CITIES DURING WORLD WAR II. THEY WERE GIVEN A RELATIVE MEASURE OF FREEDOM AND EVEN WERE ASSIGNED VARIOUS TASKS AT ROCK ISLAND ARSENAL. THESE TWO POWS ARE OPERATING BUFFING MACHINES.

On August 15, 1945, Quad-Citians joined the rest of the nation in a boisterous celebration of the end of World War II. Shotguns blasted and horns honked endlessly as cars lined up bumper-to-bumper, and people streamed into the streets by the thousands. By 7 p.m. downtown streets were jammed with cheering, snake-dancing celebrants. In Rock Island, the rejoicing was so energetic that 10 persons were injured. The commander of the Rock Island Arsenal proclaimed a two-day holiday for all government employees, the first they had had since the war had begun. As victory parades continued into the night throughout the Quad-Cities, churches held special services of thanksgiving.

The influx of people into the war plants and the impetus of the war-fueled economy had an important impact on the Quad-Cities, especially stimulating its physical and industrial growth.

Boom Follows the War

After World War II, the area underwent a rapid transformation. Davenport doubled its area and added thousands to its population. Moline and Rock Island farm equipment industries boomed. Bettendorf grew dramatically, and in all of the Quad-Cities new schools were built. Industrial expansion rolled forward, headed by the giant new Alcoa plant on Bettendorf's outskirts. That plant, employing large numbers, was nearly ready for full production at the close of 1948.

The many new industries established on both sides of the river after the war created demands for more gas and electricity. From 1946 to 1955, the area's electric consumption jumped from 286 million kilowatt hours per year to 737 million kilowatt hours annually. To meet these huge demands, large additions were built at the Riverside generating station on the Iowa side, and at the Moline generating station.

Just as it had after World War I, an element of lawlessness again gained a foothold in the Quad-Cities after the 1940s conflict. This time it took the form of widespread gambling. Games of chance flourished on both sides of the river. Tavern-owners in Scott County also tended to flout the law against serving hard liquor, legal in Illinois. Numerous raids by state agents and local law enforcement agencies did little to stop the practice. On both sides of the river, operators of taverns and nightclubs sought to separate patrons from their money with slot machines, punchboards and "jars of fun," whose winning combinations of numbers meant cash prizes for the fortunate few. Slot machines whirled merrily in many private clubs in Davenport, where they were an important source of revenue, and the slots and dice tables were busy in the backrooms of some large restaurants and nightclubs in the Illinois Quad-Cities.

An unlikely cast of characters touched off a powder keg in the fall of 1948 and helped bring gambling on the Illinois side to a sudden halt. Twenty-six-year-old Marie VanMuelbrock of Moline launched a one-woman campaign. She would enter a tavern, spot a slot machine or jar of fun and immediately summon police, waiting to determine that an arrest was made. Often, to make sure police would respond to her call, she would report a false incident, and when officers arrived to investigate would point out the gambling device and demand that the owner be arrested.

Miss VanMuelbrock raided dozens of establishments, but she too was arrested, along with the gambling proprietor, when she tossed a bottle through the window of a Rock Island tavern. She was jailed when she refused to post a $500 bond. Her crusades gained her nationwide publicity, and wire services began to refer to her as "the Joan of Arc against gambling."

While Miss VanMuehlbrock languished in jail, her mother aided by another daughter, Mathilda, took up the raiding crusade. During this time, a brick was tossed through the front window of the VanMuehlbrock home in Moline, and the women received many threatening letters. Marie remained in jail for five days, and upon her release staged a few more raids. Finally, citing public apathy to gambling, she called a truce.

A month later, though, she had a powerful ally. Bernard J. (Barney) Moran assumed the office of Rock Island County state's attorney and immediately launched a wholesale crackdown that effectively quashed gambling in the county.

Slot machines, the jars and the punchboards also began to disappear in Scott County after the State of Iowa initiated a determined anti-gambling crusade in 1951. The state legislature aided law enforcement agencies by enacting a strict gambling ordinance that provided for loss of business licenses for a year if owners were convicted of gambling in their establishments.

Just as it had had a front row seat for the emergence of radio in 1922, the Quad-Cities had an early premiere of the new miracle of communication — television. On October 31, 1949, programmed television took to the air in Iowa for the first time as WOC-TV in Davenport televised its initial two-hour program. In those early days, the *Kukla, Fran and Ollie* puppet show was shown first each night, followed by a feature film. The equipment for live programs had not yet arrived. A survey taken in 1949 showed there were 1,750 TV sets in the Quad-Cities. The world was truly ready to arrive in the area's living rooms.

TELEVISION WAS MAKING ITS IMPACT FELT ON THE QUAD-CITIES IN THE 1950S, AND EARLY CHILDREN'S PROGRAM STARS LIKE WOC-TV'S CAPTAIN KEN WERE POPULAR. WOC WAS A LEADER IN AREA TELEVISION, AS IT HAD BEEN IN EARLY RADIO.

The increasing popularity of television in the next few years, though not unique in the Quad-Cities, was soon felt by the area's many movie houses where attendance slumped drastically. Many closed their doors. A resurgence of interest as some of the newness of television wore off resulted in the revival of some theaters and construction of new, multi-unit houses on the outskirts. Some experiments, like 3-D, in which a three-dimensional effect was achieved if the audience wore special glasses, were short-lived. But the drive-in movies survived, though they seldom showed first-run films.

The Quad-City area's educational facilities continued to expand after World War II. Marycrest College had been founded in 1939 as a liberal arts school.

THIS AERIAL PHOTO CLEARLY INDICATES HOW GREATLY THE QUAD-CITY AREA HAD GROWN DURING THE PERIOD FROM 1920 TO 1960. FROM A LARGELY ISOLATED, SELF-SUFFICIENT AREA BEFORE WORLD WAR I, IT HAD EXPERIENCED TREMENDOUS POPULATION GROWTH AND ESTABLISHED ITSELF AS A MAJOR MANUFACTURING AREA.

Black Hawk College in Moline was founded in 1946 as an extension of the University of Illinois. The Moline School District took over its operation in 1948. In 1961, it became the first district community college in Illinois.

By the end of the 1950s, the number of public schools in Davenport, Rock Island and Moline had risen from just 26 in 1886 to a total of 80, and their total valuation had grown from less than $500,000 to more than $53 million. Area-wide enrollment in 1886 had totaled only 11,382, but was about 37,000 as the decade of the 1950s closed. The number of teachers had increased in that time span from 184 to more than 1,500. By the close of the decade, too, more than 4,000 Catholic students were attending nine Davenport and Bettendorf parochial schools. The multi-million dollar Assumption High School had replaced Immaculate Conception Academy and St. Ambrose Academy. Replacement costs of those parochial school buildings were estimated in 1960 at more than $7 million.

At the decade's end, St. Katharine's School in Davenport had 195 students, including 54 who made their residence there. Its $200,000 dormitory was completed in 1959. The school, in operation since 1884, was known then as St. Katharine's Hall, and was established in 1886 under the auspices of the Episcopal Diocese of Iowa, to provide a fitting place where "girls might be virtuously brought up." St. Katharine's was made possible through donations and the bequest of Miss Sarah Burr of New York. Cambria Place, the palatial residence of the Hon. John L. Davies, became the site of the school. It was a college prep school, though classes for girls ranged from nursery school through senior high. Boys were allowed to attend through fifth grade only.

At the same time, 300 students were enrolled in grades 1-12 in the Villa de Chantel, founded in 1900 in Rock Island. It was a school for girls only, though boys were admitted to Kindergarten.

Area colleges boomed at the close of World War II as returning veterans, taking advantage of the G.I. Bill, swelled classroom space to capacity. The top "G.I." year at St. Ambrose was 1948, with an enrollment of 1,256, of which 88 percent were veterans. The previous high enrollment had been 550 students. The pre-war enrollment peak at Augustana College had been 600, but it zoomed to 1,307 in 1947. By 1949, the flood of veterans lessened and enrollment in area colleges began to return to normal levels.

By the close of the 1950s, the Palmer College of Chiropractic campus in Davenport had grown to include most of the block from 8th to 11th streets on Brady and Main streets. During that period, Dr. David Palmer assumed the reins of president, succeeding his father, the late B.J. Palmer.

The post-war "baby boom" also put a strain on Quad-City area elementary schools. The question each school board faced was: where to put all of the youngsters? Emergency funds were obtained, bond issues were approved and the necessary space was provided. Almost every school district in the area wrestled with expansion plans. Within a decade in Bettendorf, for example, a new junior and senior high school were built, in addition to new elementary units.

Area industry maintained steady growth patterns, too. By the close of the 1950s, workers were earning a total annual sum of nearly $66.9 million, while annual products manufactured in the Quad-Cities surpassed $600 million in value.

The area in that period boasted 60,000 telephones, as compared to just 450 some 75 years earlier, and Davenport City Lines, formed in 1950, was providing transportation with 33 modern buses.

Scott County residents had, from early times, exhibited a streak of independence and chafed occasionally under edicts from the state capital in Des Moines. Their "State of Scott" celebrations, begun in the late 1940s, though held in fun, also underscored that veiled annoyance with orders emanating from under the capitol building's gold dome.

The event featured parades, floats, reigning queens, pretty girls in bathing suits, historical displays, pageantry and fireworks. Residents dressed up in old-time costumes and turned out in droves to watch the parades and take part in the festivities. Interest in the "State of Scott" soon waned, though, and the celebrations fizzled out in the 1950s.

Tragedies, Another War

The early years of that decade brought two major tragedies to the Quad-City area. The biggest loss of life in its history occurred on January 7, 1950, when 41 persons died in a raging fire that swept the St. Elizabeth's Hospital mental facility in Davenport. Many of the 63 inmates were trapped behind barred windows and perished before rescuers could chop through to them and they could be taken down ladders to safety. There were plenty of heroics at the scene, but no one could reach the 41 in time to save their lives. Later, a mental patient admitted that she had started the fire with a cigarette lighter.

On May 23, 1952, a fire that started in a paint room caused $500,000 damage to the Bettendorf Works of the J.I. Case Co.

Quad-Citians scarcely had time to get used to peace before their young men were once more being called up to fight in another conflict, this time in Korea. Draft quotas were increased in 1950. Once more there were scarcities, and area plants that had retooled for peace again geared up for war production.

In 1951, the J.I. Case Company plant in Rock Island received a $4.5 million order to build crankshafts for airplane engines. That same year, the Farmall Works in Rock Island turned out 75,000 tractors. The Eagle Signal Company, Davenport, worked on a $1 million order for Army teletype machines, while the Herman Nelson Corporation, Moline, was producing heating units for the government. The International Harvester Company plant in East Moline had a contract for manufacture of tank-shoe treads, and the French & Hecht Company in Davenport manufactured rocket components under a $4 million government contract. The Rock Island Arsenal increased its work force by 41.7 percent. Labor was so scarce that the Quad-Cities was listed as one of the six most critical labor shortage areas in the United States.

QUAD-CITIANS SCARCELY HAD A BREATHER FROM WORLD WAR II BEFORE IT WAS TIME TO GEAR UP ITS INDUSTRY TO PRODUCE WEAPONS AND MATERIEL FOR THE KOREAN WAR. ONCE AGAIN, THE ROCK ISLAND ARSENAL WAS IN THE FOREFRONT, PRODUCING HOWITZERS LIKE THOSE SHOWN HERE. VARIOUS PRIVATELY OWNED FIRMS ALSO TURNED OUT LARGE QUANTITIES OF MATERIEL FOR THE WAR EFFORT.

FORTY-ONE PERSONS DIED IN THE FIRE THAT DESTROYED ST. ELIZA-BETH'S HOSPITAL JANUARY 7, 1950.

DAVENPORTER JACK FLECK, BEING HONORED HERE IN HIS HOME-TOWN, ASTOUNDED THE GOLF WORLD IN 1955 WHEN HE FIRED A ONE UNDER PAR 33-36-69 TO DEFEAT VETERAN BEN HOGAN AND WIN THE NATIONAL U.S. OPEN GOLF CHAMPIONSHIP. FLECK, SEATED FOURTH FROM LEFT, PERFORMED HIS AMAZING FEAT ON THE OLYMPIC COUNTRY CLUB COURSE IN SAN FRANCISCO, CALIFORNIA.

By the end of 1951, some 3,000 Quad-Citians were in uniform. This number would eventually increase to about 7,000. The largest local contingent left on February, 15, 1952, when Rock Island's 223rd Field Artillery Battalion was called to active duty with the 44th Division.

By the time the bloody, 37-month campaign in Korea had ended, the Quad-Cities had counted 75 killed, 200 wounded and five taken prisoner. The area had sent 2,600 draftees and volunteers to fight in World War I, and 132 of them died in action. Of 10,000 area persons who took part in World War II, 244 were killed in battle.

With the Korean War's end, the Quad-Cities returned once more to peaceful pursuits. Area pride received a boost, and the Quad-Cities national attention, on June 19, 1955, when a relative unknown, Davenporter Jack Fleck, defeated veteran Ben Hogan to win the U.S. Open golf championship on the Olympic Country Club course in San Francisco, California. Fleck fired a one under par 33-36-69 to Hogan's 35-37, for a 72.

One of the most unusual area events of the decade occurred on December 17, 1952, with the surgical separation of the Brodie Siamese twins of Rock Island. They were born, joined at the head, at St. Anthony's Hospital, Rock Island. After 12 preparatory operations, a team of 17 surgeons at the University of Illinois Research Hospital performed the operation to separate them. Roger Lee died shortly after the operation, but Rodney Dee survived for a few years.

One of the major changes that occurred in the Quad-Cities in the 40-year span between 1920 and 1960 was the sharp decrease in the number of persons engaged in agriculture. In 1856, about 50 percent of area residents worked the land, but by the close of the 1950s, this had dropped to just about 15 percent.

In 1856, an investment of about $500 took care of equipment and resources, not including buildings. Even in the 1920s farming did not require an exceedingly large amount of money. But by the end of the 1950s, a farming investment could easily reach $100,000 or more, an indication of the change from labor to capital as the basis for a successful farm operation. By that time, too, the number of area farms was declining. Scott County, for example, at the decade's close had 1,850 farms, but technological advances, highways and buildings were whittling away at the total acreage.

THE SPOILS WENT TO THE FASTEST PICKER IN THE NATIONAL CORN HUSKING CONTEST WHERE ALL FOUR WINNERS SET NATIONAL RECORDS FOR PLUCKING EARS FROM HUSKS AND LOBBING THEM INTO A WAGON. A NUMBER OF NATIONAL CELEBRITIES WERE ALSO ON HAND FOR THE EVENT.

Production was up on area farms as the 1950s closed. By then, a farmer could figure on getting about 110 bushels of corn to an acre, double what could be produced just a few decades earlier. Then, it took a farmer a year to get a hog ready for market and he would feed it out to about 300 pounds, but by 1960 butcher pigs weighing from 210 to 220 pounds were ready for market in five to six months.

By that time, too, area farmers had increased food output many times over what it had been in the '20s and '30s when a farmer was lucky to produce enough food for himself and four others. By 1960, he grew enough for about 30 persons. The Scott County corn crop in that year was worth about $9 million, and swine sales totaled $13 million. The same high yields were recorded in the Illinois area farms.

Production was increased and the farmer's work load reduced by such things as pre-emergence sprays and selective weed-killers, and through new soil management practices such as crop rotation, though continuous cropping later began to find favor again with the use of more commercial fertilizers. Soil conservation had become a necessary practice by the close of the decade, and government programs, including support prices, loans, acreage allotments and quotas had become a part of every Quad-City area farm operation.

At the close of the 1950s, the area had seven hospitals with a total of 1,307 beds, more than 500 physicians and aggregate staffs of 2,355, including nurses and interns. The new 71-bed Davenport Osteopathic Hospital was completed in 1960 at a cost of $850,000. Other hospitals underwent expansion.

Scott County hospitals, all in Davenport, included at that time Mercy, St. Luke's, Davenport Osteopathic and Davenport Convalescent Hospital, operated by the Scott County Board of Supervisors. The latter had a capacity of 31 beds. Rock Island County had three hospitals: St. Anthony's in Rock Island, and Moline Public and Moline Lutheran in Moline. Special psychiatric wards at Mercy and St. Anthony's Hospitals provided a total of 53 beds, which officials felt was adequate for the area's needs. The East Moline State Hospital, located in the Watertown area, was operated by the Illinois Department of Health. It served eight counties, including Rock Island, and had a capacity of 2,000 beds for mental patients.

The Quad-City area's rapid population growth brought a corresponding increase in crime as the 1950s drew to a close, but police departments were better equipped to cope with it. By then, they had scientific detection methods that included chemicals, photography, a teletype network, radar, radio communication, more powerful cars and the opportunity for officers to train at the FBI Academy.

In the four decades after World War I, the area that came to be known as the "Quad-Cities" had grown up, matured and greatly expanded its horizons. It had survived the giddy Roaring '20s, the sobering Great Depression years of the 1930s, the demands of World War II, the tumultuous postwar years of the 1940s and the rapid expansions and changes the 1950s brought. As that decade ended, Quad-Citians were ready for new challenges. Already there were plans for a nuclear power plant in the area.

Just over the horizon was an age of space exploration, of complex computers, of such things as organ transplants and undreamed-of technological break-throughs.

Each new advance, each time of trial, would work its changes, and Quad-Citians would adapt to them as their people had in the past. They had, indeed, "seen Paree," and nothing could hold them back.

J O I N E D   B

BY DAVID COLLINS

"Thousands Cheer Kennedy at Rock Island Fieldhouse"
"Nixon Campaign Swings Through Mississippi Valley"
"Area Catholic Leaders Laud Pope's Unity Efforts"
"Quad-City Bank Debits Hit Alltime High"
"Records Set for Local Construction Projects"

Newspaper headlines appearing in the Quad-Cities during the waning months of the 1950s reflected excitement and activity. The Eisenhower years had been relatively tame and tranquil. Major international and national upheavals were few, allowing areas like the Quad-Cities to concentrate on community growth and improvement. For the most part, the decade of the '50s had been good to Quad-Citians. They hoped the years ahead would be more of the same.

And why wouldn't they share such a hope?

Bank debits (checks cleared through banks, an excellent financial barometer) were recorded at $3.1 billion dollars during 1959. Retail sales soared to $180 million. Construction permits for new residential units hit

1,024 for the year, representing $15 million in home dwellings. Another $23 million was being invested in constructing commercial buildings. Industrial payrolls were $22 million more than the previous year. Financially speaking, these were good times for the Quad-Cities.

Such figures were heralded by local Republican leaders when Richard Nixon rolled into the area in his quest for the presidency. "Keep the Good Times!" declared campaign posters and buttons. "More of the Same!" proclaimed others.

Democratic stewards, especially in Rock Island County where the party had built a strong political machine, cited John Kennedy as offering a "new frontier." The Massachusetts senator's campaign seemed to have a magic appeal for the young. Figures revealed the average Kennedy volunteer was five years younger than the average Nixon volunteer.

Adolescents turned one ear to the political realm, but remained closer tuned to the world of their own. After all, which was better listening — a presidential candidate's speech or Elvis Presley belting out "You Ain't Nothin' But a Hound Dog"? (For the more mellow teen, there was always a whitebucked Pat Boone crooning musical "Love Letters in the Sand.")

While Kennedy and Nixon commanded Quad-City attention in the political world, area residents also found themselves interested in the activities of a new leader on the other side of the world. Succeeding the conservative Pope Pius XII in 1958 as head of the Roman Catholic Church, Pope John XXIII immediately began efforts to reach out to other faiths for areas of unity and agreement.

"He's not the caretaker pontiff many thought he'd be," observed Bishop Hayes of the Davenport Diocese. "He definitely has plans of his own. I think we'll all be seeing a pulling together of denominations if Pope John XXIII has enough time to fulfill his dreams."

Bishop Hayes proved prophetic, for the aged pontiff died June 3, 1963, only six months after the first session of the Vatican Council. The prelate had hoped to lead the meeting of church leaders toward a strong unification of faiths. Pope John's successor, Pope Paul VI, returned to a more conservative direction for the Roman Catholic Church.

The death of Pope John XXIII was but one sadness endured by Quad-Citians during the 1960s. During the same year, President Kennedy was shot down by an assassin in Dallas. Carol Johnson, a Davenport resident who had served a term in Kennedy's Peace Corps, summed up the grief of many Quad-Citians.

"He was so young, so alive," Johnson observed. "He made everyone proud to be an American with his vibrant spirit, his grace and warmth. It's just so hard to believe he's gone."

Assassins' bullets claimed two other American notables in the '60s. Civil rights leader Martin Luther King Jr. was shot down in Memphis in April 1968, and Senator Robert Kennedy lost his life on a campaign trip during June of the same year.

And with the unhappiness of the deaths came a growing disillusion and confusion. The national spotlight began focusing on a military conflict in Vietnam with President Johnson becoming more adamant about an American military victory. The drafting of young men brought mixed reaction. Some felt obligated to serve their country, while others declared the United States involvement to be immoral and without purpose.

Peace marches were held throughout the Quad-Cities during the '60s. Military enlistment offices, government buildings, the arsenal — all were sites for peaceful demonstrations. Area residents took sides on whether the United States should pull out of Vietnam or fight on.

But there were no sides when a dead soldier was brought home to be buried. On both Iowa and Illinois sides of the Mississippi, family and friends gathered to bury loved ones.

QUAD-CITY RESIDENTS WHO OPPOSED THE WAR IN VIETNAM PICKETED IN FRONT OF DAVEN-PORT'S FEDERAL BUILDING. MOST DEMONSTRATIONS WERE QUIET IN THE QUAD-CITIES.

"There aren't any winners in a war like this," Max Peterson of East Moline commented after the death of his 19-year-old son, Ronald, a casualty of the conflict. "When you lose someone you love, victories and defeats have little meaning. All you feel is the grief."

Sweeping into the Quad-City area in the '60s was the hippie movement. Beards, shoulder-length hair, Navajo headbands, serapes, body paint became commonplace in the community. There were not the extremes found on the East and West coasts, but the change in dress patterns was enough to make many people shake their heads and area schools initiate dress codes. Despite the tragedies and turmoil that found their way to the Quad-City community during the '60s, positive progress was made as well. Davenport's Brady Street was widened, the city library facilities expanded, the new YM/YWCA building completed. At the Quad-City Airport, runways were extended to accommodate modern jets, a bridge was erected at Le Claire and the Interstate 74, 80 and 280 routes offered sophisticated highway arteries to and through the entire metropolitan community.

Within the business realm, farm implement dealers did a booming business which kept the agricultural factories in the area busy. Chemical plants constructed along the Mississippi further aided the local economy.

During the '60s, thousands of younger Quad-Citians received the new Sabin oral vaccine for polio. Not as welcome in many households was the oral contraception pill which caused numerous citizens to do much soul searching.

From 1959 to 1969, the cost of living rose 27 percent.

"It was impossible to get ahead financially," remembers Rock Islander Roger Schneff. "Each year I earned a little more salary, and each year the cost of everything ate up the increase."

By the end of the decade, bank debits had risen to $7.4 billion, double the amount they had been 10 years before. Housing permits numbered 1,178 units. Residential construction was booming.

Booming too was American pride. The year 1969 found two men, Neil Armstrong and Edwin Aldrin Jr., landing on the moon. The Apollo space mission climaxed intense planning and training begun in 1961.

"We all felt a part of that accomplishment," states Moliner Henry Weber. "To stand in the Quad-Cities and gaze up at the moon, and to think about two of our own Americans up there — yes, we all felt proud."

The 70's brought renewed interest in the rights of women and the protection of nature. A spirited National Organization for Women (NOW) chapter began earnest efforts in behalf of the proposed Equal Rights Amendment (ERA) to the U.S. Constitution.

"It wasn't that individual women had not recognized the inequality of men and women before," commented one NOW official. "It was just that women had not organized as an active force to work in their own behalf."

The environment also gained a spotlight in the Quad-City community. Recognizing the area's favorable haven for eagles, nature leaders and lovers led the campaign to protect a local sanctuary for the disappearing birds. Additional programs focused on means of conserving energy and natural resources.

"In school, we were made aware of everything we have," noted Mark Lundahl, a Moline resident. "We learned how important the sun was, the earth, the waters — everything. Not only did we study ecology, but we were filled with the feeling that it was un-American, even inhuman, to waste our natural resources."

Waste was on the minds of many Quad-Citians in another way as well. The Vietnam conflict had grown distasteful to Americans everywhere. Fulfilling a campaign promise, President Nixon arranged for a pullout of forces. The Quad-City community welcomed back service veterans.

But no sooner had the welcoming subsided when area residents found themselves witnessing historical revelations at the highest level of government. "Watergate" became a household word. What began as a small break-in at Democratic National Headquarters in Washington mushroomed swiftly into events that would shake the nation. Local interest intensified when the Judiciary Committee of the House of Representatives reviewed evidence to determine whether the president of the United States was guilty of impeachable offenses. Two members of the committee, Tom Railsback of Moline and Edward Mezvinsky of Iowa City, represented the Quad-City area.

National TV networks covered hearings of the House Judiciary Committee and local residents watched with keen interest. Although the committee was never called upon to vote on impeachment, community viewers expressed a favorable impression of both Railsback and Mezvinsky.

"It had to be especially hard on Tom," notes an Illinois state legislator. "Nixon had been a friend and political supporter. We were able to see Tom Railsback as a man of conscience and integrity. He served us well."

Watergate eventually led to the resignation of President Nixon, and it was not the only event to dim the feelings of Quad-Citians. Assassins attempted to kill President Gerald Ford and presidential candidate George Wallace. At the Munich Olympics, 17 Israeli athletes lost their lives, shot down in a mass execution. A spiritual leader named Jim Jones led his people to South America, then supervised a suicide of hundreds of victims. Tragedies touched the lives and spirits of many Quad-Citians.

But when 1976 arrived and it was time to observe the 200th anniversary of the nation's birth, area residents were ready. Bicentennial commissions were formed which supervised pageants, posters, parades and projects of every size.

"It was work and fun at the same time," said Moline Bicentennial chairperson Sandy Bellinger. "People came together as strangers and became friends. We really had a bang-up birthday celebration!"

Bicentennial observances pumped up pride, and during the '70s area residents showed fresh interest in pumping up their bodies as well. Joggers took to the streets, bikers to bike paths, racquetball players to their courts. Less energetic Quad-Citians discovered the fun of CB radios, mood rings, dancing "The Hustle" and wearing leisure outfits. Popular movies were often sequels to originals, disco music gathered a vast following, and television viewers enjoyed the adventures of the Bunker and Ingalls families in "All in the Family" and "Little House on the Prairie." Telephone users found they could dial-a-prayer or dial-a-story. *SMILE* and *WIN* buttons dotted many chests. A gas crunch was felt. Cable television brought added viewing pleasure, while a cinema complex in Milan proved an instant success.

But by the end of the '70s, the Quad-Cities had begun to experience major pangs of unemployment and inflation. The Rock Island Lines died an agonizing death, while area agricultural empires suffered various degrees of business illness. Construction and real estate markets suffered from high interest rates placed on money borrowers and potential builders.

The pains and problems of the '70s passed silently into a new decade. Gone were headlines proclaiming record-setting achievements of the preceding 10 years. Area residents hoped the new president, Ronald Reagan, would find solutions to the maladies besetting the national and local economies. Some area residents recalled the president's beginnings in Illinois and Iowa.

With a ratification deadline approaching for the ERA vote in the Illinois House of Representatives, both sides of the issue intensified their campaign. The nation watched as the amendment fell four votes short of the necessary 107 to pass from the House to the Senate. But area NOW leaders pledged renewed efforts and spirit in behalf of the movement.

And so the story of the Quad-Cities continues.

It is a story of faith and fun.

It is a story of fear, frustration and anger.

It is a story of hopes and dreams.

As a human tapestry, it is every color and every depth of emotion. It is the talented and the derelict. It is the builder and the destroyer.

In activity, it is every sort of event. It is a pulsating Wharton Field House when the Moline Maroons take on the Rock Island Rocks in tournament basketball action. It is a quiet neighborhood bar in East Moline where factory workers share beer and conversation after a long work day. It is a concert at Centennial Hall, an Easter egg hunt at Fejervary Park, a folk festival in Bettendorf or a walk through Black Hawk Park in autumn.

It is a winter with below zero temperatures and a summer with a week-long heat wave. It is a spring that sends flood waters over riverfronts and a fall that sends brush fires racing across dry grasslands.

Variety. That is the Quad-Cities, a collage of human beings and human events in the heartland of America.

In the years that are the immediate past, a chapter of history has been written. Some of the events are complete within themselves. Others are on-going and open-ended. Whichever they be, they are filled with the lives that have woven the Quad-City tapestry of history. In words and in pictures, the collage of the Quad-Cities continues...

SPUTNIK TRIGGERS EDUCATIONAL CHANGES

October 4, 1957.

Around the world a strange electronic beep emanated from television sets and radios. Quad-City communication centers were swamped with questions and complaints.

Soon the mystery was solved. The Soviet Union proudly declared it had successfully launched the first manmade orbiting satellite. Its name — Sputnik. The beeps? Sputnik was simply sending coded messages of its observations as it hurled through the skies.

The thought that America was in some way — any way — behind the Soviet Union shocked countless individuals. Surely the Russian space triumph was a mere fluke.

But as more and more facts about Sputnik became known, it became obvious that there were indeed weaknesses in American science. Immediately the focus fell upon education.

"The security and continued well-being of the United States depend, as never before, on the extension of scientific knowledge," observed President Eisenhower.

Rock Island Superintendent of Schools Earl Hanson echoed the president's concern. "Naturally, educators are concerned with the learning experiences that are most useful to students. We will certainly be reviewing the science curriculum within our school program. This does not mean we will be leaping into every new proposal that is suggested."

There *was* no "leaping" into rapid changes within the network of area schools. But there was increased activity in an effort to evaluate existing educational programs. Curriculum councils were organized, experts were brought in and student input was sought.

"There's no question that Sputnik shook up the world of education everywhere," reflects one Moline educator. "At that time less than half our high school graduates went on to college. Most of those who did had little science and math background. We had an immediate increase in college bound students, many of them seeking more high school science preparation."

Through passage of the National Defense Education Act, approximately $1 billion became available for state and federal education programs. Quad-City principals found their schools suddenly receiving funds for long-desired equipment, while college and graduate fellowships became available. In the decade after the Sputnik launch, Quad-City youth heading to college more than doubled.

With the launching of *Freedom 7* carrying Alan Shepard into space on May 5, 1961, many Americans felt a reborn spirit and pride. Subsequent space flights brought a new sense of peace and comfort.

"President Johnson was a big supporter of the space program," observes retired Davenport instructor Marie Caroll, "but in the mid-60s, there was a feeling we had caught up. Enrollment in high school science classes began to trickle off. The spotlight on space travel died out."

By the end of the '60s, Quad-City youth had transferred their interest to other areas of science more related to social concerns. Soviet and American scientists were cooperating in space programs. Pollution and ecological problems took the forefront. The use of napalm and defoliants in Vietnam caused many students to turn away from science.

"Then there was the return to basics," continues Caroll. "Our educational concerns in the '70s within the Quad-City community included quite a bit of experimentation. We all recognized the importance of reading, writing, math at all levels, but there were many opinions of how best results could be achieved."

New methods of math, emphasizing process as well as result, found favor within Quad-City schools. Team teaching was tried in many classrooms, students were exposed to mini-classes, mobile teaching units appeared at schools, career education programs were developed, and citizenship gained greater emphasis.

While students found changes within their educational world, Quad-City educators enjoyed greater opportunity for study through the Quad-Cities Graduate Center. Fully operative since 1969, the center draws upon the University of Iowa, Iowa State University, University of Northern Iowa, Marycrest College, University of Illinois, Northern Illinois University, Western Illinois University and Augustana College to provide courses for educators and business employees to pursue graduate work. Nine masters degree programs are currently offered. Enrollment figures find class composition to be approximately 60 percent female and 40 percent male. Area colleges, recognizing the need for continuing education, have expanded course offerings to service business and industry. Multi-media has become standard, while TV/radio communication outlets have become active campus units.

"We still cater to fulltime traditional students," comments Dr. Harold Sundelius, vice-president of academic affairs at Augustana College. "We haven't gone aggressively into attracting non-traditional students, although we may at some other time."

Cuts in federal and state aid will bring traditional financial belt tightening in the future. Staff cuts and decreased facility use are already being implemented to save dollars.

The beep of Sputnik is but a soft whisper of the past. The Quad-City educational spotlight has returned to the basics. In truth, that spotlight has seldom shifted very far away.

VOTERS PICK FIRST WOMAN, FIRST BLACK MAYORS

KATHRYN KIRSCHBAUM CAPTURED THE MAYORAL SLOT IN DAVENPORT DURING THE '70S, THUS BECOMING THE FIRST WOMAN IN THE AREA TO HOLD THE TOP EXECUTIVE OFFICE IN CITY GOVERNMENT.

"The Quad-City community is a good political thermometer for the nation," Charles Carpentier once observed. The East Moline native rose to become secretary of state in Illinois and was just about to launch a gubernatorial bid when death struck him down in 1964. He had also commented, "When a political trend starts swinging across the country, it's sure to stop off here in the Quad-Cities."

Carpentier's observations came to fruition early in the 1970s. Women and blacks were asserting new strength and power, long controlled by white male leadership. On both sides of the Mississippi, voters reflected a national mood by electing a woman and a black to head city governments.

Forty-year-old Kathryn Kirschbaum, the mother of two young sons, was serving as an alderman when she led her Democratic team to victory in 1971. National news media focused on the Kirschbaum election as "direct evidence that women are indeed making their presence known in the heartland of America."

Advocating a program of benefits for the underprivileged and disadvantaged, Kirschbaum called for "a new openness and compassion, and good faith with each other." Her city council was made up of seven Democrats and three Republicans.

Two years later Mayor Kirschbaum ran again, squeaking out a 356-vote victory margin over Republican challenger Ross Frick. Republicans captured a majority of council seats 6-4. Once again, the city leader pledged "a humane environment and benefits for all citizens of Davenport."

Hoping for a third try at Davenport's chief executive office, the mayor entered her name in the Democratic primary set for October 7, 1975. She had been openly criticized for "indecision" and "inability to cope with police matters." Fellow Democrat Dallas George bumped Mayor Kirschbaum from contention by a 2,784-2,211 vote margin. Vacating her mayoral position, Kirschbaum accepted a position with a Davenport business.

ROCK ISLAND'S JIM DAVIS WORE THE VICTOR'S SMILE AS HE LEARNED THE VOTERS HAD SELECTED HIM AS THEIR MAYOR.

On the Illinois side of the river, James Davis, a black, first became involved in city government as an activist for open housing. He was first elected to the city council in 1973.

"Too many citizens rely on elected officials or civic leaders to do all the work," Davis stated. "A city is made up of all citizens, not just a few." Successful in re-election attempts to the city council, Davis was a member when Mayor Alan Campbell died in office. Councilman Martin Galex was appointed to replace Campbell, but Galex resigned in August of 1978. Davis was named acting mayor.

In April of 1979, Davis squared off against Councilman Gerald Tyrrell. Tyrrell charged that Davis could not fulfill duties as principal of Hawthorne-Irving Elementary School while being Rock Island's mayor as well.

On April 18, 1979, Rock Island voters picked Davis by a vote of 4,045 to 3,643 for Tyrrell. The soft-spoken Davis labeled himself "the people's choice," happy that he had now been officially elected rather than appointed.

The black Mayor Davis contends he allows for no special privileges to the heavy black population who live in his city. Nor do they seek any, he affirms.

"I'm a mayor for the entire city of Rock Island," Davis asserts emphatically. "There are no racial boundaries to this office, nor geographical ones either."

The area "political thermometer" has also risen to reflect the national movement of rights for senior citizens. Although yet to back specific candidates for election, spokesmen for the elderly have shown strong force in their quest for attention and benefits.

On the local scene, a variety of organized citizens have asserted their concerns within the framework of unified groups. ACORN, Community Caring, United Neighbors and other units have campaigned actively for political and humane causes.

Less vocal and considerably less visibly in the community spotlight is the gay element. Both sides of the Mississippi have nightspots which claim predominantly gay clientele.

ZOO DRAWS VISITORS

It all began with a boy's interest in wild animals.

Today, Niabi Zoo attracts visitors from the entire Quad-City community and beyond. Recent yearly attendance figures show numbers climbing steadily toward 200,000.

Young Gordon McLain grew up fascinated with wildlife. Visiting circuses were a special treat. He became convinced that the Quad-Cities should have its own zoo.

A successful Moline masonry contractor, McLain turned his dream into reality. he acquired 234 acres of rolling land east of the Quad-Cities. Carefully, he began accumulating animals, erecting animal houses and cages. Attractive landscaping added to the site.

Having invested a quarter of a million dollars and many years, Gordon McLain opened his wild animal farm in 1959. It was a family affair with McLain's father, Byrd, serving as office manager and co-owner; his mother operating the ticket office; and Gordon's wife filling in wherever needed.

"It's a beautiful place," noted Hollywood animal trainer Gene Holder. "The buildings are ultra-modern and the animals obviously get more than their share of tender loving care."

The running of the zoo was no easy task. In addition to the McLain family, six other employees helped with the feeding and cleaning. A typical day's menu included 125 pounds of fresh meat, three bushels of produce, 20 bushels of corn and 20 bales of hay.

KATHY SH'BOOM, THE NIABI ZOO'S ELEPHANT, GREETS YOUNG WELL-WISHERS EACH YEAR ON HER BIRTHDAY IN EARLY AUGUST.

In 1961, Gordon McLain sold his zoo to Mrs. Charles Deere Wiman, who donated the complex to Rock Island County the same year.

In the years that followed, the zoo rode its own perilous merry-go-round. Although new animals replaced those that died and efforts were made to keep the zoo in decent repair, the shadows of financial strain always hovered over the successful operation of the facility.

In time, McLain's Zoo became Niabi, an Oswego word meaning "spared by the hunter." But if the animals be spared by hunters, they often came close to extinction by lack of money.

But with the efforts of a 200-member Niabi Zoological Society, designed to publicize and raise funds for the beleagured animal complex, new life was generated. From a gala ball to an annual public birthday party for elephant Kathy Shaboom, the society had filled the coffers and fed the proceeds back into zoo improvements. New fencing was erected to keep out bands of roving wild dogs which had attacked animals. Torn and rutfilled roads have been blacktopped. Efforts have been made to make the zoo open to the handicapped. A train ads a special attraction to a zoo visit.

Today, Niabi Zoo stands as a thriving memorial to a man who once had dreams as a child. Gordon McLain's boyhood dreams have brought fun and joy to countless youngsters.

"I never saw a tiger before!" exclaims a 5-year-old red-haired boy leaving Niabi. "I love every animal at this place!"

They were words Gordon McLain would have loved to hear.

MISSISSIPPI GOES ON RAMPAGE

No one could claim that the Quad-City community was not warned early enough. Those giant snowfalls of the winter of '64 left the northen lands smothering and gasping for breath. When the temperatures climbed, the heavy icy mantle began to melt.

"We're going to break some records along the Mississippi this year," one official of the National Weather Service predicted. "I'm afraid there's a 'doozie' of a flood heading our way."

Many Quad-Citians were skeptical. Sure, every spring brought the usual higher crests and inconvenience to those living near the river. Sometimes Mississippi waters even crept onto downtown river streets surrounding the levee. But a major flood? Not here. Not this year.

"It will never top the flood of '52," oldtime residents declared. "Now there's when we had problems. Water got up to 18 feet, I believe!"

But by March of 1965, much of the skepticism had faded. Even the most doubtful were beginning to appreciate the seriousness of the situation. The Army Corps of Engineers substantiated the worst fears of the National Weather Service. Bulletins listed the cities and states in the path of the forthcoming flood. The entire Quad-City community was in the middle.

Early in April the river began to climb. First to be evacuated were residents of Smith's Island west of Milan, and Enchanted Island in west Davenport. Families found refuge in the homes of relatives and friends.

By mid-April, more than 2,000 Quad-Citians had left their homes for places of safety. In city garages and along river levees, sandbags were filled and stacked. River barge traffic ceased. Area residents waited and watched.

At the official flood marker at Locks and Dam 15, anything over 15 feet is considered flooding.

Slowly the river grew higher and wider. Walls of sandbags lined the Mississippi's boundaries. The crest predictions inched upward.

16 feet.

18 feet.

21 feet.

Volunteers poured their energies into keeping dike walls secure. Senior citizens worked side by side with high school youth, lifting and packing in an effort to keep out rising flood waters.

*BETTENDORF HIGH SENIOR
KENNETH BECKER CAST A
WATCHFUL GAZE OVER THE
RISING MISSISSIPPI WATERS IN
1965.*

John O'Donnell Stadium became a giant swimming pool, as did backyards and basements. The Red Cross came in to distribute food. More families left their homes, dirty river waves licking at their heels.
Factory workers forgot their usual duties as they threw themselves into a fulltime effort to keep the Mississippi out of their plants. Some succeeded, others failed.

Special heroes emerged from the Flood of '65. College and high school students swarmed to action sites and offered their time and energy. After completing flood tasks, they stumbled home to finish homework assignments.
Never before had area cities kept in such close and constant communication. "Camanche is surrounded," one caller announced. "The dikes in Fulton have collapsed," was the reply. "They're still okay at Muscatine."
As the flood waters crept higher, the number of evacuees increased too. 8,000...9,000...10,000. The Red Cross had its hands full. National Guardsmen and helicopters became common sights throughout the area.
If aching muscles and bones could make sound, the noise would have been deafening. Trucks rolled to dike locations. Quickly the sand-filled burlap bags were unloaded by tired volunteers.
In the midst of the river gone wild there emerged a sense of spirit and dedication. Rich and poor, young and old, male and female — all pitched in to do what needed doing.
Finally, it arrived. Crest day. The river rose to 22.48 feet on April 28, 1965. Careful watch was kept for weak spots in the dikes. The slightest jet stream of water was a danger sign. New sandbags were stacked.
Many of the 12,000 residents who had been forced back from their homes made the daily inspection of their property in rowboats. On higher ground, cherry tree blossoms sprung from the trees, offering a strange contrast to the murky Mississippi water.
Then, in the same creeping manner that it had come, the river began to recede. It was a slow retreat, inch by inch. Just as it could not be stopped, it would not be hurried.

More than $10 million worth of damage had been done. Wearily, people shoveled out the dried mud. Floors lay warped and ruined. Carpeting, furniture, plastered rooms — destroyed.

But from the sadness and destruction brought by the unforgetable Flood of '65 came a new awareness of community pride and spirit. By their contributions, the youth etched a noble image of themselves in the memories of their elders. As in most times of tragedy, people had pulled together and worked as one unit.

Yes, the Mississippi had flexed her muscles.

And Quad-Citians had matched her strength.

MALLS OFFER SHOPPERS CHOICE

"To go to the mall — or to go downtown. That is the question."

Perhaps a Shakespearean paraphrase best fits the dilemma faced by Quad-City shoppers. It's a fairly recent dilemma.

General Growth Companies is the child of Matthew and Martin Bucksbaum, two brothers whose business and real estate sense approaches legend. Begun in 1952, General Growth became the largest publicly owned real estate trust in the country by 1977. It now has about 6,000 shareholders and a collection of real estate valued at well over $300 million in 25 states and Puerto Rico.

General Growth operates three shopping centers in the Quad-City area. They are Southpark in Moline, Northpark in Davenport, and Duck Creek Plaza in Bettendorf.

Northpark claims recognition as the largest shopping center in Iowa. It has waged a battle of size with Merle Hay Plaza in Des Moines ever since the Davenport mall was built on a 117-acre tract of land in 1973. A 320,000-square-foot expansion was completed in 1981. The mall has not only proven a business success, but it has been a delight for heart patients and others suffering health problems where walking is recommended. Meeting and visiting with friends at the mall is a daily experience for many Quad-Citians.

The addition of area shopping malls has posed serious problems for retail outlets elsewhere, particularly in the downtowns. City officials and merchants have worked together to keep both the shopping center and downtown businesses operating successfully.

"But it's not easy to compete with a mall," one downtown Moline businessman groans. "People today appreciate one-stop shopping. The mall also provides a social outing for many people. We're not giving up, though. There's a lot of special ingredients and personality in our downtown. And we can always count on our longtime customers. There's a lot to be said for loyalty."

ARTS FIND COMMUNITY SUPPORT

The performing arts, visual arts and literary arts have all found broad, active support within the Quad-City community. Many residents regularly head toward Chicago for a play at the Shubert or travel west for a concert at Hancher Auditorium in Iowa City, but there is constant evidence that culture does indeed thrive within the Mississippi Valley community.

One of the most recent attractions to the Quad-City artistic scene has been Circa '21 Dinner Playhouse. Spearheading the theatre is Dennis Hitchcock, who serves as producer, director and president of development. The Circa '21 playbill features non-Equity, professional theatre.

Of greater longevity are the Broadway Theatre League and Playcrafters. In its efforts to bring quality and stars to the area, the league has had both ups and downs.

"The Quad-City theatre audience is anything but predictable," notes one volunteer. "Our expenses to bring in a production are definite, yet we always have a gamble on numbers in our audience."

Playcrafters relies on community talent for a year-round program of performances. Many organizations hold charity benefits in addition to regular scheduled performances.

Combining theatre and music, the Quad-City Music Guild attracts big crowds to Moline's Prospect Park every summer. Local talent is used for the three- and sometimes four-show season.

The Tri-City Symphony audience has fluctuated over the years, but relies heavily on families of regular music lovers. Some feel Hancher's drawing power has hindered symphony attendance, but artists booked at Hancher sometimes travel to the Quad-Cities to perform.

The Davenport Art Gallery boasts an impressive permanent collection while continuing to bring quality traveling artwork to the area. Small private galleries flourish, and Studio 15 and Left Bank Art League have active, producing memberships. The offices of the Quad-City Arts Council in downtown Rock Island have frequently served as a showcase for art exhibits.

The Mississippi Valley Writers Conference was born in 1973. Its week-long writers' gathering at Augustana College sprang from a need for area enthusiasts to work with professional instructors and exchange ideas. Attendance has grown from 27 during the first year to 73 in 1981.

Five writing organizations meet regularly during the year. They include Juvenile Forum, Quad-City Writers Club, Writers' Studio, Wordsmiths and Quad-City Chapter of American Pen Women.

For the past 10 years, Writers' Studio has sponsored a one-day free writers seminar at Butterworth Center in Moline. The organization also prints a newsletter every two months.

HOSTING OUTSTANDING TRAVELING EXHIBITS AS WELL AS BOASTING A QUALITY PERMANENT COLLECTION, THE DAVENPORT ART GALLERY HAS ATTRACTED THOUSANDS OF VISITORS.

The annual Mississippi Valley Poetry Contest, sponsored by Writers'
Studio, Quad-City Writers Club and Wordsmiths, attracts hundreds of
entries each year. A Poetry Reading Night is held at Moline's Butterworth
Center.

Obviously, area residents enjoy the arts, as participants or appreciators.
Seeds of interest in opera and ballet have already been planted. There is
little doubt that the Quad-Cities will foster future artistic endeavors.

AREA INDUSTRY GROWS

Despite fluctuations in the general economy, the median buying income for
a Quad-City family after taxes stood at $22,878 in 1980. The community's
high income — which places it among the top 50 markets in the United
States — is a direct result of the productive and skilled workforce needed to
support technologically advanced manufacturing.

While most of the community's workers are employed in wholesale and
retail trade, communication, utilities, transportation and the professions,
manufacturing is the core of the Quad-City economy. Nearly 50,000 area
residents out of a total work force of 190,000 are engaged in some form of
industrial production.

The area's largest manufacturing employer, Deere & Company, claims
about 15,000 workers. Deere has five major installations in the Quad-Cities,
including its international headquarters in Moline. The company has made
major investments in the community in recent years. In 1980, Deere
completed work on its parts distribution warehouse, finished its Davenport
Works expansion program and built a new product engineering center at its
Harvester Works. Plans were announced in 1981 for two multi-million-dollar
manufacturing buildings to be constructed at East Moline's Harvester
Works. In the late 1970s, Deere's Foundry works underwent a multi-million-
dollar expansion, and the spectacular west wing was added to the
administrative center.

Deere is just one of the community's major employers that is rooted in the
agricultural industry. International Harvester, although based outside the
community, has long invested in the modernization of its plants in Rock
Island and East Moline. IH, which ranks as the Quad-Cities' third largest
employer, broke ground in 1980 for a huge computer-controlled warehouse
complex at its Rock Island Farmall plant.

The community's second largest employer, with some 7,500 workers, is the
Rock Island Arsenal. Early in the 1980s, plans were well underway for a
multi-million-dollar renovation as part of the Defense Department's Project
REARM.

The Quad-Cities is home to the world's largest aluminum rolling mill, the
Davenport Works of Alcoa, located at Riverdale. It recently increased its
capacity for heat-treating aluminum.

Caterpillar Tractor Company, another major employer with about 3,000
Quad-City workers, nearly quadrupled the size of its plant on the northern
edge of Davenport. Occupying about 650,000 square feet in 1976, the facility
had expanded to more than 2.2 million square feet by the early '80s.

Martin-Marietta also made a major investment in the Quad-Cities in the
late '70s and early '80s with construction of its $90 million cement plant in
Buffalo.

Other new industrial plants have sprung up since the late '70s. American
Honda built a $10 million parts distribution warehouse in Davenport. The
Geo. A. Hormel Company erected a new plant. Termicold located a 300,000-
square-foot freezer facility in Riverdale. Mississippi Valley Airlines located
its headquarters at the Quad-City Airport. Many other employers expanded
or renovated their facilities.

"BIX LIVES!"

It happens every July in the Quad-Cities. About the first week of the month, residents begin to snap their fingers and tap their feet. Some call it the Beiderbecke Syndrome. Others call it "Bixitis." Whatever the label, there is only one cure: attendance at the annual Bix Beiderbecke Jazz Festival along the Davenport levee on the last weekend in July.

"Bix Lives!" is the slogan for the yearly gathering of jazz lovers. The festival is the living memorial for the former Davenporter who blew a horn to worldwide acclaim in the 1920s. He was a high school dropout who burned the candle at both ends and in the middle. He drank too much and slept too little. By the age of 28, he lay alone and dead in New York City.

THE CAKEWALKIN' JASS BAND OF TOLEDO, OHIO, WITH ITS THEME SONG "CAKEWALKIN' BABES FROM HOME," HAS BECOME A FAMILIAR FEATURE OF RECENT BIX FESTS.

THE LE CLAIRE BANDSHELL GROUNDS ANNUALLY SPORT A SEA OF LAWNCHAIRS, EACH ONE FILLED WITH A DIXIELAND JAZZ ENTHUSIAST.

RUNNERS POUND THE PAVEMENT IN THE OPENING LEG OF THE BIX 7-MILE RUN, IOWA'S LARGEST RACE.

But in those 28 years Bix Beiderbecke left a mark few men manage to achieve in a full lifetime. His fellow musicians recognized his musical artistry, even genius. He was self-taught, a horn player who handled his instrument like a father handles a newborn infant.

When the first gathering of Beiderbecke fans congregated in August of 1971, there was no thought of any annual affair. A group of musicians from the East Coast — The Bix Beiderbecke Memorial Jazz Band of New Jersey — arrived in Davenport to honor Bix's memory on the 40th anniversary of the young musician's death. The visiting instrumentalists planned to visit the Beiderbecke gravesite in Oakdale Cemetery, play on a Mississippi excursion boat, hit a few nightspots where Bix had played and hold a jam session at the Holiday Inn in Davenport.

But when word got out about the jam session, more than 2,000 people flooded the Holiday Inn. Cars were lined up for a mile in both directions. It was a night to remember — and repeat.

Davenporters Esten Spurrier and Don O'Dette, who had helped the visiting New Jersey band plan their programs, were surprised and delighted. Why not an annual jazz affair?

The Bix Beiderbecke Memorial Society was formed, a non-profit group, led by O'Dette, with no money and no office. The new organization laid plans for the first Bix Beiderbecke Memorial Dixieland Jazz Festival in the Le Claire Park bandshell. Skeptics shook their heads. The first event was a fluke, they claimed. Who would support a second?

Traditional bands agreed to come, most offering to play for free. Souvenir items were designed and reproduced. Society officials worked closely with Davenport city officials.

The early phases of the first public festival went beautifully. But a downpour on Saturday night, the biggest audience drawer, plunged the event into debt.

Discouraged but undaunted, society officials turned to offering $5 membership donations. More than 1,000 people from all over the world mailed in contributions. Once more, the society was on its feet. Plans for another festival took shape.

The Beiderbecke Festival of 1973 put the BBMS on firm financial footing. Thousands of jazz lovers covered the levee. They came from all over the United States and foreign countries.

"Jazz is people music," observes Moliner Michael Roche. "It doesn't matter how old you are — this Dixieland beat and rhythm appeals to everyone. I come every year."

So do thousands of others. The festival weekend opens with a Friends of Bix Cocktail Party on Thursday night. Friday concerts begin at noon, as do the band concerts on Saturday and Sunday. After supper breaks, the music continues into the night. Even when the Le Claire gatherings break up, musicians and music lovers often head to area nightspots for additional jamming.

Jazz lovers not only cover the levee area at concert time, but they dot the river in boats of varying shape and size. To sit content in a deck chair, enjoying the soft river breezes and music is a dream world to hundreds of Mississippi boatmen.

It's impossible to know who enjoys the annual festival the most — spectators or participants. Bobbing heads, snapping fingers, quick moving feet — all attest to the young and old listeners caught up in the beat of the music.

"I love every minute I'm performing here," exclaims former Quad-Citian Bill Allred, who frequently brings a collection of fellow instrumentalists with him when he returns to the festival. "My trombone sings by itself here!"

Sing it may, while listeners snap and tap. Whatever the rhythm, July spells jazztime every year on the Davenport levee. It's a way to forget worries and troubles, to enjoy the best of Dixie beat, and to know for sure that once again, "Bix Lives!"

SPORTS ATTRACT PARTICIPANTS AND SPECTATORS

Are Quad-Citians sports minded?

For an answer, visit Brady Street Stadium on a Friday night in the fall, Wharton Field House during the winter or an area bowling center during any season. Check out the Mississippi marinas and park baseball diamonds in the spring. Go to a high school wrestling or swimming meet. Try to find an empty tennis court in June or July. For many years, the Quad-Cities have hosted national softball championships, AAU meets and league action in a variety of sports. High school area teams have brought back from state tournament action an impressive abundance of titles and trophies.

But since the early 1970s, two area athletic events have climbed their way up the ladder of national sports attention. The going hasn't always been easy, but the Quad-Cities Open has won a position of honor in the golfing spotlight, while the Quad-City Downs has brought harness racing into a respected arena for participants and spectators alike.

A dedicated golfer and member of Crow Valley Country Club, Bob McGriff was one of the founders of the first Quad-Cities Open. The first tournament, held in 1971, was a satellite of the PGA tour.

"It wasn't easing bridging the Mississippi to pull together Illinois and Iowa golfing enthusiasts," notes McGriff. "When we began work on the Open, I didn't fully understand the separation between the two states."

But bridge the sporting gap they did, and Crow Valley served as the site of the first Quad-Cities Open. By the following year, the Open had a $100,000 purse and a spot on the PGA Tour. In 1973 and 1974, the golfing classic became known as the Hardee's Quad-Cities Open. The Open moved from Crow Valley in Iowa to the Oakwood Country Club in Illinois.

Thanks to McGriff and other area golfing enthusiasts, the Quad-Cities Open has continued to grow in strength and stature. Much of the success for the event has been due to the massive number of Quad-Citians who volunteer their time and services each July. Numerous charities share the profits — when there are profits. As in most outdoor athletic events, the weather can play havoc with attendance figures. Although the tournament purse has risen to $200,000, it is still the second lowest on the tournament. Conflicts with other prestigious golf classics have also contributed to the problems with the Quad-Cities Open.

AMONG CELEBRITIES PARTIC-IPATING IN THE QUAD-CITIES OPEN WAS BOB HOPE WHO TOOK PART IN THE 1977 PGA GOLF CLASSIC HELD AT OAKWOOD COUNTRY CLUB.

Yet the annual event has brought high pitched excitement to the community every year. "Tonight" show announcer Ed McMahon for several years, lent his name to the tournament and personally helped line up celebrities to attend the event. Quad-Citians turned out in big crowds to view Bob Hope, Telly Savalas, Cornel Wilde, Ernie Banks, Tom Sullivan, Fred MacMurray and others. Attendance at the final day of the tournament was numbered up to 25,000.

"When we set out to accomplish something new or different," comments McGriff, "community people get behind us to make it happen. Whether it's media or volunteers, the support is there."

SINCE ITS OPENING IN 1973, THE QUAD-CITY DOWNS HAS ATTRACTED THOUSANDS TO THE TRACK FROM ALL OVER THE MIDWEST.

When the East Moline Downs opened in 1973, the support was less steady. Contractors and other businessmen did not get paid for their work and took the Downs owners to court. It was less than an auspicious beginning for the track and detracted from the sport of harness racing itself.

"A lot of people stayed away from the Downs at first because it was getting so much bad publicity," says Ernie Williams, a harness racing fan from Silvis. "All those problems at the start made people wonder if the place was even going to stay open from one week to the next."

Changes had to be made if the Downs was going to stay alive. The East Moline Downs became officially known as the Quad-City Downs. Court decisions and business agreements allowed the Downs to become the property of four area residents. They include Colona contractor Lee Davis, Aledo cattleman Frank McFarland, Davenport publishing representative Jim Patten and Aledo merchant Leo Henderson.

The new owners began an immediate program to improve track management and conditions. Ninety thousand dollars was spent on the racing surface of the track, the parking lot was seal coated, heating and ventilation was improved in the grooms' quarters, surrounding landscaped areas were beautified.

Just as the track itself has been improved, so too have the purses. Formerly in the range of $600, purses up to $1,500 now go to winning horsemen at the Downs. Seven hundred horses can be stabled at the facility, with 100 stalls held open for others.

There is no question about the Quad-City Downs being open from one week to the next any more. Average nightly attendance is running more than 3,000 patrons, betting a record average of $261,109. The Downs regularly attracts patrons from Peoria, Galesburg, Rockford and Dubuque. Many spectators confess to being "hooked" on the sport, while others are attracted to the remodeled restaurant.

Whether as participants or spectators, Quad-Citians are sports minded. The charismatic call of the gridiron or the basketball court is ever present. There are always those ready to answer the call.

INDOCHINESE JOIN QUAD-CITY MELTING POT

With a new decade beginning the 1980s, a new collection of people found their way to the cultural melting pot of the Quad-City community. Hundreds of Indochinese refugees, escaping the problems of their homeland regions, found fresh starts in the Mississippi Valley community. Their arrival caused local educators to seek methods to meet the needs of the children of the newly arrived families. With federal budgets slashed in numerous areas, the problem was not easily solved. Thankfully, volunteers proved useful and numerous.

The Indochinese are but the latest of nationalities to find a homeland in the Quad-City community. Each year as summer draws to a close, attention is paid the earliest settlers at the annual Black Hawk Pow Wow held at Black Hawk State Park in Rock Island. Few descendants of these people still reside in the immediate area, but the community abounds with families who can trace their roots to the German, Swedish, Belgian and Greek families who settled here during the 19th century.

The 1980 census of the Quad-City metropolitan area stands at 383,958. This figure represents a total of 8.75 percent of minority race residents as compared to the 4.8 percent recorded in the 1970 census. Scott County minority race increased from a 3.2 percent figure in 1970 to 6 percent in 1980, while Rock Island increased from 4.8 percent to 8.75 percent during the same time bracket. Now, there are approximately 6,600 blacks and 3,550 people of Spanish origin in Scott County compared to 9,800 blacks and 7,200 people of Spanish origin in Rock Island County.

Area residents of Mexican heritage actively maintain their culture with imported editions of *El Sol* from Mexico City. Spanish-speaking record albums are sold locally, and movie features appear periodically on the local scene. Mexican food is popular and featured at many restaurants.

Moline claims to be the city with the second largest Belgian population in the entire United States, with Detroit claiming first. It boasts its own Belgian counsul, Dolores Bultinck, and social gatherings often feature picks, rolle bolle and racing pigeons.

Each year Rock Island County welcomes a visiting collection of workers during the crop harvest seasons. Migrant workers arrive from the Southwestern United States. Often the families of the workers are large. They reside on the farms where they will be working. With assistance and direction from the Illinois Migrant Council which has offices in Moline, the temporary residents are provided many health, educational and social services. In early fall, the migrants return to their home areas.

GRADUALLY, INDOCHINESE NEWCOMERS TO THE QUAD-CITIES ARE SETTLING INTO THEIR NEW SURROUNDINGS, AS THIS MARKET ON MOLINE'S 7TH STREET AND OTHERS AROUND THE COMMUNITY ATTEST.

ANYONE FOR FUN?

"**A**nyone for tennis?"

"Going to the Col this weekend?"

"Don't forget Bingo this Sunday."

Activity and entertainment in the Quad-Cities run the gamut from aerial sky diving to zoo visiting. Area residents can choose active participation or passive spectatorship in a wide array of recreational events.

Long a stronghold for movies, the Quad-Cities' film centers have shifted locations. Gone are the downtown movie palaces. Visiting theatre troupes utilize the splendid RKO Orpheum, while Circa '21 dinner theatre has replaced the old Fort. Here and there an isolated moviehouse appears on the Quad-City horizon, but most have clustered in or near the shopping malls. The eight-plex Showcase Cinemas in Milan is one of the largest theatre complexes in the country. "Star Wars" holds the area record for most attended film with 250,000 having seen it in a six-month run.

Dancing is available in many area nightspots, but the Col Ballroom in Davenport remains one of the most durable of locations for "tripping the light fantastic." For 68 years, the Col has opened its doors to jitterbuggers, rock and rollers, discoers and all the rest. From Jimi Hendrix to Johnny

Cash, vocalists have taken the microphone and shared their talents. Plans call for concerts, plays and banquets to be held at the Col.

The rolling Mississippi provides plenty of opportunity for boating in the area. Marina slip space is at a premium, with waiting lists at favorite spots, such as Rock Island's Sunset Marina and Davenport's Lindsay Park Marina. Some boaters combine pleasure crafting with fishing, but many seek the waterways solely for scenic viewing and relaxation.

Each year thousands of area residents and visitors take advantage of local museums and free points of interest. The Putnam Museum in Davenport maintains an outstanding permanent collection, while often hosting traveling exhibits. Museums on Arsenal Island and at Black Hawk State Park attract a steady flow of history lovers, as do the Bettendorf Museum and the Rock Island County Historical Society.

Joggers abound in the Quad-City community, trying to keep healthy and trim. Bicyclists, too, are frequently spotted. Of recent vintage are identifiable bike trails established for the pedal pushers. One of the most popular is Duck Creek Parkway, which winds across bridges, through thickets of wildlife and beside rushing waters.

Moline's bike route to Stephen's Park, Prospect Park and down to Riverside Park is officially known as the Dan-O Watkins Memorial Bike Path. The route was named for a young Moliner who excelled in outdoor activities and leadership of youth events. Watkins lost his life in a mountain-climbing accident when he was 19.

A favorite recreation among Quad-Citians, especially senior citizens, is Bingo. More than 200 area organizations on both sides of the Mississippi sponsor regular public bingo events. Crowds range in size from 50-1,000. Up to 80 percent of the proceeds generally go toward prizes awarded participants.

"THE SKY'S THE LIMIT" FOR QUAD-CITY AERIAL ENTHUSIASTS AS THEY JAM THE MISSISSIPPI LEVEE FOR AN AFTERNOON OF FUN IN THE AIR.

With area airports so accessible, aerial activities have grown more and more popular. Piloting lessons have increased, as have sky diving interests. Ballooning has gathered fans as well, with the hot air aerostats frequently appearing over Quad-City skies.

Area artists welcome the times when they can display their offerings. The spring and fall Beaux Art Fairs held behind the Davenport Art Gallery are big attractions. Other art shows attract thousands of viewers.

The Mississippi Valley Fair in early August brings thousands of participants and spectators to auto racing contests, a midway or rides, livestock and cooking competition, demolition derbies, and featured grandstand entertainment. Harness races are often included, as well as an international art show and battle of the bands. The Rock Island County Fair offers similar entertainment each year.

Featuring a blend of multi-cultural foods, music, constume and fun, the Bettendorf Folk Festival kicks off the summer when it occurs every June. Visitors come from all over the country for the weekend festivities.

A unique feature of the Quad-Cities is the Genesius Guild operating out of Rock Island. For a quarter of a century, the theatrical group has furnished theatre goers which a classical bonanza of Greek, Shakespearian and operatic classics every summer.

Young people in the area are given opportunity for theatrical experience beyond school offerings. Davenport's Junior Theatre offers drama instruction year-round for children 4½ through high school. More recent offerings in other surrounding cities give boys and girls similar acting, dancing, singing and general experience in performing.

Although major sports have enjoyed a longtime spotlight for participation and viewing, racquetball recently snagged the attention of many Quad-Citians.

"Take me out to the ball game" is the perennial cheer of area baseball residents. Minor league baseball finds its home at John O'Donnell Stadium in Davenport in the form of the Quad-City Cubs, a Class A farm affiliation of the Chicago Cubs.

Bowling is a prime attraction in the Quad-Cities, with top tournaments often bringing in national champions.

Fishermen find activity all year long with rivers and lakes furnishing an abundance of treasure. Summer months bring channel catfish, bass and bluegill, while the autumn offers quantities of walleye and sauger. Those willing to break the winter ice will find crappie and bluegills.

For inexpensive fun, a person can find a variety of parks available. The Rock Island County Forest Preserve Commission operates the 1,600-acre Lake George area near Andalusia. Loud Thunder features 10 campgrounds, full picnic sites and boat ramps. Among Scott County's park offerings is the 1,270-acre Scott County Park located nine miles north of Davenport.

Area colleges provide quality entertainment at reasonable prices. Music fans can attend everything from rock concerts to classical musical recitals, presented by visiting artists or fulltime students. Student art exhibits, theater presentations, cable TV shows and radio programs merge education and entertainment for the viewer and listener.

For area citizens seeking activity with lesser-known sports, the opportunity is there. Both sides of the Mississippi offer ranges for archery, gymnastic studios enjoy good attendance and enthusiasts of roller skating, trap and skeet shooting and distance running can find ample opportunity to pursue their interests.

Nothing to do in the Quad-Cities? Don't you believe it.

AREA CHURCHES UNITE AND GROW

Area church history was made in April of 1971 when the longtime organization Council of Churches officially became Churches United of Scott and Rock Island Counties. The new organization represented more than 100 congregations, including 12 Roman Catholic parishes. The consolidation of community churches seemed to spring naturally out of the ecumenical upswing felt among religious persuasions around the world.
"There are many benefits to be found in actively working together," observed Monsignor T.J. Jordan, pastor of St. Pius X Church in Rock Island. "Certainly we all feel a need to assist in the social ministry within our community. We can best accomplish this by working together."
A major concern of Churches United has been related to the annual influx of migrant workers. Assistance with health, family and economical services has been provided. Clothing drives, chaplaincy services, interfaith communications, clergy management seminars, Bible study sessions — all have been coordinated by Churches United.

"FLY WITH THE EAGLE. . ."

The sight of an eagle flying majestically over the bluffs and soft waves of a river...
The sounds of a catchy melody, "Quad-Cities, USA, lookin' better every day..."
Since February of 1980 a promotional campaign has flourished, aimed at providing a unified, inspiring image of the community that is joined by a river.
"It's been a worthwhile effort," notes Illinois State Representative Tim Bell of Moline. "We've always had a place on the map geographically, but the 'Quad-Cities USA' Campaign has helped provide a positive identity to our residents and our area."
The entire promotional campaign emerged from the Quad-City Development Group. Formed in 1961, the QCDG recognized that although community cities were often considered a single economic unit, they were functioning individually in trying to promote themselves in the world of commerce and industry.
"It was a simple matter of realizing we could accomplish more working together than working apart," observes Dick Weeks, president of the group. QCDG receives funding through its 97 members and is non-profit in structure. The major thrust of its efforts is to benefit present industry and commerce, while attracting more businesses to the area.
As to the success of the campaign, within a year three out of four area residents were aware of it and had a favorable impression. The theme song, written by former Davenporter Charlie Teague, was being sung and hummed by many community citizens. Television stations had received positive input from viewers who had seen the locally produced commercials.
"It's been a good campaign," summarizes Porter McNeil, a student at MacCalester College in St. Paul, Minnesota. "People up here have now heard of the Quad-Cities, when before they only knew about their own Twin Cities. I'm glad we have it."

QUAD CITIES USA ℠

WEATHER OFFERS VARIETY

From 20 below to 100 above — from heavy, still air to tornado gusts — from a month with no precipitation to 30 days of continuous rain.

If there's one thing certain about Quad-City weather, it's the variety. Recent years have played havoc with average temperatures and weatherman predictions.

Ordinarily, July is the hottest month of the year with an average temperature of 75.6. However, in June 1980, area residents sweltered for eight straight days of near 100 degree heat. Swimming pools almost burst their seams, while air conditioners operated around the clock.

"It wouldn't have been so bad," commented Moliner Mark Lundahl. "But we'd been having such lousy winters too. It didn't seem right to have such blistering hot summers."

Although the previous winter had been bad, the winter of 1979 had been worse. In January, a three-day snowstorm had dumped a record 18.4 inches of snow on the 10 inches already on the ground. Traffic crawled along the busiest of thoroughfares, while those people fortunate enough to stay home simply hibernated.

Sudden thawing spells in northern areas sent regional rivers over their banks in 1965 and 1973. Cities and villages took immediate steps to provide floodwalls against future water overflows.

A myth that held the Quad-City community was immune to tornadoes was blown away in the early 1980s. One twister touched down in April of 1981, ripping off roofs and tossing cars parked in Moline's Holiday Inn parking lot around like toys. The resort complex reported $1 million in damage.

WHERE DO WE GROW FROM HERE ?

A driver deciding to tour the Quad-City metropolitan community would quickly make the observation that only city limit signs offer a visual division among cities. Physically, this is one big community with common problems and resources. Air, for instance, is just as polluted (or unpolluted) for the Bettendorf resident as it is for the Milan resident. Fifty-one percent of the Quad-City work force reside in a different city from where they work; therefore, unemployment figures remain relatively constant for the entire area. Crime rates, transit difficulties, cultural opportunities are consistant.

Currently, the Quad-City metropolitan community boasts a population of slightly under 390,000 with an average of 2,000 being added every year. This includes those 14 local communities claiming identification with the immediate area. Households in the Quad-City community average 2.6 persons as compared with a 2.78 national average per household. Of area cities, Bettendorf has recorded the greatest growth spurt, up 23.0 percent between 1970 and 1980. Davenport's growth is considerably less, 4.8, but steady. Both Iowa cities have much land for expansion and development to the north. With the boundaries of Rock River and Milan to the south, Rock Island and Moline are somewhat hampered. Both cities have experienced population decreases during the 1970-1980 decade, but Milan itself has a 29 percent increase.

There is little doubt that continued growth will be felt within the sales market. Variety, department and specialty stores record an average of $212 million dollars yearly, with retail trade for the metropolitan area standing at $1.7 billion annually. One-stop shopping at area malls has become commonplace with expansion plans always in progress. Downtown development projects such as Davenport's "Superblock," Rock Island's Great Plaza and Moline's Metro Center Plaza are evidence of the active efforts to promote innercity business life.

Major growth and expansion has been evident at hospital and medical facilities in the area. The newest of hospitals, Franciscan in Rock Island, opened in 1972. Other community medical facilities have added specialized units in such areas as mental health, drug treatment and alcoholism.

The metropolitan Quad-City area claims a labor force of approximately 190,000 which is about 55 percent male and 45 percent female. About half of this force make a living in trades and services, while more than one-fourth are engaged in some form of product production. The manufacturing of agricultural tools and machines has earned the region the nickname "The Farm Implement Capital of the World." Thus, the area economy is greatly influenced by the international and national agricultural economy.

Recent years have seen a merging of many local agencies, often across the Mississippi River. River Bend Library Services, Mississippi Valley Girl Scout Council, the Quad-City Development Group, the Illowa Chapter of American Red Cross — these and many more have meshed their names and services to provide benefits for both sides of the river.

"There's bound to be some consolidation of cities in the future," predicts civic leader Tish Hewitt. "One total city is not possible, since two states are involved; but there will be consolidation where it can happen. Citizens will realize it will benefit them. So much more can be achieved when cities work together rather than work apart."

Rock Island banker Charles Wilson shares such thinking. He cites "parochialism" among area cities as an obstacle to growth.

"The cities naturally fight one another to bring in new business, to get tax money in order to keep property taxes down," states Wilson. "There is no reason why communities shouldn't share the same police and fire departments to benefit from the economies of scale, which would reduce total taxes for services performed."

THE JOHN DEERE ADMINISTRATION CENTER, DESIGNED BY THE LATE EERO SAARINEN, BROUGHT A NEW LEVEL OF SOPHISTICATION TO THE QUAD-CITIES.

Although business, culture and commerce flow smoothly from city to city and across the river as well, emotional walls of individual pride are firmly instilled within many residents. Much of that pride is fostered while area residents are attending school.

"We grow up competing against crosstown rivals," noted Moline college student Scott Stoll. "We develop a strong allegiance to our own school, and in a sense, to our own city. The spirit fades a bit when we become adults, but it never disappears completely. It's hard to give up feelings we learn when we're so young and impressionable."

Dick Weeks, leader of the Quad-City Development Group, recognizes the depth of that competitive spirit. In fact, he thinks it's a good building block. "It's never been a goal of our group to do away with any boundary lines between cities," says Weeks. "But there are definitely major advantages nationally for us to be recognized as one collective business market, a single metropolitan area. To me, the Quad-Cities is a three-county metropolitan area of 14 contiguous communities. It's the largest metropolitan area on the Mississippi River between Minneapolis and St. Louis."

Of recent vintage is the active media battle for area resident reading, viewing and listening. Newspapers, television stations and radio broadcasting units have intensified their efforts to appeal far beyond their immediate localities. Both the *Rock Island Argus* and *Moline Daily Dispatch* now publish Sunday editions, joining the *Quad-City Times* in pursuit of daily readership. The arrival of cable television viewing proved immediately successful, and area colleges further supplement the selection for viewers with educational and feature programing.

"This area is heartland," observed John Hauberg, a noted historian from Rock Island and member of one of the Quad-Cities' most prominent families. "We seldom initiate anything, but rather we reflect what is the best that is initiated elsewhere. If a fad or fancy springs up on the East or West coast of our country, it is sifted through by the time it reaches us. That way we get the meat of the grain. Living here may lack the excitement of living elsewhere, but there is a sense of security and protection not found in many places. Yes, we are America's heartland. It offers a rich life, a full existence."

Surely that is what every Quad-Citian seeks in the years ahead — "a rich life, a full existence." The means of attaining that goal will vary.

And although Quad-Citians may not be initiators, there is definitely a creative spirit alive in this area. From the Quad-Cities have come writers, inventors, entertainers, artists and many more who have contributed to the finer things in life. Certainly, there is value in the craftsman, the worker in industry, the businessman, the social worker and all those who share their time and talents each day working for a better product and a better world.

Truly, Quad-Citians are joined. They are joined by a sense of pride and concern in their community. They know how to play hard and work hard. Whether times be good or bad, there is a heartland spirit, a feeling that carries a touch of the pioneer, of the law-abiding citizen, of the planner for the future.

Whether the years ahead bring consolidation of cities and towns, no one knows for sure. Already area agencies are investigating possible mergers and there is ongoing interest in consolidation for better services.

But whether the community is joined by legal boundaries, business or commerce, religion, culture or whatever, we are forever sharing a history — a history which has been molded by a long and tremendous waterway in the middle of America. Our past, our present, our future — joined by a river. This is the Quad-City story.

THIS ARCHITECT'S RENDERING SHOWS PART OF THE COMMUNITY ACTIVITY CENTER PLANNED FOR DOWNTOWN DAVENPORT. ALSO KNOWN AS THE "SUPERBLOCK IT PROMISES TO BRING A REVITALIZATION TO THE DOWNTOWN AREA.

The Contributors

Publisher Stephen M. Miller is director of business development for Lee Enterprises, Incorporated. Before joining Lee in September of 1978, he held various publishing and marketing posts with Fawcett Publications, Incorporated, and Western Publishing Company, Incorporated. A graduate of Boston College, he earned a Master of Arts at the University of Chicago and a Master of Business Administration at Fordham University.

Editor Frederick I. Anderson is managing editor of *Rental Age* magazine, published by the American Rental Association. He previously worked on the news editing staff of the *Quad-City Times* and the Lindsay-Schaub Newspapers. He is a graduate of Iowa State University, where he earned a Master of Science degree in journalism and mass communication.

Editorial adviser Roald Tweet is a professor of English at Augustana College, where he serves on the faculty of the graduate program in regional studies. He is the author of numerous publications on many aspects of the Upper Mississippi River. A graduate of St. Olaf College, he earned a Master of Arts and Doctor of Philosophy at the University of Chicago.

Art director E. Lawrence McDonald is a freelance graphic designer specializing in corporate and institutional communications. A former art director for a Quad-City art studio, he earned a Bachelor of Fine Arts degree at Northern Illinois University.

Jim Arpy has been a member of the *Quad-City Times* reporting and feature-writing staff since 1951. He is the author of the book *Legends of Our Land, a History of the Mississippi Valley*. He is a graduate of Drake University.

LaDonna Breidfjord Backmeyer is a writer, poet and researcher on ethnic subjects, history and genealogy. A graduate of Black Hawk College, she is writing a novel, the first chapter of which has been printed in *The Icelandic Canadian*, a quarterly journal.

Robert Bouilly is a historian in the Historian's Office, Headquarters, United States Army Armament Materiel Readiness Command, Rock Island Arsenal. His research in the early years of Rock Island Arsenal led to a paper which he presented to the Missouri Valley Historical Association. A graduate of Hamline University, he earned a Master of Arts and Doctor of Philosophy at the University of Missouri.

David R. Collins has been an English teacher at Woodrow Wilson Junior High School, Moline, since 1962. Since his first story was published in 1967, he has written more than two dozen books and hundreds of articles. His writing, much of it biographical and intended for youthful readers, has earned him many awards and recognition from scores of literary organizations. He is a graduate of Western Illinois University, where he earned a Master of Science degree.

Bess Pierce is a prolific writer whose work has appeared in such magazines as *Flower and Garden, Today's Health, Parents, Better Homes and Gardens* and *Mechanix Illustrated*. She writes a weekly column on the outdoors for the *Quad-City Times* and a monthly column for *Mid-West Outdoors* magazine. The author of the book *Moline: A Pictorial History*, she was a contributor to *Profiles in Leadership, Dynamic Men and Women of the Quad-Cities*.

William Roba is an instructor in English and history at Scott Community College. Formerly associated with Bi-State Metropolitan Planning Commission, he is a researcher on many aspects of Quad-City history, culture and architecture. A graduate of Augustana College, he earned a Master of Arts at Cornell University and a Doctor of Philosophy at the University of Iowa.

Jon Ryan is senior vice president of Security State Trust and Savings Bank. He is the author of numerous articles on Bettendorf history that have been published in the *Bettendorf News* and elsewhere. An Augustana College graduate, he earned a master's degree at Western Illinois University.

Kathleen Seusy is a researcher and writer on historical subjects and a volunteer worker at the Putnam Museum, where she is a member of the "Putnam Players" historical drama troupe. She is a graduate of Marycrest College.

Illustration Credits

Charles Ainsworth: 49 (*Annie Girdon*), 92 (Advertisement).

Fred Anderson: 187.

Dr. A. Henry Arp Jr.: 113.

Jim Arpy: 164.

Augustana College: 19, 22, 23, 28, 30, 31, 32, 34, 42, 43 (Harper House), 68, 88, 89, 96, 105 (Streetcar), 106, 107, 188, 132 (Dred Scott), 142 (Buddy "L"), 162 (Red Cross), 181.

Bettendorf Museum: 132, 136, 137, 138, 139, 140, 142 (City Hall), 143, 144, 145.

Davenport Chamber of Commerce: 66, 76, 80 (Library), 132, 165 (Ball), 167, 172, 176 (Downtown), 178, 190 (Jack Fleck), 217.

Davenport Public Library: 70.

Deere & Company: 86, 90, 91, 93, 95, 108, 109, 110.

East Moline Herald Printing Co.: 155.

Headquarters, United States Army Armament Materiel Readiness Command, Historical Office: 25, 94 (Dimock Gould), 97, 112 (High School), 116, 117, 119, 120 (Orphans' Home), 122, 123, 124, 125, 126, 127, 128, 129, 131 (Aerial View), 156, 184, 185, 186, 189 (Howitzers).

Larry Hetisimer: 210.

Henry Koelz: 100.

Larry McDonald: 4, 192.

Moline Dispatch: 148 (Post Office).

Martha Jamison Peterson: 149.

Bess Pierce: 94 (Pumper), 104, 114 (Auto Advertisement), 115, 168 (Rapids).

Annabelle Pinner: 158.

Putnam Museum: 12, 13, 14, 15, 18, 20, 26, 27, 36, 49 (Van Sant), 51, 52 (Huber's Brewery), 57 (Lower View), 61, 65, 66, 69, 70, 72, 74, 75, 77, 78, 79, 80 (River Carnival), 82 (Advertisement), 83 (Washing Machine), 84 (Before Fire, Liquor Permit), 85, 92 (Gould), 130, 150 (Guyer), 151, 157, 162 (Skyline), 168 (Low Water, Coffer Dam), 179 (Graf), 180, 183, 187, 190 (Corn).

Quad-City Metropolitan Airport: 114 (Airplane), 170, 179 (Airport).

Quad-City Times: 33, 50, 59, 67 (Colonel Davenport), 71, 81, 82 (Photo), 83 (Bix), 84 (After Fire), 101, 105 (Belgian Seal), 112 (Classroom), 120 (Annie Wittenmyer), 134, 165 (Billy Sunday), 176 (Chamber of Commerce), 189 (Fire), 194, 199, 200, 201, 202, 203, 204, 206, 207, 208, 209, 210, 211, 212, 213, 215.

Rock Island County Commisioners: 37 (Seal).

Rock Island County Historical Society: 38 (Harper Theatre), 39, 41, 45, 46, 48, 54, 55, 56, 57 (Upper Chute), 58, 60, 61, 62, 63, 64 (Parade), 93, 98, 102, 148 (Woodchoppers), 150 (Cornerstone), 152 (Trestle), 153, 154, 173.

Rock Island Public Library: 37, 47, 52 (McCabe's).

Silvis Public Library: 146, 160, 161.

Isabelle Smith: 159.

Lucille Tenpound: 152 (Ice Company).

Roald Tweet and Richard Oberg: 7, 8, 9, 10, 29.

U.S. Army Corps of Engineers: 40, 169.

Mrs. Parker Weeks: 56.

Basil Williams: 197.

WOC Broadcasting: 6 (Reagan).

The Robert Wright Family: 64 (Looney).

Bill Wundram: 177.

Index

This index contains the names, or at least the family names, of the major characters in Quad-City history. It also contains category headings that point to a full discussion of a subject. Whenever a discussion leaves the immediate Quad-City area — the Black Hawk War is an example — specific references to all the places and names in that discussion are not included in the index. Specific references to the Mississippi River do not appear, simply because the river is mentioned on an overwhelming majority of pages. Similarly, specific references to individual cities have been omitted when they fall within the city's own chapter. An asterisk (*) indicates an illustration on the subject.

The history of the Quad-Cities is linked closely to the businesses and industries that have breathed economic life into the community. From earliest times, commerce and industry have grown out of the needs of the people and, in turn, have attracted more people to work and live in this community which is the largest center of population between Chicago and Des Moines, Minneapolis and St. Louis.

The first firms to spring up grew naturally out of their surroundings: mills, boatyards, lumberyards, small merchants to serve the new towns, harnessmakers and blacksmiths to serve the nearby farmers. As the community grew so, too, did the places of business. And the owners of the businesses and industries returned their profits to their enterprises, in the form of expansion and diversification, and to their communities, in the forms of schools, churches, parks, opera houses.

And so the Quad-City community grew. Always in the midst of this growth have been the businesses and industries of forward-looking men and women, such as those whose profiles appear on the following pages.

No 220-page history of a community as complex as the Quad-Cities could possibly hope to include the stories of many of its leading businesses and industries without special consideration. The firms whose stories appear on these pages gave that consideration. In so doing, they have made possible a book that is richer in its historic content while remaining reasonable in price.

These, then, are the enterprises to which special thanks are due for their support of this book and of the Quad-Cities.

DEERE & COMPANY

The story of John Deere, the pioneer blacksmith who developed the world's first successful self-scouring steel plow, parallels the settlement and development of the Midwest.

John Deere was born in 1804 in Rutland, Vermont. He spent his early years in Middlebury, where he received a common school education and served a four-year apprenticeship learning the blacksmith's trade.

In 1825 he set out on his own and soon gained recognition for his careful workmanship and ingenuity. Business became depressed in the mid-1830s, however, and the future looked gloomy to the ambitious young blacksmith. Many Vermonters migrated to the "New West," and the tales of opportunity that filtered back to Vermont so stirred John Deere that he decided to move west.

He reached the village of Grand Detour, Illinois, which had been settled by others from Vermont. In his first year of blacksmithing, he learned of the serious problems Midwestern farmers had in turning the thick, fertile soil. The black loam clung to the bottom of the cast iron plows that had worked in the light, sandy New England soil.

Every few steps, farmers had to stop and scrape the soil from the plow. Cultivation became a slow, laborious task. Many settlers were discouraged and were considering moving farther west, hoping they could find soil conditions better suited to their equipment.

John Deere studied the problem and became convinced that a plow with a highly polished and properly shaped mold-board and share should turn a sharp furrow slice and scour itself at the same time. He fashioned such a plow in 1837, using, legend has it, the steel from a broken saw blade and successfully tested the plow on the farm of Lewis Crandall near Grand Detour.

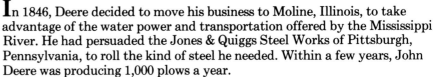

In 1846, Deere decided to move his business to Moline, Illinois, to take advantage of the water power and transportation offered by the Mississippi River. He had persuaded the Jones & Quiggs Steel Works of Pittsburgh, Pennsylvania, to roll the kind of steel he needed. Within a few years, John Deere was producing 1,000 plows a year.

In those early years, he laid down several precepts that have been followed faithfully since by the company he founded. Among those was his insistence on high standards of quality. John Deere stated frequently, "I will never put my name on a plow that does not have in it the best that is in me." Deere also realized that he had to continually improve his products to make them work better in the varying soil conditions in which they were to be used. The success of Deere's "self-polisher" in turning the rich loam of the prairies helped open the Midwest to agricultural development, along with the reaper, thresher, and other inventions. The endless fields of waving wheat and tasseled corn supplied food for millions of Americans.

John Deere believed in the new community of Moline. His company was one of many that built factories along the river front in the 1850s. Years later, after serving a term as mayor of Moline, he helped begin the Moline Public Library and other community organizations. He expressed his personal beliefs in a letter to a friend: "I never willfully wronged any man" and "I never put on the market a poorly made implement."

John Deere died in 1886. His son, Charles, was an outstanding businessman and moved the company in new directions by establishing marketing centers to distribute products to retail dealers. Besides establishing this network, Charles expanded the firm's line of products. By the time of his death in 1907, the company was making many steel plows, cultivators, corn and cotton planters and other implements.

Charles' successor was his son-in-law, William Butterworth. In 1911 he brought six non-competing farm equipment companies into the Deere organization, establishing the company as a full-line manufacturer of farm equipment. In 1918 the company purchased the Waterloo Gasoline Engine Company, just at the time agriculture was beginning to shift from animal to mechanical power.

Three of the non-competing companies and the gasoline engine company expanded the scope of Deere & Company. The Van Brunt Manufacturing Company in Horicon, Wisconsin, had become the world's leading grain drill factory. The Deere & Mansur Works in Moline was the world's largest manufacturer of corn planters. The Joseph Dain Company in Ottumwa, Iowa, was a leading maker of hay tools. By 1918, more than 8,000 Waterloo Boy tractors were manufactured by the gasoline engine company and at work on American farms. Production continued until 1923, when the first tractor to bear the John Deere name — the Model "D" — was introduced. William Butterworth stabilized the company. A Moline businessman said of him that he was the one, among the first three chief executives of Deere & Company, "who was a national figure as a man apart from a mechanized instrument, and an international figure as well."

Charles Deere Wiman, a great-grandson of John Deere, took over direction of the company in 1928. His strong emphasis on engineering and product development resulted in rapid growth. Despite the Great Depression which gripped the nation in the 1930s, the company achieved $100 million in gross sales for the first time in its history, in 1937, the year of its centennial celebration. During World War II, Wiman and war-time president Burton F. Peek continued the emphasis on product design.

As the one who continued a tradition of leadership, Wiman "was the catalyst, the spark plug, the one who inspired those about him to do well and move ahead." Under his leadership, the company became one of the nation's 100 largest manufacturers.

Under the leadership of the company's just retired chief executive, Chairman William A. Hewitt, who succeeded Charles Wiman in 1955, the John Deere organization has experienced one of its greatest periods of growth. In just five generations, the corporation has achieved annual sales in the billions of dollars. More than 600 products roll off the assembly lines at 25 factories, located in 12 nations around the world.

The Deere Administrative Center expresses the special character of Deere & Company. Designed by Eero Saarinen, the building has won numerous awards for its architectural innovations. The headquarters opened in 1964. A major addition, opened in 1978, features an interior garden, surrounded by modern office facilities.

FIRST NATIONAL BANK OF THE QUAD CITIES IN ROCK ISLAND

PHIL MITCHELL
MITCHELL & LYNDE 1885-1905
STATE BANK 1905-1927.

MITCHELL & LYNDE'S BANK – POST OFFICE BLOCK

MITCHELL & LYNDE BLOCK CONSTRUCTED IN 1891.

It took almost 129 years. But we've finally done it. The Quad-Cities' very first bank now has a name to match its seniority, its position of leadership, and its proud reputation of service to the whole Quad-Cities area. First National Bank of Rock Island is now First National Bank of the Quad Cities. The new name is our way of expressing a deep sense of pride in the new spirit of unity so recently demonstrated here in the Quad-Cities. And it's our way of telling everybody that our growth will continue to parallel the growth of the Quad-Cities, just as it has since we first opened our doors so many years ago.

First National Bank of the Quad Cities had its origins in 1852, nine years before the outbreak of the Civil War. The Quad-Cities was still a pioneer community...wild, bustling with activity, and ripe with opportunity. First of the Quad Cities actually began as a private banking house — Cook, Sargent & Parker. Three of the firm's four partners had been pioneers in Davenport, as well as successful attorneys and very prominent landowners. The establishment of the new banking house served as the cornerstone of what would eventually become the Iowa and Illinois Quad-Cities' oldest continuously operating bank, the oldest bank in Western Illinois, the fourth oldest bank in Illinois, and the oldest bank on the Mississippi River between Minneapolis and St. Louis. First National Bank of Rock Island was born.

In 1856, two enterprising Kentuckians, Philemon Mitchell and Philander Cable, arrived in the Quad-Cities with $80,000 in cash. They purchased the firm of Cook, Sargent & Parker that same year. The business was maintained under the existing name until 1860, when Judge Cornelius Lynde, Jr. acquired the Cable interest and the bank's name was changed to Mitchell & Lynde. A series of mergers and acquisitions followed, each helping to secure the bank's position of importance in the Quad-Cities. For 45 years, Mitchell & Lynde grew and prospered, and continued to provide honest, ethical banking services to Quad-Citians.

*L.B. WILSON
PRESIDENT 1937-1965
CHAIRMAN 1965-1975.*

In 1905, Mitchell & Lynde incorporated and obtained a state charter, officially changing the bank's name to State Bank of Rock Island. The growth continued; new quarters, additional staff, and multiplying assets reflected State Bank's successful record of service. But not until the dark years of the Great Depression was the public's confidence in the bank put to the acid test. Following the fatal stock market crash of 1929, growing unemployment, failing farm crops, skyrocketing inflation, and almost complete lack of faith in all government and public institutions caused universal panic. Runs on banks became common, resulting in collapse after collapse. Three hundred forty-six bank closings were reported during the first six months of 1929 alone. But customer confidence in State Bank of Rock Island helped keep the bank solvent and operating throughout those bleak years. So, during the period of recovery, State Bank of Rock Island was able to serve as an instrumental force in helping the Quad-Cities rebuild by providing critical assistance to local businesses and private citizens.

One more name change was forthcoming. Under the guidance of President Lewis B. Wilson the bank applied for a national charter in 1945.

And in January 1946, State Bank of Rock Island became First National Bank of Rock Island. Succeeding years have shown an impressive pattern of growth, both financially and physically. Modern new facilities were completed in downtown Rock Island in 1963; July 1979, First of Rock Island opened its first branch bank on 30th Street and 18th Avenue in Rock Island; and exciting new services have continually been added to help make life a little easier for Quad-Citians, like Free Checking, Interest Bearing Checking Accounts, and simplified banking with 1st Bankcard and 1st Bankmachine.

On October 2, 1981, permission was granted by the Comptroller of the Currency for the bank to officially change its name to First National Bank of the Quad Cities. At the same time, a new bank logo was introduced. The design encompasses the bank philosophy of becoming a financial institution dedicated to serving the entire Quad-City area.

THE FIRST ATM (AUTOMATIC TELLER MACHINE) IN THE QUAD-CITIES, 1973.

THE FIRST DRIVE-IN TELLER WINDOW SERVICE IN THE QUAD-CITIES, 1946.

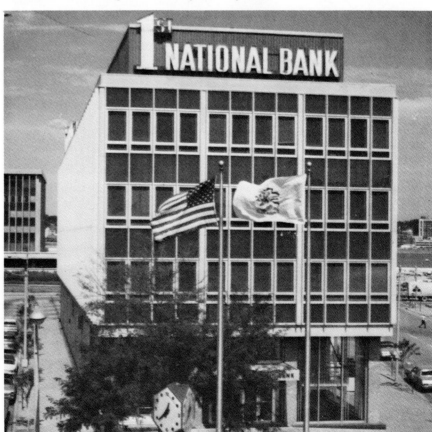

INTERNATIONAL HARVESTER
FARMALL PLANT

PRESENT LOCATION OF INTERNATIONAL HARVESTER FARMALL PLANT, 5TH AVENUE AND 42ND STREET, ROCK ISLAND.

1982, TWO-WHEEL DRIVE TRACTOR SERIES 5288.

THE 100,000TH FARMALL TRACTOR, APRIL 12, 1930.

Located on the banks of the Mississippi River in Rock Island, International Harvester's Farmall Plant is one of the major suppliers of tractors for farmers throughout the world.

In the mid-1920s, the popularity of International Harvester's "Regular" necessitated a new production plant. Farmall Plant was acquired by IH in 1924 from Moline Plow Company and in October 1926 the first *Farmall* "Regular" rolled off the assembly line in Rock Island. The world's first row-crop tractor continued in production until the early 1930s.

Since then, Farmall has enjoyed numerous production milestones. The one-millionth agricultural tractor built at the plant was produced on April 30, 1951, and in December 1978, the 2-millionth Farmall tractor was manufactured. International Harvester's complete line of tractors includes all types of agricultural, construction, garden and utility tractors, and Farmall Plant had the additional honor of building the 5-millionth IH tractor on February 1, 1974.

Before introduction of the Series 50 tractors in 1981, International Harvester launched an extensive modernization program at Farmall. Changes included new equipment, including the purchase of 300 new machines, the development of 2,000 new tractor parts, and the installation of 1,500 new machine tools.

Today the sprawling plant covers 94 acres with about 2 million square feet under roof. It is one of the most modern tractor assembly plants in the world featuring more than 150 computer-controlled machines currently in operation. Tractors are painted by computer-run robots and numerous machining functions are performed by tape-controlled electronic equipment. Production capabilities were further increased when a new $25 million automated storage and retrieval system (ASRS) went into operation in mid-1982. Additional investment in the future of Farmall was underway in the later months of 1982, when production facilities located at IH's Louisville Plant were consolidated at Farmall.

Farmall's current product line features the Series 50 and 30 tractors. The tractors range from 80 to 185 horsepower models in the standard two-wheel drive tractors and an IH exclusive lower-range horsepower line of articulated four-wheel drive "2 + 2" Series providing maximum power and mobility.

Farmall Plant is geared for the future with a reputation for quality and a dedication to serving the farming community throughout the world. Matthew J. Glogowski is the 10th plant manager to serve IH at Farmall and, despite recent modernization, people remain the plant's most important asset.

Farmall Plant holds the all-time IH safety record of more than 7.3 million consecutive manhours without a lost-time injury.

As the largest industrial employer in the city of Rock Island, Farmall Plant has a history of close cooperation with city and area governments. The plant maintains a constant awareness of its responsibilities as a corporate citizen, and in 1981, the city recognized this mutual bond by hosting an appreciation program during the observance of IH's 150th anniversary. Additionally, in August 1982, the Rock Island City Council appropriated a loan of $6 million to partially finance the transfer of production equipment from Louisville to Farmall. This loan, appropriated in recognition of the potential impact on the city's economy, clearly indicated the city's willingness to assist IH, and thus to insure the future welfare of Farmall Plant and the citizens of Rock Island.

INTERNATIONAL HARVESTER
EAST MOLINE PLANT

PRESENT LOCATION OF INTERNATIONAL HARVESTER EAST MOLINE PLANT, RIVER DRIVE AND 3RD STREET, EAST MOLINE.

Proud to be a part of the "Farm Equipment Capital of the World," International Harvester's East Moline Plant has long been established as one of the world's leading producers of grain harvesting equipment. East Moline Plant led the way into a new era of grain harvesting efficiency in 1977, with the introduction of its Axial-Flow Combine. The new combines feature a revolutionary new principle of threshing which offers greater reliability and yield.

The Axial-Flow Combine has been accorded worldwide recognition, including award of the French government's Gold Medal of Honor in March 1979, and presentation of the Challenge Cup Trophy at the Royal Agricultural Show in England in 1981. Both awards were made in recognition of the successful design of the combines built at East Moline and their contribution to world agriculture.

The East Moline plant opened in 1927 as an unheated warehouse for tractor storage. Additional building occurred during the early 1930s to accommodate the fabrication and assembly of corn pickers and harvester threshers, production of which was transferred from the company's old Deering Works in Chicago. Today, the East Moline plant includes about 156 acres along the south bank of the Mississippi River with 52 acres under roof and a floor area in excess of 2.2 million square feet.

The plant's current product line includes five models of Axial-Flow Combines, with attachments and a seasonal product, the "Early-Riser" Cyclo Air Planter. In addition, since 1976 East Moline has produced control centers (cabs) for the tractor made at the Rock Island Farmall plant as well as cabs for combines and cotton pickers. The plant specializes in assembly, sheet metal forming and fabrication operations including machining, welding and heat treating.

The International Harvester East Moline Plant is recognized as a good industrial neighbor in its community and in the Quad-City area. In combination with the International Harvester Farmall plant in Rock Island, it is a major participant in community funding for the Quad-Cities. Many IH employees are active participants in civic activities.

Roger R. Behrens is the 14th plant manager at East Moline. The plant takes great pride in its many skilled employees and their commitment to building the highest quality, most productive machines for its customers.

141 COMBINE, CIRCA 1954.

1982 MODEL, 1460 SELF-PROPELLED AXIAL FLOW COMBINE.

McGLADREY HENDRICKSON & COMPANY

With offices on both sides of the Mississippi River, McGladrey Hendrickson & Co., the Quad-Cities' largest certified public accounting firm, has truly been "joined by a river."

But it has not always been so.

McGladrey Hendrickson & Co. traces its history back to the pre-Depression era in Davenport, before the area became known as the Quad-Cities.

Ira B. McGladrey, the firm's founder, returned from service in France during World War I and joined a Des Moines-based accounting firm known as Billings, Prouty, Tompkins & Company. He was hired in 1920 to manage that firm's office in Cedar Rapids, Iowa. In 1926, he bought the Cedar Rapids office and a tiny practice in Davenport from his employers and formed what was to become the I.B. McGladrey Company.

The Davenport practice was indeed tiny. McGladrey paid a mere $500 for it. The small, one-man office was located on the third floor of the Putnam Building at 215 Main Street. For several years after the acquisition, it continued to operate under its former owners' names to keep the good will of its few clients.

Shortly after the landmark Davenport Bank Building was completed in 1932, the I.B. McGladrey Company was ready for an identity of its own in Davenport, and moved into newly completed offices on that building's ninth floor. Actually, it was half of a two-room office, shared with an insurance agent. Incidentally, the address — 917 Davenport Bank Building — remains the address of the firm's Davenport office today, 50 years later. But the firm now occupies the entire ninth floor of the building and most of the 10th.

By 1935, the firm had added another office, in Burlington, and the demands on I.B. McGladrey's time became too great for him to effectively manage the entire operation alone. He formed a partnership with two young but experienced accountants, George Hansen and Keith Dunn.

Hansen, who had been dispatched to manage the Davenport office in 1934, described its condition upon his arrival in a memoir published in 1975, when he retired from the firm:

"We didn't have more than a dozen business clients plus a few personal income tax returns. One of those clients accounted for nearly a third of the office volume...most of our few clients were going broke."

FIFTY YEARS' PROGRESS—FROM MANUAL CALCULATORS AND WORKSHEETS...

But as Davenport's economy weathered the Depression, so did the I.B. McGladrey Company. By 1939, the firm was healthy enough to acquire another accounting practice that had offices in Davenport and Omaha, Nebraska. The firm's name was also changed in 1939 to reflect the partnership made four years earlier. The firm became known as McGladrey, Hansen, Dunn & Company, the name it was to retain for nearly 40 years. World War II, and the drastic increase in income taxes required to finance mobilizing wartime industries, created a burgeoning demand for accounting services. But the challenge of rebuilding a civilian economy after the war created even more growth within the accounting profession.

In the early and mid-1950s McGladrey, Hansen, Dunn & Company's clients grew and prospered like never before. This period also marked a time of dazzling growth for the firm in the Quad-Cities.

To better meet the needs of a growing number of clients in the Illinois Quad-Cities, an office was established in Rock Island in 1950. Initially a one-man operation, that office was located in the Cleaveland Building at 1705 2nd Avenue. The "one man" was Ivan O. Bull, who later became chief executive of the firm.

As the Rock Island practice grew, so did its need for office space. As more staff were hired, it moved into larger and larger offices, finally settling in 1973 in the newly constructed quarters at 525 17th Street. That building was expanded in 1977, more than doubling its office space.

But even the growing Rock Island office was unable to keep up with the growth in demand for the firm's services in the Illinois Quad-Cities. In 1956, the firm established an office in Moline in the Fifth Avenue Building at 1630 5th Avenue. It also required more and more office space, and eventually moved into its current quarters at 3561 60th Street, Moline in 1975.

And while the firm was growing in the Quad-Cities, it was growing in other areas around the state and nation. By 1978, McGladrey, Hansen, Dunn & Company had expanded into eight states and employed 430 CPAs and another 360 staff persons in 29 offices.

Then, in November 1978, the firm consolidated its practice with that of Broeker Hendrickson & Co., a major accounting firm with headquarters in Minneapolis and St. Paul, Minnesota. The consolidation expanded the organization's reach into a total of 12 states. It also resulted in a change of the firm's name, to McGladrey Hendrickson & Co.

Today, McGladrey Hendrickson & Co. is the 13th largest certified public accounting firm in the United States. It serves the audit, accounting, tax and management advice needs of more than 48,000 clients from nearly 50 offices throughout the western two-thirds of the nation. Structured as a partnership, the firm is headed by 288 partners, and has a total employment of more than 1,400.

The firm employs nearly 150 people in its three Quad-Cities offices. Besides the more than 60 CPAs providing traditional auditing, accounting and tax services, the Quad-Cities offices include the firm's largest contingent of management consultants. Davenport has been the firm's headquarters since 1961, and is the home of its modern computer processing center and its central accounting and administrative departments.

From a failing one-man operation to the nerve center of a dynamic and rapidly growing public accounting firm, McGladrey Hendrickson & Co. has surely been "joined by a river" in the Quad-Cities.

TO COMPUTERS AND PRINTOUTS.

McLAUGHLIN BODY COMPANY

McLaughlin Body was begun in 1902 as the Wright Carriage Company. The complete operation of what was to become McLaughlin Body was contained in what is currently used solely for offices. It was before the time of automobiles, and factory production consisted solely of buggy bodies and surreys. The original company, Wright, was founded by local businessmen including Charles Deere, son of John Deere.

In 1906, the name was changed to E.H. Wilson Manufacturing Company. The product line remained the same, however, until 1914 when it became the manufacturer of automobile bodies for Velie and for Root VanDervort. Both firms built automobiles locally and sold them throughout the country. In 1916, the business was expanded to take care of war materiel produced for France. During this time, automobile body production took precedence over buggies. It was a lucrative venture until the 1927 depression which put the company into bankruptcy.

At this point, Harry McLaughlin, an engineer who "dreamed in four dimensions," teamed with Ray Cundy to form the Moline Manufacturing Corporation which became McLaughlin Body Company in 1931.

In the 1930s, McLaughlin built tractor cabs for Minneapolis-Moline, panel truck bodies for General Motors and cabs for Diamond T trucks. Harry McLaughlin nourished the concept that the company had to be more than a builder, and he worked to insure that there was involvement in his customers' products and operation. The end result has been innovation in sheet metal fabrication of cabs for trucks, farm machinery and construction equipment. The company pioneered new aluminum alloys to solve production problems, made aluminum cabs on steel tooling and built the first all-welded aluminum cab.

McLaughlin was the first to use aluminum resistance welding. In addition, the company has pioneered the drawn steel truck cab roof, farm tractor cabs, integral roll-over protection in farm tractor cabs and environmental systems for farm equipment cabs.

During the last generation of family-led growth, two of the founder's sons, J.T. McLaughlin and R.L. McLaughlin, have concentrated on the production of cabs. The company built all of the cabs for Diamond Trucks and all of the Cab-over units for International Harvester until 1976. McLaughlin has engineered and produced the last two generations of John Deere Combine cabs.

The continued success of McLaughlin Body Company can be traced to Harry McLaughlin's concept of loyalty to the customer both in word and deed as the vital ingredient for maintaining a successful business. The company continues to feel an obligation to search and work for better quality at lower cost to its customers.

MCLAUGHLIN'S EXECUTIVES EXAMINE THE FINISHED PRODUCT.

OVER 50 YEARS OF CONTINUED PROGRESS.

JOHN DEERE SOUNDGUARD
COMBINE CAB.

MODERN WOODMEN OF AMERICA

THE LEADERSHIP OF THESE MODERN WOODMEN HEAD OFFICERS, 1890-1892, SAW RAPID MEMBERSHIP GROWTH, WHICH PROMPTED THE SOCIETY TO FIND LARGER HEADQUARTERS. ROCK ISLAND, CHOSEN FROM A LIST OF SEVERAL CITIES, WAS SELECTED.

THE 12,000 MODERN WOODMEN MEMBERS WHO RECEIVED TREATMENT AT THE SOCIETY'S TUBERCULOSIS SANATORIUM IN COLORADO FROM 1909-1947 LIVED IN INDIVIDUAL HUTS.

Modern Woodmen of America was founded January 5, 1883, by Joseph Cullen Root in Lyons (now part of Clinton), Iowa. Root believed his new fraternal life insurance society would "clear away financial problems and bring much good to members and their widows and orphans." Seeing an analogy between his society and the land-clearing work of pioneer woodmen, Root chose the name Modern Woodmen, adding "of America" as a patriotic touch.

Modern Woodmen is organized into camps, local lodges to which all members belong. Pioneer Camp No. 1 at Lyons was followed by one at Fulton, Illinois, just across the Mississippi River. On May 5, 1884, the society was chartered in Illinois and the head office was moved to Fulton. Membership grew to about 50,000 by 1890.

Despite a leadership dispute, which saw Joseph Root leave the society, Modern Woodmen grew to more than 12,000 camps in the 1890s. These camps often became the social centers of their communities, fulfilling members' needs for fellowship. The ritualism of Modern Woodmen meetings, as with other fraternal organizations of the era, was immensely popular. Service to their hometown helped camp members build a sense of community within both the camp and the town. This growth prompted the society to seek a larger national headquarters, and Rock Island was chosen in 1892.

For five years, the citizens of Fulton fought in the courts to keep Modern Woodmen in their community. After a court decision in 1897, matters came to blows and the Illinois State Militia was called to protect the Modern Woodmen officials who moved the records to the society's new four-story headquarters in Rock Island. At the cornerstone laying ceremony, April 27, 1898, the speech was delivered by William Jennings Bryan, who had had a long association with Modern Woodmen. The premier orator of the day, Bryan drew a crowd of thousands to Rock Island.

Settled into its new headquarters as the century turned, Modern Woodmen continued its purpose of bringing together men who shared concern for one another's welfare and the welfare of their families. More than 1 million members had joined the society by 1910. Members paid monthly dues into a mortality fund, and payments from that fund were made to the families of members who died. The payment of monthly dues was discontinued in 1929 in favor of scheduled premium rates keyed to the age and health of each member. The society's purpose remained unchanged — providing financial security for families.

The Great Depression that soon affected the entire nation devastated the ranks of Modern Woodmen because thousands of members could no longer afford premiums for insurance of any kind. Still, the society survived, continuing to serve its members and paying all just claims. While the mission remained unchanged, two changes did occur during that period. Forester parades, a colorful element of Head Camps since 1901, met their demise in the Depression. Described as "triumphs of pageantry," the parades helped promote the society's early growth. Thousands of spectators would view the floats and drill teams dressed in a "rainbow" of colorful uniforms. The parades reached a pinnacle at the 1925 Chicago Head Camp. World War I, the Depression and changing times all took their toll, and the parades were discontinued.

The year 1929 also saw Royal Neighbors of America, until then an auxiliary of Modern Woodmen, declare its independence. Royal Neighbors began as a social club formed December 5, 1888, by wives and sisters of the Modern Woodmen camp in Council Bluffs, Iowa. In 1929, Modern Woodmen also began to issue life insurance to women and children.

MODERN WOODMEN BUILT THIS BUILDING AT 1504 THIRD AVENUE, ROCK ISLAND, WHICH SERVED AS THE SOCIETY'S HOME OFFICE FROM 1899 TO 1967. IT IS NOW THE ROCK ISLAND COUNTY OFFICE BUILDING.

S ince the earliest days of the 20th century, Modern Woodmen has provided members with fraternal benefits that respond to contemporary needs. The first such benefit was a tuberculosis sanitorium near Colorado Springs, Colorado, where more than 12,000 society members received free treatment during its 38 years of operation.

In the 1950s the society pioneered a polio benefit — called Polio Protection Plus — for members.

Today, Modern Woodmen offers a variety of fraternal benefits for members: the Orphan Benefit, College and Vocational-Technical Scholarships, the Newborn Benefit, Medic Alert Membership, Fraternal Aid Fund and Medical Information.

In the mid-1970s, the society renewed the emphasis on fraternal service to members' families and communities. The ritualistic activities of the past were replaced by a contemporary program of family life activities and community service involvement, which creates unity among the half-million members in nearly 1,000 camps throughout the United States.

The youth program, begun in 1942, is a special part of local camp activities. The more than 300 junior service clubs and teen clubs help young members learn to share and care for those in need. Reaching out to their neighbors, Modern Woodmen camps sponsor bicycle safety programs, holiday parties and other events that benefit their communities.

T oday, Modern Woodmen of America is a leader among fraternal life insurance societies. With $4 billion worth of life insurance and annuities, it ranks among the top life insurance organizations in the nation.

Modern Woodmen is a self-governing society. Delegates representing local camps throughout the nation convene every four years to review the society's progress, make needed changes in its by-laws and elect officers who will lead for the next four years.

Modern Woodmen's creed, written long ago by Edwin Markham, sums up the society's philosophy:

"There is a destiny that makes us brothers;
None goes his way alone;
All that we send into the lives of others
Comes back into our own."

A ROCK ISLAND RIVERFRONT LANDMARK, MODERN WOODMEN'S PRESENT HEADQUARTERS BUILDING OPENED IN 1967. THE CONTEMPORARY FIVE-STORY BUILDING FEATURES EXTENSIVE USE OF GLASS AND GRANITE.

ROYAL NEIGHBORS OF AMERICA

Founded as a social club on Dec. 5, 1888, Royal Neighbors of America was organized as a female auxiliary to the Modern Woodmen of America camp in Council Bluffs, Iowa, by Mrs. Marie L. Kirkland, known as "Mother of the Society." With fraternalism and Faith, Courage, Modesty, Unselfishness, and Endurance as its underlying principles, the club (consisting of wives and sisters of Modern Woodmen members) was reorganized in October 1889 as a secret social organization.

Chartered in Illinois on March 21, 1895, as a fraternal benefit organization, the Society had a membership of more than 4,000 in 100 camps, with insurance in force amounting to $576,000. By 1903, all women, whether related to members of Modern Woodmen or not, could be admitted into RNA. This allowed Royal Neighbors of America, previously limited to Modern Woodmen locations, to organize camps on a national scope.

A resolution to relocate the national headquarters from Fulton, Illinois, to Rock Island was adopted in 1908. Prominent businessmen supported the resolution, and trustees of the Rock Island Development Fund voted to donate land adjacent to the Rock Island Club building on the corner of 16th Street and 3rd Avenue — and valued at $12,000 — to RNA for its new headquarters. In 1910, the Society purchased the Rock Island Club building for nearly $14,000.

In November 1927, the cornerstone was laid for a new office building to replace the old Rock Island Club structure, which had outlived its usefulness. Constructed of Bedford limestone with a roof of slate in variegated colors, and with a granite foundation, the new three-story Supreme Office was dedicated on October 17, 1928.

The building is distinctly modern in style with no lavish display other than the crowning pediment of the Supreme Office consisting of two panels, one portraying the physical and one the spiritual side of the "Good Samaritan." Carved in stone above the bronze grills at the entrance are figures portraying womanly neighborliness, protection, and sympathy.

It was a point of particular pride to the Society's members that the total costs for completing the building were paid from funds on hand. Total cost of the building was $600,000 — an amount equal to $1 for each of the 600,000 members in good standing at the time of the dedication.

After July 8, 1929, Royal Neighbors of America ceased to be the auxiliary of Modern Woodmen of America by action of the Executive Council. For 39 years, Royal Neighbors had been affiliated with Modern Woodmen as its auxiliary; however, MWA had opened its membership to women and children not members of RNA so there no longer was any need for auxiliary status. Thereafter, the societies were legally separated, although bonds of cooperation have always been maintained.

*ROYAL NEIGHBORS OF AMERICA –
SUPREME OFFICE, ROCK ISLAND,
ILLINOIS*

ROYAL NEIGHBORS OF AMERICA – NATIONAL HOME, DAVENPORT, IOWA.

In 1930, the Society purchased a 41-acre tract of land, overlooking the Mississippi River just west of Davenport, on which to build a National Home as a haven for aged and dependent members. The architectural firm of W. Kruse, Clausen, Kruse & Klein designed the brick Georgian Colonial building, with white trim and a slate roof. The National Home, which can accommodate 52 residents, cost $321,489. It was dedicated on July 18, 1931. Although World War II created a hardship for all business organizations, Royal Neighbors of America continued, as always, to progress, as evidenced by authorization, in 1942, of payment of the Society's first dividend. In 1944, the Society began to write nonmedical insurance in all of the states where permitted by law.

Royal Neighbors of America has continually exemplified its fraternal tenets by assisting members both on a national and local level in extreme cases of need brought about by extended illness or serious accident, and by providing aid to stricken Neighbors in cases of cyclone, tornado, flood, fire, or other great public disaster. In the first two decades of the 20th century, as an example, members of RNA responded generously, helping victims of the 1906 San Francisco earthquake, the 1912 tornado in Omaha, the capsizing at Chicago of the Eastland excursion steamboat in July 1915, and the Minnesota forest fire of 1918.

The Society's fraternal benefits also include several adjunctive programs. In 1959, the Society inaugurated its "Help to Hear" program, devoted to serving the needs of the speech and hearing handicapped. Since that time, thousands of dollars have been given for assistance in the form of hearing aids, equipment for exceptional schools, and summer scholarships for hearing-impaired youngsters, in addition to volunteer hours and transportation. In conjunction with this long-standing program, the Society adopted, in 1982, the "Dogs for the Deaf" project, whereby members contribute funds for the training of dogs to be "ears" for hearing-handicapped persons.

The Fraternal Scholarship Program was instituted in 1961 to offer 5 four-year college scholarships on a competitive basis to young adult members of the Society.

Through the Orphan Benefit, adopted in 1971, junior RNA members who are fully orphaned by the death of both parents may become eligible to apply for certain benefits.

With more than 248,000 members in approximately 3,000 camps, and insurance in force amounting to nearly $600,000,000, Royal Neighbors of America is "dedicated to the members whose pioneer efforts and continuing loyalty have contributed to raising the Society to its present outstanding position and to those members who through devoted service and cooperation shall in the future raise still higher its standards of progress and achievement."

ST. LUKE'S HOSPITAL

St. Luke's Hospital has served Davenport since April 30, 1895, when it opened in a former home at 8th and Main streets. The idea for the new hospital had been conceived several years earlier when the bishop of the Episcopal Diocese of Iowa and trustees of the former Iowa Christian Home realized Davenport needed a second hospital to meet the needs of residents in the central part of town. A 22-member Board of Managers, 13 of whom were women, was formed to govern the hospital. Women, in fact, held the position of chief officer of the hospital until 1946.

After only a few months, the managers realized they needed a systematic way to train nurses. They established the Davenport Training School for Nurses August 27, 1895. It was so successful they renamed it "St. Luke's Hospital Training School" in 1897. It would train nurses to staff St. Luke's for more than 75 years.

Conditions in that first hospital — modern for its time — indicate how far health care has progressed. Lighting for surgery in the second floor operating room depended on the weather; on overcast days, surgery had to be postponed. Doctors and nurses did not wear surgical masks. Often a relative of the patient was admitted to the operating room — in street clothes.

The old hospital was remodeled in 1903, providing a "modern" surgery room, with many windows and a skylight, and accommodations for 50 patients.

With Davenport's increasing population, the hospital at 8th and Main had become inadequate by the mid-teens. Rather than remodel the aging facility, the Trustees decided to build a new hospital. Some land north of town was for sale, and the hospital took an option on a parcel bounded by the present East High and East Rusholme streets, College and Bridge avenues.

As construction at the new location progressed, changes were made at the old hospital. In the operating room, everyone now wore surgical gowns, tissue-thin gloves had become standard, and all surgical instruments were sterilized. The operating room fee for major surgery was $10, double the 1895 rate.

In 1918, St. Luke's joined 67 other hospitals nationwide as charter members of the American Hospital Association.

The new hospital building was opened in December 1919. After the new building opened, the women on the Board of Managers stepped down and reorganized as the Women's Auxiliary. So modern was the new facility that it was featured in the prestigious *Architectural Forum* magazine in December 1922.

The next year, Isabelle Craig-Anderson, who would guide the hospital for the next 21 years, became superintendent. Under Miss Craig-Anderson, St. Luke's made great progress. The daily average patient population rose from 23 to 95. The Nurses School gained recognition from the State Board of Nursing. A medical records department, the first in Iowa, was established. And the hospital was accredited by the American College of Surgeons.

A new nurses' home and training school — French Hall — was completed in June 1928, thanks to a $125,000 gift from Colonel and Mrs. George W. French.

Although the need for expansion became obvious by the late 1930s, World War II curtailed any thought of building. However, under the leadership of Leon A. Bondi, a major expansion program was begun in 1950 and completed in early 1952. The addition was six floors high, including the basement. The hospital now contained three major and two minor surgery rooms, two delivery rooms, two diagnostic X-ray rooms, two therapy X-ray rooms and more patient beds. The Women's Auxiliary opened a gift shop, began photographing newborn babies on request and provided a mobile television service.

ORIGINAL 1919 STRUCTURE OF ST. LUKE'S HOSPITAL ON HIGH STREET AND BRIDGE AVENUE AS IT APPEARED IN THE 1970S.

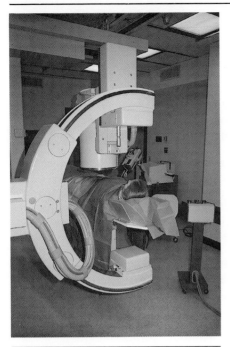

ANGIOSCOPE, A MODERN PIECE OF DIAGNOSTIC EQUIPMENT FOR USE IN CARDIAC CARE.

ST. LUKE'S HOSPITAL FACILITY ON RUSHOLME AND BRIDGE AFTER MAJOR RENOVATION, 1982.

By the late 1950s, the demand for hospital care in Davenport had increased so much that further renovation was planned. In 1963, ground was broken for a 110-bed addition, the second expansion project during Mr. Bondi's 15-year tenure. Cornerstone ceremonies on November 8 were saddened by the death the night before of R. Hovey Tinsman, president of the Board of Trustees.

Late in 1963, St. Luke's School of Nursing became the first in Iowa to receive authorization for a 24-month training program. An accelerated program made it possible to shave one year off the training needed to become a registered nurse.

Construction on the addition was completed in mid-1965. It contained an electro-encephalograph department, physical therapy, a large emergency suite, a nine-bed intensive care unit, more patient rooms, new lounges for doctors and patients' families and a new maternity section. Many of those services and others were improved in another round of construction in 1971. In 1964, the Chaplaincy Department was established. The department began a visitation program using volunteers known as "The Befrienders." The Women's Auxiliary continued to expand its services.

During 1966, modernization of the 48-year-old south wing began.

Since the late '60s, St. Luke's has been a leader in innovative treatment among Iowa hospitals. In 1969, it was the first private Iowa hospital to use the drug L-Dopa to treat Parkinson's Disease. A renal dialysis unit, opened in 1970, has expanded steadily ever since. The Maternal Health Center of Scott County was opened in French Hall in 1972, the same year husbands were allowed in St. Luke's delivery rooms during childbirth. St. Luke's brought a major surgical first to the Quad-Cities July 25, 1973, when the community's first open heart surgery was performed. The first nuclear powered pacemaker in the Quad-Cities — and in Iowa — was implanted by surgeons at St. Luke's. The seventies also saw St. Luke's develop a Medical Social Services department to meet the special needs of hospital patients and families, add new equipment in cardiac care and radiology areas, and assist in the development of several community oriented programs and services. The Maternal Health Center, Hospice Care of Scott County and Project CATCH provide special services to persons of all ages and needs. After three-fourths of a century, the St. Luke's Hospital School of Nursing accepted its final class in 1972.

During 1975 and 1976, the whole community watched as St. Luke's and Mercy hospitals considered every aspect of consolidation. Although numerous aspects of such a merger were resolved, the two hospitals ultimately decided to continue operating separately. St. Luke's then embarked on a comprehensive, hospital-wide renovation program. The project's main goal was to expand the hospital into a health care center, enhancing offerings in various service areas. A construction project in excess of $27 million was well under way as the '70s ended.

The newly renovated and expanded 232-bed hospital features larger and stronger facilities in all of its service areas. Areas of special emphasis include: emergency care; same-day surgery; physical therapy; hemodialysis, prenatal, neonatal and maternal care; cardiac services and open heart surgery.

AUGUSTANA COLLEGE

AUGUSTANA'S FIRST FOOTBALL TEAM, 1893.

After brief stays in Chicago (1860-1863) and Paxton, Illinois (1863-1875), the Swedish Lutheran pioneers who founded Augustana College purchased a tract of wooded, hilly land near the Mississippi River between Moline and Rock Island. In 1875, this site would become the permanent home of their school.

The founders intended to provide their daughters and sons, many immigrants themselves, with the education necessary to enter the American mainstream and, at the same time, provide leadership in preserving their deeply held values of faith and Scandinavian identity.

The earliest curriculum included the classical languages and such modern languages as English, German and Swedish; philosophy, Old and New Testament studies, sacred history, church history and secular history; and the standard subjects of geography, arithmetic and algebra. As early as 1879, Augustana announced a "scientific course," which included botany, zoology and chemistry. Augustana became a pioneer in American higher education when it added geology to its curriculum in the early 1880s. Thousands of Quad-Citians now benefit annually from that early decision as they view the outstanding Fryxell Geology Museum on the campus.

Who can forget the importance of music in the life of Augustana? The highly acclaimed Augustana Choir and Handel Oratorio Society have become cultural landmarks in the Quad-Cities. The Oratorio Society has now entered its second century of existence.

Augustana College continues today to live out the tradition of its founders in new ways by offering solid academic programs to more than 2,000 women and men of every economic level, of the various human races, of many ethnic communities, preparing them for responsible living in the world. The Christian values of hope, freedom, truth and community are still maintained in an ecumenical spirit.

Augustana College graduates have, by the thousands, rooted themselves in the Quad-Cities, providing leadership in business and industry, the professions, churches and synagogues and civic enterprise. In turn, the Quad-Cities has been generous in supporting Augustana. An inseparable partnership of college and community has emerged, for which Augustana is grateful.

Augustana College looks forward with confidence to the future it shares with the Quad-Cities.

TRI-CITY SYMPHONY ORCHESTRA ASSOCIATION

SALLY GOODWIN, HARPIST. ONE OF THE OUTSTANDING FEATURED ARTISTS WITH THE SYMPHONY.

Throughout its distinguished history of community service, the Tri-City Symphony Orchestra Association has maintained a strong commitment to artistic excellence. The combination of a highly trained professional ensemble of musicians, strong musical leadership, balanced programming, skilled volunteer participation and professional management has helped the Tri-City Symphony earn its first-rank position among Quad-Cities' arts organizations.

Organized in 1915, the Tri-City Symphony Orchestra was among the first orchestral ensembles in the United States to regularly present symphonic music concerts. In its early years, the Tri-City presented single concerts in many locations in the area. The first concert, conducted by Ludwig Becker, was staged in May 1916 at the Burtis Opera House. Symphony musicians, who were not compensated, performed together solely out of dedication to their craft and to their community.

The engagement of the world's finest guest artists has been an important factor in the growth and popularity of the Tri-City Symphony. Most major performing soloists since the early years of this century have appeared on stage in collaboration with the orchestra. Violinists Jascha Heifetz, Nathan Milstein and Itzhak Perlman; tenors Mario Lanza and Richard Tucker; baritones Robert Merrill and Sherrill Milnes; sopranos Marilyn Horne and Roberta Peters; clarinetist Benny Goodman; and pianists Andre Watts and Rudolf Firkusny are representative of the long and stellar list of virtuosos who have delighted Quad-City audiences for decades.

The Association has benefitted from superb musical leadership provided by the eight men who have held the title conductor and music director since the Symphony's founding. Since 1965, James Dixon has led the ensemble to its enviable reputation as an eminent regional performing group. Maestro Dixon has been granted many major awards by the nation's music community during his tenure.

Today, the association has broadened its impact on the Quad-Cities. Classified as a "metropolitan" orchestra, the association presents 18 subscription concerts in three series of six concerts each, in Rock Island and Davenport. All 85 members of the orchestra are compensated for their services and are recruited from a wide area. The association also sponsors the Tri-City Youth Symphony Orchestra, an annual in-school ensemble tour and Family Concert Series of programs for young audiences.

With a firm commitment to artistic integrity through careful programming, the continued engagement of world-class soloists, a broad range of services to its audiences and a vigorous educational organization, the Tri-City Symphony Orchestra Association is well-positioned to grow with the Quad-Cities.

CATERPILLAR TRACTOR CO.

AS A SMALL MACHINE SHOP, ENGLEHART SUPPLIED CATERPILLAR WITH NONCURRENT PARTS FOR ITS EQUIPMENT. LATER, AS A CATERPILLAR PLANT, PRODUCTION OF NONCURRENT PARTS CONTINUED.

PRODUCTION AT DAVENPORT OF CATERPILLAR'S NEW DESIGN IN TRACK-TYPE LOADERS WAS ANNOUNCED IN 1980.

THE PURCHASE OF ENGLEHART MANUFACTURING, BY CATERPILLAR TRACTOR CO. IN 1956, SIGNIFIED CAT'S FIRST MOVE INTO THE QUAD CITIES.

Caterpillar Tractor Co., headquartered in Peoria, Illinois, is the world's largest manufacturer of earthmoving, construction and material handling machinery and equipment. It is also a major producer of diesel, natural gas and turbine engines.

Some 75 facilities in 16 countries are involved in producing, marketing and supporting Caterpillar products.

Two plants — Davenport Plant and Bettendorf Remanufacturing Plant — are in the Quad-Cities.

The purchase in 1956 of Englehart Manufacturing, located near Bettendorf, signified Cat's first move into the Quad-Cities. As a small machine shop, Englehart had supplied Caterpillar with noncurrent parts for its equipment. Later, as a Caterpillar plant, production of noncurrent parts continued. Eventually, a greater percentage of current parts were also manufactured.

In 1967, the operations began moving to a newly constructed 530,000-square-foot factory and office building located just outside Davenport.

In 1973, Caterpillar remodeled its first Quad-Cities facility to function as an engine and component remanufacturing plant.

Since then, both plants have expanded. The Davenport plant now contains about 2.5 million square feet under roof, and the facility at Bettendorf added 50,000 square feet to total about 150,000 under roof.

Davenport Plant's product line has also grown to include prime products. In 1980, the first model of an entirely different design in track-type loaders was introduced.

The hydrostatic, rear-engine machines are evidence of Cat's commitment to meet the needs of an ever-changing world by designing and building the highest quality products for its customers. Dedicated, well-trained employees of the Quad-Cities plants continue, in that tradition, with pride.

FIRST TRUST & SAVINGS BANK

MODERN INTERIOR OF THE DOWNTOWN DAVENPORT LOCATION.

THIRD AND BRADY LOCATION OF FIRST TRUST & SAVINGS BANK, CIRCA 1935.

The First Trust story began in 1927 at the Bechtel Trust Company, the forerunner of today's First Trust and Savings Bank.

Bechtel became First Trust and Savings Bank in 1935 when it received a commercial bank charter. The bank's symbol was the big four-sided clock hanging on the thick outer stone walls. Inside, the bank's original grandeur is still evident: the original tiled floor, oak paneling in the former board room, terrazzo walls behind the cages in the vault and a marble desk for customers to fill out account slips next to a vintage scale.

First Trust expanded over the years. In 1959 it built the second drive-in facility in the state of Iowa. In 1961 the ornate 36 foot-high ceiling depicting nymphs and classical scenes was removed to make room for the addition of two more floors for office space. In 1969, the bank opened a northwest office at 37th and Division streets. Another office was added in November 1979 with the opening of the Cumberland Square facility in Bettendorf. A third office was added at Northgate Shopping Center early in 1981.

In 1977 a second part of First Trust's story began. Banks of Iowa, a Des Moines-based holding company, acquired the bank as a subsidiary. F. Forbes Olberg, chairman of the board of Banks of Iowa, has said recently that the bank can now "keep pace with the growth of the Quad-Cities." First Trust has retained its local character and management while enjoying the advantages of increased lending power, technical support and financial expertise.

During the last five years, the holding company has fulfilled its promise. Banks of Iowa includes 11 subsidiary banks, and all maintain their local ties and autonomy. Besides First Trust's equality with the other banks, economies of scale are enjoyed by all. The combined assets exceeding $1.5 billion offer greater benefits for the entire Quad-Cities area.

IOWA-ILLINOIS GAS & ELECTRIC COMPANY

The Quad-Cities area has been a pioneer in the electric industry for a century. In 1882, Thomas Edison's first power station in New York City was completing its first year of operations. That same year, the forerunners of Iowa-Illinois Gas and Electric Company, the Rock Island County Brush Electric Light Company, began supplying electricity to customers. Soon after, the Merchants Electric Light Company of Moline began operation. Within a few years, these companies were providing service to a large part of the community. One innovation was cooperation among the different utility companies in the Quad-Cities. In April 1888, the Moline power station provided the energy to light Rock Island's downtown street lights. Soon after, one of the first long distance power lines in the country became operational. This 2,000-volt line from Moline's hydroelectric plant carried power to light Davenport's downtown street lights.

Another innovation was the electrification of streetcars. Dr. William L. Allen was responsible for opening the Brady Street hill route on August 11, 1888. This was the second electric streetcar running in the country. It "easily climbed the hill loaded with 40 or 50 people" and was followed by another electric streetcar on the 15th Street hill in Moline.

The streetcars proved popular, and lines extended throughout the Quad-Cities area. Streetcar companies developed amusement parks at Credit Island in Davenport, Campbell's Island in East Moline and Black Hawk's Watch Tower Park on the Rock River near Rock Island. These parks were popular locations for family outings. The most famous was Watch Tower Park. It featured a chute in which daring boat riders slid down the hill into the water below.

Electrified rail lines connected Clinton and Muscatine to the metropolitan area. They were called "interurbans" because they connected cities together with daily trips. They became very popular by the 1920s with 15 round trips scheduled daily and low fares averaging 2.5 cents per mile.

Local electric and street railway companies began to merge into larger utility corporations. By 1904, People's Power Company owned all utilities in Rock Island County; People's Light and the Davenport Gas and Electric Company dominated in Scott County. Two years later, the J. G. White Engineering and Construction Company acquired all of these firms. In 1912, the United Light and Railways Company, a large interstate holding corporation, purchased and reorganized all utility companies in the Quad-Cities.

In 1942, Iowa-Illinois Gas and Electric Company appeared as United was broken up into smaller corporations. In the following years, rapid improvements in service would benefit all Quad-Citians. In the 1980s more than 170,000 residential, commercial and industrial customers in 35 communities depend on the company for electric energy.

BRADY STREET–DAVENPORT, CIRCA 1890, CIRCA 1982.

JUNIOR LEAGUE OF THE QUAD CITIES

One of the world's greatest natural resources — the Mississippi River — flows through the Quad-Cities.

In the early years, two aspects of the river caused settlers to stay. The rapids brought pilots to guide boats along the 14 miles of treacherous rapids between Le Claire and Rock Island. And the swift current attracted the forerunners of today's industry who built riverside mills to exploit it as a low-cost power source.

Ever since those early years, the Mississippi has been a center of life in the Quad-Cities. Because it still is such a profound influence on us all, the Junior League of the Quad-Cities chose "The Year of the River 1983" as a unifying theme for a full calendar of major events and educational efforts. This year-long celebration of the river has two simple goals: to increase the community's pride in and awareness of the Mississippi; and to encourage physical improvement along the river's banks. To reach these goals, the Junior League has launched "The Year of the River," with many events.

River-centered courses of study for children will be offered through Quad-Cities libraries and the Putnam Museum.

A speakers bureau will promote riverside beautification through a slide show and the establishment of a riverfront beautification fund.

The Quad-Cities Marathon will be run May 1, 1983, sponsored by the Junior League in collaboration with the Cornbelt Running Club.

A model of the Quad-Cities, "Dream of the River in the Year 2000," will be prepared by students in the School of Design at Iowa State University and displayed in the community beginning June 1, 1983.

The Year of the River Regatta will attract pleasure boaters to the Mississippi on June 25, 1983.

The Junior Theater of Davenport will present the pageant "Time and the River" August 6 and 7, 1983, at Black Hawk State Park.

A Riverfront Concert on Arsenal Island, in cooperation with the Tri-City Symphony and its Senior Board, will be presented in September, 1983.

With the help of the community, two riverfront areas, one on each side of the Mississippi, will be beautified by the end of 1984.

With this full calendar, the Junior League hopes to make all the Quad-Cities more aware of the Mississippi River's potential and leave a lasting reminder in the form of two beautified areas along the river's banks.

LEE ENTERPRISES, INCORPORATED

A. W. Lee, founder of Lee Enterprises, was fond of dreaming big dreams. He started his career as a "printer's devil" but even then, he had a vision of someday publishing his own newspaper. He promised himself that when this happened, his newspaper would never go in debt for more than it could promptly repay from current operations. His basic philosophy was that no newspaper could be an independent newspaper unless it was a self-sustaining and self-supportive newspaper. While remaining steadfast to this conviction, Lee's ambition led him to purchase the Ottumwa *Courier* in 1890 and become its publisher. He stressed responsibility to the community and to standards of writing the news truthfully. He went on to create a group of Midwestern newspapers joined in purpose yet independent in editorial viewpoint. At his death in 1907, the Lee Syndicate consisted of five newspapers, including the Davenport *Times.*

If A. W. Lee was the founder of Lee Enterprises, then E. P. Adler was the builder. At 13, he became a printer's apprentice at which time he nourished the amibition to someday own a newspaper himself. He was a young man of ability and genius working in the mechanical department of the Ottumwa *Courier* when Lee discovered him. From that point on, they were a team. Adler worked as a reporter for Lee at the *Courier* and was later appointed business manager of the Davenport *Times.* After Lee's untimely death while vacationing in Europe, Adler took the reins as president and directed the course of the publishing group for more than 40 years, continuing the traditions set down by A. W. Lee.

When the Lee group acquired the Mason City, Iowa *Globe-Gazette* in 1925, its task, under the guidance of Lee P. Loomis, first as business manager and later as publisher, was to make a good newspaper better. This accomplished, Loomis went on to expand into the field of radio, convinced that a small, local radio station would supplement and complement the services offered by the newspaper. This was the conception of radio station KGLO in Mason City. Lee Loomis went on to become the third president of the Lee group in 1949. He continued to edit the *Globe-Gazette* while taking on the responsibilities of leading a $20 million corporation. During the 1950s, he expanded the scope of the company by purchasing the Hannibal, Missouri, *Courier-Post,* the La Crosse, Wisconsin, *Tribune* and WMTV, Madison, Wisconsin while also putting a new station on the air, KHQA-TV, Hannibal Missouri. In 1960, Philip D. Adler took over as president of Lee Enterprises. He had edited the Kewanee *Star-Courier* from 1926 until 1949 when he became publisher of the Davenport *Times.* Under his leadership, Lee Enterprises acquired five Montana newspapers and a television station in West Virginia. At the same time, he reorganized the 16 independent newspapers into a new single unit, with a central office in downtown Davenport.

Adler applied technological and organizational efficiency to the workings of a communications company involved in publishing, broadcasting and graphic arts. By 1967 the Lee Stations, consisting of the radio and television stations owned by the Lee Group, had joined the Lee Enterprises corporate structure.

From 1970 to 1973, Dave Gottlieb was president. Under his direction and that of his successor, Lloyd Schermer, the decade of the '70s was highly successful. Lee Enterprises operates 18 newspapers, 4 television stations and 4 radio stations. In addition, the company serves the graphic arts industry through NAPP Systems (USA), Inc., San Marcos, California. NAPP is the world's leading producer of photosensitive polymer printing plates for newspapers. NAPP is a joint venture of Lee and Nippon Paint Company, Ltd., Osaka, Japan.

In the 1980s, the company has continued to prosper. According to Dun and Bradstreet, Lee Enterprises is "one of the 295 companies...recognized for consistently increasing dividends over the last decade."

A.W. LEE.

MARYCREST COLLEGE

Marycrest College was founded in 1939 by the Sisters of the Congregation of the Humility of Mary. Mother Mary Geraldine Upham was the charter president of the college, which began with 21 faculty members, all sisters, and 76 students. Marycrest consisted of two structures on a seven-acre campus: the former home of the Max Petersen family, which housed the sisters, and a liberal arts building, later named Upham Hall, containing classrooms and administrative offices.

None of the first students lived on campus. Because of the demand for residences, West Hall was built in 1940 and enlarged in 1958. As enrollment increased, nearby houses were bought to accommodate students until more residence halls could be built. Petersen Hall, built in 1948, provided more student quarters, a dining room and a chapel. Wings were added in 1951 and 1962. Lawlor and Rohlman residence halls were added later.

Founded as a Catholic college at the request of the bishop of the Diocese of Davenport, Marycrest existed as the women's counterpart to St. Ambrose College until 1954 when it was incorporated as a separate college. One year later the college received independent accreditation.

During Marycrest's growth, it has acquired many facilities to aid its students. The Cone Library, built in 1958, has developed into a complete resource and media center. Walsh Hall, erected in 1964, contains laboratories for the basic sciences and computer science. The nursing department acquired its own building in 1973. Communication and the theatre arts programs share the nursing facility.

In 1969, Marycrest took two dramatic new steps: it began admitting men, and it launched a master of arts program in education. Intercollegiate athletics was soon added, and a multi-use Activities Center housing basketball and tennis courts as well as the student union was constructed in 1978.

From its beginning as a small, Catholic women's liberal arts college, Marycrest has grown to serve well over 1,200 students of all ages and faiths, offering many continuing education, baccalaureate and graduate programs. Marycrest is proud of its long history of community involvement in the development of the minds of future Quad-Cities leaders.

PETERSEN MANSION.

NORTHWEST BANK & TRUST COMPANY

THE LOCUST STREET LOCATION, OPENED IN 1953.

On July 7, 1941, with only three employees, Northwest Bank & Trust Company opened for business at 1529 Washington Street, Davenport. In 1953, the bank moved to one of its present locations at 1454 West Locust Street and employed 18 persons. The drive-in facility at Locust Street was opened with a ribbon-cutting ceremony in 1960. A new motor bank at 38th and Brady streets was established in 1968, to service Davenport's fastest growing commercial area. The Locust Street facility was modernized and expanded to twice its original size in 1969. In 1972 the bank celebrated a "Founders' Day" for the original stockholders and members of their families. At that time there were 600 stockholders in the bank.

The year 1974 saw the opening of the new eight-story Northwest Bank Tower, adjacent to Northpark Shopping Center, in Davenport, with the first three stories being occupied by the bank or bank-related affiliates. In early 1975, a motor bank was consolidated into Northwest Bank Tower. On February 17, 1981, the beautiful six-story Northwest Bank Building was opened for business in Bettendorf. It featured the first drive-up automatic teller machine in the Quad-Cities area.

With the opening on February 16, 1982, of another prestigious six-floor office building at the corner of Second and Brady streets in downtown Davenport, Northwest Bank & Trust Company completed, for now, the brick and mortar plans established in 1971. It had accomplished its goal of serving all the geographical areas of its marketplace with this fourth convenient, full-service banking facility. It is the first major office building to be constructed in downtown Davenport in more than 50 years. Northwest Bank & Trust Company has been a major contributor to the development of the metropolitan area for more than 40 years.

Today, Northwest Bank & Trust Company is one of the 20 largest banks in the state of Iowa and the second largest bank in Scott County, in total assets. It employs a full-time staff of 119 and 31 bank officers. Eleven professional business persons serve on the Board of Directors, and the bank has 1,615 stockholders of record.

THE NEWEST NORTHWEST BANK FACILITY LOCATED AT 2ND AND BRADY, 1982.

DAVENPORT OSTEOPATHIC HOSPITAL

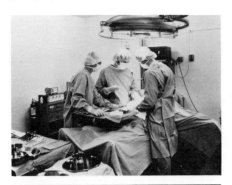

INSIDE ONE OF THE OPERATING ROOMS AT THE PRESENT DAVENPORT OSTEOPATHIC HOSPITAL.

The history of osteopathic medicine in the Quad-Cities is nearly as old as the history of formalized osteopathic medicine itself.

The first osteopathic physician, William Stirling, D.O., set up the "Tri-City Institute of Osteopathy" in downtown Davenport in 1896. This was only two years after the first school of osteopathy, located in Kirksville, Missouri, graduated its first class of 18 D.O.s (Doctors of Osteopathic Medicine).

The first roots for Davenport Osteopathic Hospital began in 1913 when Augusta Tueckes, D.O., graduated from the Kirksville school and set up practice in Davenport. Dr. Tueckes was the older sister of Dr. Lydia Jordan and Dr. Theodore Tueckes, and these three later would be among the 10 founders of the present Davenport Osteopathic Hospital.

Dr. Jordan, her husband, Dr. Holcomb Jordan, and Dr. Theodore Tueckes graduated from Kirksville in 1930. They joined with Dr. Augusta Tueckes to form the Tueckes-Jordan Clinic at 1209 Brady Street in Davenport.

The Tueckes-Jordan Clinic soon expanded and purchased a duplex across the street at 1210 Brady and equipped the building as an obstetric hospital with space for five patients. Drs. Lydia and Holcomb Jordan lived in the upstairs apartment.

Through the years more young osteopathic physicians joined the clinic, then went out to establish their own practices. The osteopathic physicians in the area soon began to see a need for a general osteopathic hospital and began to make plans.

After extensive planning, on December 6, 1945, the Davenport Osteopathic Hospital Association, Inc. was founded by Doctors Holcomb and Lydia Jordan, Augusta and Theodore Tueckes, Arthur Abramsohn, George C. Boston, John W. Campbell, Howard R. Patterson, Donald F. McDonough and L.M. Williams.

These founders, through personal philanthropic efforts, raised the money necessary to open a hospital and eventually purchased and renovated a four-story brick building at 326 East 29th Street, which became the first Davenport Osteopathic Hospital.

On September 12, 1949, Davenport Osteopathic Hospital opened its doors as a 32-bed general hospital equipped for osteopathic treatment, major and minor surgery and obstetrics.

In 1957 a county-wide drive raised $350,000 to renovate the hospital, but instead it was decided to purchase property at 1111 West Kimberly Road in Davenport and build a new hospital financed by the fund drive and the sale of bonds. The new hospital was completed in 1960.

In 1967, an additional 43-bed east wing was added. In 1976 a west wing was built to allow for upgrading services in pediatrics, the emergency room, surgery, cardiopulmonary and physical therapy.

THE FIRST DAVENPORT OSTEOPATHIC HOSPITAL LOCATED ON EAST 29TH STREET.

Today, Davenport Osteopathic Hospital is a 150-bed full service acute care hospital with 46 physicians on active staff, including two of the original founders. Three more of the founders are on honorary staff.

The hospital is a teaching hospital, with training programs for osteopathic externs, interns and residents. Davenport Osteopathic Hospital is proud to be a part of the system of more than 200 osteopathic hospitals and 20,000 osteopathic physicians providing that "something extra." In addition to all scientifically accepted methods of treatment, including surgery and the use of drugs, osteopathic physicians provide hands-on treatment — osteopathic diagnosis and treatment. They pay particular attention to the symmetry of joints, bones, muscles and nerves. By physically manipulating these elements, circulation is often improved and the body can more easily heal itself.

Throughout the history of Davenport Osteopathic Hospital, the goal has been to give Quad-Citians the best possible care at reasonable costs, while maintaining the osteopathic tradition of caring for the whole person.

QUAD-CITY TIMES

The *Quad-City Times* can trace its ancestry to 1855, when *The Iowa State Democrat* was founded. Davenport had earlier newspapers, however, beginning with Andrew Logan's *Iowa Sun and Davenport and Rock Island News*. First published August 15, 1838, Logan's weekly lasted four years. Meanwhile, other papers were being published. Among them was the *Democratic Banner*, founded in September 1848. Under a series of owners, the weekly *Banner* struggled until it finally was put up for sale in 1855. A group of Davenport businessmen sent a delegate to Peoria, Ill., to persuade David N. Richardson to come to Davenport as editor and publisher.
With his friends, George R. West and J.T. Hildreth, Richardson bought the business with $300 cash, promissory notes, a mortgage and $240 credit for supplies. The first issue of their renamed paper, *The Iowa State Democrat*, came off the press October 15, 1855.
In the fourth year of the *Democrat*'s publication, J.J. Richardson joined his older brother in Davenport to look after the paper's business interests. The Richardson brothers continued to guide the paper, which soon became a daily, for decades. D.N. was editor, J.J. advertising and business manager. After D.N. retired, J.J. took over many editorial responsibilities until his retirement well past age 70. J.J. also rose to prominence in Democratic politics and became a friend of Grover Cleveland.
The *Democrat* bought the *Davenport Gazette* in 1887 and the *Davenport Leader* in 1904. With that purchase, the paper became *The Davenport Democrat and Leader*, a name that lasted more than 40 years.

ALMOST EVERYTHING ABOUT THE NEWSPAPER HAS CHANGED OVER THE YEARS. THIS HASN'T. YOUNG MERCHANTS STILL MAKE UP THE LARGEST AND MOST RELIABLE SYSTEM OF DELIVERY.

While the *Democrat* was evolving, the *Quad-City Times'* other ancestor, *The Daily Times*, was going through changes of its own. Founded in 1878 as *The Blue Ribbon News*, Davenport's fourth weekly temperance organ, the paper was purchased the next year by E.W. Brady. Brady changed its name to *The Northwestern News*. By 1886, he had developed the paper into such a profitable venture that he was able to publish daily under a new name, *The Davenport Daily Times*.
Brady and his sons published it for 13 years. In 1899, C.D. Reimers and A.W. Lee, founder of Lee Enterprises, Incorporated, bought *The Times* for $20,000. Two years later, Lee and E.P. Adler bought out Reimers and Adler became publisher. After Lee died, Adler was elected president of the Lee group of newspapers.
As in the early days of Davenport, many other papers lived and died between the 1890s and the Great Depression. *The Times* and *The Democrat* outlived them all and carried on a friendly, but vigorous rivalry until the mid-1960s.
In 1964, the two papers merged as the *Davenport Times Democrat*, publishing morning and evening editions out of a shared newsroom. Over the decades, the two papers had occupied half a dozen premises before settling at the present East 2nd Street address. After 11 years, during which the merged paper's circulation continued to expand in the whole metropolitan area and surrounding counties, the name changed one final time — to *Quad-City Times*.

Over the last two decades, the *Times* has changed much more than its name. It was among the first newspapers in the United States to switch from "hot type" (letterpress) to "cold type" (photo-offset) printing.
The *Times* was the first newspaper in the world to convert to a totally electronic newsroom. Since the conversion in the mid-1970s, newspaper executives from all over the world have come to Davenport to inspect the *Times'* system. In the pressroom as in the newsroom, the *Times* has led in development of plastic polymer printing plates and lightweight presses. Throughout the years, *Times* journalists have won numerous awards for reporting, photography and feature writing.

ST. AMBROSE COLLEGE

CHORUS PRACTICE IN CHRIST THE KING CHAPEL.

St. Ambrose College, established more than 100 years ago in a makeshift two-room diocesan school in Davenport, has grown through the past century to become a name synonymous with quality higher education.

The institution began modestly in 1882 in the old St. Marguerite's School, site of the present Sacred Heart Cathedral. Enrollment that first year was less than 50 students. Three years later, in 1885, St. Ambrose moved to its current Locust Street location and classes were held in the new Ambrose Hall, which today is listed in the National Register of Historic Places.

St. Ambrose was incorporated in 1885 as a "literary, scientific and religious institution." The articles of incorporation stated that "No particular religious faith shall be required of any person to entitle him to admission to said seminary."

The corporation changed its name in 1908 from St. Ambrose Seminary to St. Ambrose College to meet the demand for educational facilities for those not aspiring to the priesthood.

From 1929 to 1939 the doors of the college were opened to women for late afternoon and evening classes. During World War II the United States Navy chose St. Ambrose for the training of officers.

Today St. Ambrose is a coeducational liberal arts college with a total enrollment exceeding 2,000 students. Undergraduates may choose from more than 30 major fields of study in the arts, business, education, languages and literature, philosophy, theology and social sciences.

Degrees offered at the undergraduate level include the bachelor of arts, bachelor of science, bachelor of music, bachelor of music education, bachelor of arts in special studies and bachelor of elected studies.

At the graduate level, St. Ambrose offers an evening-hour master of business administration (M.B.A.) degree program, the only campus-based program of its kind in the Quad-Cities.

Corresponding to the steady growth in enrollment through the past century, the college campus also has grown. Today the institution consists of an impressive campus occupying some seven square blocks of residential area in central Davenport. There are 11 buildings, ranging from historic Ambrose Hall to the new physical education center on which construction began in 1982 during the celebration of the college's centennial year.

AMBROSE HALL.

SCHWAB ADVERTISING SYSTEM, INCORPORATED

In early 1941, Frank M. Schwab formed his own commercial sign and outdoor advertising company. With the help of Otto F. Gerhardt, a self-taught artist who could paint the embellished pictorials popular at the time, Schwab erected scenic outdoor signs on leased property. Local businesses, such as bakeries and the brewery, were his first customers. Also, he completed extensive gold-leaf work on circus vehicles owned by Dr. B.J. Palmer.

Schwab quickly outgrew the first site of his business — a part of his home. In 1943, he purchased the U.S. Neon Sign Co. at 508 Harrison Street. The next year, he bought an Iowa City poster billboard plant and named his oldest son, Harold, manager.

During the war years, the Schwab company painted wall signs promoting War Bond sales and other patriotic themes. Perhaps the most notable one was at the northeast corner of 3rd and Main streets. The Schwab building at 508 Harrison saw the heyday of the neon trade. During the '40s, two more Schwab sons joined the firm, Richard as a salesman and Carl as an apprentice sign painter. Carl later became art director. The company employed several sign painters, neon tube benders and men to erect and service signs. In 1950, the Schwab firm moved to 312 West Locust Street. Frank Schwab Jr. completed college and joined the firm in 1954 as a sales and construction worker. Later in the '50s, Robert Schwab joined his brother in Iowa City as a salesman and artist. Now the father and all five of his sons were working together to serve the community's outdoor advertising needs.

Highway and neon sign manufacturing dominated the firm's business in the 1950s. Early in 1961, the company added small poster panels, called Junior Billboards, to its line. The first contract was for 10 spaces to advertise a local dairy. The advent of plastic signs signalled the decline of neon, and Schwab sold its neon tube bending apparatus to the University of Iowa for use in preparing laboratory glassware. The company then concentrated on painted outdoor signs and poster board sales.

In 1965, Schwab Advertising moved in April — during the height of the flood. Water came within one inch of flooding the newly occupied building at 211 Marquette Street. From this facility, which Schwab still occupies, the small poster plant matured, growing to link 10 area counties in Iowa and Illinois with spaces for outdoor advertising.

Frank Schwab Sr. incorporated the business in 1969. He forged a strong nucleus with his five sons who, together with several of his grandsons, continue to help the business grow to serve eastern Iowa and western Illinois.

SCHWAB ADVERTISING SYSTEMS' FREQUENTLY PAINTED ADVERTISING DISPLAYS ON THE SIDES OF BUILDINGS AS IN THIS WAR BOND POSTER FROM WORLD WAR II.

SEARS MANUFACTURING COMPANY

Shortly after moving to Davenport from New York, Isacc Howe Sears founded the Sears Company. In 1855 this small company began producing harnesses for farm horses in a shop in the heart of the downtown Davenport business district. Over the years the company outgrew its quarters, and it moved to 218 Perry Street in 1893.

For the next 20 years the company made harnesses, saddles, buggy whips and horse blankets. During World War I, production shifted to pup tents and pistol holders. It had moved on to other products for the Army during World War II.

Before the 1940s farmers talked about horsepower in terms of the strength and stamina of their teams rather than the size and power of their engines. As the tractor began to replace the horse, Sears began to manufacture tractor seats; 1947 marked the beginning of a new era for Sears as a supplier for motorized equipment.

In 1960 Sears Manufacturing Company moved to a modern factory on Davenport's West River Drive. With the new plant, production expanded to include all types of seating for agricultural and industrial equipment, and the work force was greatly expanded.

Sears achieved a market breakthrough in the early 1970s with the introduction of advanced mechanical suspension designs for seats. Today Sears enjoys a reputation as a leading domestic supplier of heavy duty agricultural, construction and truck seats. The company has been an innovator as well as a leading producer.

Manufacturing facilities in the 1980s include sheet metal forming and stamping, welding, automatic painting, sewing, vacuum forming and foam molding. Sears aggressively promotes its expertise with strong sales, engineering and service functions.

Sears Manufacturing Company entered the European market in 1976 when, with Coventry Motor and Sundries Co., Ltd., of Coventry, England, Sears-CMS Seating Ltd. was formed. Its manufacturing facility is located in Tafarnaubach, Wales.

Throughout its metamorphosis from small harness maker to multi national company, Sears Manufacturing has maintained a strong commitment to quality and service. Carrying on the family leadership is the company president I. Weir Sears Jr., the fourth generation of Sears to head the company. The Sears family and the employees of the company take great pride in being a part of a long-established firm and part of the history of the Quad-Cities, from which it draws its highly talented work force.

ALEXANDER SEARS (1782-1828),
ISAAC HOWE SEARS (1821-1915) AND
ISAAC LEWIS SEARS (1863-1942).

PALMER COLLEGE OF CHIROPRACTIC

Daniel David Palmer began chiropractic education in 1895 in his Davenport offices shortly after he formulated his new approach to health care. By 1904, his school had grown to the point where a move to larger quarters was necessary. The new site, on Brady Street hill, serves as the nucleus of today's campus.

One of Dr. Palmer's early students was his son, Bartlett Joshua Palmer. "B.J." soon took on administrative responsibility and later became president. The college was chartered in 1907 and clinical research began. Until he died in 1961, "B.J." led Palmer in the academic expansion required for chiropractic educational demands.

Dr. David D. Palmer succeeded his father, "B.J.," as president, a post he held until his death in 1978. During his tenure, he was responsible for directing the college on a path that led to its eventual accreditation. The college's fifth president, Dr. J.F. McAndrews, continues the Palmer tradition of accomplishment.

PALMER SCHOOL OF CHIRO-PRACTIC AS IT APPEARED IN 1910.

SECURITY STATE TRUST AND SAVINGS BANK

Security State Trust and Savings Bank opened for operation in the fall of 1965 with the dedication of the Main Bank facility at 1710 Grant Street, Bettendorf. Founded by local businessmen and professionals who saw a need for additional banking services in the growing city, the bank has been a leader in the economic growth of Bettendorf.

Security Bank's Middle Road office opened in 1974 with temporary quarters, and the permanent facility opened in October 1975. A major addition and remodeling of the Main Bank is scheduled for fall 1982 completion.

Locally owned since its origination, the bank is proud to be an independent entity. Chairman of the Board William J. Callahan, who assumed control in 1973, stresses the importance of local involvement and participation in the community. Continued growth and expanding locations are planned for the future as Security State Bank grows with Bettendorf and the Quad-Cities.

WQAD-TV ACTIVE 8
QUAD CITIES COMMUNICATIONS CORPORATION

THE MAIDEN VOYAGE OF THE ACTIVE 8 HOT AIR BALLOON ON JUNE 26, 1982

On August 15, 1963, Quad-Citians listened to their first ABC (American Broadcasting Company) television station, when Channel 8 signed on. The prime time shows from the network included such favorites as "Hootenanny," "77 Sunset Strip," "The Flintstones," "My Three Sons," "Ben Casey," "The Fugitive," "McHale's Navy" and "Wagon Train." Dr. Tom Honsa and other local businessmen had formed the Moline Television Corporation to affiliate with the ABC television network.

Network programming has changed since then, although some of those first season shows are still shown in syndication. Locally originated programming has changed as well. Many viewers will remember "The Jungle Jay Show," "Q-Deeni's Magic Shoppe," "Georgia on Q" and the late night horror show "Doctor Igor." More recent shows like "Romper Room," "Weekday Magazine" and "Weekend Magazine" have taken their place.

The seed for WQAD's commitment to quality newscasting goes back to 1966 when Jim King went on the first of two trips to South Vietnam, to talk and visit with area service men and women. Since then, film has given way to video tape. Now the WQAD Active 8 Live Van covers local news in Iowa and Illinois — the whole Quad-Cities — with news studios in Moline and Davenport.

The "Iowa Desk" is located in the first floor of the Blackhawk Hotel in Davenport, equipped with a news studio, editing facilities and staff. In July 1982 Active 8 engineers mounted a satellite receiving dish atop the Moline studio, enabling Active 8 to receive programs, news and special events from around the world.

From the early days, WQAD has served the public interest with a wide range of quality news and public affairs programs. They represent the station's policy of allowing air time for free expression of different views on public issues of importance. WQAD has been a strong supporter of the Jerry Lewis Labor Day Telethon for Muscular Dystrophy, helping to raise money for area patients. WQAD has also been involved with the annual Cerebral Palsy Telethon, The Quad-Cities Open and the Bix 7-Mile Run.

On November 1, 1977, WQAD was purchased by the *Des Moines Register & Tribune* Company, owner of one of the most prestigious newspapers in the country, recipient of several Pulitzer Prizes. The company created the Quad-Cities Communications Corporation. Always growing in the community, WQAD laid groundwork for an aggressive news gathering team, and the newly fashioned identity of ACTIVE 8 emerged.

WQAD-TV ACTIVE 8 EXISTING FACILITIES AT 3003 PARK 16TH STREET MOLINE, IN SEPTEMBER 1982.

CLIFTON PRECISION
INSTRUMENTS & LIFE SUPPORT DIVISION

The flow of knowledge and skills into Clifton Precision Instruments & Life Support's vast reservoir of experience in aerospace technology began in 1919 with the founding of Pioneer Instrument Company. The merger in 1929 of Pioneer Instrument Company with Bendix resulted in the subsequent establishment of this division.

The facility, originally built for the Victor Animatograph Corporation, a division of the Curtiss-Wright Corporation, was opened in 1948 and purchased by Bendix on December 4, 1950. Many of the Victor people transferred employment to Bendix, and some supervisors came from the new parent organization — The Eclipse-Pioneer Division. Named by Bendix the Pioneer Central Division, denoting not only a kinship with the parent organization but geographical location as well, the name was later changed to Instruments & Life Support Division. Memories from the early months of the division always bring to mind the incoming boxes and paper work marked for "operation cornfield."

In March 1982, Instruments & Life Support division was acquired by Clifton Precision and became a member of the Litton Industries family. As a division of a multi-billion dollar worldwide corporation, we are proud of its contributions to the highly technical aerospace field.

Since its beginning, the division has always been involved in aerospace products. These products, and variations of them, continue to be produced by the facility and contribute significantly to the country's welfare and security. Sonic cleaning equipment became an integral part of the product line in 1953 and health care products began in 1970. These products have since been divested.

During its lifetime, the division has had suppliers and customers from nearly every state in the union and many foreign countries.

Instruments & Life Support Division has made many contributions to the various customers it serves and to the local community. Although it is justly proud of its facilities and fine products, the real reason for its success stems from the skills and dedication of its people.

JOHNSON SHEET METAL WORKS, INCORPORATED

ANTON JOHNSON, LEFT, CIRCA 1920.

More than 60 years ago, Anton Johnson founded a tin shop in East Moline, Illinois. His grandson, C. Douglas Johnson, is now president of the firm that has grown to more than 70,000 square feet of sheet metal shop, spread over 15 acres.

Known as the "sheet metal problem solver," the company makes ventilation equipment and manufactures air pollution control devices which it also installs. It also specializes in architectural sheet metal products, such as wall panels and flashings for power plants, industrial firms, retail stores and schools.

The Johnson firm is the largest of its kind within a 150-mile radius of the Quad-Cities and is among the 100 largest in the nation. Energy conservation is a new area of expertise for the company. To save energy, Johnson engineers have devised ways to clean the air in foundries and recirculate it, rather than moving heated air outside and replacing it.

HAPPY JOE'S PIZZA & ICE CREAM PARLOR, INCORPORATED

JOE WHITTY, FOUNDER OF HAPPY JOE'S AT ONE OF HIS FRANCHISE LOCATIONS.

Back in 1972, Joe Whitty had a new idea. Why not combine pizza with an old-fashioned ice cream parlor? Unable to sell the concept here to anyone who would back him, he reluctantly took his idea to New Mexico. Finally, a Davenport banker arranged a loan through the Small Business Administration, and he returned to open his first store in East Davenport. "Without the SBA, I could never have opened," Whitty said. "It's difficult when you can't get the banks to loan money."

He received the loan, and the Happy Joe's chain was born. All of the Happy Joe's restaurants are divided into two sections. Originally, the ice cream parlor had the 1940-style fountain fittings, and sold hard candy and hand-dipped ice cream. The other section sold pizza and was decorated with many nostalgic items such as player pianos and ceiling fans. In keeping with the style of the eighties, Happy Joe's has updated its look, making use of natural tones in its decor. Joe Whitty insists on each restaurant having a home-like atmosphere so families feel welcome. Happy Joe's tries to make even the "little guy" equal, with a platform for children to watch the pizza being made behind a window.

In the 1970s, Happy Joe Whitty won the pasta crown for innovation. He introduced sauerkraut pizza, taco pizza and specialty sandwiches. More recently he added a bacon, lettuce, tomato pizza, as well as a whole wheat pizza crust. With a chain of more than 100 stores in the United States, Happy Joe's new Egyptian venture opens the Mideast for more growth in the 1980s.

KSTT/97X
QUAD CITIES BROADCASTING COMPANY

KSTT'S NEWS DEPARTMENT OF 1970.

If you remember Mark Stevens, Bootie Bottles, Lou Gutenberger, Good Guy A-Go-Go, Top 40 Surveys, Ruth and Fred, Chicken Man, Bobby Rich and Big Red, KSTT RADIO is "the station you've grown up with."

KSTT was licensed shortly after World War II, but it was in the late '50s that Quad-City audiences really began to take notice of the new radio station as it began programming a format of contemporary pop music, requests, contests, remote broadcasts and a heavy emphasis on Quad-City news with the "Big Red" mobile news cruiser.

KSTT listeners became participants as well as listeners, calling Ruth and Fred on the Phone Show, phoning in news tips, requesting songs. They visited the station on tours. They attended KSTT sponsored hootenannys and hops, ball games and picnics, concerts and Good Guy-A-Go-Go dances. And they entered contests.

KSTT listeners have searched for "Bootie Bottles" filled with gift certificates and keys to snowmobiles and motorcylces.

By the late sixties, KSTT was so much a part of the Quad-City scene that servicemen in Vietnam would request tapes of broadcasts to give them a flavor of home.

And now into the eighties, KSTT continues to reflect the contemporary Quad-Cities community, while still remembering, with nostalgia contests and "Golden Oldies," the listeners who grew up with the station in the fifties, sixties,and seventies.

In 1975, KSTT purchased the FM station, WMDR. Call letters were first changed to WHTT.

Later, when format changes were made in 1978, the call letters became WXLP, to reflect the album-oriented rock programming. Listeners call it 97X or "the X" and it is currently the top rated radio station in the Quad-City market.

In 1979, KSTT and WXLP were purchased by Guy Gannett Broadcasting Corporation of Portland, Maine, which owns several other radio and television stations in Portland; Springfield, Mass.; Miami and Cocoa Beach, Fla.; Oklahoma City, Okla. and Cedar Rapids, Iowa.

WOC BROADCASTING

THE FIRST MOBILE UNIT OF WOC RADIO.

A Rock Island music store owner named Robert Karlowa began experimenting with radio transmission as a hobby in 1907. His Morse Code broadcasting station was later granted call letters 9-BC, then 9-XR, and when Karlowa began voice broadcasting, his "Radiophone" call letters became 9-BY, followed in 1922 by the assigment of call letters WOC, barely three months after the first such assignment was granted, making WOC one of the real pioneers in the broadcast industry.

In March, 1922 WOC was purchased by B.J. Palmer, and moved to Davenport. Palmer, President of Palmer School of Chiropractic, had also been experimenting with radio broadcasting from the school on Brady Street. Palmer was quick to realize the huge potential of a medium that could bring the whole world into people's homes. He moved Karlowa's equipment to Davenport and then began installation of a totally new radio station with Western Electric equipment. This *new* WOC was dedicated October 8, 1922.

Pioneer WOC took part in many *firsts* as the broadcast industry grew and matured. It was the first to broadcast from the Iowa Legislature. It was the first station to build log records of its departments such as electrical consumption and program schedule . Most of these were finally adopted by other stations in the United States.

WOC was the first station to establish an absolute second and minute time at the beginning of all programs. WOC was the first station to offer programming on homemaking and was the first station west of Buffalo to become part of a network broadcast. In November 1926, WOC became one of the original members of the NBC radio network. WOC staff members came up with several improvements on network broadcasting equipment that later became standard in the industry.

In 1927, Dr. Palmer set up a subsidiary corporation named Central Broadcasting Company. WHO in Des Moines was purchased from Bankers Life Insurance Company on February 15, 1930. WOC and WHO set up the first system in the United States to broadcast the same programming from two different stations. When WHO became a 50,000 watt "clear channel station" in April, 1933. WOC broadcast in combination with WHO as WHO-WOC from Des Moines for a little over a year. WOC returned to Davenport in 1934 after KICK in Carter Lake, Iowa was purchased, creating available frequency.

WOC played host to many national radio stars during the early days, but its most famous on-air talent was Ronald "Dutch" Reagan, who worked at WOC for a few months in 1932 before transferring to WHO in Des Moines as part of the conversion to 50,000 watts.

WOC continued as a broadcast pioneer when B.J. Palmer applied for a television license in 1947. WOC-TV went on the air as Iowa's first commercial television station on October 31, 1949, assigned originally to channel 5. The Ryan home at 805 Brady Street was remodeled and expanded to accommodate the studio, and WOC left the Palmer campus. By December, 1950 there were an estimated 40,000 television sets in Scott and Rock Island County. WOC originally broadcast 12 hours of programming per week, but by September, 1950, national television network programming reached Davenport with the completion of a relay tower.

The current Broadcast Center was dedicated in 1963 and was designed to take advantage of the latest in broadcast technology.

The tiny pioneering beginnings of WOC, nurtured by B.J. Palmer and continued by the late Dr. David Palmer, has grown into Palmer, Incorporated, which operates not only WOC Broadcasting Company and WHO Broadcasting Company, but also KDLH Broadcasting in Duluth, Minnesota, Palmer Cablevision and Radio Naples in Naples, Florida, WTNT/WCSN in Tallahasses, Florida, and Coachella Valley Television in Palm Desert, California.

THE WOC BROADCASTING FACILITY LOCATED ON BRADY STREET IN DAVENPORT.

VISIONS, INCORPORATED

Starting out as a two person venture, tucked away in a quaint carriage house, slightly off the beaten business path, Visions' numerous successful ad promotions made it possible for rapid growth and expansion. The P.S...We Love You campaign using lions, bears and chimps, the Foster Parents campaign with the adorable little blond boy, the Peter Pan Bread campaign with the precocious curly haired girl or the Culligan campaign that changed the Culligan man to a Culligan person...all helped place Visions among the area's most respected advertising agencies. With the addition of artists, media buyers and an office staff, Visions soon outgrew their tiny studio. In 1978, Visions, Inc. purchased the Christie Mansion, restoring the historic structure to use as it's headquarters. Since that time the mansion has been bustling with creative activity. Visions has concentrated more and more on total corporate marketing for their clients, designing award winning annual reports for large corporations; entertaining thousands of people with slide and multi-media presentations; designing projects of all sizes. In the years since it began Visions has indeed become a full service advertising agency.

VISIONS, INC. LOCATED IN THE VILLAGE OF EAST DAVENPORT.

YOUNKERS, INCORPORATED

Younkers has been a part of the Quad-Cities since 1956 when on April 2 it opened its store in downtown Rock Island. Only four years later, on August 8, 1960, the present store in Duck Creek Plaza was completed. The Duck Creek store was considered large for the time, with 60,000 square feet of space, and was one of the first stores in a shopping plaza. Perhaps it was the success of this store which led to the closing in 1966 of the Rock Island unit. On July 11, 1973, Younkers opened its largest Quad-Cities store (100,000 square feet) in Northpark, followed in February 1974 by the similar 80,000 square foot store in Moline at Southpark.

In April 1979, Younkers opened a separate distribution center in Davenport to facilitate transportation of merchandise to all of its eastern Iowa stores.

Since 1956, Younkers has proudly helped to mold the buying decisions of the fashion conscious Quad-Cities consumer.

WHBF

IT BEGAN WITH A CRYSTAL MICROPHONE BACK IN THE 1920S.

Back in 1923, when raccoon coats and jazz were the rage, a railroad telegrapher at Cambridge, Illinois built an experimental radio transmitter. Two years later, Calvin Beardsley, who owned Beardsley Specialty Company in Rock Island, bought the equipment and set it up at the rear of his store. In 1925 he went on the air as WHBF, call letters resulting from a listener contest. They are said to stand for "Where Historical Blackhawk Fought." Quad-Citians tuned in with horn speakers or earphones connected to a crystal set. The station had 100 watts of power. In 1932 the station moved to Rock Island's Harms Hotel, and in November of that year the station was sold to Rock Island Broadcasting Company, formed by the John W. Potter Company, owners of the Rock Island Argus. Frequency changes came along with increasing signal strength until WHBF reached 5000 watts at 1270 kilocycles where it operates today.

At the end of World War II, the station began plans for FM broadcasting which began in 1947. Three years later the entire operation moved to its present location at the Telco Building. July 1, 1950 a new service began, with the birth of channel 4 television.

WHBF AM and FM pioneered stereo broadcasting in 1958, and in the sixties multiplex stereo and totally automated FM were added. In 1975, that FM system was replaced with a new solid state computerized system. Television viewing grew as WHBF-TV offered the first color telecast locally, then the first local color programming. The TV transmitter was moved to Orion, Illinois with installation of a 1000 foot tower. In 1982, channel 4 began transmitting from a 1385 foot tower in Bettendorf, Iowa, providing coverage of a much wider area of eastern Iowa and western Illinois.

Each of the WHBF stations is affiliated with the CBS network. In addition, the stations carry a full schedule of local news and information with live remote capability. Broadcasting now relies on satellite dishes, microwave signals, studio-transmitter links, and a host of other tools not dreamed of in earlier days, and WHBF continues to remain a leader as it updates its equipment and services.

Unusual in the Quad-Cities, WHBF radio and television stations remain locally owned and operated. From small beginnings in one room on the second floor of a building in downtown Rock Island, the WHBF activities now fill all the floors of an entire half-block!

THE DAILY DISPATCH

*CARRIERS IN THIS EARLY YEARS'
PHOTO WORE UNIFORMS,
COMPLETE WITH CAPS.*

In 1878, Oliver and Louise White, publishers of The Molly Stark, a weekly newspaper in Toulon, looked at the larger, more prosperous town of Moline — 50 miles to the northwest — and decided it needed a daily newspaper. They moved to Moline, procured a one-room shop on 3rd Avenue, hired a young assistant and were ready to go. The first issue of the Moline Daily Evening Dispatch appeared on July 31, 1878.

The newspaper hasn't missed a day of publication since.

The new enterprise faced competition which proved too much for the Whites, and they sold the paper. Two young but experienced journalists, Patterson S. McGlynn and John K. Groom, eventually purchased the paper. McGlynn's involvement was a turning point in Dispatch history. By 1891 the debt was paid off, and the newspaper was on its way.

One of McGlynn's first carriers was John Sundine, who rose through the ranks to become half-owner in 1913. Much of the early financial success is credited to his hard work and expertise. He died in 1923.

Harry A. Sward, Lee R. Blackman and August Sundine, John's brother, then joined McGlynn as owners and executives.

Blackman served the paper for more than 45 years. August Sundine became executive editor, serving until his death in 1956.

Harry Sward started his Dispatch career as a carrier in November, 1898, and rose to become treasurer in 1909. He became joint owner with August Sundine, Blackman and McGlynn in 1923, and when Blackman died, Sward and Sundine purchased his share.

It was under Harry Sward's management that The Dispatch moved from its identity with Moline to a broader relationship as a newspaper concerned and involved with a large and prosperous sector of Western Illinois.

Sward retired in 1969, and died in 1973 at the age of 88.

On February 28, 1969, Len H. Small, editor and publisher of The Daily Journal, Kankakee, purchased The Dispatch. John (Jack) Sundine, August's son, then was editor and secretary and Robert H. Sward, Harry's son, was business manager and treasurer.

Small appointed Edgar A. Shipley, former editor at Kankakee and publisher of the LaPorte, Ind., Herald-Argus, as editor and publisher of The Dispatch. Small's son, Len R. Small, joined the paper in 1971 as associate editor. He now is editor and publisher.

Shipley retired in August 1979. Len H. Small died in an automobile accident in March, 1980.

A series of mechanical and technical innovations was started in 1969. The "hot metal" method of composition was replaced by computerized photocomposition. An addition to the 5th Avenue newspaper plant was completed in 1974 — a new distribution center and pressroom — which gave Dispatch readers the first offset printed newspaper in Quad-Cities area.

The Sunday Dispatch first appeared on newsstands and doorsteps March 14, 1976, and established itself as the favorite Sunday newspaper for Illinois Quad-City readers.

The Daily and Sunday Dispatch are a part of the Small Newspaper Group, which also includes The Journal at Kankakee, The Herald-Argus, LaPorte, Ind., The Daily Times at Ottawa, Ill., The Times-Press, Streator, Ill., The Post Bulletin, Rochester, Minn., The Press Tribune, Roseville, Cal., The Pacific Palisades, Cal., Post and Scott County Publishing Company, Davenport.

The owners of the Small Newspaper Group include the family of Len H. Small. Besides Len R. Small, other family members include Jean Alice Small, editor-publisher in Kankakee and Dispatch board chairman; Tom Small, western division manager; and Jennifer Small, a news reporter in Small's Washington bureau.

*THE DISPATCH BUILDING AS IT
APPEARED DURING WORLD WAR II.*

ELLIOTT BEECHCRAFT

HERB ELLIOTT, CORPORATE PILOT, CIRCA 1938.

Herb Elliott, founder of Elliott Beechcraft, can truthfully say that his first airplane was "bought for a song." The money he earned playing bass fiddle in a dance band provided his share of the funds necessary to buy a Curtis Junior in the mid-1930's. This was the beginning of a lifelong love affair with aviation.

After receiving his commercial and flight instructor rating, Elliott decided to get into the aviation business full-time. He scouted around to find a private enterprise airport that he could run "the way an airport ought to be run." He found this in DeWitt, Iowa. In spite of primitive conditions — no electricity and no running water — the business prospered and expanded. Elliott's first appreciation of Beech products developed during this time when he became a corporate pilot on a Beech Staggerwing in 1940. However, World War II made it necessary to close the DeWitt operation. In January, 1941, Elliott left the area for Texas to serve as a civilian flight instructor for the Army Air Corps but soon enlisted in the Air Force. In 1945 the war was over and it was back to Iowa and back to business. Elliott Flying Service was reopened at Davenport's Cram Field. By 1946 the fleet had expanded and Elliott was the first to offer twin engine charter service from its Quad-City base. After opening a branch location in Des Moines in 1959, Elliott decided to move the main office to the Quad-City Airport. A third branch was established in 1972 at Flying Cloud Field near Minneapolis, Minnesota. Most recently a fourth operation was added in 1982 to service Omaha's Eppley Field.

Remembering his fondness for Beech products, Elliott entered into a mutually satisfying affiliation with Beechcraft in 1947. Today it is one of the few agencies in the country franchised by the Beech Aircraft Corporation to market the full line of Beechcraft models.

Elliott Beechcraft offers sales and service of this high quality product line and also offers the finest in personalized air travel and flight instruction. Customer service has always been the number one priority and is reflected in each fully-equipped service facility staffed with factory trained technicians, a complete parts inventory and Goodwill Ambassadors who meet each arrival, see off each departure and cater to the needs of all customers during their stay.

From its modest beginnings, Elliott Beechcraft has grown with the Quad-City area into one of the largest and most progressive general aviation sales and service operations with over 200 employees serving 7 states. Its *on demand* service provides access to 14,000 U.S. airports from each of its 4 midwestern locations.

CORPORATE HEADQUARTERS OF ELLIOTT BEECHCRAFT AT QUAD CITY AIRPORT, 1982.